Prose and Poetry of England

Executive Editor: Dr. Mary Kay Clark
Editors: Seton Staff

Printed in the United States of America.

Seton Home Study School
1350 Progress Drive
Front Royal, VA 22630
540-636-9990
540-636-1602 fax

For more information, visit us on the Web at www.setonhome.org.
Contact us by e-mail at info@setonhome.org.

ISBN: 978-1-60704-137-5

Cover: *John Henry Cardinal Newman*, John Millais

Prose and Poetry of England

Content

PREFACE ix

I ANGLO-SAXON ENGLAND
(Beginnings to 1066)

HISTORICAL AND LITERARY BACKGROUND 1

Roman Occupation - Anglo-Saxon Invasion - Coming of Christianity - Golden Age of Anglo-Saxon Literature - Danish Invaders and the Age of Alfred - The First Anglo-Saxon Prose - Old English Poetry - Anglo-Saxon Language - Narrative Poetry - Classification of Poetry - The Epic - Beowulf.

Charles W. Kennedy, translator BEOWULF 14
Bede, translated by Alfred THE ECCLESIASTICAL HISTORY OF ENGLAND 28

II THE MIDDLE ENGLISH PERIOD 31
(1066-1450)

Character of the Normans - Union of Saxons and Normans - A Time of Upheaval - Changes in the Language - Religious Literature - Secular Lyrics - Medieval Story Telling - The Ballad

English and Scottish Ballads SIR PATRICK SPENS 38
EDWARD, EDWARD 40
GET UP AND BAR THE DOOR 42
THE WIFE OF USHER S WELL 43

THE METRICAL TALE 45

Geoffrey Chaucer THE PROLOGUE TO THE CANTERBURY TALES 49
THE NUN'S PRIEST'S TALE 57

THE DRAMA IN MEDIEVAL ENGLAND 67

A Morality Play EVERYMAN 69

III THE RENAISSANCE AND THE ELIZABETHAN AGE
(1500-1603)

HISTORICAL AND LITERARY BACKROUND 78

The Early Renaissance - St. Thomas More - More's Place in Literature

Thomas More RICHARD III 81
William Roper ST. THOMAS MORE'S DEFENSE AND EXECUTION 84

THE ELIZABETHAN AGE (1558-1603) 89

Mary, Queen of Scots - Patriotism, Peace, and Prosperity -
The Poetry of Edmund Spenser - The Faerie Queene

Edmund Spenser — THE FAERIE QUEENE 94

LYRIC POETRY 98

Christopher Marlowe — THE PASSIONATE SHEPHERD TO HIS LOVE 99
Sir Walter Raleigh — THE NYMPH'S REPLY TO THE SHEPHERD 100
Robert Southwell — THE BURNING BABE 101
Ben Jonson — TO CELIA 102
TO THE MEMORY OF MY BELOVED MASTER, WILLIAMSHAKESPEARE 103

THE SONNET 106

Edmund Spenser — SONNET FROM THE AMORETTI 106
William Shakespeare — SONNET XXIX-WHEN IN DISGRACE WITH FORTUNE AND MEN'S EYES 108
SONNET XXX-WHEN TO THE SESSIONS OF SWEET SILENT THOUGHT 109
SONNET LV-NOT MARBLE, NOR THE GILDED MONUMENTS 109
SONNET CXVI-LET ME NOT TO THE MARRIAGE OF TRUE MINDS 110
SONNET LXXIII-THAT TIME OF YEAR THOU MAY'ST IN ME BEHOLD 110

Philip Sidney — SONNET FORTY-ONE 113

THE BIBLE 114

Douay Bible — THE SACRIFICE OF ISAAC 117
Edward J. Kissane, The Book of Job
POEM ON WISDOM 119

THE BOOK OF PSALMS 122

Pontifical Biblical Institute, translators
PSALM 22 123
PSALM 72 124
Michael J. Gruenthaner, S.J., translator
THE SUFFERING MESSIAS 126
Ronald A. Knox, translator — PAUL'S SPEECH AT ATHENS 129

ELIZABETHAN PROSE 131

THE ENGLISH ESSAY MAKES ITS BOW 133

Francis Bacon — OF STUDIES 134

THE DEVELOPMENT OF ENGLISH DRAMA 137

IV THE SEVENTEENTH AND EIGHTEENTH CENTURIES
(1603-1780)

HISTORICAL AND LITERARY BACKGROUND 141

The Stuart Interval (1603-1625) - The Puritan Age (1625-1660)-Protestants Divided - King Charles I Put to Death

CAVALIER POETS 143

Thomas Carew	A SONG	144
Richard Lovelace	TO LUCASTA, ON GOING TO THE WARS	145
	TO ALTHEA, FROM PRISON	146
Robert Herrick	TO THE VIRGINS	148
Sir John Suckling	WHY SO PALE AND WAN?	149

METAPHYSICAL POETRY 150

John Donne	REPENTANCE	151
	BATTER MY HEART	152
Richard Crashaw	ON THE GLORIOUS ASSUMPTION OF OUR BLESSED LADY (Selection)	153
	THE FLAMING HEART (selection)	154
George Herbert	THE PULLEY	155

PURITAN PROSE AND POETRY 156

John Milton	ON HIS BLINDNESS	158
	PARADISE LOST (selection)	159

THE RESTORATION (1660-1688) 167

THE AGE OF POPE (1689-1740) 170

Alexander Pope	AN ESSAY ON CRITICISM (selection)	174
Joseph Addison and Richard Steele	SIR ROGER AT CHURCH	180

THE AGE OF JOHNSON (1740-1780) 184

James Boswell	(from) LIFE OF JOHNSON	185

THE TRANSITION FROM CLASSICISM TO ROMANTICISM (1780-1798) 192

Thomas Gray	ELEGY WRITTEN IN A COUNTRY CHURCHYARD	193
Robert Burns	JOHN ANDERSON, MY JO	199
	A MAN'S A MAN FOR A' THAT	200
William Blake	AUGURIES OF INNOCENCE	202
	THE TIGER	202
	THE LITTLE BLACK BOY	204

V THE AGE OF ROMANTICISM
(1780-1840)

HISTORICAL AND LITERARY BACKGROUND 206

The Defeat of Napoleon - The Rediscovery of Old Ballads - Romanticism and Exaggerated Romanticism - Revolt Against Artificiality - Nature and the Eternal

William Wordsworth	SHE DWELT AMONG THE UNTRODDEN WAYS	212
	SHE WAS A PHANTOM OF DELIGHT	213
	THE TABLES TURNED	214
	LINES WRITTEN IN EARLY SPRING	215
	THE SOLITARY REAPER	216
	COMPOSED UPON WESTMINSTER BRIDGE	217
	THE WORLD IS TOO MUCH WITH US	218
Samuel Taylor Coleridge	KUBLA KHAN	220
Walter Scott	AVE MARIA	222
George Gordon, Lord Byron	THE EVE OF WATERLOO	224
	THE COLISEUM	227
	THE DESTRUCTION OF SENNACHERIB	229
	SHE WALKS IN BEAUTY	231
Percy Bysshe Shelley	OZYMANDIAS	232
	THE CLOUD	233
	TO A SKYLARK	235
	ODE TO THE WEST WIND	239
John Keats	ON FIRST LOOKING INTO CHAPMAN'S HOMER	242
	ODE TO A NIGHTINGALE	244
	ODE ON A GRECIAN URN	247
	BRIGHT STAR! WOULD I WERE STEADFAST AS THOU ART	250

VI THE VICTORIAN ERA
(1840-1900)

HISTORICAL AND LITERARY BACKGROUND 252

Changing England - Democracy on the March - Victorian Writers - Outstanding Poets - The Short Story Appears in England - Victorian Drama

Thomas Babington Macaulay	RANKE'S HISTORY OF THE POPES *(selection)*	258
Thomas Carlyle	THE STORMING OF THE BASTILLE	260
Alfred Tennyson	BREAK, BREAK, BREAK	265
	IN MEMORIAM *(selection)*	266
	ULYSSES	270
	LOCKSLEY HALL	273
Robert Browning	THE YEAR'S AT THE SPRING	274
	HOME THOUGHTS FROM ABROAD	274
	RABBI BEN EZRA (selection)	275
	PROSPICE (LOOK AHEAD!)	277
	MY LAST DUCHESS	278

Elizabeth Barrett Browning	HOW DO I LOVE THEE	281
Matthew Arnold	DOVER BEACH	283
Dante Gabriel Rossetti	LOST DAYS	285
Christina Rossetti	UP-HILL	286
Rudyard Kipling	GUNGA DIN	287
	RECESSIONAL	289

THE OXFORD MOVEMENT AND THE CATHOLIC REVIVAL 291

John Henry Newman	APOLOGIA PRO VITA SUA (selection)	293
	THE IDEA OF A UNIVERSITY (selections)	297
	LITERATURE AND LIFE	300

VII THE TWENTIETH CENTURY HISTORICAL AND LITERARY BACKGROUND 302

Political and Social Changes - The Rise of the Labor Party - England Suffered from World Wars - Literature Reflects Complexity of the Age - The Catholic Revival - The Short Story - Short Stories of Today

Graham Greene	THE HINT OF AN EXPLANATION	309

THE MODERN NOVEL 319

NONFICTION: BIOGRAPHY 322

Evelyn Waugh	EDMUND CAMPION (selection)	324

TWENTIETH CENTURY POETRY 331

A. E. Housman	TO AN ATHLETE DYING YOUNG	333
William Butler Yeats	THE LAKE ISLE OF INNISFREE	334
	WHEN YOU ARE OLD	335
	THE SECOND COMING	336
John Masefield	A CONSECRATION	338
Walter de la Mare	IN MEMORY OF G. K. CHESTERTON	340
Rupert Brooke	THE SOLDIER	341
W. W. Gibson	SIGHT	342
Siegfried Sassoon	AFTERMATH	343
	DREAMERS	344
Stephen Spender	THE EXPRESS	345
W. H. Auden	THE UNKNOWN CITIZEN	347
T. S. Eliot	CHORUS NO. 1 OF "THE ROCK"	348
	JOURNEY OF THE MAGI	350
Hilaire Belloc	TO DIVES	352
Roy Campbell	TO THE SUN	354

	ESSAYS	355
Hilaire Belloc	THE PATH TO ROME	356
Dylan Thomas	REMINISCENCES OF CHILDHOOD	361
Gilbert Keith Chesterton	THE ROMANCE OF ORTHODOXY	365
	MODERN DRAMA	369

PREFACE

In this completely revised edition of *Prose and Poetry of England, St. Thomas More Series,* the editors have necessarily kept in mind the viewpoint of both the student and the teacher.

In editing the text from the viewpoint of the student, the editors presuppose that the superior as well as the average and slower student will use the text. For that reason, some of the selections and study aids have been chosen for the superior student alone. The entire text need not (and should not) be studied by every student. On the other hand, more than sufficient materials for the intellectual capacity of the average 12th grade student have been included.

By offering challenging as well as easily comprehended selections and study materials, the editors have consciously attempted to avoid any intimation of "the canonization of mediocrity," so increasingly apparent in American high school education. From long years of actual classroom experience, the editors are convinced that too many teachers underestimate the capacity of our American youth for intellectual and cultural development. The Christian teacher should help the student acquire an intellectual maturity befitting an intelligent Christian citizen, rather than allow him to seek and find the level of the mass mind.

The *St. Thomas More Series* makes the honest claim that all the selections have been completely edited from a totally Catholic viewpoint. This does not mean that Catholic writing alone is represented. The editors feel that it is more valuable for the young Catholic student to study critically the great masterpieces of the English literary tradition, although at times they may be at variance with Catholic tradition, than for him to devote himself exclusively to Catholic literary art. A critical evaluation of all philosophies is a very effective way for the student to see the truth in Catholic thought and criticism, since he must live his life in a world which reflects pagan and heretical as well as Christian influences.

With proper teacher motivation, the student should attain from the study of this text a fairly high level of (a) mastery of the various types of prose and poetry; (b) a realistic and practical Catholic application of what is read and studied to contemporary social, cultural, and religious life; (c) an introduction to the cultural past as integrated with the present; (d) an extension of vocabulary and reading skills; (e) a critical appreciation and personal cultural enrichment.

For many teachers, the study aids accompanying each selection will serve only as suggestions to be used as they fit individual teacher plans. However, the editors do feel that the detailed analyses of the abundant selections in this book should provide useful material for both the experienced and inexperienced teacher.

It is hoped that, in teaching a selection, the primary emphasis will be placed upon the explanation of the text both for understanding and literary and critical appreciation. For that reason, larger selections of a specific type of prose and poetry have been included in this revision.

Thus, for example, one-third of the epic *Beowulf* and almost one-half of the metrical romance *Sir Gawain and the Green Knight* have been printed in the text. In this way, the selection can be studied as representative of an entire epic or metrical romance.

Other objectives in teaching a selection should be the evaluation of an individual piece for its (a) technique and (b) the application of its thought content to life as the student lives it and will live it. Minimal emphasis should be placed on historical background and biographical material.

For those teachers who follow the type rather than the chronological approach to literature, there will be found throughout the book detailed treatment of each type of prose and poetry. A table of contents by types is also included.

The editors sincerely hope that the end result of the teaching of this text will be a more mature enrichment of the Catholic adolescent mind, a deeper appreciation of his place in society, and a glimpse, at least, of the contemporary world as a part of Western culture—a culture which has been bequeathed to him by the English Catholic literary giants from the age of *Beowulf* and Chaucer and Thomas More down to Chesterton and the other twentieth century Christian writers.

The arming and departure of the knights

I. ANGLO-SAXON ENGLAND

BEGINNINGS TO 1066

The student who would appreciate the richness and variety of English expression should know something of the soil in which the English language and English literature grew. And for a Catholic, it is important to note that much of English thought is associated with Catholic traditions centuries old.

The dark-haired, blue-eyed Iberians were the first inhabitants of Britain. Of them we know little, since they left no written literature or history. They did leave behind them, however, their impressive stone structures, ruins of which still survive at Stonehenge and Avebury.

Several centuries before the birth of Christ, successive waves of Britons or Brythonic Celts swept across the east of England, subjugating and absorbing, to a large extent, the Iberians. Rude and primitive as the Britons were, their literature shows that they were both fierce in battle and keenly appreciative of the beauties of nature and the charm of womanhood, which they held in great respect. In their thatched huts, before the peat fires, their poets sang of the great warrior Cuchulainn[1] and of Deirdre[2] the beautiful.

In 55 B.C., Caesar, with his temporary expedition, made the British Isles a part of Roman history. Very shortly after the death of the British King, Cymbeline, in the first century after Christ, the Roman legions made a permanent invasion and for four centuries the Roman eagles soared over the British Isles. The Romans brought with them the elements of order, culture, and stability. Strong stone roads, high walls, lighthouses, elaborate villas, baths, and coins stamped the land with civilization. The Latin language now made possible exchange of ideas with the continent. Soon, by ways unknown to us, Christianity came to the Romanized Britons.

With Christianity came literature. The earliest book known to have been written on British soil was the *Commentary of St. Paul* by the heretic Pelagius.[3] The British Church had an established hierarchy by the late third century. At the Council of Arles in 314, she was represented by three bishops. Many of the sons of the British Church suffered martyrdom under Diocletian. Even while the Roman empire was tottering and crying out for assistance from her British legions, Fastidious, a British bishop, was calmly writing a Latin book on "The Christian Life." He wrote: "He is a Christian who follows the life of Christ, who imitates Christ in all things."

[1]CUCHULAINN (kōō·kŭl´ĭn)—Irish legendary hero who appears in many of the great tales of early Celtic literature.

[2]DEIRDRE (dēr´drê)—Tragic heroine of early Celtic literature.

[3]PELAGIUS (pê·lā´jĭ·ŭs)—Early Christian heretic against whom St. Augustine wrote. Pelagius denied Original Sin and Christian grace.

When the Roman legions were recalled to help save a hopelessly collapsing Empire in the beginning of the fifth century, the British people found themselves without protection from their savage border neighbors, the Picts and the Scots.

THE ANGLO-SAXON INVASION

About 449 A.D. the Angles, Saxons, and Jutes—tribes from the woods of northern Germany and the marshy shores of the North Sea and the Baltic—drove their swift, shallow boats onto the defenseless beachheads of Britain's eastern coast. From the coast they swarmed westward in raid after raid, tearing down the Roman towers, burning fields and dwellings, stealing and enslaving the helpless Celts. The Britons, who had become used to letting the Romans do their fighting for them, fell easy victims to the Anglo-Saxon invaders. The British survivors were driven back into the mountainous districts of Wales, Devonshire, and Cornwall.[4] The new invaders were little interested in learning the British language and adopted only a few words from the Celtic tongue or from the Latin language as spoken by the Britons.

But we must not think of these Germanic tribes as pirates by nature or trade. They were a hardy, powerful, determined race, who found the struggle for existence a

[4]CORNWALL—There is a tradition that the British King Arthur dwelt in Tintagel in Cornwall and that Cornwall is the original setting of Arthur and his Round Table.

bloody affair. A warlike people in need of more land for wives and children, impatient of government, fiercely jealous of their personal liberty, they fought their bloody way into British territory. It was these Angles, Saxons, and Jutes who were eventually to determine the basic language and culture of the English race. After their wild spell of pillaging and looting, they settled down into numerous kingdoms, the most important of which were Northumbria in the north, Mercia in the Midlands, and Wessex in the south. The Angles occupied Northumbria, and from them Britain came to be called "Angle-lond."

The Anglo-Saxons lived, not in towns built and walled with stone as the Romans had done, but in groups of wooden houses surrounded by a wooden stockade. The words for such communities were *tun* or *ham,* words which still remain in modern English as *town* and *home.* Each chieftain was surrounded by a band of freemen, called thanes, who ate at their lord's table and defended him with their lives. These warriors wore shirts of mail called *byrnies;* their helmets were crowned with boars' heads and other decorations; their arms were swords, spears, bows and arrows. Generosity was the quality most admired in their leader. Thus he was referred to as "the ring-giver."

The peasants lived in their tiny huts around the great halls of their lords. The mead halls, so graphically described in *Beowulf,* were designed to serve as emergency stockades and were powerfully constructed. High and drafty, their stone masonry and massive beams were smoke-blackened and gaunt. Around the walls, heavy oaken tables, hacked by the trencher knives of roistering guests, supported enormous piles of roasted venison, fish, and many fowls. Ale and mead—a potent beverage brewed from honey—were their drinks. And as the drinking horn made the rounds, the delight of the men was to listen to the scop[5] or the bard recalling the bloodcurdling adventures of some hero whose exploits became more wonderful and more fraught with danger as the legend of his fame was unfolded from generation to generation. It was undoubtedly through such retelling that the historical figure of King Alfred and his brave defense of Celtic liberty against the invading Saxon tribes grew into the golden legend that we know.

The Anglo-Saxon invaders were heathens, worshipping the old German gods, Odin and Thor, and believing in charms, man-eating monsters, and in Wyrd, the iron fate that determines all. The world of their songs was an heroic world of warriors who were supermen, of fabulous exploits on land and sea. They told their tales and sang their songs from memory.

COMING OF CHRISTIANITY

To these hearty thanes, Christianity came about 600 A.D. Missionaries arrived in Britain almost simultaneously from two directions; and, as might be expected, the challenge of Christ captured the wild enthusiasm and restless imagination of this spirited people. Catholicism was spread through the north by some of those vigorous Irish monks who at this period were carrying the light of the

[5]SCOP—An Anglo-Saxon court poet.

Gospel and secular learning to every part of the world. Oswald, king of Northumbria, had been converted while in exile by St. Columba, the Irish poet, scholar, statesman, ruler, and saint. From Columba's school, Oswald brought back Aidan, to establish a similar school at Lindisfarne. It was this school which became the fountain of culture and learning for northern England.

Meanwhile, some years before Aidan's arrival, Christianity had entered England by another door. St. Augustine, sent by Pope Gregory the Great, landed with his fellow missionaries at Kent in 597. They sang a *Te Deum* in the ruins of an old pre-Saxon church and made this spot the wellspring of Christianity for the southern kingdoms of England. Though Augustine and his men had remarkable success, the work of conversion was carried on against heavy odds. Many Anglo-Saxons turned back to the worship of Odin and Thor before Christian victory was finally complete.

THE GOLDEN AGE OF ANGLO-SAXON LITERATURE

The eighth century marked the golden summit of Anglo-Saxon culture and learning. The Celtic warmth and feeling which Irish monks had given to Northumbria, and the Roman organization which Augustine and his missionaries brought to the south, joined hands and ushered in the first dawn of English learning and literature. It was the Christian missionaries who brought the Anglo-Saxons into contact with the literature of Greece and Rome. Theodore from distant Tarsus, and Hadrian from Africa, wandered up and down the length and breadth of the Island, setting up schools, preaching and teaching everywhere, dispensing their knowledge of Greek and Latin as well as divine literature.

Monasteries were founded which became the haven of literature and arts. In these monasteries, great libraries were built up; in them was taught the rhythm of the liturgical chant, which worked itself into the very fiber of English verse; in fact, practically all the poetry that has come down to us from this period of English history was written in the monasteries and by the monks.

It was the monks who gathered up the ancient folk tales and preserved them in writing. It was a monk who composed *Beowulf,* the folk epic which gives us a splendid picture of Anglo-Saxon life and character. It was the monks, too, who taught these war-like folk new songs in which the heroes were Christ and His Apostles. Evidence of this can be seen in the sublimely beautiful and genuinely Christian poetry of Cynewulf whose *Christ, The Dream of the Rood,* and *Elene* mark the highest level to which Old English poetry attained.

In Saint Bede (673-735), a native Anglo-Saxon, who even in his life won the title of Venerable, we have one of the greatest scholars of all time. He wrote almost one hundred books, among which is his *Ecclesiastical History of England.* This most important primary source book of English history was originally written in Latin but was later translated into Anglo-Saxon prose by King Alfred. It is in his *History* that Bede tells the story of Caedmon, the ignorant cowherd at the monastery of Whitby, who received in a vision the gift of song. The fragment of Caedmon's song quoted by Bede is the earliest recorded piece of Old English poetry.

Unfortunately, these buds of culture, which gave such promise of great things to be, were destroyed by the invasion of a new enemy, the Danes. In the ninth century, legions of Vikings swept silently up the British rivers in their black, dragonprowed ships; and from them the blond giants stormed across the north country, leveling the monasteries and mead halls, burning and destroying until the land became desolate. Then they pushed southward across the Thames, and within a century would likely have devastated the whole Island had not their steadily advancing masses met Alfred in the great battle of Edington. Elsewhere the natives had huddled together like sheep without a shepherd, but now at last England had a leader—and a great one. At battle's close, the Danes had been routed; and Alfred, the noble Christian of the West Saxons, rolled back the tide of conquest. It is this routing of the new pagan invasion by Alfred which Gilbert K. Chesterton makes the theme of his ringing *Ballad of the White Horse.*

DANISH INVADERS AND THE AGE OF ALFRED

But in the long struggle with the Danes, Anglo-Saxon culture had lost its vitality. Alfred had no sooner forced the Danes to peace than he turned his attention to the problems of reconstruction. All that was left of the great monasteries of the north was uncleared rubble. Alfred set about to attract scholars to him and to establish schools where "every freeborn youth who possessed the means should abide at his book until he could well understand English writing." In his educational program Alfred chose to emphasize the importance of a native language and literature as a means for developing a national spirit. Even the old warriors of the court were put to school, and there are amusing stories of how many of them insisted that they much preferred struggling with the Danes to struggling with the alphabet!

In order that there might be English writings for his people to read, Alfred, together with his scholars, translated many books from the Latin into Anglo-Saxon. Among others, he selected four outstanding works of the previous century: Orosius' *History of the World,* Boethius' *Consolation of Philosophy,* Bede's *Ecclesiastical History of England,* and Pope Gregory's *Pastoral Care.* Alfred wrote prefaces to all these works, one of the most famous being that to the *Pastoral Care* in which he points out to the clergy both the glorious heritage and tradition that is theirs, and their obligation to pass on this heritage to the faithful. He also revived the old *Anglo-Saxon Chronicle,* which before his time had been a memorandum of English events of unequal importance. He was to make this *Chronicle* a valuable source book for English historians. Alfred's work is remarkable to this day for its compelling power of thought and expression, and he well deserves the title of "Father of English Prose."

THE FIRST ANGLO-SAXON PROSE

In spite of all his efforts, Alfred did not succeed during his lifetime in re-educating his people to the degree of culture they had obtained in the days of Venerable Bede. After his death, however, disorder and invasion slowly gave way to peace. Christianity gained a solid foothold. The monasteries were restored under Benedictine rule and became once again

centers of learning and refinement. The court, the church, the monastery, the school, the farm, and the marketplace became the pivotal points in English life.

Old English prose reached its golden summit in the late tenth and early eleventh centuries. The most important development was the homily, a sermon with a moral lesson that became a thing of art under the polished pens of the learned monks and bishops. In the history of English prose, the Old English homily is important since it began a prose tradition which has lasted to modern times. The manner and style of the homily with its narrative illustrations, its varied use of allegory, its appeal to the will rather than to the intellect, can be traced through the thirteenth and fourteenth century devotional literature to the prose of the fifteenth century. Its influence was felt in the Renaissance in the prose of St. Thomas More and even in such literary forms as the Elizabethan drama. We find it in the allegories of John Bunyan, whose *Pilgrim's Progress* introduced the Puritan homily to American literature.

Outstanding among the Old English sermons of the tenth and eleventh centuries were the *Blickling Homilies;* the sermons of Bishop Wulfstan, Archbishop of York; and the sermons of the greatest writer of his day, Aelfric. He it was who carried Old English prose to its height in the generation before the Norman conquest. In life, character, and love of books and learning, Aelfric greatly resembles Bede. No other Old English prose writer had such a marked influence on the English people of his own time and a greater molding power over English literature to come.

In the last days of the Saxon dominion, poetic forms disappeared, and the primitive majesty and simple grandeur of the earlier poetry died away. Yet in the British genius there still lives an energy and endurance born of these early poets. Now and again through the centuries there flash glimpses of the ships and swords, the ploughshares, and the jeweled crosses of those early days. And though the heroes and the monsters disappeared, English poetry still shows a closeness to nature, a devotion to family, a fierce defending of liberty, a thread of brooding melancholy, an abiding love of the sea—heritages all of its Anglo-Saxon ancestry.

OLD ENGLISH POETRY

The Anglo-Saxons loved their books with a passionate revere“”nce. The great Bede tells us that he took delight in reading and writing, and placed books first when naming the treasures brought home by monks from their journeys to Rome. And it was Alfred who wrote: “Through learning is belief held, and every man who loves wisdom is happy.” The unknown author of the strange poem known as “Salamon and Saturn” sums up what the first writers of English literature thought of books:

> Books are glorious; they give in earnest
> a wise will to him who wonders.
> They heal the heart’s mood of every man,
> heal the distress of daily life;
> they found and make firm the strong thought.
> Strong is he who tastes of book lore;
> He is ever wiser in wielding power.
> Books bring triumph to true-hearted men,
> health of mind to him who loves them.[6]

Of the vast storehouse of Old English literary writings which must have existed, comparatively few manuscripts have come down to us. And little wonder, when we recall how often the priceless treasuries of the monastery libraries were ravaged by invasion and raid; how many thousands of manuscripts were burnt and destroyed by the persecutors of the Church under Henry VIII and Elizabeth. Among the old English records, four are outstanding and contain the greater number of poems written before the eleventh century: *The Junius Manuscript,* now in Bodleian Library, Oxford University, which contains the poems at one time attributed to Caedmon; *The Exeter Book,* which contains the largest collection of Old English Poetry which has come down to us; *The Vercelli Manuscript;* and *The Cotton Vitellius* A 15, which was almost destroyed by fire in 1731. This precious manuscript contains the only surviving handwritten copy of *Beowulf.*

[6]“Salamon and Saturn” from *Word Hoard*—Passages from Old English Literature from the Sixth to the Eleventh Centuries, translated and arranged by Margaret Williams, M.A., copyright, 1940, by Sheed and Ward, Inc., New York.

The language found in the greater number of these manuscripts is the Wessex dialect of the tenth century. Much of the poetry was originally composed in the earlier forms of the Northumbrian and Mercian dialects, but the original copies perished in the Danish invasions. When the Wessex scribes made copies of the earlier manuscripts in the tenth century, they transformed the Northumbrian and Mercian dialects into their own West Saxon, which was then known as the "King's English."

We must not think that Old English poetry was primitive or crude. Its poetic rules were highly technical. Each line contained four accents with a pause in the middle of the line. The strongest word in each half-line, or hemistich, alliterated with the strongest accent in the second half-line. Each half-line had two strong accents and one or several light syllables. This rise and fall of accented and light beats in each line could be varied into five distinct accent patterns. The result was a strong rhythm, without rhyme, and without stanza form—and very suggestive of modern free verse. In Old English poetry, nouns were considered the strongest parts of speech, then adjectives, then verbs. Sometimes the alliteration was double in one or both half-lines.

Here are two typical lines from *Beowulf:*

Gre´ndel gong´an. God´es yr´re baer
(Grendel going. God's ire [he] bore.)

Flo´ta fam´ ig-heals fú gel gelí cost.
(Foamy-neck floaters, like unto fowls.)

The translation which you will read has imitated the important features of the original poem. Again notice that each line had four major accents, and that every line is marked by alliteration:

Grendel, fated, fled to the fens
or
The stranger from far, the stalwart and strong.

The influence of Anglo-Saxon poetic technique is felt in our day, especially in the versification of Gerard Manley Hopkins. Hopkins admitted that he found the movement of his "new rhythm" in *Piers Plowman,* the great poem of the fourteenth century, which was written according to the rules of Old English poetry.

ANGLO-SAXON LANGUAGE

The Anglo-Saxon people spoke a form of Low German dialect which eventually became the root from which our English language sprang. Although it is true that many of the Old English words have disappeared, it is also true that most of the short, everyday words are direct descendants of this early English speech. Examples of such basic words are *day, father, mother, man, wife, drink, sleep, fight,* the personal pronouns and the numerals. Old English had its own pronunciation and spelling, and its own grammar with many inflectional forms, which show its kinship to Greek and Latin.

The resemblances and the differences between the Anglo-Saxon and Modern English are easily illustrated in the Old English version of the Our Father:

Faeder ūre, thū the eart on heofunum,
Sī thīn nama gehālgod.
Tobecume thīn rīce.
Gewurthe thīn Willa on earthan swā swā on heofunum.
Ure gehaeghwāmlican hlāf syle ūs tō daeg.
And forgyf ūs ūre gyltas, swā swā wē forgyfath ūrum gyltendum.
And ne gelǣd thū ūs on costnunge,
Ac ālys ūs of yfele. Sōthlīce.

An important characteristic of the Germanic languages is that they form new words by joining two or more old words. The Anglo-Saxon word for *vocabulary* was *word-hoard*; for *drowning* was *sea-death.* Modern English has kept this capacity for forming compounds, but it is usually more convenient for us to make new words by using Latin and Greek stems, prefixes, and suffixes. And so though we have expressions like *schoolhouse, railroad,* and *playwright,* we also say *depend* (not *under-hang*) and *submarine* (not *under-sea-boat).*

The Anglo-Saxons had an amazing poetic vocabulary—vivid, singing words. They had as many as twenty synonyms for such words as *sea, horse, warriors.* Adjectives had a double richness, like *thought-hard, winter-weary, battle-bright.* Their love for compounds often gave us such imaginative expressions as *World-father* for *Creator,* and *foamy-necked floaters* for *boats.* They had a real fondness for figures of speech, especially for metaphor and personification. The sun was a *sky-candle,* the sea, *the whale's road,* the ship, the *sea-horse,* the shield was the *linden-wood.* The use of these metaphorical compounds is so characteristic of their poetry that it is recognized as a particular figure of speech and called a *kenning.*

Old English prose first followed the Latin pattern, since it had been translated from the Latin. Its sentence structure was awkward and its grammar was inadequate. If the poetic vocabulary was complete, its vocabulary for the more abstract ideas required in prose was very limited. But as learning progressed and the Danes stopped pillaging the monasteries, prose developed. The spade work of Alfred gave growth to the rich flowering of the writing of Aelfric, the cultured teacher of the eleventh century.

NARRATIVE POETRY

In almost every language, the earliest literature is poetry rather than prose. The reasons for this are, perhaps, that the first literature was oral rather than written, and that it was sung or chanted in connection with some religious or tribal celebration; hence, poetry was a more natural medium of communication.

THE CLASSIFICATION OF POETRY

Poetry is generally classified as narrative, lyric, or dramatic. Why the earliest form of poetry should be narrative or story-telling poetry is easy to understand. Just like the child, all simple and primitive peoples are naturally interested in the common things they know, and the fantastic things they do not know and sometimes fear. So the blind Homer sang of Circe and the Enchantress, the singing Sirens, and one-eyed giants, as well as the banquet feast, the funeral pyres, and the tenderness of love. Scops and troubadours wandered from castle to castle in Saxon and Norman times, with their tales of fiery dragons, magic swords, and ladies in distress. And in our own time the American cowboy riding under the stars, the lumberjack around his camp fire, and the hill dweller in his mountain home have added to the wealth of American folklore the simple, naive, and sometimes violent tales which represent in part the life they know, and in part the life they hunger for.

Perhaps we have taken stories for granted, like our food and friends; but why do stories fascinate people? The most interesting adventure in the world is life, and stories give us a large or small cross-section of life, lived by *someone, somewhere, somehow.* An analysis of the simplest story, as well as of the most complex novel, will invariably reveal that *someone* (the character), *somewhere* (the setting), came up against some odds, some decision, the outcome of which *somehow* (sequence, story, or plot) influences his life and the lives of others. A story is then interesting because it portrays life. Life is interesting because it is a vital activity, often a clash of opposing forces, external to man, or within his soul. And since the outcome of such a clash is never certain because of man's free will, there inevitably will be *interest* and *suspense.*

Narrative poetry is generally divided into four types: (1) the epic, (2) the ballad, (3) the metrical romance, (4) the metrical tale. This book includes examples of all of these forms.

An epic is a long narrative poem, the highest, the most dignified, and the most sublime form of narrative poetry. It has been defined by the Greek, Aristotle, who said that an epic is an "imitation of life which is narrative in form and poetic in meter . . . it has for its subject a single action, whole and complete . . . The characters celebrated should be of lofty type." The essential story is usually quite simple, and progress is made throughout towards a definite goal. But the path taken is seldom the shortest one. Numerous episodes and "flash backs" lead to detours. In other words, the epic moves slowly, developing (in detail) the characteristics of greatness of its leading man, the epic hero.

There is always one central heroic character who embodies, to some extent, the outstanding characteristics of his race. He is usually involved in a struggle against opposing forces of nature, of men and supermen; it is through his deeds and by his efforts as a *representative* of his people that the episodes, each one of which is often complete in itself, are linked together and unified in a continuous narrative. As Professor Kerr points out in his *Epic and Romance,* "the grandeur and magnitude of the epic lies not so much in the elevated language, nor in the greatness of theme, nor in the length of the poem as in the greatness of soul of the hero." It is because of his "king-size" manner that the words, rhythm, and subordinate characters of the poem must take on suitable and like proportions.

THE EPIC

There are two types of epic, the *folk epic* and the *literary epic.* The folk epic originated among the people, and passed through a long period of telling before it reached its written form. The poet who finally made it a unified poem is usually unknown. *The Iliad* and *The Odyssey* of Homer, which tell of the last days of the Trojan War and the struggle of Ulysses to reach and save his own kingdom of Ithaca, after the fall of Troy, are the finest examples of the folk epic in the literature of the world. *The Nibelungenlied,* the German folk epic, tells the stories of the Germanic characters of the sixth and seventh centuries, Brunhild, Siegfried, and Hagen, later commemorated in the operas of Wagner. *The Song of Roland,* the great epic of France, recounts how Roland, one of Charlemagne's Twelve Peers, dies bravely because of the treachery of his own stepfather in betraying the cause of Charlemagne in his fight against the Saracens. *Beowulf* is the only folk epic in the English language.

The literary epic is the conscious product of one known writer. But the poet chooses his materials from respected traditions. To some extent, the literary epic also reflects the thought and opinions of the age in which it was written. The greatest literary epic in the English language is Milton's *Paradise Lost.* Other epics are Virgil's *Aeneid* and Dante's *Divine Comedy,* the latter perhaps the greatest piece of writing of all time, whose vast theme is the salvation of the human soul.

We may briefly summarize the essential elements of the epic as follows: The plot is a unified story whose direct action is short, but whose implied action is on a sweeping scale. There is one central, heroic character, plus some other superhuman and lesser characters. The setting is in the distant past, either legendary or supernatural. The mood is noble and dignified, religious and sublime. The poetic form often employs certain devices such as a formal introduction called "the invocation," a *roll-call of important characters,* and *lofty speeches* descriptive of persons, places, and events.

THE EPIC
BEOWULF

Beowulf is the oldest epic in any modern European language. Written in the eighth century by an unknown monk, the poem gives us a splendid example of the epic tradition. Although its material is Scandinavian in background, its structure is in the tradition of the literary epic, and there is no doubt of the Christian influence in its spirit. Much of the subject matter of the poem was originally collected through oral transmission; and the poem itself may have been developed from an earlier series of epic tales, though none of these has survived. But *Beowulf,* in the form in which it has come to us, is a single, unified poem.

The Christian author of *Beowulf* took the primitive material derived from pagan folk-lore and legend and infused into it a Christian spirit which colors the entire poem. The thoughts and judgments, the actions and the motives of the noble characters are Christian. Pagan elements still remain, however. For example, side by side we find references to the blind power of *Wyrd,* or Fate, and to the omnipotence and providence of the true God. But just as often it is implied that Fate is controlled by the Christian God. Again, the origin of Grendel and his dam or mother from the Scandinavian water troll is lost in the poet's identification of these monsters as the adversaries of God. Reference to the Old Testament runs throughout the poem in unmistakably Christian terms.

The character of Beowulf is suffused with the Christian spirit. Again and again he asks for divine guidance and acknowledges the assistance of God in his heroic deeds. The Christian way of life motivates the conduct of the noble characters. No more beautiful expression of Christian wisdom can be found than that of the advice of Hrothgar to Beowulf at the height of his triumphs.

Beowulf is a story of the pagan past of the ancestors of the eighth century Anglo-Saxon, retold in the light of Christian teachings of the Golden Age of Anglo-Saxon literature. It is a tale in which the endurance, loyalty, and courage of the heroic age are tempered with Christian virtues and graced with the courtly manners which were to characterize all subsequent English medieval literature.

There can be little doubt that the epic *Beowulf* was composed under the influence of the Virgilian epic. In general form and movement it manifests a literary quality of form and movement, an epic dignity of speech and action, a well-developed theme not derived from the Scandinavian tale. Virgil's *Aeneid* was well known in the early Middle Ages. Venerable Bede and Alcuin were lovers of Virgil. Surely the educated poet of the Age of Bede who fashioned *Beowulf* must have had in mind the *Aeneid* as the model of the classical epic.

Was the epic composed by a Christian monk to give an example of a noble king and the Christian ideal? Edmund Spenser, who wrote the *Faerie Queene,* said that the purpose of his book "is to fashion a gentleman or noble person in virtuous and gentle discipline." Although we have no such statement of the purpose of the author of *Beowulf,* many passages in the poem suggest that he wrote the poem not merely to retell an heroic pagan story, but to give his age a narrative of an heroic Christian king who would serve as a model for noble living.

The spirit of the poem is the spirit of England, and its poetic ideal is the Christian ideal. It is a poem suited to the Christian court. Its English strain is felt in its tone of pondering sadness and lament, as well as its moral temper. Both the youthful and the aged Beowulf illustrate that chivalrous spirit which gave birth to the knight errant of the medieval courtly romance.

"Beyond the call of duty" was the theme of Beowulf's life. Courage, strength united to gentleness, solicitude for the needs and dangers of others, a sense of honor and valor ennobled by unselfish service, faith and trust in God—these are some of the lessons of life that come to the modern world from the pages of *Beowulf.*

Beowulf

TRANSLATED BY CHARLES W. KENNEDY

The story begins in the land of the Danes in the reign of King Hrothgar. The glory of his rule was symbolized in the great hall which he built and called Heorot[1] or Hall of the Hart.[2] But in time disaster came to the land in the form of two monsters: Grendel and his dam or mother, both of hideous shape and superhuman size.

To Hrothgar was granted glory in war,
Success in battle; retainers bold
Obeyed him gladly; his band increased
To a mighty host. Then his mind was moved
To have men fashion a high-built hall,
A mightier mead-hall than man had known,
Wherein to portion to old and young
All goodly treasure that God had given,
Save only the folk-land, and lives of men.
His word was published to many a people
Far and wide o'er the ways of the earth
To rear a folk-stead richly adorned;
The task was speeded, the time soon came
That the famous mead-hall was finished and done.
To distant nations its name was known,
The Hall of the Hart; and the king kept well
His pledge and promise to deal out gifts,
Rings at the banquet. The great hall rose
High and horn-gabled, holding its place
Till the battle-surge of consuming flame
Should swallow it up. . . .
Then an evil spirit who dwelt in the darkness
Endured it ill that he heard each day
The din of revelry ring through the hall,
The sound of the harp, and the scop's sweet song.
A skillful bard sang the ancient story
Of man's creation; how the Maker wrought
The shining earth with its circling waters;
In splendor established the sun and moon
As lights to illumine the land of men;
Fairly adorning the fields of earth
With leaves and branches; creating life
In every creature that breathes and moves.
So the lordly warriors lived in gladness,
At ease and happy, till a fiend from hell
Began a series of savage crimes.
They called him Grendel, a demon grim
Haunting the fen-lands, holding the moors,
Ranging the wastes, where the wretched wight

[1]HEOROT (hā´ō·rŏt).

[2]HART—Deer.

38. FEN-LANDS—Marshes.

39. WIGHT—A creature, a living being, from the Anglo-Saxon.

Made his lair with the monster kin;
He bore the curse of the seed of Cain
Whereby God punished the grievous guilt
Of Abel's murder. Nor ever had Cain
Cause to boast of that deed of blood;
God banished him far from the fields of men;
Of his blood was begotten an evil brood,
Marauding monsters and menacing trolls,
Goblins and giants who battled with God
A long time. Grimly He gave them reward!

[Night raids by Grendel gradually diminished the number of Hrothgar's warriors and turned the hall into a place of fear and dread. For twelve years this terror lay upon the land.

But news of this dire calamity which was afflicting the Danes reached the land of the Geats in southern Sweden, where it came to the knowledge of the hero Beowulf. Against the advice of his uncle, Hygelac, and eager for fame and adventure, Beowulf with a small band of followers sailed for Denmark to match his strength against Grendel.]

Then tales of the terrible deeds of Grendel
Reached Hygelac's thane in his home with the Geats;
Of living strong men he was the strongest,
Fearless and gallant and great of heart.
He gave command for a goodly vessel
Fitted and furnished; he fain would sail
Over the swan-road to seek the king
Who suffered so sorely for need of men.

47. TROLLS—A troll is a preternatural being, celebrated in Scandinavian folk-lore. It is sometimes referred to as a dwarf, sometimes as a giant, which inhabits caves, hills and the sea. The myth of the trolls has been woven into the story of *The Song of Norway*, the modern light opera.

And his bold retainers found little to blame
In his daring venture, dear though he was;
They viewed the omens, and urged him on.
Brave was the band he had gathered about him,
Fourteen stalwarts seasoned and bold,
Seeking the shore where the ship lay waiting,
A sea-skilled mariner sighting the landmarks.
Came the hour of boarding; the boat was riding
The waves of the harbor under the hill
The eager mariners mounted the prow;
Billows were breaking, sea against sand.
In the ship's hold snugly they stowed their trappings,
Gleaming armor and battle-gear;
Launched the vessel, the well-braced bark,
Seaward bound on a joyous journey.
Over breaking billows, with bellying sail
And foamy beak, like a flying bird
The ship sped on, till the next day's sun
Showed sea-cliffs shining, towering hills
And stretching headlands. The sea was crossed,
The voyage ended, the vessel moored.
And the Weder people waded ashore
With clatter of trappings and coats of mail;
Gave thanks to God that His grace had granted
Sea-paths safe for their ocean-journey.

[Beowulf and his company landed and were challenged by the Danish coast-guard, who noted the princely form and bearing of Beowulf. After learning his name and his mission, the coast-guard led the company over the stone-paved streets where the Hall of the Hart gleamed in its glory. They piled their

war-gear and boar-crested helmets outside the hall. A warrior bore the news of their coming to Hrothgar. Beowulf entered proudly.]

Then the bold one rose with his band around him,
A splendid massing of mighty thanes;
A few stood guard as the Geat gave bidding
Over the weapons stacked by the wall.
They followed in haste on the heels of their leader
Under Heorot's roof. Full ready and bold
The helmeted warrior strode to the hearth;
Beowulf spoke; his byrny glittered,
His war-net woven by cunning of smith:
"Hail! King Hrothgar! I am Hygelac's thane,
Hygelac's kinsman. Many a deed
Of honor and daring I've done in my youth
This business of Grendel was brought to my ears
On my native soil. The seafarers say
This best of buildings, this boasted hall,
Stands dark and deserted when sun is set,
When darkening shadows gather with dusk.
The best of my people, prudent and brave,
Urged me, King Hrothgar, to seek you out;
They had in remembrance my courage and might.
Many had seen me come safe from the conflict,
Bloody from battle; five foes I bound
Of the giant kindred, and crushed their clan.
Hard-driven in danger and darkness of night
I slew the nicors that swam the sea,
Avenged the woe they had caused the Weders,
And ended their evil—they needed the lesson!
And now with Grendel, the fearful fiend,
Single-handed I'll settle the strife!
Lord of nations, and leader of men,
I beg one favor—refuse me not,
Since I come thus faring from far-off lands—
That I may alone with my loyal earls,
With this hardy company, cleanse Hart-Hall.
I have heard that the demon in proud disdain
Spurns all weapons; and I too scorn—
May Hygelac's heart have joy of the deed—
To bear my sword, or sheltering shield,
Or yellow buckler, to battle the fiend.
With hand-grip only I'll grapple with Grendel;
Foe against foe I'll fight to the death,
And the one who is taken must trust to God's grace!"

107. NICOR—A water monster.

ðꞃeah ſyð þan hie þæſ laðan laſt ſcea
ƿedon ƿeꞃᵹan ᵹaſteſ ƿæſ ꝥ ᵹe ƿin to

[Hrothgar gratefully welcomed Beowulf amid royal entertainment and entrusted to Beowulf and his band the task of freeing Heorot from the scourge of Grendel. At the height of the celebration the jealous and proud Danish courtier, Unferth, alluded to a swimming match between Beowulf and Breca in which Unferth claimed that Breca had bested Beowulf. Breca predicted an evil fate for Beowulf if he dared to encounter Grendel. But Beowulf replied:]

"My good friend Unferth, addled with beer
Much have you made of the deeds of Breca!
I count it true that I had more courage,
More strength in swimming than any other man.
In our youth we boasted—we were both of us boys—
We would risk our lives in the raging sea.
And we made it good! We gripped in our hands
Naked swords, as we swam in the waves,
Guarding us well from the whales' assault.
In the breaking seas he could not outstrip me,
Nor would I leave him. For five nights long
Side by side we strove in the waters
Till racing combers wrenched us apart,
Freezing squalls, and the falling night,
And a bitter north wind's icy blast.
Rough were the waves; the wrath of the sea-fish
Was fiercely roused; but my firm-linked byrny,
The gold-adorned corselet that covered my breast,
Gave firm defense from the clutching foe.
Down to the bottom a savage sea-beast
Fiercely dragged me and held me fast
In a deadly grip; nonetheless it was granted me
To pierce the monster with a point of steel.
Death swept it away with the swing of my sword.
The grisly sea-beasts again and again
Beset me sore; but I served them home
With my faithful blade as was well-befitting.
Bloody with wounds, at the break of day,
They lay on the sea-beach slain with the sword.
No more would they cumber the mariner's course
On the ocean deep. From the east came the sun,
Bright beacon of God, and the seas subsided;
I beheld the headlands, the windy walls.
Fate often delivers an undoomed earl
If his spirit be gallant! And so I was granted
To slay with the sword-edge nine of the nicors.
I have never heard tell of more terrible strife
Under dome of heaven in darkness of night,
Nor of man harder pressed on the paths of ocean.
But I freed my life from the grip of the foe
Though spent with the struggle.
The billows bore me,
The swirling currents and surging seas,
To the land of the Finns. And little I've heard
Of any such valiant adventures from you!
Neither Breca nor you in the press of battle

Ever showed such daring with dripping swords—
Though I boast not of it! But you stained your blade
With blood of your brothers, your closest of kin;
And for that you'll endure damnation in hell,
Sharp as you are! I say for a truth,
Son of Ecglaf, never had Grendel
Wrought such havoc and woe in the hall,
That horrid demon so harried your king,
If your heart were as brave as you'd have men think!
But Grendel has found that he never need fear
Revenge from your people, or valiant attack
From the Victor-Scyldings, he takes his toll,
Sparing none of the Danish stock.
But soon will I show him the stuff of the Geats,
Their courage in battle and strength in the strife."

[Hrothgar's hopes were high as he listened to Beowulf's bold resolve. At nightfall, Beowulf and his men took over the hall, sleeping with their weapons at hand. Then suddenly out of the mist and darkness, Grendel burst in upon them.]

From the stretching moors, from the misty hollows,
Grendel came creeping, accursed of God,
A murderous ravager minded to snare
Spoils of heroes in high-built hall.
Under clouded heavens he held his way
Till there rose before him the high-roofed house,
Wine-hall of warriors gleaming with gold.
Storming the building he burst the portal,
Though fastened of iron, with fiendish strength;
Forced open the entrance in savage fury
And rushed in rage o'er the shining floor.
A baleful glare from his eyes was gleaming
Most like to a flame. He found in the hall
Many a warrior sealed in slumber,
A host of kinsmen. His heart rejoiced;
The savage monster was minded to sever
Lives from bodies ere break of day,
To feast his fill of the flesh of men.
But he was not fated to glut his greed
With more of mankind when night was ended!
The hardy kinsman of Hygelac waited
To see how the monster would make his attack.
The demon delayed not, but quickly clutched
A sleeping thane in his swift assault,
Tore him in pieces, bit through the bones,
Gulped the blood, and gobbled the flesh,
Greedily gorged on the lifeless corpse,
The hands and the feet. Then the fiend stepped nearer,
Sprang on the Sea-Geat lying outstretched,
Clasping him close with his monstrous claw.
But Beowulf grappled and gripped him hard,
Struggled up on his elbow; the shepherd of sins
Soon found that never before had he felt
In any man other in all the earth

181. VICTOR-SCHYLDINGS (shil´dingz) — Descendants of Scyld. Danes.

A mightier hand-grip; his mood was humbled,
His courage fled; but he found no escape!
He was fain to be gone; he would flee to the darkness,
The fellowship of devils. Far different his fate
From that which befell him in former days!
The hardy hero, Hygelac's kinsman,
Remembered the boast he had made at the banquet;
He sprang to his feet, clutched Grendel fast,
Though fingers were cracking, the fiend pulled free.
The earl pressed after; the monster was minded
To win his freedom and flee to the fens.
He knew that his fingers were fast in the grip
Of a savage foe. Sorry the venture,
The raid that the ravager made on the hall.
There was din in Heorot. For all the Danes,
The city-dwellers, the stalwart Scyldings,
That was a bitter spilling of beer!
The walls resounded, the fight was fierce,
Savage the strife as the warriors struggled.
The wonder was that the lofty wine-hall
Withstood the struggle, nor crashed to earth,
The house so fair; it was firmly fastened
Within and without with iron bands
Cunningly smithied; though men have said
That many a mead-bench gleaming with gold
Sprang from its sill as the warriors strove.
The Scylding wise men had never weened

That any ravage could wreck the building
Till the time when the swelter and surge of fire
Should swallow it up in a swirl of flame.
Continuous tumult filled the hall;
A terror fell on the Danish folk
As they heard through the wall the horrible wailing,
The groans of Grendel, the foe of God
Howling his hideous hymn of pain,
The hell-thane shrieking in sore defeat.
He was fast in the grip of the man who was greatest
Of mortal men in the strength of his might,
Who would never rest while the wretch was living,
Counting his life-days a menace to man.
Many an earl of Beowulf brandished
His ancient iron to guard his lord,
To shelter safely the peerless prince.
They had no knowledge, these daring thanes,
When they drew their weapons to hack and hew,
To thrust to the heart, that the sharpest sword,
The choicest iron in all the world,
Could work no harm to the hideous foe.
On every sword he had laid a spell,
On every blade; but a bitter death
Was to be his fate; far was the journey
The monster made to the home of fiends.
Then he who had wrought such wrong to men,
With grim delight as he warred with God,
Soon found that his strength was feeble and failing
In the crushing hold of Hygelac's thane.
Each loathed the other while life should last!
There Grendel suffered a grievous hurt,
A wound in the shoulder, gaping and wide;
Sinews snapped and bone-joints broke,
And Beowulf gained the glory of battle.
Grendel, fated, fled to the fens,
To his joyless dwelling, sick unto death.
He knew in his heart that his hours were numbered,
His days at an end. For all the Danes
Their wish was fulfilled in the fall of Grendel.
The lord of the Geats made good to the East-Danes
The boast he had uttered; he ended their ill.
The token was clear when the bold in battle
Laid down the shoulder and dripping claw—
Grendel's arm—in the gabled hall!

[With morning came joy as the Danes gathered in the Hall to view the huge claw of Grendel. They traced the bloody steps of the monster to the edge of the dark pool. As they returned from the fen to Heorot, with horses proudly prancing, a minstrel sang a song in praise of Beowulf. A great feast was prepared at which Hrothgar honored Beowulf and his men with many gifts in the banquet hall. Hour after hour the revelry continued.

But the coming of night brought new horror in the person of Grendel's mother who came to avenge her son's death. She entered among the sleeping Danish thanes, woke them to struggle, and carried off Aeschere, the beloved comrade of Hrothgar. The Danes were filled with despair. In the morning, the aged Hrothgar speedily summoned Beowulf, who had no knowledge of the new attack.]

The hero came tramping into the hall
With his chosen band—the boards re-sounded—
Greeted the leader, the Ingwine lord,
And asked if the night had been peaceful and pleasant.
Hrothgar spoke, the lord of the Scyldings:
"Ask not of pleasure; pain is renewed
For the Danish people. Aeschere is dead!
He was my comrade, closest of counsellors,
My shoulder-companion as side by side
We fought for our lives in the welter of war,
As an earl should be, a prince without peer,
Such was Aeschere, slain in the hall
By the wandering demon! I know not whither
She fled to shelter, proud of her spoil,
Gorged to the full . . .
Oft in the hall I have heard my people,
Comrades and counsellors, telling a tale
Of evil spirits their eyes have sighted,
Two mighty marauders who haunt the moors.
One shape, as clearly as men could see,
Seemed woman's likeness, and one seemed man,
An outcast wretch of another world,
And huger far than a human form.
Grendel my countrymen called him, not knowing
What monster-brood spawned him, what sire begot.
Wild and lonely the land they live in,
Wind-swept ridges and wolf-retreats.
Dread tracts of fen where the falling torrent
Downward dips into gloom and shadow
Under the dusk of the darkening cliff.
Not far in miles lies the lonely mere
Where trees firm-rooted and hung with frost
Overshroud the wave with shadowing gloom.
And there a portent appears each night,
A flame in the water; no man so wise
Who knows the bounds of its bottom-less depth.
The heather-stepper, the horned stag,
The antlered hart hard driven by hounds,
Invading that forest in flight from afar
Will turn at bay and die on the brink
Ere ever he'll plunge in that haunted pool.
'Tis an eerie spot! Its tossing spray
Mounts dark to heaven when high winds stir
The driving storm, and the sky is murky,
And with foul weather the heavens weep.
On your arm only rests all our hope!
Not yet have you tempted those terrible reaches
The region that shelters that sinful wight.
Go if you dare! I will give requital
With ancient treasure and twisted gold.
As I formerly gave in guerdon of battle,
If out of that combat you come alive."
Beowulf spoke, the son of Ecgtheow:
"Sorrow not, brave one! Better for man
To avenge a friend than much to mourn.
All men must die; let him who may
Win glory ere death. That guerdon is best
For a noble man when his name survives him.

292. INGWINE (ĭng´wĭ·nă)—Danes.

320. MERE—A lake or pool.

340. GUERDON (gûr´dŭn)—A reward.

342. ECGTHEOW (ĕj´thĕ·ō)—Father of Beowulf.

Then let us rise up, O ward of the realm,
And haste us forth to behold the track
Of Grendel's dam."

[Hrothgar leaped up and thanked God for the hero's words. Then the Danes and the Geats journeyed together over the moorlands to the watery depths. Beowulf girded himself with his war-gear and Unferth gave him his sword, Hrunting. Beowulf accepted the sword and asked that all his treasure be sent to Hygelac if he died in the combat.]

After these words the prince of the Weders
Awaited no answer, but turned to the task,
Straightway plunged in the swirling pool.
Nigh unto a day he endured the depths
Ere he first had view of the vast sea-bottom.
Soon she found, who had haunted the flood,
A ravening hag, for a hundred half-years,
Greedy and grim, that a man was groping
In daring search through the sea-troll's home.
Swift she grappled and grasped the warrior
With horrid grip, but could work no harm,
No hurt to his body; the ring-locked byrny
Cloaked his life from her clutching claw;
Nor could she tear through the tempered mail
With her savage fingers. The she-wolf bore
The ring-prince down through the watery depths
To her den at the bottom; nor could Beowulf draw
His blade for battle, though brave his mood.
Many a sea-beast, strange sea-monsters,
Tasked him hard with their menacing tusks,
Broke his byrny and smote him sore.
Then he found himself in a fearsome hall
Where water came not to work him hurt,
But the flood was stayed by the sheltering roof.
There in the glow of the firelight gleaming
The hero had view of the huge sea-troll.
He swung his war-sword with all his strength,
Withheld not the blow, and the savage blade
Sang on her head its hymn of hate.
But the bold one found that the battle-flasher
Would bite no longer, nor harm her life.
The sword-edge failed at his sorest need.
But fixed of purpose and firm of mood
Hygelac's earl was mindful of honor;
In wrath, undaunted, he dashed to earth
The jewelled sword with its scrolled design,
The blade of steel; staked all on strength,
On the might of his hand, as a man must do
Who thinks to win in the welter of battle
Enduring glory; he fears not death.

[Beowulf gripped the shoulder of Grendel's dam and hurled her to the ground. In the tussle, she staggered Beowulf, knelt upon him and drew her dagger, but the steel of his corslet shielded his breast. Swiftly he sprang

to his feet, seized a heavy sword from her war-gear, and struck with fury.]

Thrust at the throat, broke through the bone-rings;
The stout blade stabbed through her fated flesh.
She sank in death; the sword was bloody;
The hero joyed in the work of his hand.
The gleaming radiance shimmered and shone
As the candle of heaven shines clear from the sky.

[The Danes who had watched at the edge of the pool believed Beowulf had been killed when they saw the water suddenly stained with blood. In despair they returned to Heorot. But the loyal Geats waited until at last Beowulf swam up from the depths bearing Grendel's head and the hilt of the sword whose blade had melted. Joyfully his companions accompanied him to the Hall of the Hart. Here again Hrothgar celebrated with an elaborate feast and giving of gifts. When all were silent Hrothgar praised the young hero who had been strong and loyal, and bade young Beowulf to strive for virtue, as the ancient Danish King Heremod did not.]

"Strive for virtue! I speak for your good.
'Tis a wondrous marvel how mighty God
In gracious spirit bestows on men
The gift of wisdom, and goodly lands,
And princely power! He rules over all!
He suffers a man of lordly line
To set his heart on his own desires,
Awards him fullness of worldly joy,
A fair home-land, and the sway of cities,
The wide dominion of many a realm,
An ample kingdom, till, cursed with folly,
The thoughts of his heart take no heed of his end.

He lives in luxury, knowing not want,
Knowing no shadow of sickness or age;
No haunting sorrow darkens his spirit,
No hatred or discord deepens to war;
The world is sweet to his every desire,
And evil assails not—until in his heart
Pride overpowering gathers and grows.
Then is his heart pierced, under his helm,His soul in his bosom, with bitter dart.
He has no defense for the fierce assaults
Of the loathsome Fiend. What he long has cherished
Seems all too little! In anger and greed
He gives no guerdon of plated rings.
Since God has granted him glory and wealth
He forgets the future, unmindful of Fate.
But it comes to pass in the day appointed
His feeble body withers and fails;
Death descends, and another seizes
His hoarded riches and rashly spends
The princely treasure, imprudent of heart.
Beloved Beowulf, best of warriors,
Avoid such evil and seek the good,
The heavenly wisdom. Beware of pride!"

[With the morning light Beowulf came to take his leave. He returned Hrunting with thanks to Unferth, and with his companions triumphantly took sail for home.]

The ship was launched.
Cleaving the combers of open sea
They dropped the shoreline of Denmark astern.
A stretching sea-cloth, a bellying sail,
Was bent on the mast; there was groaning of timbers;
A gale was blowing; the boat drove on.
The foamy-necked plunger plowed through the billows,
The ring-stemmed ship through the breaking seas,
Till at last they sighted the sea-cliffs of Geatland.
The well-known headlands; and, whipped by the wind,
The boat drove shoreward and beached on the sand.

[Upon their arrival in the land of the Geats, they were royally welcomed and feasted by Hygelac and his court. Beowulf recounted his wonderful adventures and shared with Hygelac and the queen the gifts which Hrothgar had given him. Hygelac, in turn, gave Beowulf a gift of a costly sword, and a stately hall with a large estate. So ends the first section of the narrative.

Years went by and at last Beowulf ruled the kingdom of the Geats. During his old age a fire dragon ravaged his land after one of his men stole a golden flagon from a huge treasure which the dragon had guarded for three hundred years. With fire and flame the dragon burned dwellings and filled all hearts with terror. Beowulf prepared for battle against this menace to his people. Armed with his sword, Naegling, and an iron shield, the king, with eleven comrades, was guided by the thief to the dragon's fen.]

The thirteenth man in the hurrying throng
Was the sorrowful captive who caused the feud.

[Standing near the stone entrance from which hot steam poured forth, Beowulf and the dragon entered into mortal combat. His sword, Naegling, broke. All of his companions turned and fled into the forest to save their lives except the youthful Wiglat.]

he saw his king
Under his helmet smitten with heat.
He thought of the gifts which his lord had given,
The wealth and the land of the Waegmunding line
And all the folk-rights his father had owned;
Wiglaf spoke in sorrow of soul,
With bitter reproach rebuking his comrades:
"I remember the time, as we drank in the mead-hall,
When we swore to our lord who bestowed these rings
That we would repay for the war-gear and armor,
The hard swords and helmets, if need like this
Should ever befall him.
Now is the day that our lord has need
Of the strength and the courage of stalwart men.
Let us haste to succor his sore distress
In the horrible heat and merciless flame.
God knows I had rather the fire should enfold
My body and limbs with my gold-friend and lord."

[Finally the dragon fastened his fangs in Beowulf's throat and the hero suffered a deadly wound. Wiglaf thrust his sword into the dragon's body and Beowulf with dying strength cut the beast in two with his dagger. Now dying Beowulf spoke:]

"My armor and sword I would leave to my son
Had Fate but granted, born of my body,
An heir to follow me after I'm gone.
For fifty winters I've ruled this realm,
And never a lord of a neighboring land
Dared strike with terror or seek with sword.
In my life I abode by the lot assigned,
Kept well what was mine, courted no quarrels,
Swore no false oaths. And now for all this
Though my hurt is grievous, my heart is glad.
When life leaves body, the Lord of mankind
Cannot lay to my charge the killing of kinsmen!"

[Beowulf asked Wiglaf to gaze on the gold of dragon's loot. Wiglaf returned to his dying lord with heaps of the treasure. As he looked upon the spoils, Beowulf gave thanks to God who gave the grace to win these riches for his people. He spoke again to young Wiglaf:]

"Heed well the wants, the need of my people;
My hour is come, and my end is near.
Bid warriors build, when they burn my body,
A stately barrow on the headland's height.
It shall be for remembrance among my people
As it towers high on the Cape of the Whale,
And sailors shall know it as Beowulf's Barrow,
Sea-faring mariners driving their ships
Through fogs of ocean from far countries."

448. WAE´GMUNDING (wag'mŭn-dĭng)—The family to which Wiglaf and Beowulf belonged.

478. BARROW—A grave covered by an earthen mound.

Then the great-hearted king unclasped from his throat
A collar of gold, and gave to his thane;
Gave the young hero his gold-decked helmet,
His ring and his byrny, and wished him well.
"You are the last of the Waegmunding line.
All my kinsmen, earls in their glory,
Fate has sent to their final doom,
And I must follow." These words were the last
The old king spoke ere the pyre received him,
The leaping flames of the funeral blaze,
And his breath went forth from his bosom, his soul
Went forth from the flesh, to the joys of the just.

[The cowardly thanes crept back and looked at Wiglaf as he sat by the king's body. Wiglaf again upbraided them and told of the contempt with which the cowardly deed would be spoken of in future years. A messenger rode along the cliffs relating the sad news of Beowulf's people and prophesying the fall of the nation. The body of the dead dragon was tumbled over the cliff into the sea. In accordance with Beowulf's dying wish, a funeral pyre was built on the headland and a barrow constructed in which was buried the dragon's treasure. The funeral pyre was kindled, and round the pyre wound the mourning warriors as they proclaimed his virtue and fame.]

They sang their dirge and spoke of the hero
Vaunting his valor and venturous deeds.
So is it proper a man should praise
His friendly lord with a loving heart,
When his soul must forth from the fleeting flesh.
So the folk of the Geats, the friends of his hearth,
Bemoaned the fall of their mighty lord;
Said he was the kindest of worldly kings,
Mildest, most gentle, most eager for fame.

WORD STUDY

1. Give several synonyms for the following words: *addled, harried, baleful, marauding, murky, swelter, eerie, wrought.*

2. Show how the word *ominous* is related to *omen*. What does *portent* mean? What is the difference between *cumber* and *combers*? What is the connection between the word *mere* and the Latin word *mare?*

3. In translating Beowulf into modern English, Professor Kennedy has kept the strong action verbs, the epithets or vivid picture adjectives, and the compound words of the Anglo-Saxons. Carefully select several examples of such verbs and adjectives.

FOR DISCUSSION

1. What information in the first 36 lines is given us to indicate that Hrothgar was a successful Christian king?

2. What details are we given about Grendel in lines 37-49?

3. Briefly describe the journey of Beowulf from the land of the Geats to Denmark.

4. Discuss the contents of Beowulf's first speech before Hrothgar in lines 90-124. How did Hrothgar receive Beowulf?

5. How did Beowulf refute the charge of Unferth that Beowulf had been bested in the swimming match with Breca? Is there any irony or sarcasm in his reply? Explain.

6. Briefly describe the encounter of Beowulf with Grendel. Was Grendel slain by a sword? Explain.

7. Was Beowulf present in the mead-hall when Grendel's dam slew Aeschere?

8. Briefly describe Beowulf's encounter with Grendel's dam. Was Unferth's sword, Hrunting, effective in slaying her? Explain. What did Beowulf carry with him when he arose to the surface of the pool?

9. What and who provoked the Fire Dragon to lay waste the land of the Geats during the last years of Beowulf's reign?

10. Contrast the actions of Wiglaf with those of the other thanes in Beowulf's tragic combat with the Fire Dragon. How did Beowulf suffer his mortal wound? How was the fire dragon killed?

11. What were Beowulf's parting requests as spoken to Wiglaf?

12. Enumerate the details which conclude the epic.

FOR APPRECIATION

1. The selection from *Beowulf* which you have read is filled with many beautiful *kennings* like *swan-road, heather-stepper,* and *foamy-necked plunger.* Select at least ten *kennings* from the text.

2. Choose from the text at least ten lines in which the translator was particularly successful in imitating the alliterative form of the original Anglo-Saxon verse.

3. The hero of an epic sums up in himself the characteristics of the ideal man of the country in which the epic was written. Write a character sketch of Beowulf pointing out the virtues portrayed in him which the Christian Anglo-Saxon of the eighth century admired.

4. Reread and study carefully lines 397-431, which contain the advice of Hrothgar to Beowulf. Could the modern ruler as well as the average man profit from such advice? Discuss. Is this advice of Hrothgar solid spiritual advice? Explain.

5. An interesting study for those who have studied the *Aeneid* would be to 1) compare the *Aeneid* and *Beowulf* as examples of epic poetry; 2) compare the descriptions of the seas and the storms in *Beowulf* with some of those in the *Aeneid*; 3) analyze the similarities of setting and imagery in lines 315-334 of *Beowulf* with lines 479-591 of the Seventh Book of the *Aeneid.*

6. Do you find any evidence that the author of *Beowulf* would have his hero stand for Christ and his companions for the Apostles? Discuss.

PROJECTS

1. Write one or more brief prose descriptions modeled after the descriptions in lines 65-82; lines 315-338; lines 432-442.

2. Reread the treatment of the epic as a form of narrative poetry and show how *Beowulf* conforms to the epic tradition.

RELATED READING

Every student will want to read the entire poem in the translation by Professor Kennedy.

The *Seafarer* is one of the earliest English poems of the sea. This poem as well as excerpts from Cynewulf's majestically beautiful poems, *The Christ, Elene,* and *The Dream of the Rood,* may be found in modern translation in Margaret Williams' *Word-Hoard.*

You are urged to read the thrilling *Song of Roland* in the excellent modern English translation by Frederick Bliss Luquiens.

THE ECCLESIASTICAL HISTORY OF ENGLAND

THE VENERABLE BEDE

Translated by Alfred

The famous passage below, taken from Bede's ECCLESIASTICAL HISTORY, *tells the story of the first English Christian poet and of how he acquired his miraculous gift of song while living at the monastery of the Abbess Hilda. The selection also gives us a fine example of the rough, alliterative rhythm of early English prose.*

In the monastery of this Abbess (Saint Hilda) was a certain brother wonderfully gifted and honoured with God's grace, because he was in the habit of putting into song the things that tended to piety and virtue, so that whatever he learned through scribes of holy lore, that he adorned after a little while with song-speech, with the greatest sweetness and zeal, and always put it in the English tongue, and through his songs the hearts of many men were often set burning with scorn of the world and with attraction to the heavenly life. And thus many others after him among the English began to make holy songs, but no other could do it like to him, because he learned songcraft not at all from men but was helped divinely, and through God's gift received songcraft.

"The Ecclesiastical History of England" by Bede and translated by Alfred from *Word Hoard—Passages from Old English Literature from the Sixth to the Eleventh Centuries,* translated and arranged by Margaret Williams, M.A., copyright, 1940, by Sheed and Ward, Inc., New York.

And for this he could not work a lie nor an idle song, but only those which led to piety and which it became a godly tongue to sing.

He was a man living in the worldly state until the time when he was advanced in years, and he had never learned any song, and for this often at the beer drinking, when it was deemed for the sake of bliss that they all, each in turn, should sing to the harp, then arose he for shame from the feasting, and went home to his house. When he had done that one time, left the house of the beer drinking and was going out to the cattleshed (the care of them was given to him that night), and when he there at the fitting time laid his limbs on the bed and slept, then stood by him a man in a dream, and hailed him and greeted him and named him by name: "Caedmon, sing me somewhat." Then answered he and said: "I cannot sing, for that I came out of the beer drinking and came hither, because I could not." Then he said that was speaking with him: "But thou canst sing to me." Said he: "What shall I sing?" Said he: "Sing me the first shaping." When he received this answer, then began he straight to sing in praise of God the Shaper verses and words he had never heard, and they went thus:

Now must we praise heaven's keeper,
the might of the ruler and His heart's thought,
the work of glory-father of every wonder
He made the beginning everlasting Lord.
He first shaped for the children of men
the skies for a roof, holy maker.
then afterwards mankind's keeper
made the earth, the soil for man,
almighty ruler and endless Lord.

Then arose he from sleep, and he had fast in mind all that he sang sleeping, and to those words straightway added he many words in the same measure to the song worthy of God. Then came he in the morning to the town-reeve who was the ealdorman, and told him what gift he had received, and he straightway led him to the Abbess, and said it and told it to her. Then she bade be gathered the most learned men, and the disciples, and bade him tell the dream before them, and sing that song, that it might be decided by the judgment of all of them, what and whence it was. Then it was plain to them all what it was, that it was a heavenly gift given by the Lord Himself. Then they related and told to him a holy story and words of godly lore. They bade him, then, if he could, change it into song, and into the harmony of verse. When he had heard it, then went he home to his house, and came again in the morning and sang to them a well-wrought poem, and gave to them what they had bidden.

Then began the Abbess to embrace and love God's gift in the man, and she advised and taught him that he should leave his worldly state and enter monk-hood, and he liked it well, and she received him into the monastery with his goods and added him to the company of God's servants, and bade him be taught the account of the holy story and tale, and all that he could learn with his hearing, that he turned in his mind, and as a clean beast ruminating[1] he turned it into the sweetest song, and his verses were so winsome to hear that his teachers themselves learned and wrote from his mouth. He sang first the shaping of earth and the beginning of mankind, and all the

[1]RUMINATING—Meditating; also, chewing the cud.

story of Genesis, that is the First Book of Moses, and then the outgoing of Israel's folk from the Egyptians' land, and the ingoing into the promised land, and about many others of the holy writing of the Canoni cal Books, and about Christ's manhood and His suffering, and His rising into Heaven, and about the coming of the Holy Ghost, and the teaching of the Apostles, and then about the terror of the Doom to come, and the fear of the pain full of torments, and about the sweetness of the Kingdom of heaven he made many songs; and also many others about God's benefits and dooms he wrought. In all these he earnestly tried to draw men from the love of sin and of evil deeds, for he was a very godly man and humbly subject to the discipline of the rule, and against those who would do otherwise he burned with zeal, and for this he finished and ended his life in a fair wise.

FOR DISCUSSION

1. What special significance does the story of Caedmon have for a Catholic writer? Discuss.

2. Compare the sentence structure of the passage with that of modern prose. In what ways do they differ? In three or four well chosen adjectives, sum up the qualities of Bede's style as seen in Alfred's translation.

WORD STUDY

Discuss the meaning of these early English words: *songspeech, holy lore, song-craft, first shaping, town-reeve.*

PROJECTS

Write a brief sketch of the life, works, and importance of Bede.

The Last Chapter, by J. Doyle Penrose (1902) Bede translating the Gospel of John on his deathbed

THE MIDDLE ENGLISH PERIOD

1066-1450

In the eleventh century, England's peace was threatened from across the Channel. Edward the Confessor, a Saxon king who spent his youth in France, disastrously welcomed influential Norman leaders to his court. This mistake paid off when Edward's successor, Harold, came to the throne. The Normans prepared to invade England and waited for the Danes to break out in one of their perennial uprisings in the north. Then the Normans landed on the beaches of the south of England in great on-rushing waves. Harold, "the last of the Saxons," moved his poorly equipped troops to meet this unexpected terror. On October 12, 1066, Harold's forces faced the troops of William the Conqueror at Hastings. As the *Anglo-Saxon Chronicle* relates: "Then beginning the *Song of Roland*, the standard was raised and waved, the trumpets and bugles sounded, and, invoking the aid of heavenly powers, they (the Normans) began the battle." From dawn to sunset the Saxon stood against the long-range bows of the French. Harold fell wounded, the army buckled, and William of Normandy became William the Conqueror of England.

The road to London now lay open to the Normans. Tersely does the *Anglo-Saxon Chronicle* tell of William's conquest and crowning: "William over-ran the land, and came to Westminster, and Ealdred the Archbishop hallowed him King, and men paid him tribute, and gave him hostages, and after bought their land."

The new conquerors were of a different cut from the Angles, Saxons, and Danes. The Normans were both Christian and civilized. They were descendants of Scandinavian Vikings who had seeped into northern France and so ravaged Christendom that a new invocation was added to the Litany of the Saints: "From the peril of Northmen, O Lord, deliver us." Soon they changed their Germanic tongue for the French of the conquered people. With their conversion to Christianity, they absorbed the Christian culture. This new people became an integral part of the French kingdom, and it was in Normandy that the French genius was best expressed in literature, in architecture, in chivalry.

CHARACTER OF THE NORMANS

Under the new regime, most of the great estates passed into the hands of William's followers, and the English bishops and abbots were supplanted by Norman churchmen. The new Norman nobility built thick-walled strongholds in which to defend themselves from the hostile Saxons; but as time went on and the opposition between Saxon and Norman lessened, these cumbersome structures were replaced by beautiful Norman castles which formed the background for a richer, gayer life than the rough Saxons had known. The Norman bishops likewise brought a new grandeur to cathedral and monastery. Durham, Ely, and the older parts of Canterbury still bear witness to the beauty of Norman architecture. At the hands of the conquerors, the government was gradually feudalized and centralized in the court. There was also a great increase in growth and importance of town and city life. Many businesses moved to England from the Continent and laid the foundations for modern English towns as commercial centers. In the century that followed the Conquest, French language and French laughter were heard at the court. Norman chroniclers told in rich Latin how William bent England to his will. But that century was a century of silence for native English literature.

The Normans, especially under Henry I (1100–1135) and Henry II (1154–1189), introduced the notions of chivalry and knighthood. This was the time of the Crusades, and with the Crusaders came back new ideas, new mannerisms, and new luxuries from the Orient. The two universities of Oxford and Cambridge, founded during this period, helped to increase learning and to spread many new ideas that were appearing.

The assimilation of Norman culture by the native Saxons came about only after much bloodshed, cruelty, and hard feeling. But different in so many respects, these two peoples knelt at the same altar. Religion was a common denominator that made an ultimate fusion of the two cultures possible. The Anglo-Saxons did gradually absorb the refinements of the Normans, so that by the year 1300, two centuries after the Conquest, there was a new culture and a new language which was neither entirely Norman nor strictly Anglo-Saxon.

UNION OF SAXONS AND NORMANS

The Magna Carta, wrung from King John in 1215, was to prove potent in welding the minds and hearts of the people together. It was the first important step in the long journey towards democracy. A free man could no longer be imprisoned or tortured except after lawful trial. Fines were fixed by law. No taxes could be levied without the consent of the Council. The Church was granted freedom from royal interference.

The march of equality advanced another step in 1265, when for the first time Parliament sat, not just as agents of the clergy and nobility, but with representatives of the common people—an assembly which was to become the English House of Commons.

England by the thirteenth century was "Merrie England." Exhilaration was in the air. Men explored the whole world of adventure and romance with a vigor which still holds us spellbound. Knights went bravely riding off to the Crusades; gay companies of ladies, squires, and monks made pilgrimages to distant shrines; scholars hastened to Rome. It was an age when the miraculous and supernatural were taken for granted. Men lived on intimate, easy terms with their patron saints and saw God as the center of their lives and Heaven as their ultimate home. It was an age of merriment—because men realized they were children of God.

However, in the fourteenth century, a series of misfortunes worked widespread havoc not only to Catholicism, the soul of medieval England, but to England at large. These unfortunate events began with another war—this time over holdings which the Norman kings still retained in France. Before it terminated, the Hundred Years' War cost England all her French territory and in 1349 brought the Black Death to the Island. This terrible plague destroyed one-third of the population and swept away two-thirds of the clergy and the monks who had been the teachers of England through the centuries. Unprepared, and in some cases, even unworthy men were ordained to take their places, with the result that not only religion but culture in general suffered.

A TIME OF UPHEAVAL

With the Battle of Crécy, the cannon replaced the traditional bow as an instrument of war, and spelt doom for the armored knight and the age of chivalry. The Black Death brought hunger in its wake, and hunger led to revolt. As weaving developed into an industry of primary importance, peasants left the manors to find work in the crowded towns. Boroughs and cities grew boisterous. Tax collectors were stoned off the streets and hardly a day passed without some dignitary being burned in effigy. People flocked to the country fairs, spending days and nights on the highways crowded with merchants and packmen. There were mountebanks and magicians to entice the country bumpkins, and pastry stalls that did a furious business. There were wines and silks and trinkets to be had after endless heckling. These were nervous, turbulent times when almost anything could happen—and usually did.

The great social contribution of the age was the system of guilds among the tradesmen and craftsmen, similar in many respects to our modern trade unions. As we shall see later, the guilds played a tremendous part in the development and sponsoring of the medieval drama.

As we have seen, it took more than a century for the Anglo-Saxon and Norman cultures to unite. During the first century after the Conquest, French became the language of the court and society. What literature there was, was written in either French or Latin. Anglo-Saxon was outlawed from the schools and was considered a mark of social inferiority. But in the country and among the simple people, the Old English tongue persisted.

CHANGES IN THE LANGUAGE

It gradually assimilated Norman words and turns of expression, until by the end of the thirteenth century, Old English had become Middle English, a language much closer to our modern tongue than was the old Anglo-Saxon. The new language retained much of the Anglo-Saxon vigor, but through the Norman influence gained considerably in lightness and flexibility.

The first effect of this fusion was a tremendous increase in the English vocabulary. Words were multiplied both numerically and expressively.

In our language today, we often have a choice of Saxon or Norman words to express a particular meaning for what we want to say. For example, *house* from the Saxon indicates an ordinary dwelling, but *mansion* and *manse* from the French *maison* indicate special kinds of houses. Usually the Anglo-Saxon words are the ones with the humble or common meaning, and the Norman-French have become the dressed-up or specialized words.

The Norman-French was a *Romance* language—that is, it was a modification of the Latin which had been spoken by the Roman soldiers who conquered Gaul. Thus English received through the Norman-French a great store of Latin derivatives. Today, we make use not only of the Anglo-Saxon word *red*, but also of words like *rouge, ruby,* and *rubicund* derived from the Latin through the Norman-French. Another fund of Latin words kept coming into English use directly, through the studies of churchmen and scholars.

The absorption of French and Latin words into English gave our language the capacity to make thousands of new words by using prefixes and suffixes. At the same time, it retained the picturesque, though sometimes cumbersome, knack of making compounds. The blend of Teutonic and Romance characteristics has resulted in giving modern English the most flexible and expressive vocabulary of all the living languages.

The second change that took place was a remarkable simplification of English grammar. Both Latin and Anglo-Saxon were highly inflected languages—that is, the various uses of words were indicated by changes in form of the words themelves. In learning a new language, these inflections are the most difficult to master. And so when Saxon and Norman got to talking together, they picked up each other's words and let the inflected endings go. The resulting simplification of inflections was further aided by the adoption of a simple or normal sentence order and by the substitution of natural gender for the confusing system of grammatical gender.

With a greatly increased vocabulary and a greatly simplified grammatical structure, a vital, flexible language emerged during the Middle English period.

It was this language that was to be the raw material which Chaucer, Shakespeare, Milton, and the other great English authors were to use in creating the masterpieces of English literature.

MIDDLE ENGLISH LITERATURE

Although Middle English literature reached its high water mark with Chaucer, Langland, the Pearl Poet, and Malory in the fourteenth and fifteenth centuries, we must not suppose that there was no literary activity in the English tongue during the two previous centuries. We shall mention but a few of the less known but important contributions to later English literature before studying in detail the ballad, the metrical romance, and the metrical tale—all distinct products of medieval literature.

The Beastiary, composed of allegorical tales of the animal kingdom, and punch-packed with moral lessons, was translated into English by an unknown poet of East Anglia in the thirteenth century. Both medieval preacher and poet drew upon these tales for their sermons and their literary writings.

The Owl and the Nightingale is one of the greatest of the medieval debate poems. It was developed according to the art form of the contentio (debate) of the *Eclogues* of Virgil and made popular in England by such scholars as Alcuin. The allegory in the poem has the owl sing of what is serious and traditional in life, while the nightingale sings of what is joyous, daring, and new. The influence of this debate poetry can be seen both in the metaphysical poets of the seventeenth century and in Dryden's famous allegorical satire, *The Hind and the Panther.*

RELIGIOUS LITERATURE

Much of the literature of the Middle Ages reflects the close connection between the monastic cloister and the world. Outstanding among the religious poetry and prose of this period are the *Ancren Riwle* by the Dominican Friar Robert Bacon and *The Form of Perfect Living* and the religious lyrics by Richard Rolle. Hundreds of other religious lyrics still survive whose authorship is unknown and whose poetic themes are the love of Franciscan poverty, love of Our Lady, and love of Christ, the ideal Knight. As a piece of prose literature, the *Ancren Riwle* molded the style of medieval English prose for centuries.

SECULAR LYRICS

The origins of the lyrics of Shakespeare as well as the moderns can be found not only in the Renaissance writers but also in the outpourings of the medieval wandering scholar and of the professional troubadour. The overcrowded universities of the time were unable to house the thousands of boys, for the most part irresponsible young clerics, who attended these seats of learning but were forced to sing for their livelihood. Unconsciously, these wandering young poets accomplished for literature what no professional poet could have done. With the hymns of the Church and the poetry of Horace ringing in their ears, they created a vernacular lyric of their own. The stanza forms and especially the rhymes were derived from the Church's liturgy. Often the Latin and the English languages were woven together into what is called macaronic verse. Of Our Lady they could sing:

Of one that is so fayr and bright
    Velut maris stella
Brighter than the day is light,
    Parens et puella.

Their love songs and nature songs were bright and gay, echoing the happy sounds of children on the village green.

Springtime is come with love to earth,
With blossoms and with bird's mirth
    That all this bliss bringeth.
Day's-eyes in the dales,
Notes sweet of nightingales,
    Every bird singeth.[1]

MEDIEVAL STORY TELLING

With no television or radio to fill up their leisure hours, the people of the Middle Ages welcomed a good story from any source. The author of the *Gesta Romanorum* tells us that "on stormy winter nights after supper the family gathers around the fireplace to tell old stories."

John Mandeville's *Travels* is the best known of these collections of stories. Originally written in French, they were translated into Middle English. In the *Gesta Romanorum,* a collection of 380 stories whose subject matter ranged from classical mythology to the realm of the preternatural, we have a storehouse of pointed narratives from which Shakespeare and many others drew heavily. For example, we find in it the tale of the bond concerning the pound of flesh and the story of "Androcles and the Lion," so popular with children of all ages.

By the end of the fourteenth century, writing came to be looked upon as an art to be developed for its own sake, and for the first time story collections were written by men who

[1] "Old English Lyric" from *Glee Wood—Passages from Middle English Literature from the Eleventh Century to the Fifteenth,* translated and arranged by Margaret Williams, M.A., copyright, 1949, by Sheed and Ward, Inc., New York.

might be called our first professional writers. Outstanding among these collections were Chaucer's *Canterbury Tales* and John Gower's poetic allegory, *Confessio Amantis.*

THE BALLAD

The ballad may be defined as a comparatively short narrative poem originally composed to be sung. Most of the ballads were composed between the twelfth and sixteenth centuries. Handed down from generation to generation through oral transmission, they acquired many additions and variations and were finally written down for permanent record in the eighteenth century.

The popular or folk ballad resembles the folk epic in its origins, but differs in other respects. The composers of both types of narrative poetry are unknown, and their subject matter comes from tradition. But whereas the epic deals with an heroic theme in an heroic manner, the ballad is simple in theme and often crude in form, employing commonplace words and country dialects. Ballads vary in length from a simple episode like that of "The Wife of Usher's Well" to several episodes strung together into a long loose narrative, like those of the *Robin Hood* cycle. They treat of themes which stir the imagination of the common folk. Love, jealousy, war, revenge, death, and the preternatural are the staple subjects, and the treatment is usually tragic.

Like all primitive poetry which tells a story for its own sake, the ballad is strictly objective. It contains no suggestion of how the author has been moved by the event, and it therein resembles a modern news report in which the reactions of the reporter are carefully omitted.

In the ballad, the action is generally not presented as a straight narrative. The first two stanzas give us an identification of the hero and the next two stanzas a bit of narrative. In the remaining stanzas, the action is given by a succession of little scenes. Much of the action is presented through dialogue, and the characters generally speak for themselves. The motives of the characters are suggested and implied rather than directly expressed. To appreciate the complete story of the ballad, there must be much reading between the lines. As in most poetry, the concrete is preferred to the abstract. The theme of the ballad is expressed in vivid and concrete details. Its moral is generally suggested and very rarely directly expressed.

The ballads are composed in stanzas of one of two kinds, either in couplets of iambic pentameter or in the *ballad stanza,* a quatrain rhyming *a b c b,* with alternating iambic tetrameter and iambic trimeter lines. Often the ballad has a refrain with what is known as "incremental repetition," that is, a stanza that repeats the preceding stanza with the variations necessary to continue the story. The ballad "Edward, Edward" illustrates both the refrain and the repetition.

A distinction is often made between the more crude form of the folk ballad and the more polished ballads composed by the minstrels, and hence called *minstrel* ballads. These ballads were sung before the courtly assemblage, and this accounts both for the more polished language and the more romantic theme. Fine examples of the minstrel ballads are "The Boy and the Mantle" and "King Arthur and King Cornwall."

Versions of the old English and Scottish ballads may be heard today in the mountains of Kentucky, Tennessee, and West Virginia. Yet most of our present day ballad singers have no idea that these songs were brought to America from England three or four centuries ago.

Sir Patrick Spens

Artistically speaking, "Sir Patrick Spens" is one of the best, if not the best, of the old ballads. It is usually classified as an historical ballad, because it so closely parallels the story of the daughter of Alexander III, Margaret. She was married to the king of Norway, Eric, and all the knights and nobles who had accompanied her to Norway perished on the voyage home. Sir Patrick Spens is not an historical figure. Shipwrecks were of frequent occurrence off the coast of Scotland, and since ballad singers mixed fact and fiction, the details of this ballad are probably the result of a combination of several different stories.

The king sits in Dumferling toune,
  Drinking the blude-reid wine:
"O whar will I get guid sailor,
  To sail this schip of mine?"

Up and spak an eldern knicht,
  Sat at the kings richt kne:
"Sir Patrick Spens is the best sailor
  That sails upon the se."

The king has written a braid letter,
  And signd it wi his hand,
And sent it to Sir Patrick Spens,
  Was walking on the sand.

The first line that Sir Patrick red,
  A loud lauch lauched he;
The next line that Sir Patrick red,
  The teir blinded his ee.

"O wha is this has don this deid,
  This ill deid don to me,
To send me out this time o' the yeir,
  To sail upon the se!

"Mak haste, mak haste, my mirry men all,
  Our guid schip sails the morne:"
"O say na sae, my master deir,
  For I feir a deadlie storme.

5. ELDERN KNICHT—An older knight.
9. BRAID LETTER—A long letter.
14. LOUD LAUCH—A loud laugh laughed he.
16. EE—Eye.

"Late late yestreen I saw the new
moone,
Wi the auld moone in hir arme,
And I feir, I feir, my deir master,
That we will cum to harme."

O our Scots nobles wer richt laith
To wet their cork-heild schoone;
Bot lang owre a' the play wer played,
Thair hats they swam aboone.

25-26—It is still a superstition among sailors that when the dark part of the moon can be seen inside the horn of the new moon, a storm will follow.
29. RICHT LAITH—Right loath, very unwilling.
30. SCHOONE—Shoes.
31. LANG OWRE—Long before.
32. THAIR HATS THEY SWAM ABOONE—Their hats swam above them, that is, they drowned.

O lang, lang may their ladies sit,
Wi thair fans into their hand,
Or eir they se Sir Patrick Spens
Cum sailing to the land.

O lang, lang may the ladies stand,
Wi thair gold kems in their hair,
Waiting for thair ain deir lords,
For they'll se thame na mair.

Haf owre, haf owre to Aberdour,
It's fiftie fadom deip,
And thair lies guid Sir Patrick Spens,
Wi the Scots lords at his feit.

38. KEMS—Combs.
41. HAF OWRE, TO ABERDOUR—Half over, half over to Aberdour, a small town near Edinburgh.

FOR APPRECIATION

1. The calamity of the shipwreck which brought death to Sir Patrick and his men, together with the loneliness of the fair ladies who wait for their lords' return—these constitute the tragedy of the ballad. More than half the lines of the ballad are devoted to emphasizing this theme. Less than half of the lines treat of the external framework of events which are responsible for the tragedy. Select the lines in the ballad which simply tell the story. Select those lines which emphasize the tragedy.

2. Note the implied actions and motives which can be read between the lines. Why does the king drink blood-red wine in line 2? Why does the king want someone to sail his ship? Has he lost many good sailors before? What is the character of the eldern knight? Do you think he has some personal grudge against Sir Patrick?

3. Stanzas five, six, and seven contain a climactic undertone of the tragedy to come. How are these fears confirmed in stanza eight? Explain.

4. In line 30, why does the poet use the word "cork-heeled"? Is there any connection between drowning and cork?

5. Does line 41 suggest that Sir Patrick and his men were drowned on the *return* voyage? Explain.

6. Reread paragraph 4 of the introduction to the ballads, then show how "Sir Patrick Spens" follows the typical ballad organization and development.

The use of the fan and the comb is a typical ballad convention. The poor, who delighted in these stories, equally disliked long descriptions, so certain details were chosen to suggest the type of characters. To the poor, golden combs and fans stood for all that they longed for and never had. They suggested luxury, nobility, and wealth.

The final stanza of a ballad usually contains a "punch line." We are prepared for the tragedy, but when it comes, we are nonetheless affected by the scene in the final two lines.

Edward, Edward

"Edward, Edward" is a famous ballad of domestic tragedy. It gives, dramatically, by a series of seven questions and answers, the dialogue between a son, guilty of patricide, and his mother who persuaded him to do the deed.

"Why dois your brand sae drap wi bluid,
Edward, Edward,
Why dois your brand sae drap wi bluid,
And why sae sad gang yee O?"
"O I hae killed my hauke sae guid,
Mither, mither,
I hae killed my hauke sae guid,
And I had nae mair bot hee O."

"Your haukis bluid was nevir sae reid,
Edward, Edward,
Your hauke bluid was nevir sae reid,
My deir son I tell thee O."
"O I hae killed my reid-roan steid,
Mither, mither,
I hae killed my reid-roan steid,
That erst wae sae fair and frie O."

"Your steid was auld, and ye hae gat mair,
Edward, Edward,
Your steid was auld, and ye hae gat mair,
Sum other dŏle ye drie O."
"O I hae killed my fadir deir,
Mither, mither,
I hae killed my fadir deir,
Alas, and wae is mee O!"

"And whatten penance wul ye drie for that,
Edward, Edward?
And whatten penance will ye drie for that?
My deir son, now tell me O."
"Ile set my feit in yonder boat,
Mither, mither,
Ile set my feit in yonder boat,
And Ile fare ovir the sea O."

"And what wul ye doe wi your towirs and your ha,
Edward, Edward?
And what wul you doe wi your towirs and your ha,
That were sae fair to see O?"
"Ile let thame stand tul they doun fa,
Mither, mither,
Ile let thame stand tul they doun fa,
For here nevir mair maun I bee O."

"And what wul ye leive to your bairns and your wife,
Edward, Edward?
And what wul ye leive to your bairns and your wife,
Whan ye gang ovir the sea O?"
"The warld is room, late them beg thrae life,
Mither, mither,
The warld is room, late them beg thrae life,
For thame nevir mair wul I see O."

1. BRAND—Sword.
4. GANG—Go.
5. HAUKE—Hawk, falcon.
16. THAT ERST. . .FRIE—That once was fair and spirited.
20. DULE. . .DRIE—Grief...suffer, undergo.
33. HA—Hall.
39. TUL—Till.
41. BAIRNS—Children.

"And what wul ye leive to your ain mither
deir,
Edward, Edward?
And what wul ye leive to your ain mither
deir?
My deir son, now tell me O."
"The curse of hell frae me sall ye beir
Mither, mither,
The curse of hell frae me sall ye beir,
Sic counseils ye gave to me O."

FOR APPRECIATION

1. Explain in detail how the action of the ballad is expressed indirectly rather than directly.

2. What details in the ballad indicate that Edward is a knight? What is the relationship between the mother and the son? How would you sum up the mother's character? Why did not Edward come out immediately and say that he murdered his father? Where is the climax of the story?

3. Show how the ballad is a good example of the use of refrain and incremental repetition.

Get Up and Bar the Door

After a rather steady diet of old ballad tragedy, it is delightful to discover an occasional burst of good humor. "Get Up and Bar the Door" is a good example both of ballad humor and of the traditional medieval friendly feud between husband and wife. In this instance, the wife comes out victorious.

It fell about the Martinmas time,
  And a gay time it was then,
When our good wife got puddings to make,
  And she's boild them in the pan.

The wind sae cauld blew south and
    north,
  And blew into the floor;
Quoth our goodman to our goodwife,
  "Gae out and bar the door."

"My hand is in my hussyfskap,
  Goodman, as ye may see;
An it should nae be barrd this hundred
    year,
  It's no be barrd for me."

They made a paction tween them twa,
  They made it firm and sure,
That the first word whaeer should speak,
  Shoud rise and bar the door.

Then there came two gentlemen,
  At twelve o clock at night,
And they could see neither house nor hall,
  Nor coal nor candle-light.

"Now whether is this a rich man's house,
  Or whether is it a poor?"
But neer a word wad ane o them speak,
  For barring of the door.

And first they ate the white puddings
  And then they ate the black;
Tho muckle thought the goodwife to
    hersel,
  Yet neer a word she spake.

Then said the one unto the other,
  "Here, man, tak ye my knife;
Do ye tak off the auld man's beard,
  And I'll kiss the goodwife."

"But there's nae water in the house,
  And what shall we do than?"
"What ails ye at the pudding-broo,
  That boils into the pan?"

1. MARTINMAS—The feast of St. Martin on November 11, a religious festival in the Middle Ages.
7. GOODMAN—It was the custom in the Middle Ages to call the husband "goodman."
9. USSYFSKAP—The chores of a housewife.
12. FOR ME—So far as I am concerned.
13. PACTION—Agreement.
27. MUCKLE—Much.
35. "What is the matter with the pudding broth?" The sauce of the pudding was made from liquor.

O up then started our goodman,
  An angry man was he:
"Will ye kiss my wife before my een,
  And scad me wi' pudding-bree?"

40. SCAD—Scald.

Then up and started our goodwife,
  Gied three skips on the floor:
"Goodman, you've spoken the foremost
    word,
  Get up and bar the door."

FOR APPRECIATION

1. In your own words, supply the action in the ballad which is implied.

2. What was the pact between husband and wife? Did the wife have to exercise a great amount of restraint during the midnight visit of the strangers? Explain. What caused the husband to lose his bet?

3. Is the stanza form and meter used in the ballad the traditional *ballad* stanza and meter? Explain.

The Wife of Usher's Well

In reading this very famous ballad, we should be not so much concerned with the few simple facts of the story, but rather with the undertones of grief and horror which are suggested through a series of vivid and concrete little scenes.

There lived a wife at Usher's Well,
  And a wealthy wife was she;
She had three stout and stalwart sons,
  And sent them oer the sea.

They hadna been a week from her
  A week but barely ane,
Whan word came to the carline wife
  That her three sons were gane.

They hadna been a week from her,
  A week but barely three,
Whan word came to the carlin wife
  That her sons she'd never see.

"I wish the wind may never cease,
  Nor fashes in the flood,
Till my three sons come hame to me,
  In earthly flesh and blood."

It fell about the Martinmass,
  When nights are lang and mirk,
The carlin wife's three sons came hame,
  And their hats were o the birk.

It neither grew in syke nor ditch
  Nor yet in ony sheugh;
But at the gates o Paradise,
  That birk grew fair eneugh.

"The Wife of Usher's Well" (Old English Ballad) from *English and Scottish Popular Ballads,* edited by Sargent & Kittredge, copyright, 1904, 1932, by George Lyman Kittredge, used by permission of Houghton Mifflin Company.

7. CARLINE—Old woman.

14. CASHES—Troubles.
18. MIRK—Dark, gloomy.
20. BIRK—Birch.
21. SYKE—Trench.
22. SHEUGH—Furrow.

"Blow up the fire, my maidens,
  Bring water from the well;
For a' my house shall feast this night,
  Since my three sons are well."

And she has made to them a bed,
  She's made it large and wide,
And she's taen her mantle her about,
  Sat down at the bed-side.

Up then crew the red, red cock,
  And up and crew the gray;
The eldest to the youngest said,
  " 'T is time we were away."

The cock he hadna crawd but once,
  And clappd his wings at a',
When the youngest to the eldest said,
  "Brother, we must awa.

"The cock doth craw, the day doth daw,
  The channerin worm doth chide;
Gin we be mist out o our place,
  A sair pain we maun bide;

"Fare ye weel, my mother dear!
  Fareweel to barn and byre!
And fare ye weel, the bonny lass
  That kindles my mother's fire!"

27. A'—All.

42. CHANNERIN—Devouring.
44. SAIR... MAUN—Sore ... must.
46. BYRE—COW shed.

FOR APPRECIATION

1. Two popular superstitions are found in this poem. The first is that if a person wishes hard enough, even the dead must come back from their graves. The second is that all ghosts must vanish at the crowing of the cock. Discuss the application of these superstitions in the ballad.

2. In stanzas five and six, how are we told that the sons are coming home as spirits and not in flesh and blood? Is this an example of an abstract fact expressed poetically? Explain. How would you state the simple fact of their return in prose? Do these stanzas give us the key to the ending of the poem? Explain.

3. Analyze stanzas seven and eight. What emotions of the mother are expressed? Are these emotions expressed directly or implied from the action? Discuss.

4. In the last four stanzas how are the emotions of fear and dread expressed? Does the simple understatement in the lines: " 'T is time we were away," and "Brother, we must awa," heighten the terror? Discuss.

5. Discuss how effectively the ballad poet contrasts life and death, the warmth of the living and the horror of the grave, in stanzas 11 and 12. What precise, concrete details did the poet select to show this contrast?

THE METRICAL TALE

The metrical tale is a narrative poem in which a story is told as simply and realistically as possible. It may deal with any phase of life, and its theme may be either allegorical or literal. In many ways, the metrical tale may be compared to the modern short-story, especially in its relative brevity and its unity of impression. As we shall see, Chaucer, in his *Canterbury Tales*, was a master of the metrical tale.

CHAUCER AND ENGLAND

The ordinary man of the fourteenth century was apt to view his world as being old, sophisticated, and corrupt. New developments in the government and organization of society were replacing the crumbling feudal system. Kings and royalty were being supplanted by the new rich who had made vast fortunes out of the commercialism of trade and finance. The common people were beginning to stir and revolt. Corruption in the Church, the state, and in individual lives was the frequent target of satirical writers. Chief among these satirists were two outstanding English poets: William Langland and Goeffrey Chaucer.

VISION OF PIERS PLOWMAN

Both Chaucer and Langland were citizens of London. But, unlike Chaucer, the court poet, the gaunt and hungry Langland lived his nights and days among the underprivileged, making a sparse living by singing psalms for the souls of the wealthy departed. The restless man burned with pity and indignation at the evils of his world. He wrote his thoughts and dreams into his *Vision of Piers Plowman.* With a sharp and angry pen, he cried out against social injustice, challenged both churchmen and the wealthy to reform, and stingingly satirized the unworthy clergy, monks, and friars. But he differed radically from the early reformer, Wyclif, who would have overthrown the Church and existing society. Langland wanted to reconstruct and revitalize society with a new spiritual vigor.

Piers Plowman is like a rough pageant of his century, in which we brush shoulders with the common man as he wears the smell of the streets on his tattered clothing. We hear the laughter and the cries of the poor as they act and talk, sometimes raucously and rowdily, sometimes gravely and profoundly. But throughout the poem there is the quest of Piers, the common Englishman, for Truth which is God and for Christ who can solve man's problems.

The poem is written in the south-Midland dialect and in the old alliterative meter of the Anglo-Saxons, which was revived in the fourteenth century.

The Vision of Piers Plowman is a long allegory composed of twenty sections, with Long Will, the author, as the dreamer. In sections one to seven, the world is seen as a field of folk between the Tower of Heaven and the Pit of Hell. The folk seem to be unmindful of everything except the making of money. Holy Church warns that a reasonable care for the business of the world is good, but that the real vocation of man is to follow Truth and Love. In this section, Langland satirizes the corruption and injustices both of the secular government and the common man. The poet represents Penance, Contrition, Confession, and Reparation as fighting against these abuses. The reparation imposed upon all men is to seek Saint Truth. To Piers Plowman is entrusted a pardon sent from Truth which states that whoever lives according to Truth, Love, Conscience, Reason, Penance, and Labor is in a State of Grace and will win Salvation. This is to "Do Well."

In sections eight to fifteen, Piers meets the characters Thought, Study, Clergy, Scripture, and Imagination. To each he puts the question, "What is Do Well?" Each supplies an answer not only to that question but to the question, "What are Do Better and Do Best?" In brief, the answer to Do Well is: be honest, God-fearing, neighborly, hard working, and obedient to the Church. In addition to these, Do Better should teach the ignorant, heal the suffering, and practice what you teach. Do Best should be outstanding in all these virtues and should also guide and administer the Church. In each of these three vocations, we have an allegorical interpretation of the life of the good layman, the good priest, and the good bishop.

In sections sixteen to twenty, the poet explains how Do Better is exemplified in the teaching, healing, and suffering of the true priest, as these were exemplified in Christ. He further shows that the triple vocation of Do Well, Do Better, and Do Best is found perfectly in Christ.

After Christ's Ascension and the coming of the Holy Ghost, Christ taught Piers to build a great Barn of Unity or "Holy Church in English." But the Barn built by Piers (who is now a symbol of papal authority) is stormed by forces of evil amassed against it. In the final battle, Piers vanishes, as the Pope seemed to have vanished in the great Western Schism.

Langland ends the poem in a black hour, but in the last line, we are reminded that Christ, triumphant on Easter Day, cannot fail.

CHAUCER AND THE CANTERBURY TALES

Geoffrey Chaucer was a polished courtier, statesman, professional man of letters, and man of the world. He, too, was well aware of the problems of his day, but his satire was more artistic and certainly more detached than Langland's. Chaucer never directly argues or preaches. He merely presents the corruption, the exaggerated pomp, the foolishness and rascality of the men and women of his age, and allows his readers to draw their own conclusions. His is the indirect dramatic method of the modern novelists. Langland employed the tactics of the medieval preacher. Chaucer's satire is softened throughout by his humor, his awareness of beauty, his rich love of life, and his international outlook.

In common with the Pearl Poet, Chaucer was a conscious artist. In his early years, he wrote in the traditional allegorical manner and gave us such masterpieces as *The Parliament of Fowls* and *Troilus and Criseyde.* But he did not use the alliterative meter nor the Old English poetic diction of the romances. His meter and verse forms he borrowed from the French schools, and the diction he used was that of cultivated people of London.

GEOFFREY CHAUCER

In the *Canterbury Tales,* Chaucer becomes the storyteller *par excellence.* With his emphasis on realism, he gives the whole work the character of a novel. Chaucer's greatness lies in his ability to portray character. For the most part, the stories which he tells are not original. There are legends, love stories, adventures, satires, allegories, and fables; all are borrowed from Italian, French, and English story collections, and from oral tradition. Chaucer's originality stems from his ability to tell the tales in masterly, brilliant versification; the idea of the pilgrimage as a framework and a source of unity for his tales; and the vitality, vividness, and satiric humor that permeate both the stories and the characters of the storytellers.

In Chaucer's day, pilgrimages to various shrines were common. One of the journeys most frequently undertaken was that to the shrine of Thomas à Becket, archbishop of Canterbury, who had been murdered during the reign of Henry II. It was the custom of the pilgrims desiring to visit this shrine to gather at the Tabard Inn across the Thames River from London. Here they waited until a sufficient number came to make the journey pleasant and safe. Chaucer presents a group of these pilgrims in his *Canterbury Tales* and in the prologue gives a description of each of them.

THE MURDER OF THOMAS À BECKET

As a result of a suggestion of Harry Bailly, the jovial host of the inn, who proposed to ride with the company to Canterbury as its guide, each pilgrim was to tell four tales, two during the ride to Canterbury and two during the return. Whoever was judged to be the best storyteller would be given a fine supper by all the rest when they returned.

This plan, of course, was but a device enabling Chaucer to tell a great number of stories. Had he carried out his plan there would have been more than one hundred tales, for there were twenty-nine pilgrims. Only twenty-four were written, but they cover a wide range of subject matter.

In the prologue, Chaucer's characterization is at its best, and the prologue has been called "one of the most perfect pieces of composition in the English language." In it we have clear-cut pictures with sharp details of dress and mannerisms, and a shrewd appraisal of character. It has been called an album of medieval England and her people. Although Chaucer has given us a fairly representative cross section of medieval characters, selected from the various social levels, professions, and occupations, we must not suppose that he is sketching for us representative types. Chaucer, like the nineteenth century Dickens, was a master of caricature. All his characters were exaggerated for literary reasons. Just as it is the custom of the storyteller to make his characters larger than life, so Chaucer consciously and artistically overdrew his characters to make them interesting. Many of the people he included in the prologue had a foundation in fact in his own personal life or personal prejudices. In his days, there were certainly too large a number of wordly nuns, immoral friars, wealthy monks, rowdy millers, covetous doctors, and women of the world like the Wife of Bath. These and others Chaucer satirized, but certainly not as typical of their class. For he knew too well that despite the large number of citizens in all walks of life who followed the primrose path of ease and luxury, there were abundantly more who followed the Ten Commandments.

The Canterbury Tales

TRANSLATED BY THEODORE MORRISON

The following selections include a portion of the prologue and THE NUN'S PRIEST'S TALE. *As the portraits of the characters in the prologue unfold, it is as if the reader were living for a while in the "Merrie England" of the fourteenth century.*

To get the feel of Chaucer's verse, one should read it in the original. However, six hundred years have made enough changes in spelling and pronunciation to puzzle the general reader, and so first acquaintance should come through a modern translation. As a sample of the original, the first eighteen lines are presented in Middle English, with a parallel reading in modern English. To get the effect of Chaucer's pronunciation, the final e's should be pronounced and the vowels should be given the sounds they have in most European languages. Long Ā is AH, Ē is Ā; Ī is ĒĒ; O͞O is Ō, E͞E is Ā; OU or OW is O͞O. Final Ë is pronounced like the final A in VIRGINIA.

PROLOGUE

MIDDLE ENGLISH VERSION

Whan that Aprille with his shourës so͞otë
The droghte of Marche hath percëd to the ro͞otë,
And bathëd every veyne in swich licour,
Of which vertu engendrëd is the flour;
Whan Zephirus eek with his swetë bre͞eth
Inspirëd hath in every holt and he͞eth
The tendrë croppës, and the yongë sonnë
Hath in the Ram his halfë course yronnë,
And smalë fowlës maken melodyë,
That slepen al the nyght with open yë,
So priketh hem nature in hir coragës:
Than longen folk to goon on pilgrymagës,

A MODERN ENGLISH TRANSLATION

As soon as April pierces to the root
The drought of March, and bathes each bud and shoot
Through every vein of sap with gentle showers
From whose engendering liquor spring the flowers;
When zephyrs have breathed softly all about
Inspiring every wood and field to sprout,
And in the zodiac the youthful sun
His journey halfway through the Ram has run;
When little birds are busy with their song
Who sleep with open eyes the whole night long
Life stirs their hearts and tingles in them so,
On pilgrimages people long to go

4. ENGENDERING—Life producing.

8. HALFWAY THROUGH THE RAM HAS RUN—People of the Middle Ages were familiar with all the signs of the zodiac. This was a common way of indicating early April.

And palmers for to seken straungë strondës,
To fernë halwës couthe in sondry londës:
And specially, from every shirës endë
Of Engelond, to Caunterbury they wendë,
The holy, blisful martir for to sekë,
That hem hath holpen whan that they were seeke.

13. PALMERS—Pilgrims returned from the Holy Land, carrying palm leaves as evidence of their journey.

And palmers to set out for distant strands
And foreign shrines renowned in many lands.
And specially in England people ride
To Canterbury from every countryside

To visit there the blessed martyred saint
Who gave them strength when they were sick and faint.

17. MARTYRED SAINT—St. Thomas à Becket

In Southwark at the Tabard one spring day
It happened, as I stopped there on my way,
Myself a pilgrim with a heart devout
Ready for Canterbury to set out,

19. THE TABARD—The name of a real inn in a suburb of London.

At night came all of twenty-nine assorted
Travelers, and to that same inn resorted,
Who by a turn of fortune chanced to fall
In fellowship together, and they were all

Pilgrims who had it in their minds to ride
Toward Canterbury. The stable doors were wide,
The rooms were large, and we enjoyed the best,
And shortly, when the sun had gone to rest,
I had so talked with each that presently
I was a member of their company
And promised to rise early the next day
To start, as I shall show, upon our way.
But none the less, while I have time and space,
Before this tale has gone a further pace,
I should in reason tell you the condition
Of each of them, his rank and his position,
And also what array they all were in;
And so then, with a knight I will begin.

A KNIGHT was with us, and an excellent man,
Who from the earliest moment he began
To follow his career loved chivalry,
Truth, openhandedness, and courtesy.
He was a stout man in the king's campaigns
And in that cause had gripped his horse's reins
In Christian lands and pagan through the earth,
None farther, and always honored for his worth.
Meek as a girl and gentle in his ways.
He had never spoken ignobly all his days
To any man by even a rude inflection.
He was a knight in all things to perfection.
He rode a good horse, but his gear was plain,
For he had lately served on a campaign.
His tunic was still spattered by the rust
Left by his coat of mail, for he had just
Returned and set out on his pilgrimage.

His son was with him, a young SQUIRE, in age
Some twenty years as near as I could guess.
His hair curled as if taken from a press.
He was a lover and would become a knight.
In stature he was of a moderate height
But powerful and wonderfully quick.
He had been in Flanders, riding in the thick
Of forays in Artois and Picardy,
And bore up well for one so young as he,
Still hoping by his exploits in such places
To stand the better in his lady's graces.
He wore embroidered flowers, red and white,
And blazed like a spring meadow to the sight.
He sang or played his flute the livelong day.
He was as lusty as the month of May.
His coat was short, its sleeves were long and wide.
He sat his horse well, and knew how to ride,
And how to make a song and use his lance,
And he could write and draw well, too, and dance.
So hot his love that when the moon rose pale
He got no more sleep than a nightingale.
He was modest, and helped whomever he was able,

51. INFLECTION—Tone of voice.

60. AS IF TAKEN FROM A PRESS—Men as well as women used various devices for putting a curl in naturally straight hair. Older men curled and waved their beards.

And carved as his father's squire at the table.

There was also a NUN, A PRIORESS,
Whose smile was gentle and full of guilelessness.
"By St. Loy!" was the worst oath she would say.
She sang mass well, in a becoming way,
Intoning through her nose the words divine,
And she was known as Madame Eglantine.
She spoke good French, as taught at Stratford-Bow,
For the Parisian French she did not know.
She was schooled to eat so primly and so well
That from her lips no morsel ever fell.
She wet her fingers lightly in the dish
Of sauce, for courtesy was her first wish.
With every bite she did her skillful best
To see that no drop fell upon her breast.
She always wiped her upper lip so clean
That in her cup was never to be seen
A hint of grease when she had drunk her share.
She reached out for her meat with comely air.
She was a great delight, and always tried
To imitate court ways, and had her pride,
Both amiable and gracious in her dealings.
As for her charity and tender feelings,
She melted at whatever was piteous.
She would weep if she but came upon a mouse
Caught in a trap, if it were dead or bleeding.
Some little dogs that she took pleasure feeding
On roasted meat or milk or good wheat bread
She had, but how she wept to find one dead
Or yelping from a blow that made it smart,
And all was sympathy and loving heart.
Neat was her wimple in its every plait,
Her nose well formed, her eyes as gray as slate.
Her mouth was very small and soft and red.
She had so wide a brow I think her head
Was nearly a span broad, for certainly
She was not undergrown, as all could see.
She wore her cloak with dignity and charm,
And had her rosary about her arm,
The small beads coral and the larger green,
And from them hung a brooch of golden sheen,
On it a large A and a crown above;
Beneath, "All things are subject unto love."
A Priest accompanied her toward Canterbury,
And an attendant Nun, her secretary.

There was a MONK, and nowhere was his peer,
A hunter, and a roving overseer.
He was a manly man, and fully able
To be an abbot. He kept a hunting stable,
And when he rode the neighborhood could hear
His bridle jingling in the wind as clear
And loud as if it were a chapel bell.
Wherever he was master of a cell

83. "BY ST. LOY"—An oath by St. Loy was the mildest kind of swearing.

87. STRATFORD-BOW—A Benedictine convent near London. The French taught here was Anglo-Norman French, not the pure French of Paris.

111. HER WIMPLE—The veil of her habit, worn over the head and around the neck and chin.

The principles of good St. Benedict,
For being a little old and somewhat strict,
Were honored in the breach, as past their prime.
He lived by the fashion of a newer time.
He would have swapped that text for a plucked hen
Which says that hunters are not holy men,
Or a monk outside his discipline and rule
Is too much like a fish outside his pool;
That is to say, a monk outside his cloister.
But such a text he deemed not worth an oyster.
I told him his opinion made me glad.
Why should he study always and go mad,
Mewed in his cell with only a book for neighbor?
Or why, as Augustine commanded, labor
And sweat his hands? How shall the world be served?
To Augustine be all such toil reserved!
And so he hunted, as was only right.
He had greyhounds as swift as birds in flight.
His taste was all for tracking down the hare,
And what his sport might cost he did not care.
His sleeves I noticed, where they met his hand,
Trimmed with gray fur, the finest in the land.
His hood was fastened with a curious pin
Made of wrought gold and clasped beneath his chin,
A love knot at the tip. His head might pass,
Bald as it was, for a lump of shining glass,
And his face was glistening as if anointed.
Fat as a lord he was, and well appointed.
His eyes were large, and rolled inside his head
As if they gleamed from a furnace of hot lead.
His boots were supple, his horse superbly kept.
He was a prelate to dream of while you slept.
He was not pale nor peaked like a ghost.
He relished a plump swan as his favorite roast.
He rode a palfrey brown as a ripe berry.

There was an OXFORD STUDENT too, it chanced,
Already in his logic well advanced.
He rode a mount as skinny as a rake,
And he was hardly fat. For learning's sake
He let himself look hollow and sober enough.
He wore an outer coat of threadbare stuff,
For he had no benefice for his enjoyment
And was too unworldly for some lay employment.

133. ST. BENEDICT—St. Benedict established the Order of Benedictine monks in 529 at Monte Cassino, Italy. The Order was introduced into England about 600.

143. This line is obvious satire. Here Chaucer, the Catholic poet, is indulging in irony at the expense of the worldly monk.

145. MEWED—To be enclosed or confined in a cage.

146. AUGUSTINE—The great St. Augustine of Hippo who founded the Canons Regular of St. Augustine. The Rule of St. Augustine was and still is the Rule of many religious congregations.

167. PALFREY—A saddle horse.

174. BENEFICE—The Oxford student was a cleric in Minor Orders who did not receive revenue from any endowed church.

He much preferred to have beside his bed
His twenty volumes bound in black or red
All packed with Aristotle from end to middle
Than a sumptuous wardrobe or a merry fiddle.
For though he knew what learning had to offer
There was little coin to jingle in his coffer.
Whatever he got by touching up a friend
On books and learning he would promptly spend
And busily pray for the soul of anybody
Who furnished him the wherewithal for study.
His scholarship was what he truly heeded.
He never spoke a word more than was needed,
And that was said with dignity and force,
And quick and brief. He was of grave discourse,
Giving new weight to virtue by his speech,
And gladly would he learn and gladly teach.

There were five Guildsmen, in the livery
Of one august and great fraternity,
A WEAVER, a DYER, and a CARPENTER.
A TAPESTRY-MAKER and a HABERDASHER.
Their gear was furbished new and clean as glass.
The mountings of their knives were not of brass
But silver. Their pouches were well made and neat,
And each of them, it seemed, deserved a seat
On the platform at the Guildhall, for each one
Was likely timber to make an alderman
They had goods enough, and money to be spent,
Also their wives would willingly consent
And would have been at fault if they had not.
For to be "Madamed" is a pleasant lot,
And to march in first at feasts for being well married,
And royally to have their mantles carried.

For the pilgrimage these Guildsmen brought their own
COOK to boil their chicken and marrow bone
With seasoning powder and capers and sharp spice.
In judging London ale his taste was nice.
He well knew how to roast and broil and fry,
To mix a stew, and bake a good meat pie,
Or capon creamed with almond, rice, and egg.
Pity he had an ulcer on his leg!

A worthy WOMAN there was from near the city
Of Bath, but somewhat deaf, and more's the pity.
For weaving she possessed so great a bent
She outdid the people of Ypres and of Ghent.
No other woman dreamed of such a thing
As to precede her at the offering,

178. ARISTOTLE—Greek philosopher of the fourth century B.C. His works throughout the Middle Ages and even today are considered the ground-work of all philosophical knowledge.

219. YPRES AND GHENT—Two cities in West Flanders famous for their fine weaving.

Or if any did, she fell in such a wrath
She dried up all the charity in Bath.
She wore fine kerchiefs of old-fashioned air,
And on a Sunday morning, I could swear,
She had ten pounds of linen on her head.
Her stockings were of finest scarlet-red,
Laced tightly, and her shoes were soft and new.
Bold was her face, and fair, and red in hue.
She had been an excellent woman all her life.
Five men in turn had taken her to wife,
Omitting other youthful company—
But let that pass for now! Over the sea
She had traveled freely; many a distant stream
She crossed, and visited Jerusalem
Three times. She had been at Rome and at Boulogne,
At the shrine of Compostella, and at Cologne.
She had wandered by the way through many a scene.
Her teeth were set with little gaps between.
Easily on her ambling horse she sat.
She was well wimpled, and she wore a hat
As wide in circuit as a shield or targe.
A skirt swathed up her hips, and they were large.
Upon her feet she wore sharp-roweled spurs.
She was a good fellow; a ready tongue was hers.
All remedies of love she knew by name,
For she had all the tricks of that old game.

There was a good man of the priest's vocation,
A poor town PARSON of true consecration,
But he was rich in holy thought and work.
Learned he was, in the truest sense a clerk
Who meant Christ's Gospel faithfully to preach
And truly his parishioners to teach.
He was a kind man, full of industry,
Many times tested by adversity
And always patient. If tithes were in arrears,
He was loth to threaten any man with fears
Of excommunication; past a doubt
He would rather spread his offering about
To his poor flock, or spend his property.
To him a little meant sufficiency.
Wide was his parish, with houses far asunder,
But he would not be kept by rain or thunder,
If any had suffered a sickness or a blow,
From visiting the farthest, high or low,
Plodding his way on foot, his staff in hand.
He was a model his flock could understand,
For first he did and afterward he taught
That precept from the Gospel he had caught,

244. SHARP-ROWELED—A rowel is a little wheel with sharp points attached to spurs.

248. In the following lines, Chaucer gives us a picture of the ideal parish priest and the one sincere religious man in the pilgrimage. In Langland's *Piers Plowman*, the parish priest comes in for his share of censure, along with the monks and the friars.

258. EXCOMMUNICATION—According to Church Law, the faithful were bound to pay tithes or Church taxes, as commanded by God in the Old Testament. Stubborn refusal on the part of those who could afford to pay could result in their being deprived of the spiritual benefits of the Church. Abuses, of course, crept in when unworthy churchmen demanded such payment from the poor.

And he added as a metaphor thereto,
"If the gold rusts, what will the iron do?"
For if a priest is foul, in whom we trust,
No wonder a layman shows a little rust.
A priest should take to heart the shameful scene
Of shepherds filthy while the sheep are clean.
By his own purity a priest should give
The example to his sheep, how they should live.
He did not rent his benefice for hire,
Leaving his flock to flounder in the mire,
And run to London, happiest of goals,
To sing paid masses in St. Paul's for souls,
Or as chaplain from some rich guild take his keep,
But dwelt at home and guarded well his sheep
So that no wolf should make his flock miscarry.
He was a shepherd, and not a mercenary.
And though himself a man of strict vocation
He was not harsh to weak souls in temptation,
Not overbearing nor haughty in his speech,
But wise and kind in all he tried to teach.
By good example and just words to turn
Sinners to heaven was his whole concern.
But should a man in truth prove obstinate,
Whoever he was, of rich or mean estate,
The Parson would give him a snub to meet the case.
I doubt there was a priest in any place
His better. He did not stand on dignity
Nor affect in conscience too much nicety,
But Christ's and his disciples' word he sought
To teach, and first he followed what he taught.

[The other characters introduced in the prologue include a Yeoman (who rode with the Knight), a Friar, a Merchant, a Lawyer, a Franklin (or Country Squire), a Sailor, a Physician, a Plowman (brother of the Poor Parson), a Bailiff, a Steward for a group of lawyers, a Miller, and a Summoner to Ecclesiastical Courts. The last 144 lines introduce the jolly host of the Tabard Inn, who proposes the storytelling contest and who decides to join the pilgrims and act as master of ceremonies on the journey.]

278-281. The meaning of these lines is this: The Parish priest did not hire someone to discharge his own local parish duties, which brought little monetary return, and leave for the gayer life of London to live an easy life singing Masses in St. Paul's great church, where he would receive larger stipends from the rich Mass foundations.

WORD STUDY

1. *Spattered, peaked, swathed,* and *ambled* are picturesque words. Why?

2. Explain the meaning of *sumptuous, deemed, furbished.* Give antonyms for *ignoble* and *prim.*

FOR APPRECIATION

1. Enumerate the signs of spring which Chaucer details in the first fifteen lines of the prologue.

2. Would you say that Chaucer is poking fun at the dress of the Squire? Explain. Have the Squire and the modern "young man about town" anything in common? Explain.

3. What precise details in Chaucer's description of the Nun would make you conclude that she was a rather worldly woman? What was Chaucer's attitude toward her? What is your reaction?

4. Discuss in detail the satire contained in the description of the Monk. What is the difference between a Monk and a Friar? If you read Chaucer's description of his Friar in the prologue, you will find he is much harder on the Friar than on the Monk. What may be the reason for this?

5. In your own words, give a brief sketch of the Wife of Bath.

6. What was Chaucer's attitude toward the Parish priest? Discuss. Give at least five characteristics of the good parish priest as described for us by Chaucer.

7. Which characters of the prologue do you think are the most effectively sketched? Give your reasons. Chaucer purposely employed caricature as a literary device. Point out lines in which caricature is employed.

8. What precise details of medieval dress, manners, customs, and attitude could you learn from reading the prologue?

9. From your knowledge of history, what evidence can you give that Chaucer's characters are not completely typical of the men and women whom he portrays?

THE NUN'S PRIEST'S TALE

During the Middle Ages, the tale of the Rooster and Fox appeared in numerous fables and in several versions of the beast-epic, the romance of Reynard. In the twelfth and thirteenth centuries, these stories in which beasts and birds could speak took on a literary form, and served as a medium of satire on court and clergy as well as sermon material for the medieval preacher.

In the tale told by Sir John, the nun's confessor, Chaucer uses this fable to show some of the weaknesses of humanity thinly guised in the feathered costumes of rooster and hens. It is a masterpiece of mock-heroic verse, enriched by Chaucer's knowledge of human nature, philosophy, religion, learning, and medieval science.

The rooster, Chanticleer, and the hen, Partlet, represent man and woman, lord and lady. As the medieval lady, Partlet reviews the qualities that should be found in an ideal husband. Chanticleer refutes her learned arguments with the skill of a medieval scholar. Sir Russell Fox ranks with the most infamous traitors in history.

As you read the tale, look for the humor and the satire.

Once a poor widow, aging year by year,
Lived in a tiny cottage that stood near
A clump of shade trees rising in a dale.
This widow, of whom I tell you in my tale,
Since the last day that she had been a wife
Had led a very patient, simple life.
She had but few possessions to content her.
By thrift and husbandry of what God sent her
She and two daughters found the means to dine.
She had no more than three well-fattened swine,
As many cows, and one sheep, Moll by name.
Her bower and hall were black from the hearth-flame
Where she had eaten many a slender meal.
No dainty morsel did her palate feel
And no sharp sauce was needed with her pottage.
Her table was in keeping with her cottage.
Excess had never given her disquiet.
Her only doctor was a moderate diet,
And exercise, and a heart that was contented.
If she did not dance, at least no gout prevented;
No apoplexy had destroyed her head.
She never drank wine, whether white or red.
She served brown bread and milk, loaves white or black,
Singed bacon, all this with no sense of lack,
And now and then an egg or two. In short,
She was a dairy woman of a sort.
She had a yard, on the inside fenced about
With hedges, and an empty ditch without,
In which she kept a cock, called Chanticleer.
In all the realm of crowing he had no peer.
His voice was merrier than the merry sound
Of the church organ grumbling out its ground
Upon a saint's day. Stouter was this cock
In crowing than the loudest abbey clock.
Of astronomy instinctively aware,
He kept the sun's hours with celestial care,
For when through each fifteen degrees it moved,
He crowed so that it couldn't be improved.
His comb, like a crenelated castle wall,
Red as fine coral, stood up proud and tall.
And he was azure-legged and azure-toed.
As lilies were his nails, they were so white;
Like burnished gold his hue, it shone so bright.
This cock had in his princely sway and measure
Seven hens to satisfy his every pleasure,
Who were his sisters and his sweethearts true,
Each wonderfully like him in her hue,
Of whom the fairest-feathered throat to see
Was fair Dame Partlet. Courteous was she,
Discreet, and always acted debonairly.
She was sociable, and bore herself so fairly,

8. HUSBANDRY—Wise management.

39. CRENELATED—Furnished with battlements. A battlement was a decorative device used in medieval architecture; an elevated wall with open spaces surrounding the medieval castle.

Since the very time that she was seven nights old,
The heart of Chanticleer was in her hold
As if she had him locked up, every limb.
He loved her so that all was well with him.
It was a joy, when up the sun would spring,
To hear them both together sweetly sing,
"My love has gone to the country, far away!"
For as I understand it, in that day
The animals and birds could sing and speak.
Now as this cock, one morning at daybreak,
With each of the seven hens that he called spouse,
Sat on his perch inside the widow's house,
And next him fair Dame Partlet, in his throat
This Chanticleer produced a hideous note
And groaned like a man who is having a bad dream;
And Partlet, when she heard her husband scream,
Was all aghast, and said, "Soul of my passion,
What ails you that you groan in such a fashion?
You are always a sound sleeper. Fie, for shame!"
And Chanticleer awoke and answered, "Dame,
Take no offense, I beg you, on this score.
I dreamt, by God, I was in a plight so sore
Just now, my heart still quivers from the fright.
Now God see that my dream turns out all right
And keep my flesh and body from foul seizure!
I dreamed I was strutting in our yard at leisure
When there I saw, among the weeds and vines,
A beast, he was like a hound, and had designs
Upon my person, and would have killed me dead.
His coat was not quite yellow, not quite red,
And both his ears and tail were tipped with black
Unlike the fur along his sides and back.
He had a small snout and a fiery eye.
His look for fear still makes me almost die.
This is what made me groan, I have no doubt."
"For shame! Fie on you, faint heart!" she burst out.
"Alas," she said, "by the great God above,
Now you have lost my heart and all my love!
I cannot love a coward, as I'm blest!
Whatever any woman may protest,
We all want, could it be so, for our part,
Husbands who are wise and stout of heart,
No blabber, and no niggard, and no fool,
Nor afraid of every weapon or sharp tool,
No braggart either, by the God above!
How dare you say, for shame, to your true love
That there is anything you ever feared?
Have you no man's heart, when you have a beard?
Alas, and can a nightmare set you screaming?
God knows there's only vanity in dreaming!
Dreams are produced by such unseemly capers

95. NIGGARD—Miser.

As overeating; they come from stomach vapors
When a man's humors aren't behaving right
From some excess. This dream you had tonight,
It comes straight from the superfluity
Of your red choler, certain as can be.
Cato, that has been thought so wise a man,
Didn't he tell us, 'Put no stock in dreams'?'
"Madame," he answered, "thanks for all your lore.
But still, to speak of Cato, though his name
For wisdom has enjoyed so great a fame,
And though he counseled us there was no need
To be afraid of dreams, by God, men read
Of many a man of more authority
Than this Don Cato could pretend to be
Who in old books declare the opposite,
And by experience they have settled it,
That dreams are omens and prefigurations
Both of good fortune and of tribulations
That life and its vicissitudes present.
This question leaves no room for argument.
The very upshot makes it plain, indeed.
Yes, in St. Kenelm's life I have also read—
He was the son of Cynewulf, the king
Of Mercia—how this Kenelm dreamed a thing.
One day, as the time when he was killed drew near,
He saw his murder in a dream appear.
His nurse explained his dream in each detail,
And warned him to be wary without fail
Of treason; yet he was but seven years old,
And therefore any dream he could but hold
Of little weight, in heart he was so pure.
I'd give my shirt, by God, you may be sure,
If you had read his story through like me!
Moreover, Partlet, I tell you truthfully,
Macrobius writes—and by his book we know
The African vision of great Scipio—
Confirming dreams, and holds that they may be
Forewarnings of events that men shall see.
Again, I beg, look well at what is meant
By the Book of Daniel in the Old Testament,
Whether *he* held that dreams are vanity!

103-106. According to medieval science, too much food or drink caused vapors to arise from the stomach to the brain.

109. CATO—Dionysius Cato, who composed a book of sayings in the fourth century.

119. In the following lines, Chaucer has Chanticleer argue like a medieval scholar by quoting other authorities to prove his point. His aim is to give more and better authorities than Partlet can. The stories are *exempla*, found in medieval sermon books.

125. ST. KENELM'S LIFE—When Kenulphus, king of Mercia, died in 821, he left his throne to his son Kenelm, aged 7. Kenelm dreamed that he saw a tree with wax lights upon it, and that he climbed to the top. When one of his friends cut it down, he was turned into a little bird and flew to Heaven. The bird was his soul, the flight his death. Shortly afterwards, his ambitious aunt had him murdered and buried under a tree; a heavenly light over the tree led to the discovery of the place of his burial.

138. MACROBIUS—About the year 400, Macrobius wrote a commentary on Cicero's *Somnium Scipionis* (The Dreams of Scipio). This work had a great influence on medieval literature, especially upon Chaucer.

143. Read the story of Daniel's dream in the Book of Daniel, Chapter 4.

Read also about Joseph. You shall see
That dreams, or some of them—I don't say all—
Warn us of things that afterward befall.
Think of the king of Egypt, Don Pharaoh;
Of his butler and his baker think also,
Whether they found that dreams have no result.
Whoever will search through kingdoms and consult
Their histories reads many a wondrous thing
Of dreams. What about Croesus, Lydian king—
Didn't he dream he was sitting on a tree,
Which meant he would be hanged? Andromache,
The woman who was once great Hector's wife,
On the day that Hector was to lose his life,
The very night before his blood was spilled
She dreamed of how her husband would be killed
If he went out to battle on that day.
She warned him; but he would not heed nor stay.
In spite of her he rode out on the plain,
And by Achilles he was promptly slain.
But all that story is too long to tell,
And it is nearly day. I must not dwell
Upon this matter. Briefly, in conclusion,
I say this dream will bring me to confusion
And mischief of some sort. And furthermore,
On laxatives, I say, I set no store,
For they are poisonous, I'm sure of it.
I do not trust them! I like them not one bit!
Now let's talk cheerfully, and forget all this.
My pretty Partlet, by my hope of bliss,
In one thing God has sent me ample grace,
For when I see the beauty of your face,
You are so scarlet-red about the eye,
It is enough to make my terrors die.
For just as true as *In principio*
Mulier est hominis confusio—
And Madame, what this Latin means is this:
'Woman is man's whole comfort and true bliss'—
I am then so full of pure felicity
That I defy whatever sort of dream!"
And day being come, he flew down from the beam
And with him his hens fluttered, one and all;
And with a "cluck, cluck" he began to call
His wives to where a kernel had been tossed.
He was a prince, his fears entirely lost.
Grim as a lion he strolled to and fro,
And strutted only on his either toe.
He would not deign to set foot on the ground.
"Cluck, cluck," he said, whenever he had found
A kernel, and his wives came running all.
Thus royal as a monarch in his hall

145. The story of Joseph is contained in the Book of Genesis.

153. The dream of Croesus is related in the "Monk's Tale."

155. ANDROMACHE (ăn·drŏm′*a*·kė)—Chaucer's knowledge of the story of Andromache was not taken from Homer (Greek was little known in the Middle Ages), but from Dares Phrygius.

156. Both Hector and Achilles were heroes of the Trojan War.

178-179. The translation of this Latin medieval proverb is: "From the very beginning woman is the confusion of man." Note that Chanticleer's false translation is not detected by Partlet.

I leave to his delights this Chanticleer,
And presently the sequel you shall hear.
After the month in which the world began,
The month of March, when God created man,
Had passed, and when the season had run through
Since March began just thirty days and two,
It happened that Chanticleer, in all his pride,
While his seven hens were walking by his side,
Lifted his eyes, beholding the bright sun,
Which in the sign of Taurus had then run
Twenty and one degrees and somewhat more,
And knew by instinct, not by learned lore,
It was the hour of prime. He raised his head
And crowed with lordly voice. "The sun," he said,
"Forty and one degrees and more in height
Has climbed the sky. Partlet, my world's delight,
Hear all these birds, how happily they sing,
And see the pretty flowers, how they spring
With solace and with joy my spirits dance!"
But suddenly he met a sore mischance,
For in the end joys ever turn to woes.
Quickly the joys of earth are gone, God knows.
A sly iniquitous fox, with black-tipped ears,
Who had lived in the neighboring wood for some three years,
His fated fancy swollen to a height,
Had broken through the hedges that same night
Into the yard where in his pride sublime
Chanticleer with his seven wives passed the time.
Quietly in a bed of herbs he lay
Till it was past the middle of the day,
Waiting his hour on Chanticleer to fall
As gladly do these murderers, one and all,
Who lie in wait, concealed, to murder men.
O murderer, lurking traitorous in your den!
O new Iscariot, second Ganelon,
False hypocrite, Greek Sinon, who brought on
The utter woe of Troy and all her sorrow!
O Chanticleer, accursed be that morrow
When to the yard you flew down from the beams!
That day, as you were well warned in your dreams,
Would threaten you with dire catastrophe.
Women have many times, as wise men hold,
Offered advice that left men in the cold.
A woman's counsel brought us first to woe
And out of Paradise made Adam go
Where he lived a merry life and one of ease.
But since I don't know whom I may displease
By giving women's words an ill report,
Pass over it; I only spoke in sport.

198. THE MONTH OF MARCH—According to the ancient tradition, the world was created at the time of the vernal equinox.

229. GANELON—Ganelon betrayed Roland, the hero of *The Song of Roland*.

230. GREEK SINON—Sinon invented the Trojan horse which was responsible for the fall of Troy.

There are books about it you can read or skim in,
And you'll discover what they say of women.
I'm telling you the cock's words, and not mine.
Harm in no woman at all can I divine.
Merrily bathing where the sand was dry
Lay Partlet, with her sisters all near by,
And Chanticleer, as regal as could be,
Sang merrily as the mermaid in the sea;
For the *Physiologus* itself declares
That they know how to sing the merriest airs.
And so it happened that as he fixed his eye
Among the herbs upon a butterfly,
He caught sight of this fox who crouched there low.
He felt no impulse then to strut or crow,
But cried "cucock!" and gave a fearful start
Like a man who has been frightened to the heart.
For instinctively, if he should chance to see
His opposite, a beast desires to flee,
Even the first time that it meets his eye.
This Chanticleer, no sooner did he spy
The fox than promptly enough he would have fled.
But "Where are you going, kind sir?" the fox said.
"Are you afraid of me, who am your friend?
Truly, I'd be a devil from end to end
If I meant you any harm or villainy.
I have not come to invade your privacy.
In truth, the only reason that could bring
This visit of mine was just to hear you sing.
Beyond a doubt, you have as fine a voice
As any angel who makes heaven rejoice.
Also you have more feeling in your note
Than Boëthius, or any tuneful throat.
Milord your father once—and may God bless
His soul—your noble mother too, no less,
Have been inside my house, to my great ease.
And verily sir, I should be glad to please
You also. But for singing, I declare,
As I enjoy my eyes, that precious pair,
Save you, I never heard a man so sing
As your father did when night was on the wing.
Straight from the heart, in truth, came all his song,
And to make his voice more resonant and strong
He would strain until he shut his either eye,
So loud and lordly would he make his cry,
And stand up on his tiptoes therewithal
And stretch his neck till it grew long and small.
He had such excellent discretion, too,
That whether his singing, all the region through,
Or his wisdom, there was no one to surpass."
Blind to all treachery, Chanticleer began
To beat his wings, like one who cannot see
The traitor, ravished by his flattery.

252. PHYSIOLOGUS (fĭź´ĭ·ŏl´ŏ·jŭs)—The reference is to a Latin beastiary. There is a chapter in the book on sirens and mermaids.

275. BOËTHIUS (bô·ē´thĭ·*us*)—(470-525) was the author of *De Consolatione Philosophiae* which was translated into Anglo-Saxon by Alfred's scholars and later into Middle English by Chaucer. Boethius was admired not only as a philosopher but also as a musician.

This Chanticleer stood tiptoe at full height.
He stretched his neck, he shut his eyelids tight,
And he began to crow a lordly note.
The fox, Don Russell, seized him by the throat
At once, and on his back bore Chanticleer
Off toward his den that in the grove stood near,
For no one yet had threatened to pursue.
O destiny, that no man may eschew!
Alas, that he left his safe perch on the beams!
Alas, that Partlet took no stock in dreams!
In truth, no lamentation ever rose,
No shriek of ladies when before its foes
Ilium fell, and Pyrrhus with drawn blade
Had seized King Priam by the beard and made
An end of him—the *Aeneid* tells the tale—
Such as the hens made with their piteous wail
In their enclosure, seeing the dread sight
Of Chanticleer. But at the shrillest height
Shrieked Partlet. She shrieked louder than the wife
Of Hasdrubal, when her husband lost his life
And the Romans burned down Carthage; for her state
Of torment and of frenzy was so great
She willfully chose the fire for her part,
Leaped in, and burned herself with steadfast heart.
Unhappy hens, you shrieked as when for pity,
While the tyrant Nero put to flames the city
Of Rome, rang out the shriek of senators' wives
Because their husbands had all lost their lives;
This Nero put to death these innocent men.
But I will come back to my tale again.
Now this good widow and her two daughters heard
These woeful hens shriek when the crime occurred,
And sprang outdoors as quickly as they could
And saw the fox, who was making for the wood
Bearing this Chanticleer across his back.
"Help, help!" they cried. They cried, "Alas! Alack!
The fox, the fox!" and after him they ran,
And armed with clubs came running many a man.
Ran Coll the dog, and led a yelping band;
Ran Malkyn, with a distaff in her hand;
Ran cow and calf, and even the very hogs,
By the yelping and the barking of the dogs
And men's and women's shouts so terrified
They ran till it seemed their hearts would burst inside;
They squealed like fiends in the pit, with none to still them.
The ducks quacked as if men were going to kill them.
The geese for very fear flew over the trees.
Out of the beehive came the swarm of bees.

308-310. Priam, the last King of Troy, was slain by Pyrrhus, when the Greeks conquered that city. The story is told in the Second Book of Virgil's *Aeneid*.

315. HASDRUBAL (hăz´drōō·băl)—King of Carthage. When the Romans burned the city in 146 B.C., he slew himself, and his wife and sons burned themselves.

Now hear me, you good people, one and all!
Fortune, I say, will suddenly override
Her enemy in his very hope and pride!
This cock, as on the fox's back he lay,
Plucked up his courage to speak to him and say.
"God be my help, sir, but I'd tell them all,
That is, if I were you, 'Plague on you fall!
Go back, proud fools! Now that I've reached the wood,
I'll eat the cock at once, for all the good
Your noise can do. Here Chanticleer shall stay.' "
"Fine!" said the fox. "I'll do just what you say."
But the cock, as he was speaking, suddenly
Out of his jaws lurched expeditiously,
And flew at once high up into a tree.
And when the fox saw that the cock was free,
"Alas," he said, "alas, O Chanticleer!
Inasmuch as I have given you cause for fear
By seizing you and bearing you away,
I have done you wrong, I am prepared to say.
But, sir, I did it with no ill intent.
Come down, and I shall tell you what I meant.
So help me God, it's truth I'll offer you!"
"No, no," said he. "We're both fools, through and through.
But curse my blood and bones for the chief dunce
If you deceive me oftener than once!
You shall never again by flattery persuade me
To sing and wink my eyes, by him that made me.
For he that willfully winks when he should see,
God never bless him with prosperity!"
"Ah," said the fox, "with mischief may God greet
The man ungoverned, rash, and indiscreet
Who babbles when to hold his tongue were needful!"
Such is it to be reckless and unheedful
And trust in flattery. But you who hold
That this is a mere trifle I have told,
Concerning only a fox, or a cock and hen,
Think twice, and take the moral, my good men!
For truly, of whatever is written, all
Is written for our doctrine, says St. Paul.

381-382. The reference here is to St. Paul's Epistle to the Romans, Chapter 15, verse 4.

Then take the fruit, and let the chaff lie still.
Now, gracious God, if it should be your will,
As my Lord teaches, make us all good men
And bring us to your holy bliss! Amen.

WORD STUDY

1. Write original phrases in which the following words are used: *azure, burnished, lurking, debonair, wary*. What is the color of *jet?*

2. Is there a difference in meaning between *superfluous* and *abundant*? What is the relationship between *discreet* and *cautious*? *iniquitous* and *evil*? *vicissitude* and *burden*? Explain.

FOR APPRECIATION

1. Why does Chaucer begin the tale by contrasting the poverty of the widow with the splendor of the rooster? Is there any social satire implied here? Discuss. Is it possible that Chanticleer and the hens with their fine airs may symbolize the Norman culture? Discuss.

2. Study in detail the imagery which Chaucer employs in his description of Chanticleer in lines 39-44, and of the fox in lines 79-86. Is there any connection between Chanticleer's physical beauty, his vanity, and his future fall? Discuss.

3. What artistic device is contained in lines 60-61?

4. Enumerate and discuss the details of the ideal husband as given by Partlet in lines 91-99.

5. Does Chanticleer's dream in lines 74-87 prepare us for his later misfortune? Explain.

6. What kind of arguments does Chanticleer use to refute Partlet's conviction that dreams are of no account? Enumerate these arguments. What type of human being might be symbolized in the learned Chanticleer? Discuss.

7. By what trickery was Chanticleer taken captive by the fox? Explain. How did he ultimately outfox the fox?

8. Select and discuss those lines which contain the medieval attitude towards women as found in many of the writings of that age. Note lines 246-247; is this a common artistic device?

9. Discuss the satire of the entire Tale, especially in lines 100; 178-181; 267-292.

10. What is the moral of the Tale as given by Chaucer at the conclusion of the story?

11. Chaucer wrote in what is known as the "heroic couplet." Explain this verse form and scan several of the lines.

RELATED READING

Chaucer's *The Pardoner's Tale* and *The Nun's Tale* should be required reading. In addition to these literary classics, you should read at least one of the following: *The Knight's Tale* or *The Clerk's Tale* or *The Man of Law's Tale.* These and other works of Chaucer may be read in the excellent modern translations by Nevill Coghill in the Penguin Books edition; in the *Portable Chaucer*, edited by Theodore Morrison in the Viking Portable Library; or in the translation of J. U. Nicholson.

Read at least one Passus or section of Langland's *Vision of Piers Plowman.* This has been translated into modern English by Henry W. Wells.

THE DRAMA IN MEDIEVAL ENGLAND

In modern times, Church and stage have been uneasy bedfellows. The same was true in the first centuries of Christianity when the Church and the early Fathers had no use for actors. In Saint Augustine's time, a pagan actor who was converted to Christianity had to give up his profession. There was reason for such action, for drama had degenerated from the high level of the ancient Grecian tragedy which had its origin in religious worship. The only survivals of the drama left to the people of the Early Middle Ages were low forms of Roman comedy.

But like their modern counterparts, the common people had to be entertained. The ancient *mime*, a form of popular comedy, was taken over by the minstrels to satisfy the appetite of the populace for buffoonery. Rope walkers, monkey trainers, tumblers, and dancers often joined these troupers and performed wherever an open space and an audience could be found.

Classic drama, on the other hand, withdrew to the quiet of the monasteries during the hectic centuries following the fall of Rome. In one such monastery, Roswitha, a Benedictine nun, wrote six plays in the classical tradition. Although composed against the background of the iron tenth century, they showed marvelous literary powers. But Roswitha was a literary personage born out of time, and her tenth century plays had little if any influence on the candle-lit drama that was rising in England.

THE MYSTERY AND MIRACLE PLAYS

The new medieval drama, like that of the Greeks, had its germ in religious worship. Born at the base of the altar, at the foot of the pulpit, it was, in its simpler form, merely illustrative of incidents in the life of Christ. The earliest preserved text, the *Quem-quaeritis*[1] trope[2] found at St. Gall, has divided a chorus at the Easter Mass into two antiphonal groups,[3] with the angels standing guard over Christ's sepulchre on one side and the women seeking Christ's Body on the other. The angels chant: "Whom seek ye in the sepulchre, O followers of Christ?" and the women respond that they have come in search of Jesus of Nazareth. Then the angels proclaim joyously that He has risen. The news is greeted with a glorious *Te Deum* sung by the whole congregation. Out of the episode of the three Marys at the tomb developed the Easter cycle; out of the Shepherds' quest came the Christmas cycle. Still later the day of doom was added, so that in the full-grown mystery cycle we have the sublime panoramic view extending from the creation of the world to the Last Judgment.

By gradual transition, the strictly Biblical subject matter was supplemented by stories from the lives of the great saints and martyrs of the Church. These saint-plays were called

[1]*Quem-Quaretis*—Whom do you seek.
[2] TROPE—A trope is a further development of a passage in the Liturgy of the Church. Thus the "Whom do you seek" of the Easter angel was amplified into an Easter play.
[3]ANTIPHONAL GROUPS—Groups which alternately sing or chant a musical response.

miracles in contradistinction to the *mysteries* which dealt with the life of Christ. About 1250, however, many bishops were inclined to prohibit the clergy from taking part in these plays and to forbid the use of the church for their presentation. This attitude was not really intolerant, since in the momentum of dramatic development the performances were tending to take on the nature of comedy. Noah's wife stubbornly refused to leave dry land; always she made Noah's life miserable by her garrulous scolding. The devils, too, were a problem, jabbing the cherubs with their pitchforks. So the whole hilarious business was thrown out of church, bag and baggage.

Once outside, holiday crowds swarmed over the church yards and into the fields, and to accommodate their audience, the Guilds developed a system of high-wheeled carts that moved from one street to another, each stopping to present its scene of the cycle. By the year 1400 in most of the leading English towns such as York, Chester, and Coventry, the Guilds had taken over these plays. In York, for example, there was developed a series of forty-eight plays. In this cycle an attempt was made to dramatize the Biblical story from the creation of the world to the Resurrection of Christ and the Harrowing of Hell. The various scenes were divided among the different Guilds with a naive appropriateness. In the York Cycle, for example, the creation of the earth was

THEATERS ON WHEELS

presented by the plasterers' guild, the building of the Ark by the shipwrights, the turning of water into wine at Cana by the vintners, the Last Supper by the bakers; and at Chester the Harrowing of Hell was presented by the cooks and innkeepers. The expense list for one production included such items as "a pair of gloves for God—four pair of angels' wings—a pound of hemp to mend the angels' heads—and a torch for setting the world on fire."

In the fifteenth century, there developed another type of play known as the *morality.* Allegorical figures were introduced to explain the point, the moral of the tale. Finally, the stories departed entirely from their Biblical foundation and told of ordinary man and his struggle for salvation. Saintly characters wore gilt hair and beards; souls were dressed in black or white coats depending on their destination; angels won admiring gasps from the audience with skins of gold and wings that flapped. But by popular acclaim the "star" was still the Devil. As stormy a villain as ever, he strode the boards, dressed in black or red, sometimes breathing smoke from his mouth, and often endowed with a long and agile tail. At his heels came Vice, in fool's clothes, whose duty it was to tease audience and Devil alike. Ultimately both were swept back by the Virtues into a gaping hell-mouth—smoky and sulphurous and, if it was an elaborate production, belching red flames at intervals.

Everyman

A MORALITY PLAY

The greatest of all moralities is the famous fifteenth-century EVERYMAN. *This morality is the story of how Everyman on his journey is abandoned by all but his Good Deeds, who alone will accompany him to the judgment seat of God and plead for him. Death hovers convincingly in the background like one of Holbein's spectral skeletons. The following selection will give a fair idea of the pathos, humanity, and exaltation of the play.*

Here beginneth a treatise how the High Father of Heaven sendeth Death to summon every creature to come and give account of their lives in this world and is in manner of a moral play.

MESSENGER. I pray you all give your audience,
And hear this matter with reverence,
By figure a moral play—

3. BY FIGURE—In form.

The *Summoning of Everyman* called it is,
That of our lives and ending shows
How transitory we be all day.
The story saith, — Man, in the beginning,
Look well, and take good heed to the ending,
Be you never so gay!
Ye think sin in the beginning full sweet,
Which in the end causeth thy soul to weep,
When the body lieth in clay.
Here shall you see how Fellowship and Jollity,
Both Strength, Pleasure, and Beauty
Will fade from thee as flower in May.
For ye shall hear, how our heaven king
Calleth Everyman to a general reckoning:
Give audience, and hear what he cloth say.

GOD. I perceive here in my majesty,
How that all creatures be to me unkind,
Living without dread in worldly prosperity:
Of ghostly sight the people be so blind,
Drowned in sin, they know me not for their God;
In worldly riches is all their mind,
They fear not my rightwiseness, the sharp rod;
My law that I shewed, when I for them died,
They forget clean, and shedding of my blood red;
I hanged between two, it cannot be denied;
To get them life I suffered to be dead;
I healed their feet, with thorns hurt was my head:
I could do no more than I did truly,
And now I see the people do clean forsake me.
They thank me not for the pleasure that I to them meant,
Nor yet for their being that I them have lent;
I proffered the people great multitude of mercy,
And few there be that asketh it heartily;
They be so cumbered with worldly riches,
That needs on them I must do justice,
On Everyman living without fear.
Where art thou, Death, thou mighty messenger?

DEATH. Almighty God, I am here at your will,
Your commandment to fulfil.

GOD. Go thou to Everyman,
And show him in my name
A pilgrimage he must on him take,
Which he in no wise may escape;
And that he bring with him a sure reckoning
Without delay or any tarrying.

DEATH. Lord, I will in the world go run over all,
And cruelly outsearch both great and small;
Every man will I beset that liveth beastly
Out of God's laws, and dreadeth not fully:
He that loveth riches I will strike with my dart,
His sight to blind, and from heaven to depart,
Except that alms be his good friend,
In hell for to dwell, world without end
Lo, yonder I see Everyman walking;
Full little he thinketh on my coming;
His mind is on fleshly lusts and his treasure,
And great pain it shall cause him to endure
Before the Lord Heaven King.
Everyman, stand still; whither art thou going
Thus gaily? Hast thou thy Maker forget?

EVERYMAN. Why askst thou?
Wouldest thou wete?

22. GHOSTLY—Spiritual.
26. SHEWED—Showed.
50. OUTSEARCH—Seek out.
65. WETE—Know.

DEATH. Yea, sir, I will show you;
In great haste I am sent to thee
From God out of his majesty.
EVERYMAN. What, sent to me?
DEATH. Yea, certainly.
Though thou have forget him here,
He thinketh on thee in the heavenly sphere,
As, or we depart, thou shalt know
EVERYMAN. What desireth God of me?
DEATH. That shall I show thee;
A reckoning he will needs have
Without any longer respite.
EVERYMAN. To give a reckoning longer leisure I crave;
This blind matter troubleth my wit.
DEATH. On thee thou must take a long journey:
Therefore thy book of count with thee thou bring;
For turn again thou cannot by no way,
And look thou be sure of thy reckoning:
For before God thou shalt answer, and show
Thy many bad deeds and good but a few;
How thou hast spent thy life, and in what wise,
Before the chief lord of paradise.
EVERYMAN. Full unready I am such reckoning to give.
I know thee not: what messenger art thou?
DEATH. I am Death, that no man dreadeth.
For every man I rest and no man spareth;
For it is God's commandment
That all to me should be obedient.
EVERYMAN. O Death, thou comest when I had thee least in mind;
In thy power it lieth me to save,
Yet of my good will I give thee, if ye will be kind,
Yea, a thousand pound shalt thou have,
And defer this matter till another day.
DEATH. Everyman, it may not be by no way;
I set not by gold, silver, nor riches,
Ne by pope, emperor, king, duke, ne princes.
For and I would receive gifts great,
All the world I might get;
But my custom is clean contrary.
I give thee no respite: come hence, and not tarry.
EVERYMAN. Alas, shall I have no longer respite?
I may say Death giveth no warning:
To think on thee, it maketh my heart sick,
For all unready is my book of reckoning.
Wherefore, Death, I pray thee, for God's mercy,
Spare me till I be provided of remedy.
DEATH. Thee availeth not to cry, weep, and pray:
But haste thee lightly that you were gone the journey,
And prove thy friends if thou can.
EVERYMAN.
Death, if I should this pilgrimage take,
And my reckoning surely make,
Show me, for saint charity,
Should I not come again shortly?
DEATH. No, Everyman; and thou be once there,
Thou mayst never more come here,
Trust me verily.
EVERYMAN. O gracious God, in the high seat celestial,
Have mercy on me in this most need;

73. OR—Before.
79. WIT—Mind.
88. FULL—Most
91. REST—Arrest.
96. GOOD—Goods.
101. NE—Not.
107. SAINT—Holy.

Shall I have no company from this vale terrestrial
Of mine acquaintance that way me to lead?

DEATH. Yea, if any be so hardy,
That would go with thee and bear thee company.
And now out of thy sight I will me hie;
See thou make thee ready shortly,
For thou mayst say this is the day
That no man living may scape away.

EVERYMAN. Alas, I may well weep with sighs deep;
Now have I no manner of company
To help me in my journey, and me to keep;
I would to God I had never be gete!
To my soul a full great profit it had be;
For now I fear pains huge and great.
The time passeth; Lord, help that all wrought;
For though I mourn it availeth nought.
To whom were I best my complaint to make?
What, and I to Fellowship thereof spake?
We have in the world so many a day
Be on good friends in sport and play.
I see him yonder, certainly;
I trust that he will bear me company;
Therefore to him will I speak to ease my sorrow.
Well met, good Fellowship, and good morrow!

FELLOWSHIP SPEAKETH. Everyman, good morrow by this day,
Sir, why lookest thou so piteously?
If any thing be amiss, I pray thee, me say,

128. HIE—Betake.
131. SCAPE—Escape.
135. GETE—Born.

141. WHAT, AND I TO FELLOWSHIP THEREOF SPAKE?—What if I should speak of this matter to *Fellowship*?

That I may help to remedy.
EVERYMAN. Yea, good Fellowship, yea,
I am in great jeopardy.
FELLOWSHIP. Sir, I must needs know your heaviness;
I have pity to see you in any distress;
If any have you wronged ye shall revenged be,
Though I on the ground be slain for thee,—
Though that I know before that I should die.
EVERYMAN. Verily, Fellowship, gramercy.
FELLOWSHIP. Tush! by thy thank I set not a straw.
Show me your grief, and say no more.
EVERYMAN. I shall show you how it is;
Commanded I am to go a journey,
A long way, hard and dangerous,
And give a strait count without delay
Before the high judge Adonai.
Wherefore I pray you, bear me company
As ye have promised, in this journey.
FELLOWSHIP. That is matter indeed! Promise is duty,
But, and I should take such a voyage on me,
I know it well, it should be to my pain:
Also it make me afeard, certain.
But let us take counsel here as well as we can,
For your words would fear a strong man.
EVERYMAN. Why, ye said, If I had need,
Ye would me never forsake, quick nor dead,
Though it were to hell truly.
FELLOWSHIP. So I said, certainly,
And yet if thou wilt eat, and drink, and make good cheer,
Or haunt to women, the lusty company,
I would not forsake you, while the day is clear,
Trust me verily!
EVERYMAN. Yea, thereto ye would be ready;
To go to mirth, solace, and play,
Your mind will sooner apply
Than to bear me company in my long journey.
FELLOWSHIP. Now, in good faith, I will not that way.
But and thou wilt murder, or any man kill,
In that I will help thee with a good will!
EVERYMAN. O that is a simple advice indeed!
Gentle fellow, help me in my necessity;
We have loved long, and now I need,
And now, gentle Fellowship, remember me.
FELLOWSHIP. Whether ye have loved me or no,
By Saint John, I will not with thee go.
EVERYMAN. Yet I pray thee, take the labour, and do so much for me
To bring me forward, for saint charity,
And comfort me till I come without the town.
FELLOWSHIP. Nay, and thou would give me a new gown,
I will not a foot with thee go;
But and you had tarried I would not have left thee so.
And as now, God speed thee in thy journey,
For from thee I will depart as fast as I may.
EVERYMAN. Wither away, fellowship? Will you forsake me?

159. GRAMERCY—Thanks.
165. STRAIT—Strict.
166. ADONAI—God.
170. AND—If.
170. VOYAGE—Journey.
174. FEAR—Frighten.
176. QUICK—Living.
187. WILL NOT—Have no desire.
190. A SIMPLE ADVICE—A silly idea.

FELLOWSHIP. Yea, by my fay, to God I betake thee.
EVERYMAN. Farewell, good Fellowship; for this my heart is sore;
Adieu for ever, I shall see thee no more
FELLOWSHIP. In faith, Everyman, farewell now at the end;
For you I will remember that parting is mourning.
FELLOWSHIP. Alack! shall we thus depart indeed?
Lo, Fellowship forsaketh me in my most need:
Yet in my mind a thing there is;—
All my life I have loved riches;
If that my good now help me might,
He would make my heart full light.
I will speak to him in this distress.—
Where art though, my Goods and riches?
GOODS. Who calleth me? Everyman? What haste thou hast!
I lie here in corners, trussed and piled so high,
And in chests I am locked so fast,
Also sacked in bags, though mayst see with thine eye,
I cannot stir; in packs low I lie.
What would ye have, lightly me say.
EVERYMAN. Come hither, Goods, in all the haste though may,
For of counsel I must desire thee.
GOODS. Sir, and ye in the world have trouble or adversity,
That can I help you to remedy shortly.
EVERYMAN. It is another disease that grieveth me;
In this world it is not, I tell thee so.
I am sent for another way to go,
To give a straight account general
Before the highest Jupiter of all;
And all my life I have had joy and pleasure in thee.
Therefore I pray thee go with me,
For, peradventure, thou mayst before God Almighty
My reckoning help to clean and purify;
For it is said ever among,
That money maketh all right that is wrong.
GOODS. Nay, Everyman, I sing another song,
I follow no man in such voyages;
For and I went with thee
Thou shouldst fare much the worse for me;
For because on me thou did set thy mind,
Thy reckoning I have made blotted and blind,
My condition is man's soul to kill;
If I save one, a thousand I do spill;
Weenest thou that I will follow thee?
Nay, from this world, not verily.
EVERYMAN. I had wend otherwise.
GOODS. Therefore to thy soul Good is a thief;
For when thou art dead, this is my guise
Another to deceive in the same wise
As I have done thee, and all to his soul's reprief.
EVERYMAN. O false Good, cursed thou be!
Thou traitor to God, that hast deceived me,
And caught me in thy snare.
GOODS. Marry, thou brought thyself in care,
Whereof I am glad,
I must needs laugh, I can not be sad.
EVERYMAN. Ah, Good, thou hast had long my heartly love
I gave thee that which should be the Lord's above.
But wilt thou not go with me in deed?
I pray thee truth to say.

205. FAY—Faith.
210. DEPART—Separate.
235. PERADVENTURE—Perchance.
246. SPILL—Destroy.
251. GIUSE—Practice.
253. REPRIEF—Reproof, shame.

GOODS. No, so God me speed,
Therefore farewell, and have good day.
EVERYMAN. Of whom shall I now counsel take?
I think that I shall never speed
Till that I go to my Good-Deed,
But alas, she is so weak,
That she can neither go nor speak;
Yet will I venture on her now.—
My Good-Deeds, where be you?
GOOD-DEEDS. Here I lie cold in the ground;
Thy sins hath me sore bound.
EVERYMAN. Good-Deeds, I pray you, help me in this need,
Or else I am for ever damned indeed;
Therefore help me to make reckoning
Before the redeemer of all thing,
That king is, and was, and ever shall.
GOOD-DEEDS. Everyman, I am sorry of your fall,
And fain would I help you, and I were able.
EVERYMAN. Good-Deeds, your counsel I pray you give me.
GOOD-DEEDS. That shall I do verily;
Though that on my feet I may not go,
I have a sister, that shall with you also,
Called Knowledge, which shall with you abide,
To help you to make that dreadful reckoning.
KNOWLEDGE. Everyman, I will go with thee, and be thy guide,
In thy most need to go by thy side.
EVERYMAN. My Good-Deeds, gramercy;
I am well content, certainly,
With your words sweet.
KNOWLEDGE. Now go we together lovingly,
To Confession, that cleansing river.
EVERYMAN. For joy I weep; I would we were there;
But, I pray you, give me cognition
Where dwelleth that holy man, Confession.
KNOWLEDGE. In the house of salvation:
We shall find him in that place,
That shall us comfort by God's grace.
To, this is Confession; kneel down and ask mercy,
For he is in good conceit with God almighty.
EVERYMAN. O glorious fountain that all uncleanness doth clarify,
Wash from me the spots of vices unclean,
That on me no sin may be seen;
I come with Knowledge for my redemption,
Repent with hearty and full contrition;
For I am commanded a pilgrimage to take,
And great accounts before God to make.
Now, I pray you, Shrift, mother of salvation,
Help my good deeds for my piteous exclamation.
CONFESSION. I know your sorrow well, Everyman;
Because with Knowledge ye come to me,
I will you comfort as well as I can,
And a precious jewel I will give thee,
Called penance, wise voider of adversity;
Therewith shall your body chastised be,
With abstinence and perseverance in God's service:
Here shall you receive that scourge of me,
Which is penance strong, that ye must endure,
To remember thy Saviour was scouraged for thee

273. IN—On.

296. COGNITION—Information.
302. CONCEIT—Favor.
310. SHRIFT—Absolution.

With sharp scourages, and suffered it patiently;
So must thou, or thou scape that painful pilgrimage;
Knowledge, keep him in this voyage,
And by that time Good-Deeds will be with thee.
But in any wise, be sure of mercy,
For your time draweth fast, and ye will saved be;
Ask God mercy, and He will grant truly,
When with the scourage of penance man doth him bind,
The oil of forgiveness then shall he find.

EVERYMAN. O eternal God, O heavenly figure,
O way of rightwiseness, O goodly vision,
Which descended down in a virgin pure
Because he would Everyman redeem,
Which Adam forfeited by his disobedience:
O blessed Godhead, elect and high-divine,
Forgive my grievous offence;
Here I cry thee mercy in this presence.
O ghostly treasure, O ransomer and redeemer
Of all the world, hope and conductor,
Mirror of joy, and founder of mercy,
Which illumineth heaven and earth thereby,
Hear my clamorous complaint, though it late be;
Receive my prayers; unworthy in this heavy life,
Though I be, a sinner most abominable,
Yet let my name be written in Moses' table;
O Mary, pray to the Maker of all thing,
Me for to help at my ending,
And save me from the power of my enemy,
For Death assaileth me strongly;
And, Lady, that I may by means of thy prayer
Of your Son's glory to be partaker,
By means of his passion I it crave,
I beseech you, help my soul to save.—
Knowledge, give me the scourage of penance;
My flesh therewith shall give a quittance:
I will now begin, if God give me grace.

KNOWLEDGE. Now, Everyman, be merry and glad;
Your Good-Deeds cometh now; ye may not be sad;
Now is your Good-Deeds whole and sound,
Going upright upon the ground.

GOOD-DEEDS. Everyman, pilgrim, my special friend,
Blessed be thou without end;
For thee is prepared the eternal glory.
Ye have me made whole and sound,
Therefore I will abide by thee in every stound.

EVERYMAN. Gramercy, Good-Deeds: now may I true friends see;
They have forsaken me every one;
I loved them better than my Good-Deeds alone.
Knowledge, will ye forsake me also?

KNOWLEDGE. Yea, Everyman, when ye to death do go:
But not yet for no manner of danger.

EVERYMAN. Gramercy, Knowledge, with all my heart.

KNOWLEDGE. Nay, yet I will not from hence depart,
Till I see where ye shall be come.

EVERYMAN. Methinketh, alas, that I must be gone,
To make my reckoning and my debts pay,
For I see my time is nigh spent away.

366. STOUND—Season.

Take example, all ye that this do hear or see,
How they that I loved best do forsake me,
Except my Good-Deeds that bideth truly.
GOOD-DEEDS. All earthly things is but vanity:
Beauty, Strength, and Discretion, do man forsake,
Foolish friends and kinsmen, that fair spake,
All fleeth save Good-Deeds, and that am I.
EVERYMAN. Have mercy on me, God most mighty;
And stand by me, thou Mother and Maid, holy Mary.
GOOD-DEEDS. Fear not, I will speak for thee.
EVERYMAN. Here I cry God mercy.
GOOD-DEEDS. Short our end, and minish our pain;
Let us go and never come again.
EVERYMAN. Into thy hands, Lord, my soul I commend;
Receive it, Lord, that it be not lost;
As thou me boughtest, so me defend,
And save me from the fiend's boast,
That I may appear with that blessed host
That shall be saved at the day of doom.
In manus tuas—of might's most
For ever—*commendo spiritum meum.*

398. *In manus tuas . . .* —"Into Thy hands I commend my spirit."

FOR DISCUSSION

1. What is the reaction of Everyman to the summons which he receives? What companions does he wish to bring with him on his journey? Which companions can accompany him, and which cannot? Explain.

2. What does Knowledge do for him? Enumerate in detail what Confession does for him.

3. Explain the meaning of lines 245-253.

4. Explain just why the play is an allegory.

5. How does a Catholic sense of values help in the appreciation of the play? Discuss.

6. What qualities in this play give it as much appeal to a twentieth-century audience as it gave to a fifteenth-century one?

7. It has been said that there is no tragedy in medieval drama. Why is this true of *Everyman*, even though the protagonist or leading character descends to the grave?

RELATED READING

Read at least one of the following mystery plays: *Noah, Abraham and Isaac, The Second Shepherd's Play*. They can be found in C. G. Child's edition of *Early English Plays.*

THE RENAISSANCE AND THE ELIZABETHAN AGE

1500-1603

The century after Chaucer's death was one of political confusion, of civil and foreign wars, and of economic disasters. In 1485, Henry Tudor brought the civil War of the Roses to an end with his victory over Richard III on Bosworth Field. Henry VII was officially recognized as king by Parliament, and thus began the reign of the Tudors which was to have such a devastating effect on English Catholic history.

During the early hectic years of the fifteenth century, there was little literary activity. In the last quarter of the century, however, William Caxton took up the new art of printing and began publishing English books. An enthusiastic admirer of both Chaucer and Malory, he edited the *Canterbury Tales* and *Morte d'Arthur* and wrote an introduction to both.

THE EARLY RENAISANCE

Renaissance means "rebirth" and is intended to describe a renewed interest in the classics and the Graeco-Roman culture which took fire in Italy and swept over the rest of Europe in the fifteenth and sixteenth centuries. Unfortunately, in Italy this "new learning" with its emphasis on the natural man led to rank paganism. Many Italians not only highly esteemed the beauty of Homer, Aristotle, Plato, the Greek tragedians, Virgil, and Cicero, but they also made the pagan ideal of life their own. Italian writers like Boccaccio and Petrarch portrayed the Kingdom of Man as more desirable than the Kingdom of God. In their enthusiasm for the natural beauty of the pagan ideal, they exaggerated man's importance as the center of the universe to the neglect of his highest dignity—his relationship to God and his supernatural destiny. Thus, in contrast to the spirit of the Middle Ages, the universe of man's thoughts and actions became *homocentric* (man-centered) rather than *theocentric* (God-centered).

It would be a mistake, however, to consider the Renaissance as a complete reaction against the teachings and culture of the Middle Ages. In fact, modern scholars are now beginning to see that the Renaissance was a natural outgrowth of the Middle Ages in many respects. Classical literature had been known and studied throughout the Middle Ages. It was the medieval monks who copied the ancient classics before the time of the printing press and preserved them for future generations. The whole culture of the Middle Ages was built upon ancient Latin and Greek thought that had been Christianized. The interest which men had taken in philosophy and theology for centuries led to a natural reaction in favor of the humanities—the literature of Greece and Rome. The emphasis shifted from a search for truth to a search for beauty. But the greatest beauty of the Renaissance was in the Cathedral, the religious painting and sculpture of men like Michelangelo and Raphael, men working in the great Catholic tradition of St. Augustine of Hippo, St. Bernard, St. Thomas Aquinas, Dante, and Chaucer.

The intoxication that was found in the beauty of art and literature, as contrasted with the more sober discipline of logic and philosophy, led many men to condemn philosophy and theology and even to replace religion by an adoration of human beauty. It must be admitted that a great many of these excesses could have been avoided if the great philosophy of St. Thomas Aquinas had not fallen into disrepute during the late fourteenth and fifteenth centuries.

There were, then, two currents of Renaissance thinking. One carried on the Catholic tradition and incorporated it into art, letters, Christian philosophy, religion, the sacredness of love, and the supernatural dignity of man. The other emphasized the material, the carnal, and the pagan pursuit of beauty and natural perfection. It stood for freedom from law and the shackles of the Catholic Church, and for the "infinite desire" to perfect the natural capacities of man as an individual.

SAINT THOMAS MORE

The beginnings of the Renaissance in England were a much more balanced affair simply because its early leaders and scholars were Catholic humanists. Men like Colet, Linacre, Grocyn, St. Thomas More, and St. John Fisher brought to the love of the classics and the humanistic ideal the spirit of Christian humility and the total understanding of man's natural and supernatural relationship to God—his final end and ultimate source of wisdom and beauty.

In St. Thomas More we have one of the greatest of all great Englishmen. From his birth in 1478 until his execution by his old friend Henry VIII in 1535, he gave England and posterity an example of Christian sanity, sanctity, statesmanship, and scholarship perhaps never before nor since combined in one man.

More rose rapidly in his profession as a lawyer and at twenty-six was sent to Parliament. He successively and successfully became Under-Sheriff of London, a member of the King's Council, Under-Treasurer of England, Speaker of the House of Commons, and finally at fifty-one Lord Chancellor of the Realm—the first layman ever to hold that position. As a statesman and trusted adviser of Henry VIII, he represented that monarch on the most difficult diplomatic missions. A devoted husband and father, he was a friend of the poor, a champion of peace, an ardent apologist against the new heresies, and a defender of the Papacy. A man of the world who daily brushed shoulders with the high and mighty as well as with the outcast, a man whose sense of laughter made him live "for the next world but was merry withal," an heroic saint, who daily wore a hair-shirt, "whose soul was more pure than snow"—this is but a brief etching of More, the man of letters, who stands as the bridge which spans the medieval and the modern world. He is "one of the founders of modern literature," and he is the connecting link in the continuity of English Catholic thought from Bede and Chaucer to Chesterton.

Thomas More was undoubtedly a man of the Renaissance. In the field of the humanities, he was as much a pioneer as his distinguished teacher, Colet, and his intimate friend, Erasmus, the Dutch humanist, who had been invited to teach Greek at Oxford at the request of that other great humanist, St. John Fisher. More's *Utopia,* a delightful satire on government, society, and economic repression was England's first significant contribution to Renaissance literature. In it we see the influence of Plato's *Republic,* Plutarch's *Lives,* St. Augustine's *City of God,* and Amerigo Vespucci's *Voyages.* But the Christian humanist is at work in the *Utopia,* where More artistically portrays a dream world in which pagans guided by reason only seem to regard Christian values more highly than Christians do.

It is unfortunate that More is known only for his *Utopia* which, because of its apparently revolutionary ideas on society's and man's mode of living, has had an appeal for the radical in every century. Very few realize that More wrote controversy in English prose and that his *Richard III, Four Last Things,* and *Dialogue of Comfort* were recognized by both his contemporaries and later critics as outstanding examples of literary composition. In the preface to More's collected *Works,* published in 1557, William Rastell wrote that More had written "books so many and so well, as no one Englishman ever wrote the like, whereby his works be worthy to be had and read of every English man that is desirous to know and learn, not only the eloquence and property of the English tongue, but also the true doctrine of Christ's Catholic Church."

MORE'S PLACE IN LITERATURE

It may surprise us to learn that during the Age of Elizabeth *Richard III* was printed five times within a space of twenty years. It formed the basis of Shakespeare's play and was called by an Elizabethan critic "the best written part of all our Chronicles." In the days of the Stuarts, More was regarded as among the half-dozen English writers who "speak the best and purest English," and Ben Jonson, in his *English Grammar,* quotes More more frequently than any other prose work.

In his last official act as Chancellor, More wrote a long defense of liberal education and the study of Greek, which he sent to the faculty of Oxford University. This was done to thwart some of the more conservative clergy who were attempting to make a seminary out of Oxford. It is ironic that the same Henry who approved this course of action was very shortly to condemn More to the executioner's axe. It is also ironic and tragic that Henry turned from More's book *Utopia,* which he had admired so much for its gentle philosophy of government, to the infamous *Il Principe (The Prince)* by the Italian, Machiavelli. Encouraged by Thomas Cromwell to study Machiavelli, Henry was transformed from a Defender of the Faith, a lover of the arts, and the great friend of Thomas More into being his own pope, the destroyer of the culture of the ages, and executioner of his dearest friend. Since Henry's day *The Prince* has been the guide of many another ruthless dictator and tyrant.

With the beheading of Sir Thomas More and John Fisher, the early bloom of a truly Christian Renaissance in England was blighted, if not entirely killed; for More and Fisher gave an example of what a Christian Renaissance could have been and, perhaps, in our own day, may yet be.

The death of these two martyrs indicates another phase of Henry VIII's reign which had a tremendous effect on England's future history and literature. These men died because they refused to acknowledge Henry as supreme head of the Church of England. Henry had cut himself, and would soon cut his realm, from the Church. He ordered the devastation of the monasteries and the filling of the royal coffers with their wealth and property. Not since the invasion of the Danes had there been such pillaging and wanton destruction of priceless relics and manuscripts. The glass of Lincoln Cathedral was used as a mark for crossbow practice, and few remonstrated.

The revolt from the ancient Catholic Faith grew under Henry's daughter, Elizabeth. From that time on, England was gradually Protestantized, but the culture which several centuries of Catholicism had given her lived on in her literature.

RICHARD III

THOMAS MORE

The historical piece, Richard III, *is a fragment of what Sir Thomas More had planned to be a complete history of his own times. However, engaged as he was with his controversial works and with the completion of* Utopia, *the history was never finished. Nevertheless, the fragment holds a high place in English historical prose. Shakespeare was heavily indebted to it for his play,* Richard III. *It can be said truly that with his dramatic narrative power, More initiated the art of modern historical writing in England.*

The selection which appears below is a short passage from the history. More has shown how the Duke of Gloucester, appointed protector to the boy-king, Edward V, has had himself declared King Richard III and has determined to rid himself of his nephews, Edward and the younger brother, Richard. The King entrusted the job to his henchman, Sir James Tyrell, who in turn employed assassins to murder the princes in the Tower. In the passage below, More depicts the murder, and then relates the tragic end of the King and his assassins. When Henry VII defeated Richard on the field of Bosworth in 1485, he brought to an end the Civil War of the Roses and inaugurated the Tudor dynasty.

For Sir James Tyrell[1] devised that they should be murdered in their beds. To the execution whereof he appointed Miles Forest, one of the four that kept them, a fellow fleshed in murder before-time. To him he joined one John Dighton, his own horsekeeper, a big broad square strong knave. Then all the others being removed from them, this Miles Forest and John Dighton about midnight (the sely[2] children lying their beds) came into the chamber, and suddenly lapped them up among the clothes, so bewrapped them and entangled them, keeping down by force the featherbed and pillows hard unto their mouths, that within a while smored[3] and stifled, their breath failing, they gave up to God their innocent souls into the joys of heaven, leaving to the tormentors their bodies dead in the bed. Which after that the wretches perceived, first by the struggling with the pains of death, and after long lying still to be thoroughly dead, they laid their bodies naked out upon the bed, and fetched Sir James to see them. Which upon the sight of them, caused those murderers to bury them at the stair foot, meetly[4] deep in the ground under a great heap of stones. Then rode Sir James in great haste to King Richard, and showed him all the manner of the murder; who gave him great thanks and, as some say, there made him knight. But he allowed not, as I have heard, the burying in so vile a corner, saying that he would have them buried in a better place, because they were a King's sons. Lo, the honourable courage of a King! Whereupon, they say that a priest of Sir Robert Brakenbery[5] took up the bodies again, and secretly interred them in such a place as, by the occasion of his death which only knew it,[6] could never since come to light. Very truth is it and well knowen, that at such time as Sir James Tyrell was in the Tower for treason committed against the most famous prince King Henry the seventh,[7] both Dighton and he were examined and confessed the murder in manner above written; but whither the bodies were removed they could nothing tell.

And thus as I have learned of them that much knew and little cause had to lie, were these two noble princes, these innocent tender children, born of most royal blood, brought up in great wealth, likely long to live to reign and rule in the realm, by traitorous tyranny taken, deprived of their estate, shortly shut up in prison, and privily slain and murdered, their bodies cast God wot[8] where, by the cruel ambition of their unnatural uncle and his dispiteous[9] tormentors. Which things on every part well pondered, God never gave this world a more notable example, neither in what unsurety standeth this worldly weal, or what mischief worketh the proud enterprise of an high heart, or finally what wretched

[1]SIR JAMES TYRELL—Tyrell was a strong supporter of the Yorkists and became Richard's Master of the Horse. He was later taken into favor by Henry VII but was ultimately beheaded for conspiracy against Henry in 1502.

[2]SELY—Innocent.

[3]SMORED—Smothered.

[4]MEETLY—Here the word means "moderately."

[5]SIR ROBERT BRAKENBERY—Keeper of London Tower to whom the Duke of Clarence related his horrible dream. See Shakespeare's *Richard III*, Act 1, Sc. 4.

[6]BY THE OCCASION OF HIS DEATH WHICH ONLY KNEW IT—"when he—the only one who knew it—died." That is, the priest of Sir Robert of Brakenbery was the only one who knew where the princes were reburied, and when he died the secret died with him.

[7]KING HENRY THE SEVENTH—Henry defeated Richard III at Bosworth.

[8]WOT—To know, the present tense of "wit."

[9]DISIPITEOUS—Pitiless, merciless.

end ensueth such dispiteous cruelty. For first, to begin with the ministers, Miles Forest at Saint Martin's piecemeal rotted away. Dighton indeed yet walketh on alive, in good possibility to be hanged ere he die. But Sir James Tyrell died at Tower Hill, beheaded for treason. King Richard himself, as ye shall hereafter hear, slain in the field, hacked and hewed of his enemies' hands, harried on horseback dead, his hair in despite torn and togged[10] like a cur dog: and the mischief that he took, within less than three years of the mischief that he did. And yet all the mean time spent in much pain and trouble outward, much fear, anguish, and sorrow within. For I have heard by credible report of such as were secret with his chamberers, that after this abominable deed done, he never had quiet in his mind, he never thought himself sure. Where he went abroad, his eyen whirled about, his body privily fenced, his hand ever on his dagger, his countenance and manner like one alway ready to strike again; he took ill rest a nights, lay long waking and musing, sore wearied with care and watch, rather slumbered than slept, troubled with fearful dreams, suddenly sometime sterte up, leape out of his bed and runne[11] about the chamber, so was his restless heart continually tossed and tumbled with the tedious impression and stormy remembrance of his abominable deed.

[10] TOGGED—Pulled about, mauled.

[11] STERTE, LEAPE, RUNNE—These are old past tenses of "start," "leap," "run."

FOR DISCUSSION

1. Study the balance and rhythm of More's sentences, his use of alliteration, his colorful and graphic action words. Choose several sentences in the passage and analyze them for the above qualities.

2. Explain the satire in More's remark: "Lo, the honourable courage of a King!" Is there something almost prophetic in this statement? What happened to More?

3. Note how dramatically More describes Richard's reaction to the murder. Mention several other tyrants in history and literature who suffered similar fates.

PROJECTS

1. Compare More's description of the murder with that in Shakespeare's *Richard III*, Act IV, Sc. 3.

2. Give the historical background of the War of the Roses.

3. Write a description of the tragic end of some tyrant. Be as graphic and dramatic as possible.

ST. THOMAS MORE'S DEFENSE AND EXECUTION

WILLIAM ROPER

Here we are interested in More the man and the saint, whom Swift called "the person of the greatest virtue this Kingdom ever produced." Since his canonization in 1935, many books have been written about him; but all of them must rely upon his first biographer, his son-in-law, William Roper. Roper has the distinction not only of having written an excellent life of St. Thomas More, but also of having written the first biography in the English language.

The selections which we shall read have been re-written in modern English. A few lines of the original will be quoted at the end of the passage.

The Jury found him guilty. And immediately upon their verdict the Lord Chancellor, beginning to proceed in judgment against him, Sir Thomas More said to him: "My Lord, when I practiced Law, the manner in such case was to ask the prisoner before judgment why judgment should not be given against him." Whereupon the Lord Chancellor, staying his judgment, wherein he had partly proceeded, demanded of him what he was able to say to the contrary. More then most humbly made answer as follows:

"For as much, my Lord," said he, "this indictment is grounded upon an Act of Parliament[1] directly repugnant to the laws of God and His holy Church, the supreme government of which, or any part thereof, may no temporal prince presume by any law to take upon him, as rightfully belonging to the See of Rome, a spiritual pre-eminence specially granted by special prerogative by the mouth of our Savior Himself, personally present on earth, only to St. Peter and his successors, Bishops of the same See. It is therefore in law among Christian men insufficient to charge any Christian man." And for proof thereof, he declared that this Realm, being but one member and a small part of the Church, might not make a particular law disagreeable with the general law of Christ's universal Catholic Church. No more than the city of London, being but

[1]ACT OF PARLIAMENT—On March 30, 1534, an Act of Parliament was passed requiring from all subjects an oath limiting the succession of the crown to the children of Henry VIII and Anne Boleyn. Parliament prescribed no definite form of the oath but Henry's commissioners drafted a form which not only insured Elizabeth's right to succession but invalidated Henry's marriage to Catherine, made valid Henry's marriage to Anne, and repudiated any oath that had been taken "to any foreign authority, prince, or potentate."

one poor member in respect of the whole realm, might make a law against an Act of Parliament to bind the whole realm. He further showed that it was contrary both to the laws and statutes of our own Land yet unrepealed, as they might easily perceive in the *Magna Charta:*[2] *Quod ecclesia Anglicans libera sit, et habeat omnia Jura sus Integra et libertates suas illaesas.*[3] It was also contrary to that sacred oath which the King's Highness himself and every other Christian prince always with great solemnity received at the coronations. He alleged moreover that no more might this Realm of England refuse obedience to the See of Rome than might the child refuse obedience to his own natural father. For as St. Paul said of the Corinthians: "I have regenerated you, my children, in Christ." So might St. Gregory, Pope of Rome, of whom, by St. Augustine,[4] his messenger, we first received the Christian faith, of us Englishmen truly say: "You are my children, because I have given to you everlasting salvation, a far higher and better inheritance than any carnal father can leave to his child, and by regeneration made you my spiritual children in Christ."

[The Lord Chancellor then accused More of "stiffly sticking" contrary to the Bishops and learned men of the Realm. More claimed the support of the Clergy and learned men of the past and affirmed that he was not bound to "conform my conscience to the Council of One Realm against the general Council of Christendom." The Lord Chancellor, not desiring to have the burden of judgment entirely upon himself, asked the advice of Lord FitzJames, Chief Justice of the King's Bench. The Chief Justice replied that "if the Act of Parliament be lawful, then the Indictment is good enough." Sentence was then passed against More and he returned to the Tower led by Sir William Kingston, Constable of the Tower and a dear friend of More. More comforts Kingston by saying: "Trouble not yourself but be of good cheer; for I will pray for you, and my good Lady, your wife, that we may meet in heaven together, where we shall be merry for ever and ever." We now continue in Roper's own words.]

When Sir Thomas More came to Westminster to the Tower[5] again, his daughter, my wife, desirous to see her father, whom she thought she would never see in this world again, and also to have his final blessing, watched at the Tower Wharf, where she knew he would pass by, before he could enter the Tower. As soon as she saw him, after reverently receiving his blessing on her knees she hastened towards him, without consideration or care of herself, pressed into the midst of the throng and company of the guard that were round about him, hastily ran to him, and there openly in the sight of them all embraced him and took him about the neck and kissed him. . . .

So remained Sir Thomas More in the Tower, more than a week after his trial.

[2]MAGNA CHARTA—The Great Charter which the English barons forced King John to sign at Runnymede in 1215. It laid the foundation for English religious, political, and personal freedom.

[3]*Quod ecclesia . . . suas illaesas.*—An article of the Magna Charta which gave autonomy or self-government to the English Church: "That the English Church should be free, that all its rights should be held inviolate, and that its liberties should be unimpaired."

[4]ST. AUGUSTINE—St. Augustine was sent by St. Gregory to convert the Anglo-Saxons in 597.

[5]TOWER—The Tower was the official prison of London.

Whence, the day before he suffered, he sent his shirt of hair,[6] not willing to have it seen, to my wife, his dearly beloved daughter, and a letter written with a piece of charcoal, plainly expressing the fervent desire he had to be executed on the morrow. The letter said: "I cumber you, good Margaret, much, but I would be sorry if it should be any longer than tomorrow. For tomorrow is St. Thomas' even, the sixth of July; and therefore tomorrow I long to go to God. It is a day very meet and convenient for me. I never liked your manner better towards me than when you kissed me last. For I like when daughterly love and dear charity hath no leisure to look to worldly courtesy."

And so on the next morning, being Tuesday, St. Thomas' even, in the year of our Lord 1535, according as he in his letter the day before had wished, early in the morning came to him Sir Thomas Pope, his very good friend, with a message from the King and the Council, that he should before nine of the clock of the same morning suffer death; and that therefore he should forthwith prepare himself thereto.

"Master Pope," said he, "for your tidings I heartily thank you. I have been always much bounden to the King's Highness for the benefits and honors that he has from time to time most bountifully heaped upon me; and yet I am more bound to His Grace for putting me into this place, where I have had convenient time and space to think about my end. And so help me God, most of all, Master Pope, am I bound to His Highness, because it pleases him so shortly to rid me out of the miseries of this wretched world; and therefore I will not fail earnestly to pray for His Grace, both here, and also in the world to come."

[6] SHIRT OF HAIR—A shirt made of horse hair, used as an instrument of penance.

"The King's pleasure is further," said Master Pope, "that at your execution you shall not use many words."

"Master Pope," More replied, "you do well to give me warning of His Grace's pleasure; for other wise, at that time I purposed to have spoken at some length; but of no matter wherewith His Grace or any other should have cause to be offended. Nevertheless, whatsoever I had intended to say I am ready obediently to conform myself to His Grace's commandment; and I beseech you, Master Pope, to arrange with His Highness that my daughter Margaret may be at my burial."

"The King has consented already," said Master Pope, "that your wife, children, and other friends shall have liberty to be present thereat."

"O how much beholden, then," said Thomas More, "am I unto His Grace, who permits me to have so gracious consideration at my poor burial!"

Wherewithal, Master Pope, taking his leave of him, could not refrain from weeping. Sir Thomas More perceiving this, comforted him in this wise: "Quiet yourself, good Master Pope, and be not discomforted, for I trust that we shall some time see each other in heaven full merrily, where we shall be sure to live and love together, in joyful bliss eternally."

Upon this departure, Sir Thomas More, as one that has been invited to some solemn feast, changed himself into his best apparel. Master Lieutenant observing, advised him to put it off, saying that he who should have it was but a rascal.

"What, Master Lieutenant?" quoth he, "shall I account him a rascal that shall do me this day so singular a benefit? Nay, I assure

you, were it cloth of gold, I think it well bestowed on him, as St. Cyprian[7] did, who gave his executioner thirty pieces of gold." And although at length through Master Lieutenant's importunate persuasion, he altered his apparel; yet, after the example of the holy martyr St. Cyprian, he gave of the little money that was left him a coin of gold to his executioner.

And so he was brought by Master Lieutenant out of the Tower, and from thence led towards the place of execution. Going up to the scaffold, which was so weak that it was ready to fall, he said merrily to the Lieutenant, "I pray you, Master Lieutenant, see me safe up: and for my coming down let me shift for myself."

And then he desired all the people thereabout to pray for him, and to bear witness with him, that he should suffer death in and for the faith of the holy Catholic Church. Which done, he kneeled down, and after his prayers were said, turned to the executioner with a cheerful countenance, and said to him, "Pluck up thy spirits, man, and be not afraid to do your office. My neck is very short. Take heed, therefore, that you do not strike awry."

So passed Sir Thomas More out of this world to God, upon the very same day which he most desired.

[The following is a brief selection from Roper's original. It is a good example of English prose in transition from Middle English. Note the difference in spelling.]

And so was he by master Leiuetenaunte brought out of the Tower, and from thence led to [wardes] the place of execution. Where, goinge uppe the scaffold, which was

[7]ST. CYPRIAN—Bishop of Carthage and martyr. Famous apologist of the third century.

so weake that it was ready to fall, he saide merilye to master Leiuetenaunte: "I pray you, master Leiuetenaunte, see me salf uppe, and for my cominge downe let me shifte for my self."

Then desired he all the people thereaboute to pray for him, and to beare witness with him that he should (nowe there) suffer death in and for the faith of the holy chatholik churche. Whiche done, he kneled downe, and after his prayers said, turned to the executioner; and with a cheerefull countenaunce spake (thus) to him: "Plucke upp thy spirites, man, and be not afrayde to do thine office; my necke is very shorte nor; take heede therefore thow strike not awrye, for savinge of thine honestye."

So passed Sir Thomas More out of this world to god uppon the very same daye in which himself had most desired.

FOR DISCUSSION

1. Note the simplicity of Roper's style. Judging from the selection you have just read, do you think Roper is a good biographer? Explain.

2. Was Margaret More's public display of affection for her father dangerous? Explain.

3. Outline the arguments which More used to show that the Act of Parliament was against the laws of God and His Church.

4. Why did More wish to die on July 6?

5. What evidence of heroic sanctity is found in the selection?

6. Discuss this comment of Addison written two centuries after More's death: "The innocent mirth which had been so conspicuous in his life, did not forsake him to the last."

WORD STUDY

What does *knave* mean today? What did it mean in More's day? Look up the definition of *weal* and *cumber.* What is the connection between *weal* and *commonwealth*? Explain the meaning of the expression *a fellow fleshed in murder.* Make sure you know the meaning of *prerogative, allege, interred.*

PROJECTS

1. Read and be prepared to discuss More's defense of a liberal education as quoted in Charles A. Brady's *Stage of Fools,* pp. 230-235.

2. More's *Utopia* is a widely discussed book. Class members may take certain chapters from the book for special reports and class discussion. Basis for discussion: Why does *Utopia* interest the twentieth century world?

3. In his epilogue to his *Life of More,* Christopher Hollis writes that four things were killed when More was killed: learning, justice, laughter, and holiness. Read the two-page epilogue and make an oral or written report on it.

4. St. Thomas More was executed at Tyburn, a place sacred in the history of English Catholicism. Mention several other English martyrs who were executed there.

5. Write a brief biographical sketch of "More, the Ideal Family Man."

RELATED READING

Read the article on Thomas More in *Jubilee,* July 1954.

You must read Charles A. Brady's *Stage of Fools,* an excellent dramatic and historical presentation of the life and times of Thomas More, written in the form of a novel.

A great scholar's estimate of More may be found in R. W. Chambers' *Thomas More* and in his *The Place of St. Thomas More in English Literature and History.*

THE ELIZABETHAN AGE

1558-1603

When the daughter of Henry VIII and Anne Boleyn took the throne, England's future looked rather meager. The treasury was empty, the army disbanded, the navy second-rate. But Elizabeth, whatever else she may have been, was no fool. And along with a red wig and a sharp tongue, she possessed a will of iron.

Forty-five years she reigned successfully. Under her rule the monarchy was established, and England attained great material prestige and prosperity. It was a swaggering, swashbuckling age given to exalting itself, its wealth, its achievements. And the people were persuaded to associate all this with her whom her subjects called their "virgin queen."

Mary, Queen of Scotland, one-time Queen of France, and now claimant to the English throne through her grandmother, the daughter of Henry VII, threatened Elizabeth's security. Graciously lovely at nineteen, Catholic, and rich in foreign influence, Mary was unwelcome at Elizabeth's court where she had fled from Scotland. Political expediency favored her death, but Elizabeth kept her prisoner for twenty years before she sent her to her death on a charge of plotting against the queen's life. The tragic Queen of Scots moved all who met her to pity, but her death brought unity and strength to England. Under condemnation of death, Mary had appealed to Philip of Spain to avenge her and to secure the throne for her son. At her death, Philip assembled a large fleet and army, which set out in 1588. Elizabeth made hasty preparations to meet the invasion, and the smaller English fleet under Sir Francis Drake attacked the enemy spread out in a seven-mile crescent across the English Channel. Of the hundred and fifty vessels in the Spanish Armada, less than a third escaped. Although the victory was due as much to weather conditions favoring the English as to their skill and daring, the victory was nonetheless a tremendous one. It marked England's emergence as a world power, and patriotic enthusiasm ran high. Pride in the British navy has ever since been traditional.

MARY, QUEEN OF SCOTS

Elizabeth's reign was distinguished for her policy of colonization. We who live in a world that has shrunk to a neighborhood, whose farthest point—the air-line advertisements tell us—is at most forty hours from our doorstep, can hardly realize what an impact the discovery of the vast new continent of America in 1492 had on people's minds. Men set out to hunt fabulous silver mines and rivers whose waters rolled over precious stones. The expeditions were manned by "apt young men" from the West country, and financed in part by the great Queen herself. And as the ships swung down the tide, untold wealth seemed to be had only for the questing. Large merchant companies such as the Hudson Bay Company and the East India Company were chartered to trade with Russia and the Far East. And there were freebooters like Drake, Hawkins, and Sir Walter Raleigh who came back to England with hoards of gold pirated from Spanish vessels. The new attitude, whereby man was willing to undergo very great risks in the hope of exorbitant gains, was likewise responsible for a

multitude of get-rich-quick schemes. Everything from alchemy[1] to the retrieving of drowned lands was attempted.

Manufacturing received promotion and encouragement. Agriculture was studied and improved. The bourgeoisie came into economic and political power. The capitalist system was taking shape. From within, the feudal system had been dissipated by the general breakdown of medieval civilization, and from without by the economic and social policies of Henry VIII and Elizabeth. It was an age of production for profit and self-aggrandizement, of exploitation of the dispossessed, of new methods of "mass-production" and tenant-farming.

As far back as the time of Chaucer, educated Englishmen had been traveling abroad and had been gradually assimilating the Italian Renaissance ideal with its emphasis on the individual. The wide accomplishments of such universal geniuses as Michelangelo and Leonardo da Vinci stirred men's ambition. The gradual advance in the sciences and arts of the continent coupled with the discoveries of new lands made the possibility of human progress seem limitless. The whole political and economic structure was undergoing a change. With all these new ideas in the air, together with the introduction of the printing press, it is not to be wondered at that this was one of the most productive eras of English literature.

PATRIOTISM, PEACE, AND PROSPERITY

Elizabeth's chief contributions to England were these: she gave it fifty years of comparative peace, she brought it wealth, and above all she developed a sense of nationalism by playing up the Spanish threat and by building up the English navy. The poets and prose writers alike wrote long flattering works on "the bountiful good Queen Bess." With their tongues in their cheeks, they traced her lineage back to the great King Arthur. She encouraged the flattery but did very little in a material way to aid the flatterers. She herself was fairly well versed in literature and the arts. We are familiar with the picture which represents her, during one of her visits to Oxford, listening to the handsome young Edmund Campion addressing her eloquently in Greek. (She later had him hanged, drawn, and quartered for giving a no less eloquent defense of the Catholic Faith.) Spenser, who paid her exaggerated homage in *The Faerie Queene*, hoping thereby to obtain preferment at court, learned in his Irish exile how cheaply she bought her flattery.

[1]ALCHEMY (ăl´kê-mĭ)—A combination of science and magic practiced in medieval times; one objective was to change cheap metals into gold.

Like travelers today, nearly everybody who took a voyage or made an expedition came home and wrote a book about it. Richard Hakluyt published his *Principal Navigations*, which gives accounts of the voyages of all of the great Elizabethans and their predecessors. Sidney's *Arcadia* is full of the charm that hangs about distant lands; Spenser speaks of the colony which his friend Sir Walter Raleigh attempted to found in Virginia; and Shakespeare's *Tempest* pictures the conflict between civilization and savagery on a romantic island.

But more than anything else, the new spirit of nationalism was like heady wine to the writers and poets. All the historical plays of Shakespeare surge with pride in England. There is the same patriotic rapture in Spenser's *Faerie Queene* with its glorification of Elizabeth and its vilification of Mary Stuart, Queen of Scots, and of his Catholic Majesty, Philip II of Spain. Besides these, a great number of chronicles and histories were written exalting England and the Tudor dynasty.

The Renaissance emphasis on the individual, the notion of courtly love, and the general enthusiasm of the age gave rise to a wealth of lyric poetry. Almost every Elizabethan writer tried his hand at writing sonnets. A profusion of pure lyrical songs saturated the plays of Shakespeare, Ben Jonson, Beaumont, and Fletcher. Marlowe, Raleigh, and Spenser wrote in the popular pastoral form. The lyrics of Thomas Campion were as well known by the Elizabethan populace as are the outpourings of the modern songwriter.

But by far the greatest literary achievement of the age was the flowering of the drama in the hands of Marlowe, Shakespeare, Ben Jonson, and other lesser known writers like Greene and Dekker. With Shakespeare the summits were reached. As Carlton Hayes says of Shakespeare's plays, "they are individual and nationalist, medieval and modern, Italian and classical, and above all, English."

Time out of mind there have been debates and disputes over whether or not Shakespeare was a Catholic. Even though the latest scholarship seems to indicate that he was, the point is not too important. What is important is that his plays are Catholic—as Carlyle puts it, "the outflowering of the Catholic middle ages."

No single period ever again produced such names as Marlowe, Ben Jonson, Shakespeare, Sidney, Spenser, and Francis Bacon. This was the age of literary giants who wrote their works "to last until the stars are out."

THE POETRY OF EDMUND SPENSER

We might compare the poetical works of Edmund Spenser to a mirror in which are reflected the various influences of the Renaissance on Elizabethan life and letters, the political and religious turmoil of the period, and the growing national consciousness of England, with her pride in her ancestry and her position as a rising international power. From his knowledge of the classics and the Renaissance emphasis on the courtly ideal, Spenser attempted to portray what he conceived to be the ideal commonwealth and the ideal courtier or private man.

In his *Shepherd's Calendar*, a book of twelve poems, Spenser followed a fashion, made popular by the Italian Renaissance writers, of imitating the pastoral poems of Theocritus and Virgil. Pastoral poetry treats of rural life not in a realistic but in an idealistic and allegorical manner. It is an artificial form of poetry in which the setting is always some form of Arcadia or never-never-land where men live an ideal existence, free from the strife of civilization, where nature is always kind and men live very simple lives. The characters in a pastoral poem are represented as shepherds. Sheep and cattle represent wealth. In some form or other, almost all the Elizabethan writers attempted the pastoral style.

EDMUND SPENSER

Spenser added satire to the pastoral with his many references in the *Shepherd's Calendar* to the religious conditions of his time. He further used it as a medium for flattering Elizabeth, the queen of the shepherds, and for praising poetry and its place in the life of the courtier.

THE FAERIE QUEENE

It was Spenser's great ambition to write an epic of his age in which he would "imitate earlier epic poets in showing how a noble person should be fashioned." During the Renaissance, epic poetry was regarded as idealized history to which were added the ideal ruler and the ideal courtier or private citizen.

The Faerie Queene is Spenser's attempt to attain these purposes. Although it is not an epic, it is a great metrical romance and places its author among the five highest ranking English poets.

Just as Virgil traced the origin of Rome to Troy, so Spenser, in the *Faerie Queene*, makes his theme the origin of the English nation. In Elizabeth, Spenser saw the return of Arthur, the fulfillment of the prophecy of the legend that Arthur would return to rule England. The Tudors were Welsh and belonged to ancient British stock like Arthur of Britain. The "glorious reign" of Elizabeth was the return of England through the Tudors to the race of Arthur. As the theme of each of the twelve books of *The Faerie Queene,* Spenser treats of those basic virtues which he considers to constitute the national and individual character. Each book is devoted to the adventures of a Knight who represents these virtues.

Prince Arthur is supposed to represent the virtue of *Magnificence* which the Greek philosopher Aristotle taught represented the sum total of all other virtues. Other virtues symbolized in the romance are *Holiness* represented by the Red Cross Knight; *Temperance* symbolized by Sir Guyon; *Chastity,* by Britomartis; and *Courtesy,* by Calidore. Prince Arthur sees in a vision Glorianna, the Faerie Queene, and is so captivated by her beauty that he resolves to seek her out in fairy land. The adventures that befall him on the way constitute the main plot and serve as the connecting link in the story. It is the custom of the Faerie Queene to hold an annual feast which lasts twelve days. On each day she sends forth a Knight to aid some distressed person who has begged her aid. To right each separate wrong calls for the exercise of a special virtue on the part of the Knight.

GENERAL PLAN

The allegorical references employed in the poem are drawn from the vast fount of Spenser's knowledge of the Bible, Greek and Latin poets, writers of the Italian and French Renaissance, and medieval literature. His debt both to Chaucer and the medieval romance is very large. In keeping with the contemporary conviction that the purpose of poetry was to teach, *The Faerie Queene* has moral significance; it is not the morality of the Catholic medieval tradition, however, but rather that of the good pagan and the new Protestantism of his day.

Moreover, the poem contains a great fund of historical references and political and religious satire under the guise of the allegory. Dryden tells us that every one of the Knights of Spenser's poem was then living at the court of Elizabeth, among them Sidney and Leicester. Religious satire abounds in the secondary or implied allegory. In the first book, Duessa symbolizes Roman Catholicism and Una the Anglican religion. Archimago stands for the Pope, and the supposed Jesuit plots are hinted at in the flattery and designs of Duessa and Archimago.

As a narrative poet, Spenser can be tedious, and very few read the entire poem today. His allegories are too involved and the later books lack unity and consistency. His greatness lies in his mastery of color, of imagery, of melodic cadence, his use of assonance and alliteration, and the unique nine-line stanza which he invented. *The Faerie Queene* is a magnificent picture book which no poet has ever successfully imitated.

The Spenserian stanza is composed of nine lines, eight of which are written in iambic pentameter and the ninth in iambic hexameter. This last line is called an *Alexandrine.* The ninth line is a conclusion to the preceding eight; in it the musical cadence of the preceding lines comes to a triumphant or quiet close. The rhyme scheme of the stanza is: *ab ab bc bc c.*

In Book I, Holiness, the Red Cross Knight, sets forth as champion of Una, Truth, to slay the Dragon that is ravaging her father's country. In her company, he fights successfully against Error, but is soon led by the deceiver Archimago, Guile and Fraud, to distrust the integrity of his

SYNOPSIS OF BOOKS I AND II

Lady and to take Duessa in her stead. The Red Cross Knight is able to defeat the pagan Knights Sans Foy and Sans Joy, but falls an easy victim to the Giant of Pride, Orgoglio. Una brings to his aid the divine strength of Arthur. Though rescued from the sin of pride, the Red Cross Knight is weakened by suffering and remorse, and narrowly escapes the clutches of Despayre. It is only after dwelling in the House of Holiness and there learning the full way of the Christian faith that he gains strength to overcome the Dragon and becomes worthy to marry Una.

In Book II, Sir Guyon represents Temperance. In the Castle of Medina, he learns that the secret of virtue is moderation. Sent out to destroy a wicked enchantress who enslaves men through base desires, Guyon overcomes Furor (Anger) and Atin (Malignity) but is seduced temporarily by Phaedria (Idleness). In the Cave of Mammon (Wealth) he overcomes Avarice and Ambition. When Guyon is reduced to exhaustion as a result of his sojourn in the Underworld, Arthur comes to his rescue. In the final canto of the Book, Guyon rejects the supreme temptation of the sensuous life in the Bower of Bliss.

(FROM) *The Faerie Queene*

EDMUND SPENSER

The setting of the following passage is the Underworld, where Guyon meets Mammon (Wealth and Worldliness). In the previous adventures of Book II, Sir Guyon was accompanied by "his trustie guyde," the palmer, who represents the virtue of temperance. His very last adventure ended with his rescue from the "Ydle lake" into which he had plunged to escape from an enchanted island where Phaedria (Idle Mirth) tempted him to spend his life in self-gratification.

So Guyon having lost his trustie guyde,
Late left beyond that Ydle lake, proceedes
Yet on his way, of none accompanyde;
And evermore himselfe with comfort feedes
Of his own vertues and praise-worthie dedes,
So long he yode, yet no adventure found,
Which fame of her shrill trompet worthy reedes;
For still he traveild through wide, wastefull ground,
That nought but desert wildernesse shewed all around.
At last he came unto a gloomy glade,

Covered with boughes and shrubs from heavens light,
Whereas he sitting found in secret shade
An uncouth, salvage, and uncivile wight,
Of griesly hew, and fowle ill favoured sight;
His face with smoke was tand, and eies were bleard,
His head and beard with sout were ill bedight,
His cole-blacke hands did seeme to have ben seard
In smithes fire-spitting forge, and nayles like clawes appeared.

His yron coate, all overgrowne with rust,
Was underneath envelopéd with gold;
Whose glistring glosse, darkned with filthy dust,
Well yet appeared to have beene of old
A worke of rich entayle, and curious mould,
Woven with antickes and wyld ymagery;
And in his lap a masse of coyne he told,
And turned upside downe, to feede his eye
And covetous desire with his huge threasury.
And round about him lay on every side
Great heapes of gold that never could be spent:
Of which some were rude owre, not purifide
Of Mulcibers devouring element;
Some others were new driven, and distent
Into great ingowes and to wedges square;
Some in round plates withouten moniment;
But most were stampt, and in their metal bare
The antique shapes of kings and kesars straunge and rare.

6. YODE—Went.
7. REEDES—Judges.
11. HEAVENS LIGHT—Here and throughout the poem, no apostrophe indicates the possessive case.
13. UNCOUTH, SALVAGE, AND UNCIVILE WIGHT—Strange, wild, and ill-mannered creature.
14. GRIESLY—Grisly, horrible, ghastly.
15. TAND—Tanned.
16. SOUT—Soot.
16. BEDIGHT—Disfigured.
21. GLISTRING—Glittering, shining.
23. ENTAYLE—Carving.
24. ANTICKES—Ancient or strange designs.
31. MULCIBER—Vulcan, god of fire.
32. DISTENT—Stretched.
33. INGOWES—Ingot.
34. MONIMENT—Identifying mark.
36. KESARS—Emperors, from Caesar. Note the connection with modern Kaiser.

[As soon as he saw Sir Guyon, he hastily arose in fright and began to pour all the metal into a vast open hole. But Guyon withheld his arm and spoke:)

"What art thou man—(if man at all thou art)
That here in desert hast thine habitaunce,
And these rich heapes of wealth doest hide apart
From the worldes eye, and from her right usaunce?"
Thereat with staring eyes fixed askaunce,
In great disdaine, he answered: "Hardy Elfe,
That darest vew my direfull countenaunce,
I read thee rash and heedlesse of thy selfe,
To trouble my still seate, and heapes of pretious pelfe.

"God of the world and worldlings I me call
Great Mammon, greatest god below the skye,
That of my plenty poure out unto all,
And unto none my graces do envye:
Riches, renowne, and principality,
Honour, estate, and all this worldes good,
For which men swinck and sweat incessantly,
Fro me do flow into an ample flood,
And in the hollow earth have their eternall brood.

"Wherefore, if me thou deigne to serve and sew,
At thy command lo all these mountaines bee;
Or if to thy great mind, or greedy vew,
All these may not suffise, there shall to thee
Ten times so much be numbred francke and free."
"Mammon," said he, "thy godheads vaunt is vaine,
And idle offers of thy golden fee;

40. USAUNCE—Usage.
41. ASKUANCE—Sideways, the word connotes disfavor.
44. READ—Perceive.
45. PELFE—Wealth.
52. SWINCK—Toil.
55. SEW—Follow.
59. FRANCKE—Generously.
60. GODHEADS VAUNT—Godlike exhibition; your attempt at being a god.

To them that covet such eye-glutting gaine
Proffer thy giftes, and fitter servaunts entertaine."

[Guyon continues to reject Mammon's offer by saying that knightly deeds and not riches are becoming his vocation. To this Mammon replies:]

"Vaine glorious Elfe," said he, "doest not thou weet,
That money can thy wantes at will supply?
Sheilds, steeds, and armes, and all things for thee meet
It can purvay in twinckling of an eye;

And crownes and kingdomes to thee multiply.
Do not I kings create, and throw the crowne
Sometimes to him, that low in dust doth ly?
And him that raigned, into his rowme thrust downe,
And whom I lust, do heape with glory and renowne?"

[Guyon answers:]

"All otherwise," said he, "I riches read,
And deeme them roote of all disquietnesse;
First got with guile, and then preserv'd with dread,
And after spent with pride and lavishnesse,
Leaving behind them griefe and heavinesse.
Infinite mischiefes of them do arize,
Strife, and debate, bloodshed, and bitternesse,
Outrageous wrong, and hellish covetize,
That noble heart as great dishonour doth despize.

"Ne thine be kingdomes, ne the scepters thine;
But realmes and rulers thou doest both confound,
And loyall truth to treason doest incline;
Witnessese the guiltlesse bloud pourd oft on ground,
The crownéd often slaine, the slayer cround;
The sacred Diademe in peeces rent,
And purple robe goréd with many a wound;
Castles surprizd, great cities sackt and brent;
So mak'st thou kings, and gaynest wrongfull government."

64. WEET—Know.
67. PURVAY—Provide.
71. ROWME—Place, region.
72. LUST—Desire, choose.
73. READ—Regard.
80. COVETIZE—Covetousness.
82. NE . . . NE—Neither . . . Nor.
89. BRENT—burned.

WORD STUDY

Spenser deliberately used words which were obsolete in his day, and even coined new words for metrical effect. He chose words which though still in use in his day were passing out of fashion. Hence such words as *ne, uncouth, Wight, eke, whilome,* infrequently used by Shakespeare, were constantly used by Spenser. Yet his vocabulary is basically composed of simple English words. He deliberately avoided the involved mannerisms so popular in many of the Elizabethan writers.

1. Spenser used such words as *francke* (generous, free), *bayt* (deceit), *sleight* (trick), and *pelfe* (pelf). Are these words still used today in such expressions as "a Congressman's franking privileges," "fish-bait," and "sleight-of-hand"? Explain.

2. Look up the origin and give the meaning of: *grisly* and *uncouth*. Has the common meaning of the word *lust* changed from Spenser's day? How do the words *subtile* and *subtle* differ in meaning?

FOR DISCUSSION

1. Describe Mammon as Spenser pictures him in lines 13-27. Explain the meaning of lines 46-54. What was Guyon's answer to the temptation of Mammon expressed in lines 55-59? What arguments does Mammon use to further state his case in lines 64-72? Discuss in detail Guyon's further reply in lines 73-90. Do past and present history prove that Guyon was correct? Explain.

FOR APPRECIATION

1. Study the meter and the rhyme scheme, as well as the imagery in the stanza beginning with line 64.

2. Select several lines which impressed you with their musical cadence, their assonance and alliteration.

LYRIC POETRY

The distinguishing feature of narrative poems is their *objectivity.* By that is meant that a narrative poem tells a story for its own sake—that the reader is interested in the story told and not in the author's personal feelings, emotions, or views of life.

Lyric poetry, on the contrary, is highly *subjective*; that is, a lyric poem is the expression of some personal feeling, emotion, or point of view of the author. It is chiefly concerned with a definite experience of the author, in which he portrays his personal moods and reflections. Lyric poetry may tell a story, but not for its own sake. The story serves as a medium only for the expression of the author's attitude and philosophy of life.

Besides its subjectivity, a lyric poem is characterized by a definite unity, relative brevity, and an intense emotional expression. Its unity is secured by its expression of one single thought, feeling, or situation. Since the lyric is generally short, the emotion is necessarily compressed and intensified.

The chief value of the lyrical poem for us may be summarized as follows: endowed by nature and training to express the feelings of the human heart more deeply and the beauty of the universe more perfectly than the ordinary man, the poet can produce an experience which the ordinary man can feel but vaguely and express inadequately. By means of his poem, the poet interprets for us the worlds within and without us in terms of truth and beauty.

The most majestic type of lyric poetry is the ode, characterized by an elevated thought and an intense intellectual and emotional seriousness. Other types of lyrics are the sonnet; the elegy, a poem written to honor someone who has died; the simple lyric; the descriptive lyric; and the meditative lyric, which is solemn, serious, and philosophical in tone.

Since the lyric is highly individualistic, it is little wonder that the Elizabethan poets, steeped in the atmosphere of the Renaissance with its emphasis on the individual, produced a profusion of lyrics.

The Passionate Shepherd To His Love

CHRISTOPHER MARLOWE

Although Marlowe was primarily a dramatist, he wrote many flawless lyrics, the best known of which is "The Passionate Shepherd to His Love." The poem was so popular in his own day that many replies were written to it, the most famous being Raleigh's. In this poem Marlowe employs the typical pastoral style of the Renaissance and gives us the Elizabethan notion of perfect love or the ideal courtship.

Come live with me and be my love,
And we will all the pleasures prove
That hills and valleys, dales and fields,
Woods or steepy mountain yields.

And we will sit upon the rocks,
Seeing the shepherds feed their flocks,
By shallow rivers, to whose falls
Melodious birds sing madrigals.

And I will make thee beds of roses,
And a thousand fragrant posies,
A cap of flowers, and a kirtle
Embroidered all with leaves of myrtle;

A gown made of the finest wool,
Which from our pretty lambs we pull;
Fair linèd slippers for the cold,
With buckles of the purest gold;

A belt of straw and ivy buds
With coral clasps and amber studs;
And if these pleasures may thee move,
Come live with me and be my love.

Thy silver dishes for thy meat
As precious as the gods do eat,
Shall on an ivory table be
Prepared each day for thee and me.

8. MADRIGALS—Love songs.

11. KIRTLE—Gown.

The shepherd swains shall dance and
sing
For thy delight each May morning;
If these delights thy mind may move,
Then live with me and be my love.

FOR APPRECIATION

1. Select the particular and concrete details which the poet chose to convey to his love the assurance that she will want for nothing.

2. What particular joys does the poet paint as being of the essence of happiness? Has he omitted some important ones? Discuss.

3. Is there any similarity between this type of love song and the modern love song? Discuss. Is there any harmful effect in both, if taken too seriously? Explain.

4. Analyze the poem for its melodic cadence. Scan at least one stanza.

The Nymph's Reply to the Shepherd

SIR WALTER RALEIGH

Raleigh's poetry is more realistic than that of his contemporaries. Humor, satire, and sometimes bitterness will be found in it. Note the acidity of his reply and the deftness with which he pierces the golden bubble of Marlowe's idyll.

If all the world and love were young,
And truth in every shepherd's tongue,
These pretty pleasures might me move
To live with thee and be thy love.

Time drives the flocks from field to fold,
Where rivers rage, and rocks grow cold;
And Philomel becometh dumb;
The rest complains of cares to come.

The flowers do fade, and wanton fields
To wayward Winter reckoning yields;
A honey tongue, a heart of gall,
Is fancy's spring, but sorrow's fall.

Thy gowns, thy shoes, thy beds of roses,
Thy cap, thy kirtle, and thy posies,
Soon break, soon wither, soon forgotten,
In folly ripe, in reason rotten.

Thy belt of straw and ivy buds,
Thy coral clasps and amber studs,
All these in me no means can move
To come to thee and be thy love.

But could youth last, and love still breed,
Had joys no date, nor age no need,
Then these delights my mind might move
To live with thee and be thy love.

7. PHILOMEL—The nightingale.
22. NO DATE—No end.

FOR APPRECIATION

1. Discuss in detail how Raleigh answers Marlowe. Is his reply effective? Why? Does he write in the pastoral form?

2. Select lines which may be satirical and ironic. Discuss their effectiveness.

3. Which of the two poems do you consider to be the more artistic by reason of meter, cadence, imagery, etc.? Discuss. Which of the two do you prefer? Why?

4. Explain the meaning of lines 11-12; line 16; lines 21-22.

5. Does Raleigh give the complete Catholic answer to the problem of love and courtship? Why or why not?

The Burning Babe

ROBERT SOUTHWELL

Like Thomas More and Edmund Campion, Robert Southwell, S.J., suffered the usual fate of literary oblivion simply because he was a Catholic and a martyr. It is strange that poetry which was highly praised by both Shakespeare and Ben Jonson should have been neglected until our own day. But Southwell has been rediscovered, and critics are again giving him his rightful place as one of the better minor Elizabethan poets.

"The Burning Babe" is his most popular poem, and as a Christmas poem, it is unique. Written in the cold cell of London Tower, where he was imprisoned by the priest-hunters of Elizabeth, it realistically paints the Infant Christ not in the sweet simplicity of the Babe of Bethlehem, but as the Infant Redeemer on fire with a love which men have scorned. Here we have the martyr's insight into the Sacred Heart of Christ.

As I in hoary winter's night
  Stood shivering in the snow,
Surprised I was with sudden heat,
  Which made my heart to glow;

And lifting up a fearful eye
  To view what fire was near,
A pretty Babe, all burning bright,
  Did in the air appear;

Who, scorchèd with excessive heat,
  Such floods of tears did shed,
As though His floods should quench His flames,
  Which with His tears were bred.

"Alas!" quoth He, "but newly born,
  In fiery heats, I fry,
Yet none approach to warm their hearts
  Or feel my heart, but I;

14. FRY—To burn, the regular meaning of this word in Elizabethan times.

"My faultless breast the furnace is,
  The fuel, wounding thorns;
Love is the fire, and sighs the smoke,
  The ashes, shame and scorns.

"The fuel Justice layeth on,
  And Mercy blows the coals,
The metal in this furnace wrought
  Are men's defilèd souls.

"For which, as now on fire I am,
  To work them to their good,
So will I melt into a bath,
  To wash them in My blood."

With this He vanished out of sight,
  And swiftly shrunk away,
And straight I called unto my mind
  That it was Christmas Day.

FOR APPRECIATION

1. Precisely how does this poem differ from the usual Christmas theme? Discuss.

2. The poem is developed by a series of comparisons. Select several of these. Do you think them overdone?

3. Interpret the words spoken by the Infant in the vision. Explain the meaning of *fiery heats; wounding thorns; the fuel; the coals.*

4. Analyze lines 11-12. This is an example of an Elizabethan conceit which you will discuss when you study Donne's sonnet.

5. What is the meaning of *hoary*?

6. Can you find the underlying doctrine of devotion to the Sacred Heart in this poem? Discuss.

To Celia

BEN JONSON

Probably no finer compliment can be paid to a woman than to have a beautiful poem written to her. When the poem can be set to music, the compliment is doubly enhanced. Such a poem is the following—a poem which the world has been singing for almost four centuries.

Drink to me only with thine eyes,
  And I will pledge with mine;
Or leave a kiss but in the cup
  And I'll not look for wine.
The thirst that from the soul doth rise
  Doth ask a drink divine;
But might I of Jove's nectar sup,
  I would not change for thine.

I sent thee late a rosy wreath,
  Not so much honoring thee
As giving it a hope that there
  It could not withered be;
But thou thereon didst only breathe
  And sent'st it back to me;
Since when it grows, and smells, I swear
  Not of itself, but thee!

7. JOVE—Father of the gods.

7. NECTAR—A drink prepared for the gods.

FOR APPRECIATION

1. In the old days it was customary, whenever the occasion offered, to drink a toast to the fair ladies present. In the opening line the poet substitutes something in the place of the wine. What is it?

2. In line 3 the poet says that if the fair lady will but touch her lips to the cup, it will suffice for him and the wine will be unnecessary. What further compliment is paid Celia in the first stanza?

3. What is the theme? What is the central thought?

To the Memory of My Beloved Master, William Shakespeare

BEN JONSON

There were but ten years between the birth dates of Shakespeare and Jonson. We are told they were great friends. "I loved the man," said Jonson, "and do honor his memory, on this side idolatry." In this light, we can understand the beauty of his poem.

To draw no envy, Shakespeare, on thy name,
Am I thus ample to thy book and fame;
While I confess thy writings to be such
As neither man nor muse can praise too much.
'Tis true, and all men's suffrage. But these ways
Were not the paths I meant unto thy praise;
For silliest ignorance on these may light,
Which, when it sounds at best, but echoes right;
Or blind affection, which doth ne'er advance
The truth, but gropes, and urgeth all by chance;
Or crafty malice might pretend this praise,
And think to ruin, where it seemed to raise. . . .
But thou art proof against them, and, indeed,
Above the ill fortune of them, or the need.
I therefore will begin. Soul of the age,
The applause, delight, the wonder of our stage,
My Shakespeare, rise! I will not lodge thee by
Chaucer, or Spenser, or bid Beaumont lie
A little further, to make thee a room:

2. AMPLE—Abundant in praise.
4. MUSE—The Muses were goddesses of song, poetry, and the arts.
5. SUFFRAGE—Opinion, decision.
18. CHAUCER, SPENSER, BEAUMONT—Chaucer was an earlier English poet, sometimes called the "father of English literature." Spenser and Beaumont were Shakespeare's contemporaries.

Thou art a monument without a tomb,
And art alive still while thy book doth live,
And we have wits to read and praise to give.
That I not mix thee so my brain excuses—
I mean with great, but disproportioned Muses;
For if I thought my judgment were of years,
I should commit thee surely with thy peers,
And tell how far thou didst our Lyly outshine,
Or sporting Kyd, or Marlowe's mighty line.
And though thou hadst small Latin and less Greek,
From thence to honor thee, I would not seek
For names, but call forth thundering Æschylus,
Euripides, and Sophocles to us,
Pacuvius, Accius, him of Cordova dead,
To life again, to hear thy buskin tread,
And shake a stage; or when thy socks were on,
Leave thee alone for the comparison
Of all that insolent Greece or haughty Rome
Sent forth, or since did from their ashes Come.
Triumph, my Britain, thou hast one to show
To whom all scenes of Europe homage owe.
He was not of an age, but for all time!
And all the Muses still were in their prime,
When, like Apollo, he came forth to warm
Our ears, or like a Mercury to charm.
Nature herself was proud of his designs
And joyed to wear the dressing of his lines,
Which were so richly spun, and woven so fit,
As, since, she will vouchsafe no other wit.
The merry Greek, tart Aristophanes,
Neat Terence, witty Plautus, now not please,
But antiquated and deserted lie,
As they were not of Nature's family.
Yet must I not give Nature all; thy art,
My gentle Shakespeare, must enjoy a part;
For though the poet's matter nature be,
His art doth give the fashion; and that he
Who casts to write a living line must sweat,
(Such as thine are) and strike the second heat
Upon the Muses' anvil, turn the same
(And himself with it) that he thinks to frame,
Or, for the laurel, he may gain a scorn;
For a good poet's made, as well as born.
And such wert thou; look how the father's face
Lives in his issue, even so the race

25. OF YEARS—That is, mature.
26. COMMIT—Compare.
27-28. LYLY, KYD, MARLOWE—Dramatists of Shakespeare's day.
31-32. FAESCHYLUS, EURIPIDES, SOPHOCLES—Dramatists of ancient Greece.
33. PACUVIUS, ACCIUS—Dramatists of ancient Rome.
33. HIM OF CORDOVA—Seneca, a Roman dramatist.
34. BUSKIN—A very thick-soled high boot worn by actors of tragedy.
35. SOCKS—Thin-soled low slippers worn by actors of comedy.
43. APOLLO—God of the sun.
44. MERCURY—Messenger of the gods.
49. ARISTOPHANES—A writer of ancient Greek comedy.
50. TERENCE, PLAUTUS—Writers of Roman comedy.
57. CASTS—Attempts.
61. LAUREL—A symbol of victory or achievement.

Of Shakespeare's mind and manners
brightly shines
In his well turnèd and filèd lines,
In each of which he seems to shake a lance,
As brandished at the eyes of ignorance.
Sweet Swan of Avon! what a sight it were
To see thee in our waters yet appear,
And make those flights upon the banks
of Thames,
That so did take Eliza and our James!
But stay, I see thee in the hemisphere
Advanced, and made a constellation there!
Shine forth, thou Star of poets, and with
rage
Or influence chide or cheer the drooping
stage,
Which, since thy flight from hence, hath
mourned like night,
And despairs day, but for thy volume's light.

72. ELIZA AND OUR JAMES—Queen Elizabeth, and her successor, King James I.

FOR APPRECIATION

1. What are the theme and the central thought of the poem? Break down the poem into at least five distinct thought divisions. Give a heading for each.

2. Explain the meaning of the following lines. Line 20: *Thou art a monument without a tomb;* lines 34-35: *thy buskin tread . . . when thy socks were on.*

3. Describe the art of writing as Jonson sees it in lines 55-63.

4. Summarize in one or two paragraphs Jonson's tribute to Shakespeare. Include his opinions of Shakespeare's writings, the opinions of others, the immortality of his verse, the men whom Shakespeare surpasses.

5. Select several lines which you consider memorable. What are the meter and the stanza form of the poem?

WORD STUDY

1. Describe the color of *coral, amber, orient pearl.* Describe the taste suggested by *nectar, gall, tart.* Is *nectar* a word used frequently today? Explain. What is the connotation of the word *gall* in the slang expression "He has his gall"?

2. What kind of ideas are suggested by *laurel* and *myrtle?* What is the origin of their figurative meaning?

3. Give synonyms for *tread, ample, chide, brandished.* What is the difference between a *peer* and a *swain?* What does *peerless* mean? Is the word *swain* used today? Why or why not? Explain the complete meaning of *suffrage* in the phrase "the right of suffrage."

THE SONNET

The sonnet is a specialized type of lyric poetry which was popular in the Elizabethan period. It is a poem of fourteen lines, written in iambic pentameter, with a definite rhyme scheme. Two forms of the sonnet have been used in English poetry: the Italian, and the English or Shakespearean. The Italian form consists of an *octave,* the first eight lines which present the subject matter of the poem, and the *sestet,* the last six lines which contain the poet's reflections on that subject matter. The rhyme-scheme of the octave is *a b b a, a b b a.* In the sestet the rhyme-scheme may be *c d e, c d e* or *c d, c d, c d.*

The English or the Shakespearean sonnet consists of three quatrains and a couplet, rhyming *a b a b, c d c d, e f e f, g g.* Like the Italian sonnet, it contains two waves of thought. In the English sonnet, however, the first wave of twelve lines expresses the problem, and the couplet contains the poet's reflections or solution of that problem.

The sonnet had its origin in Italy in the thirteenth century and was popular with Dante, Petrarch, and Tasso. It was introduced into England during the reign of Henry VIII by Thomas Wyatt and became very popular when the Earl of Surrey experimented with a new sonnet form. Richard Tottel's *Miscellany,* the first English anthology of poetry, printed in 1557, contained 271 "Songs and Sonnettes," written for the most part by Wyatt and Surrey.

As a result of their experimentation with the Italian sonnet, Wyatt and Surrey produced the English sonnet form employed by the great Elizabethan sonnet writers, Sidney, Spenser, and Shakespeare.

Sonnets may be written as single, independent pieces, or may be grouped together in sequences. They may express the development of an emotional experience in the life of the poet, or may actually tell a story. During the Elizabethan Period, it was fashionable to write sonnet cycles, the most famous of which are *The Amoretti* of Spenser, *Astrophel and Stella* of Sidney, and Shakespeare's immortal sequence which remained unnamed.

Sonnet from the Amoretti

EDMUND SPENSER

Like the sonnets of Shakespeare and Sidney, love is the theme of Spenser's AMORETTI *or "Little Loves." But unlike many other Elizabethan sonnets, they are sincere; for they are the sonnets of a real courtship, inspired by Spenser's future wife, Mary Boyle. Sonnet LXI is a glowing tribute to the woman who embodied for Spenser the ideal of pure and chaste love.*

LXI

The glorious image of the Maker's beauty,
My sovereign saint, the idol of my thought,
Dare not henceforth, above the bounds of duty,
T' accuse of pride, or rashly blame for ought.
For being, as she is, divinely wrought,
And of the brood of angels heavenly born,
And with the crew of blessed saints upbrought,
Each of which did her with their gifts adorn—
The bud of joy, the blossom of the morn,
The beam of light, whom mortal eyes admire;
What reason is it then but she should scorn
Base things that to her love too bold aspire!
Such heavenly forms ought rather worshipt be
Than dare be loved by men of mean degree.

1. IMAGE OF THE MAKER'S BEAUTY—See Genesis 1:26. Is Spenser here speaking of material or spiritual beauty? Or both?
14. MEAN—Low.

FOR APPRECIATION

1. Elizabethan love poetry was greatly influenced by the Renaissance concept of love as expressed in Castiglione's *Courtier*. According to this concept, love is a yearning of the soul after true beauty. "True love of beauty is good, holy, and brings forth fruit in the souls of them that with the bridle of reason restrain the ill disposition of sense."

The subject of the sonnet is Spenser's wife-to-be. Analyze the sonnet carefully and show that "idealized love" is the theme of the sonnet. Select the particular and concrete details which develop this theme.

2. Explain the meaning of lines 11 and 12. Do lines 13 and 14 restate the theme of the poem? Discuss. May lines 13 and 14 also imply that the poet is fortunate in having such a being for his betrothed? Discuss.

3. Give the rhyme scheme of the sonnet. Does it differ from the Shakespearean form? Explain.

Sonnets

WILLIAM SHAKESPEARE

For purely poetic expression of thoughts, nothing can quite equal Shakespeare's sonnets. Lyrics by other poets of his day sparkled with conceits (artificial expressions) and glittering extravagances. Shakespeare's sonnets are rich and deep with unforgettable beauty. We do not know who inspired them, but their affection survives "death's dateless night" in immortal lines.

XXIX

When in disgrace with fortune and men's eyes
I all alone beweep my outcast state,
And trouble deaf heaven with my bootless cries,
And look upon myself, and curse my fate,

1. FORTUNE—The Elizabethan writers frequently used the Greek and Roman notion of *fortune.* In that sense it means, not chance or luck, but destiny.

2. MEN'S EYES—Shakespeare may have been out of favor with his literary patron. Again we must remember he was an actor and a playwright. He may refer here to the changing popularity of actors and plays.

3. BOOTLESS—Useless; unavailing. It would be interesting to trace the meaning of this word from the Old English.

WILLIAM SHAKESPEARE

Wishing me like to one more rich in hope,
Featured like him, like him with friends possessed,
Desiring this man's art, and that man's scope,
With what I most enjoy contented least;
Yet in these thoughts myself almost despising,
Haply I think on thee,—and then my state,
(Like to the lark at break of day arising
From sullen earth,) sings hymns at heaven's gate;
For thy sweet love remembered, such wealth brings
That then I scorn to change my state with kings.

7. DESIRING THIS MAN'S ART . . . SCOPE—Jealous of this man's ability to get things done or his skill in writing and acting. Scope can mean here his broad outlook on life, his universal interest.

XXX

When to the sessions of sweet silent thought
I summon up remembrance of things past,
I sigh the lack of many a thing I sought,
And with old woes new wail my dear time's waste;
Then can I drown an eye, unused to flow,
For precious friends hid in death's dateless night,
And weep afresh love's long-since-canceled woe,
And moan the expense of many a vanished sight.
Then can I grieve at grievances foregone,
And heavily from woe to woe tell o'er
The sad account of fore-bemoanèd moan
Which I new pay as if not paid before;
But if the while I think on thee, dear friend,
All losses are restored, and sorrows end.

LV

Not marble, nor the gilded monuments
Of princes, shall outlive this powerful rhyme;
But you shall shine more bright in these contents
Than unswept stone, besmeared with sluttish time.
When wasteful war shall statues overturn,
And broils root out the work of masonry,
Nor Mars his sword nor war's quick fire shall burn
The living record of your memory.
'Gainst death and all-oblivious enmity
Shall you pace forth; your praise shall still find room
Even in the eyes of all posterity
That wear this world out to the ending doom.
So, till the judgment that yourself arise
You live in this, and dwell in lovers' eyes.

7. NOR MARS HIS SWORD . . . BURN—Here we have an example of the Elizabethan possessive. We would say "the sword of Mars and the fire of war."

CXVI

Let me not to the marriage of true minds
Admit impediments. Love is not love
Which alters when it alteration finds,
Or bends with the remover to remove:
O, no! it is an ever-fixèd mark,
That looks on tempests and is never shaken;
It is the star to every wand'ring bark,
Whose worth's unknown, although his height be taken.
Love's not Time's fool, though rosy lips and cheeks
Within his bending sickle's compass come;
Love alters not with his brief hours and weeks,
But bears it out even to the edge of doom.
  If this be error and upon me proved,
  I never writ, nor no man ever loved.

9. LOVE'S NOT TIME'S FOOL—Love does not vanish as the beloved grows older.

LXXIII

That time of year thou may'st in me behold
When yellow leaves, or none, or few, do hang
Upon those boughs which shake against the cold,
Bare ruined choirs, where late the sweet birds sang.

4. BARE RUINED CHOIRS—Could it be that Shakespeare is here referring to the destruction of the monasteries and the sweet birds (the monks) who chanted the Divine Office?

In me thou see'st the twilight of such day
As after sunset fadeth in the west;
Which by and by black night doth take away,
Death's second self, that seals up all in rest.
In me thou see'st the glowing of such fire
That on the ashes of his youth doth lie,
As the death-bed whereon it must expire,
Consumed with that which it was nourished by.
This thou perceiv'st, which makes thy love more strong
To love that well which thou must leave ere long.

8. DEATH'S SECOND SELF—This notion of sleep occurs frequently in Shakespeare's poetry. Compare with the metaphor in *Macbeth*, Act II, Sc. 2, line 37.

12. CONSUMED—A fire is finally choked by the ashes of the fuel which fed it. Compare this fire with that in Southwell's "Burning Babe," stanza 3.

FOR APPRECIATION

SONNET XXIX:

1. What universal experience is expressed in lines 3-8? In a few words describe this experience.

2. What thought has the power to break the mood described in the first eight lines? Find lines in the first part of the sonnet that are in exact contrast to lines 12, 13, 14.

3. What poetic devices does the poet employ to attain the weighty, solemn, and heavy movement in the first 8 lines and the rapid, light, and gay movement in the last 6 lines? Discuss. Do the two movements express the different moods of the poem? Study the rich contrast in imagery between *lark at break of day arising* with *sullen earth.* Does *sullen earth* restate the mood of the first 8 lines? Explain.

4. Scan the sonnet. Is the rhyme scheme Shakespearean or Italian?

5. The lark is famous in English literature. List several poems in which it is commemorated.

SONNET XXX:

1. In the sonnet Shakespeare uses the figure of a summons to a court session. What experiences are summoned?

2. Note the use of constant alliteration. Select the lines which illustrate this figure.

3. Shakespeare employs many Elizabethan conceits. Here is one: "old woes new wail my dear time's waste." Can you choose another?

4. Explain the meaning of lines 10-12.

5. In a simple phrase, express the figure, "drown an eye."

6. Which sonnet do you prefer, 29 or 30? Discuss.

SONNET LV:

1. This poem could be used as a splendid introduction to the study of literature. Why? Shakespeare is not only immortalizing love but poetry. Select the lines which express the author's conviction that this poem would be immortal.

2. Horace wrote in one of his odes, "I have built a monument more lasting than bronze." The same idea is expressed in this sonnet. Explain how the things of the mind, the great thoughts of great men, outlast wars and conflagrations, death and "all-oblivious enmity."

3. What are the qualities in literature which make it immortal? Here you are studying a sonnet written four hundred years ago. Why

has Shakespeare's prophecy in the sonnet been fulfilled?

4. Apply lines 5-8 to the wars of the modern world.

5. Let each member of the class describe the mental picture that lines 11 and 12 awaken in him. If you were an artist, how would you portray the idea contained there?

6. Give the rhyme scheme of the sonnet. Is this a true Shakespearean sonnet?

SONNET CXVI:

1. Work out in detail the images in the poem. Is the imagery in the sonnet consistent or confused? Explain.

2. What might be some other "impediments" to the marriage of true minds? Is Shakespeare speaking of real love or infatuation? Discuss. Discuss the place of self-sacrifice in love.

3. Explain the meaning of "Love's not Time's fool." What is the connection between "Time" and "bending sickle's compass"?

SONNET LXXIII:

1. Shakespeare uses three figures taken from three manifestations of nature to tell us his age. Explain these figures. Which do you consider the most suitable and most poetically expressed?

2. Was Shakespeare really an old man when he wrote this sonnet, or was he looking at old age from afar?

3. Discuss in detail the choice of his diction to develop the movement and mood of the poem.

4. Is the sonnet developed in two waves of 12 and 2 lines or in two waves of 8 and 6 lines?

5. Explain the meaning of lines 13 and 14. Discuss some popular songs which have the same theme."

PROJECT

As a class project, try composing a Shakespearean sonnet. Agree on a topic, perhaps some humorous subject, and have one person write the lines on the blackboard as they are suggested by the class. Or, plan the content of each of the three quatrains and the final couplet, and divide the class into committees for the actual writing. Remember to use the right rhyme scheme and iambic pentameter lines.

Shakespeare at home.

Sonnet Forty-One

PHILIP SIDNEY

Human nature changes little from age to age. Sidney, a skilled horseman, wins the tourney prize and attributes his success to the inspiration of his Stella, watching in the stands. Today the hero of the football field or basketball court outdoes himself because the twenty-first-century counterpart of Stella is cheering for her athlete as she "sends forth her beams" of approval from the sidelines.

Having this day my horse, my hand, my lance
Guided so well that I obtained the prize,
Both by the judgment of the English eyes
And of some sent from that sweet enemy France,
Horsemen my skill in horsemanship advance,
Town folks my strength; a daintier judge applies
His praise to sleight which from good use doth rise;
Some lucky wits impute it but to chance;
Others, because of both sides I do take
My blood from them who did excel in this,
Think Nature me a man-at-arms did make.
How far they shot awry! the true cause is,
Stella looked on, and from her heavenly face
Sent forth the beams which made so fair my race.

1. HAVING—This word goes with "guided" in line 2.

5. ADVANCE—Speak well of.

7. SLEIGHT—Cunning.

9-10. OTHERS . . . THIS—Others say I won the prize because my ancestors on both sides were skilled in tournament play.

12. SHOT AWRY—Missed the mark.

13. STELLA—The poetic name, meaning "a star," which Sidney used in his lyrics for Miss Penelope Devereaux.

FOR APPRECIATION

1. To the Elizabethan, Philip Sidney was the typical Renaissance courtier. Select those details in the poem which might portray such a picture.

2. Does the first wave of thought end with the eighth or the twelfth line? Scan the sonnet carefully and give the rhyme scheme.

WORD STUDY: SONNETS

The effectiveness of the poetic image in poetry is secured by the choice of the exact connotative adjective, called an epithet. Find epithets in the preceding sonnets; give their literal and denotative meanings, for example: *deaf heaven, sluttish time, gilded monuments, bare ruined choirs.*

THE BIBLE

IMPORTANCE AND INFLUENCE

Will it surprise you to know that THE best-seller of the past four hundred years has been the Bible? Did you know that the book which has influenced English literature more than any other book is the Bible?

Old English literature owed its heaviest literary debt to the Bible. Throughout the Middle Ages the layman was well versed in Bible stories. And in the works of Shakespeare, Milton, Dryden, Browning, and Tennyson there are found Biblical characters, Biblical events, Biblical allusions and turns of expression. To the present day, writers have been influenced, consciously or not, by the Bible's imagery, its noble cadences and rhythms. The Bible's proverbs, more than the colorful aphorisms of Shakespeare and the epigrams of Pope, have woven themselves into the very texture of our ordinary speech. The terse and expressive figures of Biblical writers, such as "idol with feet of clay," and "handwriting on the wall," are so commonplace to us that we never question their origin. In the Bible we find models for every literary type developed in English writing: simple narrative, graphic descriptions, lucid explanations, and logical arguments. For the study of English literature, for the writing of English prose and poetry, a real knowledge of the Bible is the best possible preparation.

HISTORY

We know the Bible as one book. In reality it is a complete library, for it is a collection of seventy-three books, whose composition spanned fifteen hundred years. These books—forty-six in the Old Testament, twenty-seven in the New Testament—have been gathered and guarded by the Church, which has placed them in the "Canon of Sacred Scriptures," the list of books declared by the Church to have been inspired by God.

Broadly speaking, the original language of the Old Testament was Hebrew; that of the New Testament was Greek. When the Jews were scattered throughout the known world after the exile, in what is historically known as the "Dispersion," it was necessary to translate the Sacred Books into other languages. When Christianity rapidly spread in the first century, the New Testament was also translated into other languages. Before the time of Christ, the Jews at Alexandria made their Septuagint translation into Greek. For the early Christians, there were the translations into Armenian, Syriac, Arabic, Ethiopian, and Latin. At the close of the fourth century, the great scholar St. Jerome made his famous Vulgate translation. It is this Latin translation that has been held as the official text by the Catholic Church. In the Middle Ages the people who could read at all could read Latin. Thus there was little need for the Church to issue Scriptures in another language. Yet in many lands (and in England), there were translations into the native tongue before the days of printing.

The Protestant reformers of the sixteenth century have charged Catholicism with keeping the Bible as a closed book. They venerate Wyclif (d. 1384) and Tyndale (d. 1536) as "morning stars of the Reformation" for their work in bringing out the Bible. Protestantism accepted the Bible from the Church, but with important changes: seven of the books were dropped from the Canon; the Scriptures alone were regarded as "the only safe guide for faith"; Tradition as a second source of Revelation was rejected; and the Church's authority was denied in the "liberalism of private and individual interpretation."

ATTITUDE OF THE REFORMERS

It is a too common fallacy to believe that John Wyclif was the first to make an English translation of the Scriptures in 1382. In the seventh century there was the *Poem on Genesis;* in the eighth, the translations of Bede, of Eadhelm, of Guthlac, of Egbert. All of these were in the Saxon language understood and spoken by the Christians of the time. There were the free translations of King Alfred and his scholars, and of Aelfric, archbishop of Canterbury. There were popular renderings like the *Book of Durham,* the *Rushworth Gloss,* and others which have survived.

Consequent upon the Norman Conquest (1066), Anglo-Norman became the language of England, and several specimens are still known of translations into this intermediate language—the *Paraphrases of Orm, Salus Animae,* and the translations of William Shoreman and Richard Rolle. Saint Thomas More in his arguments against the Tyndale edition points out that "the whole Bible long before Wyclif's day was by virtuous and well-learned men translated into the English tongue, and by good and godly people with devotion and soberness well and reverently read. . . . The Clergy keep no Bibles from the laity but such translations as be either not yet approved for good, or such as be already reproved for naught as Wyclif's was." *(Dialogues, III).* Cranmer, the archbishop of Canterbury, who more than any other (as Belloc shows in his historical study, *Cranmer*) was responsible for the theft of Roman Catholicism from the English people, substantiates More's arguments in his preface to the Great Bible of 1540: "The Holy Bible was translated and read in the Saxon tongue, which at that time was our mother tongue, whereof there remaineth yet divers copies found in old Abbeys, of such antique manner of writing and speaking that few men now be able to read and understand them." And Protestant Foxe offers this strong testimony: "If histories be well examined, both before the conquest and after, as well before John Wyclif was born, as since, the whole body of Scripture by sundry men [was] translated into our native tongue."

But it is the authentic Bible alone that contains the Inspired Word. And it is the Bible correctly interpreted that the Church desires the faithful to read; for St. Peter's words still ring true: "In which are certain things hard to be understood, which the learned and unstable wrest, as they do also the other scriptures, to their own destruction." (II Peter 3:6.) As the Guardian of the Scriptures, the Church's authorization and acceptance are necessary for an acceptable translation or edition of any of the Sacred Books.

THE AUTHORITY OF THE CHURCH

Thus the translation of Wyclif, shot through as it was with the heretical teachings of the Lollards, was condemned by the Church. In 1408, the Synod of Bishops at Oxford prohibited the translation of any part of the Bible into English by any unauthorized person, and the reading of any version before it was formally approved. Thus, too, the first Bible printed in English, the anti-Catholic version of the New Testament published by William Tyndale in 1525, was rejected. Tyndale had embodied in his version Luther's notes and explanations of texts, which were full of hatred against Rome. The learned Thomas More attacked Tyndale in his *Defence Against Heretics,* stating that "to find errors in Tyndale's book were like studying to find water in the sea." King Henry VIII, who was to wear for a few years the Roman title of "Defender of the Faith," published an edict that "the translation of the Scripture corrupted by William Tyndale should be utterly expelled, rejected, and put away out of the hands of the people. . . . "

But after Henry's break with the Church of Rome, there came a whole flood of versions and translations. Coverdale completed Tyndale's work in 1536. The Great Bible, sometimes called Cranmer's, was published in 1539. By Royal Proclamation this volume was ordered to be put in every church in England. In 1557, William Wittingham edited another translation. The Geneva Bible with marginal notes that were fiercely Calvinistic appeared in 1560. This version became so popular with the English people that the Elizabethan bishops hastened to get out the Bishops' Bible under Matthew Parker, archbishop of Canterbury, in 1568. With none of these, however, were the various factions in the English church satisfied. Under James I, a group of fifty-four scholars was assigned to bring out another edition. This, the King James or Authorized Version, was published in 1611. It proved to be the best Protestant version that ever appeared, and it is this version that has had the greatest influence on subsequent English prose.

In very recent years, a thoroughly modern version of the King James Bible has been written by Protestant Biblical scholars.

The persecuted Catholics in England were under a great disadvantage. The exiled Cardinal Allen had erected at Douai, France, a college for the training of priests for the English mission. Huguenot riots forced the removal of the college to Rheims. It was at Rheims in 1582 that Gregory Martin and Robert Bristow, working under Cardinal Allen, brought out the Catholic translation of the New Testament from St. Jerome's Vulgate. In 1593, the college returned to Douai. There, in 1609, the translation of the Old Testament was added, and the entire version was called the Douai-Rheims edition. It is Bishop Challoner's revision (1749-50) of the Douai-Rheims with which we are most familiar.

WORK OF CATHOLICS

A revival of Biblical interest and studies in the late nineteenth century has led to new Catholic versions and translations. The Westminster Version, a translation of the New Testament from the original Greek and Hebrew texts, was completed by English and American scholars in 1935. In 1937 was published the second edition of the Reverend F. A. Spencer's translation of the New Testament from the Greek. The Confraternity New Testament, a revision of the Challoner-Rheims version based on the Latin Vulgate, was published in 1941, under the patronage of the Episcopal Committee of the Confraternity of Christian Doctrine. Monsignor Ronald A. Knox published his translation of the New Testament from the Latin

Vulgate in 1944. He completed the translation of the Old Testament in 1948. Monsignor Knox has remarkably succeeded in presenting the New Testament in the attractive garb of the modern English idiom.

Another Catholic translation of the New Testament into contemporary prose appeared in 1954, the work of Father James A. Kleist, S.J., and Father Joseph L. Lilly, C.M.

THE SACRIFICE OF ISAAC

(Genesis 22:1-18)

Genesis, the first book of the Old Testament, contains the story of the creation, the fall of our first parents, and the call of the fathers of the Hebrew race.

Abram of Ur has been called by God and has been blessed by the priestly King Melchisedech. God has changed his name to Abraham and has made a solemn pact whereby He promised Abraham, "I will make nations of thee, and kings shall come out of thee." To Abraham's barren wife, Sara, was born Isaac; and in him and through him rests the fulfillment of God's promise. And now Abraham's loyalty and obedience are thus tested by God.

This selection is from the Douai-Rheims version.

1. After these things, God tempted Abraham, and said to him: Abraham, Abraham. And he answered: Here I am.

2. He said to him: Take thy only begotten son Isaac, whom thou lovest, and go into the land of vision: and there thou shalt offer him for an holocaust upon one of the mountains which I will shew thee.

3. So Abraham rising up in the night, saddled his ass: and took with him two young men, and Isaac his son: and when he had cut wood for the holocaust he went his way to the place which God had commanded him.

4. And on the third day, lifting his eyes, he saw the place afar off.

5. And he said to his young men: Stay you here with the ass: I and the boy will go with speed as far as yonder, and after we have worshipped, will return to you.

6. And he took the wood for the holocaust, and laid it upon Isaac his son: and he himself carried in his hands fire and a sword. And as they two went on together,

7. Isaac said to his father: My father. And he answered: What wilt thou, son? Behold,

saith he, fire and wood: where is the victim for the holocaust?

8 And Abraham said: God will provide himself a victim for an holocaust, my son. So they went on together.

9 And they came to the place which God had shewn him, where he built an altar, and laid the wood in order upon it: and when he had bound Isaac his son, he laid him on the altar upon the pile of wood.

10 And he put forth his hand and took the sword, to sacrifice his son.

11 And behold an angel of the Lord from heaven called to him, saying: Abraham, Abraham. And he answered: Here I am.

12 And he said to him: Lay not thy hand upon the boy, neither do thou anything to him: now I know that thou fearest God, and hast not spared thy only begotten son for my sake.

13 Abraham lifted up his eyes, and saw behind his back a ram amongst the briers sticking fast by the horns, which he took and offered for a holocaust instead of his son.

14 And he called the name of that place, The Lord Seeth. Whereupon even to this day it is said: In the mountain the Lord will see.

The Sacrifice of Isaac

15 And the angel of the Lord called to Abraham a second time from heaven, saying:

16 By my own self have I sworn, saith the Lord: because thou hast done this thing, and hast not spared thy only begotten son for my sake:

17 I will bless thee, and I will multiply thy seed as the stars of heaven, and as the sand that is by the sea shore: thy seed shall possess the gates of their enemies.

18 And in thy seed shall all the nations of the earth be blessed, because thou hast obeyed my voice.

WORD STUDY

Give a complete history of the word *holocaust.*

FOR DISCUSSION

1. Give a thumb-nail sketch of Abraham's character as it is implicitly portrayed in the narrative.

2. What important spiritual lessons can be learned from this story?

3. What figures of speech are contained in verse 17?

4. What is the complete meaning of verse 18?

5. Explain why this selection is a fine example of the simple narrative. Note the absolute simplicity of the style, intelligible to any child.

A PROJECT

Discuss orally or in a written paper the relationships between the sacrifice of Isaac and the Sacrifice of the Mass.

RELATED READING

Read chapter 14 of the Book of Exodus.

Poem on Wisdom

THE BOOK OF JOB

The Book of Job is a discussion in dialogue form of the problem of retribution. Is there a contradiction between the doctrine of the justice of God and the facts of human experience? We must remember that the Jewish concept of the future life did not have the fullness of our Christian Revelation. The reader is informed at the beginning that Job's sufferings are merely a test of his fidelity. But the solution expressed by Job (and endorsed by God's final speeches) is not more than negative: suffering is not always the result of sin, nor is there a necessary connection between happiness and virtue. This negative solution was a preparation for the fuller revelation of the new dispensation—the true reward of the just is eternal life in the presence of God. The "Poem on Wisdom" which now forms the twenty-eighth chapter of the Book is regarded by most critics as an independent poem set within the dialogue between Job and his friends.

The basis of Hebrew versification is thought-arrangement and not word-arrangement. In Hebrew poetry the meter is given in the balance of thought or parallelism that exists between the two parts of each verse. This thought-contrast will be more noticeable in the translation of the Psalms.

Nothing is known of the writer, except what can be deduced from this work. The thoughts are those of a Palestinian Jew of the post-Exilic period. The date of composition cannot be fixed more exactly than the fifth to third century before Christ.

This selection is taken from Reverend Edward J. Kissane's work, THE BOOK OF *JOB.*

1 When there is a mine for silver,
And a place where gold is refined,
2 Iron is taken out of the earth,
And stone is melted into copper,
3 Man putteth an end to darkness,
And to the uttermost bound he searcheth.
4 The stone of darkness and death-shade
Is pierced with channels by man's agency;
Those which were forgotten of the foot
Diminish, they are diverted by man.
5 The earth out of which cometh bread,
Underneath is turned up by fire;
6 The stones thereof are the place of sapphires,
That have dust of gold;
7 Man putteth forth his hand to the flint,
He overturneth mountains by the roots;
8 In the rocks he cleaveth canals,
Whatever is precious his eye seeth;
9 The beds of rivers he searcheth,
And what was hidden he bringeth to light.
10 But Wisdom, where can it be found?
And where is the place of understanding?
11 Man knoweth not the way thereto,
And it is not found in the land of the living;
12 The path no bird of prey knoweth,

VERSES 1-4: In his search for precious metals, man labors unceasingly. He is undeterred by darkness or distance; he tunnels through rock; he changes the course of rivers.

"Poem on Wisdom" from *The Book of Job*, translation by Monsignor Edward J. Kissane, reprinted by permission of Browne & Nolan Limited, Dublin.

VERSES 5-9: The earth's surface gives food to man; from its interior he tears precious stones. Overcoming all obstacles, he searches the beds of rivers and the depths of the earth, and he finds his desire.

And the vulture's eye hath not seen it;
13 The proud beasts have not trodden it,
The lion hath not passed thereby;
14 The Abyss saith: 'It is not in me,'
And the Sea saith: 'It is not with me.'
15 Gold cannot be given in exchange for it,
Nor silver weighed as the price thereof;
16 It cannot be valued with the gold of Ophir,
With the precious onyx or the sapphire;
17 Gold and glass cannot equal it,
Nor can the exchange thereof be vessels of fine gold.
18 Coral and crystal need not be mentioned.
The excellence of wisdom is above pearls;
19 The topaz of Ethiopia cannot equal it,
Neither can it be valued with fine gold.
20 But Wisdom, whence cometh it?
And where is the place of understanding?
21 It is hidden from the eyes of all living,
And from the fowls of the air it is concealed;
22 Abaddon and Death say:
With our ears we have heard a rumour thereof:
23 God understandeth the way thereof,

VERSES 10-14: But man cannot attain the abode of Wisdom; not even if like the wild beasts he sweeps the ends of the earth. For Wisdom is not to be found in the surroundings of the earth nor in the sea.

VERSES 15-19: Man's precious stones can buy many things, but not Wisdom.

22. ABADDON—A Hebrew word meaning destruction or the place of the lost—the bottomless pit.

And He knoweth the place thereof;
24 For he looketh to the ends of the earth,
And seeth what is under the whole heavens.
25 When He made a weight for the wind,
And meted out the waters by measure,
26 When He made an ordinance for the rain,
And a way for the thunderstorm;
27 Then He saw and reckoned it,
He had established it, yea, He had searched it out;
28 And He said unto man:
Lo, the fear of the Lord is wisdom,
And to depart from evil is understanding.

VERSES 20-24: Whence Wisdom, no creature can tell. God alone knows, He who knows all things.

VERSES 25-28: God is the Creator and the Orderer; His plan is Wisdom. Man's task is to fulfill his appointed place in that plan.

FOR APPRECIATION

1. Note the relationship in structure between Anglo-Saxon poetry and the balance of thought of Scriptural poetry.

2. How is this poem significant in the light of the Atomic Age? Discuss man's material progress and his spiritual retrogression. May it be said that verses 1-9 contain the history of scientific research?

3. Is there an implicit argument against pantheism in the poem? Explain.

4. Choose at least three significant figures of speech from the poem.

PROJECTS

1. "Lo, the fear of the Lord is Wisdom,
   And to repent from evil is understanding."

Write an editorial taking as your theme the above text, with practical applications to the modern world. Show how repentance and humility can improve mankind.

2. See the *Catholic Encyclopedia* for the story of Job.

3. Explain what you mean by "the patience of Job."

RELATED READING

Read chapters 24 and 28 from the Book of Job in the Douai-Rheims version.

THE BOOK OF PSALMS

The book which is poetic above all others in the Old Testament is the Book of Psalms. The Psalms are a collection of the lyric poetry of ancient Israel, a storehouse of pure and lofty song. Most of the Psalms were composed in the days of King David, about a thousand years before Christ. Perhaps half of the poems were made by David himself; of the other authors, we know almost nothing.

But the Book of Psalms is not merely an anthology of Hebrew poetry. It is a collection of the Sacred Chants meant to be used in the worship of God. They are great poetry, poetry that is for all time, for they express man as man. But more, they breathe the very essence of true religion: they are God's inspired word concerning the never-changing relations of the soul with God.

In the Old Dispensation, they were used in the liturgy of the Hebrew worship. From earliest times the Psalms always have been cherished by the Church. By far the greater part of the Office of the Breviary daily recited or chanted by priests and religious is composed of the Psalms. Psalms are recited in the Mass, and they so enter into every liturgical function that they have been called "the prayer book of the liturgy."

Of the Psalms and their variety of subject matter, St. Athanasius wrote: "They seem to be a kind of mirror for everyone who sings them, in which he may observe the motions of the soul, and as he observes them give to them in words. . . . Methinks that in the words of this book you may find an exact survey and delineation of the whole life of man, the dispositions of the soul and the movements of the mind. If a man has need of patience and confession, if affliction or temptation has overtaken him, if he has been persecuted or has been delivered from the plots of his enemies, if he is in sorrow or trouble, or if he wishes to praise and give thanks and bless the Lord, he finds instruction in the Psalms."

The following selections from the Psalms are based on the new Latin translation made by the professors of the Pontifical Biblical Institute. This new translation has removed many of the inaccuracies which obscured the meaning of the original Hebrew text.

Psalm 22

A PSALM OF DAVID

1 The Lord is my shepherd: I want
for nothing; he makes me to lie in
greenpastures,
2 He leads me to waters where I may rest;
he restores my soul.
3 He guides me along the right paths for
his name's sake.
4 Although I walk in a darksome valley,
shall fear no evil, for thou art with me.
Thy crook and thy staff: these comfort
me.
5 Thou preparest a table for me before the
eyes of my foes;
Thou anointest my head with oil; my cup
brims over.
6 Goodness and kindness will follow me
all the days of my life,
And I shall dwell in the house of the
Lord days without end.

FOR DISCUSSION

1. The Oriental mind prefers the concrete, the individual picture to a general discussion of the abstract. What attribute of God has the Psalmist here portrayed from his experience?

2. Why is enumeration of deeds more effective than straight description of the Good Shepherd?

3. How is the Lord pictured in verses 5 and 6? What individual details of ancient Jewish hospitality are depicted?

4. What is the general attitude towards God on the part of the Psalmist?

PROJECTS

1. You should be acquainted with Marc Connolly's famous play, *The Green Pastures.* Why is his title a good one? Would you say this play is a comedy? Why or why not?

2. Explain the place of the "crook and staff" in the Church's liturgy.

RELATED READING

Read the parable of the Good Shepherd in Luke 15 and the bestowal of the Primacy on St. Peter in John 21.

Psalm 72

A PSALM OF ASAPH

1 How good is God to the upright; the Lord, to them that are pure of heart.
2 But my feet almost wavered, my steps almost slipped,
3 For I was envious of the ungodly, seeing the prosperity of sinners.
4 For they have no torments, healthy and fat is their body.
5 In the hardships of mortals they have no part, and they are not scourged like other men.
6 Therefore pride encircles them like a necklace, and violence covers them like a robe.
7 Their iniquity comes forth from a gross heart, the thoughts of their mind break forth.
8 They jeer and they speak spitefully, they threaten proudly.
9 They set their mouth against heaven, and their tongue ranges over the earth.
10 Therefore my people turns to them, and they gulp down great draughts of water.
11 And they say: "How does God know and is there knowledge in the Most High?"
12 Behold, the wicked are like that, and, always untroubled, they increase their power.
13 Have I, then, in vain kept my heart clean, and washed my hands in innocence?
14 For I suffer scourges all the time, and chastisement every day.
15 If I were to think: I will talk like them, I should abandon the generation of thy children.
16 Therefore I took thought that I might know this thing: but it seemed hard to me,
17 Until I went into the sanctuary of God, and considered their end.
18 Truly thou dost set them on a slippery way; thou castest them down in ruins.
19 How they fell in a moment, they have ceased to be, they are utterly consumed by a great terror.
20 Like a dream, when one awakes, O Lord, so, when thou risest up, thou shalt despise their image.
21 When my mind was being provoked, and my heart was being striken,
22 I was foolish and without understanding: I was like a brute beast before thee.

23 But I will be with thee always: thou hast taken my right hand;
24 By thy counsel thou wilt lead me, and at length thou wilt receive me into glory.
25 Whom have I in heaven but thee? And earth does not delight me if I am with thee.
26 My flesh and my heart melt away, the Rock of my heart and my portion, God forever.
27 For, behold, they that go away from thee shall perish, thou destroyest all that are unfaithful to thee.
28 But it is good for me to be near God, to put my refuge in the Lord God.
I will declare all thy works in the gates of the daughter of Sion.

FOR DISCUSSION

1. Here is another treatment (as in the Book of Job) of the great question: Why do the wicked prosper and the good suffer? What is the attitude of the Psalmist in verses 1-12? What has brought on the temptation?

2. Is there any change of mood in verses 13-17? Explain.

3. Verses 18-20 and 23-28 portray the final lot of the wicked and the just man; how does the Psalmist develop the contrast between the two states? Is the technique effective?

4. The solution here offered is outstanding in the Old Testament. How does it compare with the teaching on immortality in our Christian Revelation? Do the two have much in common?

WORD STUDY

Explain the phrases: *gross heart* in verse 7 and *my mind was being provoked* in verse 21.

PROJECTS

1. Choose at least five figures of speech from the Psalm and explain the meaning of each.

2. Explain the famous figure in verse 28. The "daughter of Sion" referred to is Jerusalem.

RELATED READING

Read and study Psalms 1 and 120. They are rich in meaning.

King David Composes the Psalms.

The Suffering Messias

(ISAIAS 52:13-53:12)

Isaias, the most literary of the prophets, has been called the Evangelist of the Old Testament. Here is his well-known prophecy of the atonement of the Messias and His exaltation. This is one of the most famous passages of the Old Testament. The translation was made by Reverend Michael J. Gruenthaner, S.J.

52:13 Behold, the Wise One, my Servant,
shall be exalted,
He shall be raised up and be high
exceedingly.
Just as many were appalled at him—
14 So marred from that of man was
his appearance,
And his form from that of the
children of men—
15 So shall he cause many nations
to rise up;
Kings shall hold their mouths
because of him.
For they shall see things of which
they had not been told;
They shall understand things of
which they had not heard.
53:1 Who could have believed what
we have heard?
And to whom was the Lord's
might revealed?
2 And he grew up as a slender
shoot before Him,
And as a root out of the dry ground.
He had no form nor charm that
we should gaze upon him,
No beauty that we should admire
him.
3 He was despised and forsaken
of men,
A man of sorrows, acquainted
with pain,
Like one from whom men hide
their faces.
He was despised and we
esteemed him not.
4 Nevertheless, it was our pains that
he bore,
And our sorrows that he carried,
While we accounted him stricken,
Smitten by God and afflicted.
5 But he was wounded for our
transgressions,
Crushed for our iniquities;
The chastisement that brought
us peace was upon him,
And by his stripes we were healed.
6 Like sheep, we all had gone astray:
We had turned each one his own
way,
But the Lord laid upon him the
punishment of us all.
7 When tortured, he submitted and
opened not his mouth.
Like a lamb that is led to the
slaughter,

Like a ewe before her shearers,
He was mute and opened not his
mouth.
8 Through oppression in judgment he
was taken away.
As for his contemporaries,
who considered
That he was cut off from the
land of the living
Smitten for the sin of my
people.
9 They appointed his grave with
transgressors
And with criminals when he should
die,
Although he had done no
violence,
And there was no deceit in his
mouth.
10 But the Lord saw fit to afflict him
with suffering.
When his life shall have offered
atonement for sin
He shall see posterity, prolong his
days,
And the Lord's design will prosper
in his hands.
11 He shall see the fruit of
his mortal travail;
He shall be content with what he
shall perceive
The Just One, my Servant, shall
bring justice to many,
And he shall carry their sins.
12 Therefore, I will assign him a
multitude as his portion
And great numbers as his spoil,
Because he poured out his life into
death,
And was numbered with
transgressors.
Yea, he bore the sin of many and
interposed for transgressors.

OUTLINE OF ARGUMENT

(The Poet speaks in the Name of God)

52:13-15 Exaltation of the Servant emphasized by repetition, by contrast, and by enumeration of those offering homage and their reactions.

(The Poet speaks in the name of the Hearers)

53:1-2 Amazement at this revelation: that God's power should be revealed in this extraordinary way in this Servant. For this Servant grew up in humble circumstances.

2-3 Yes, this Servant—without beauty, despised, full of sorrows—like a leper was shunned and scorned.

4-9 But all His suffering was for us; all His pains, the price of our sins. This notion of vicarious suffering is driven home by many repetitions.

11-12 (The Poet speaks in the Name of God.)

10-12 God allowed this suffering—as atonement for sin; the reward to this Servant, and to the redeemed.

FOR DISCUSSION

1. This prophecy concerning the sufferings of Christ is presented simply yet with great appeal. Can you give a few reasons for its literary worth?

2. Point out the strength of the contrast in 52:13-15.

3. List the attributes of Christ as given in 53:2-3. How many times is our guilt assigned as the cause of Christ's sufferings?

4. Is sadness the final effect, or does the prophet see God's goodness and generosity as the overall view?

PROJECTS

1. Prepare explanations of the references to this prophecy in Luke 22:37, Matthew 8:17, and I Peter 2:22.

2. Discuss why Christ's atonement should have been necessary.

RELATED READING

Note the points of similarity in Psalm 21.

Read the accounts of the Passion in Matthew 27, Mark 15, and Luke 23; and, to understand Christ's motivation in these sufferings, John 14-17.

Carrying of the Cross

PAUL'S SPEECH AT ATHENS

(Acts 17:15-34)

The Acts of the Apostles is St. Luke's partial account of the earliest days of the Church, from Our Lord's Ascension until St. Paul's first imprisonment at Rome. Luke's concern is with the beginnings, the spread of the Gospel into new territory. Naturally, the dominating character is St. Paul and his labors throughout the Roman Empire.

Paul's second missionary journey has taken him on another long trip through the Roman provinces. The vision of the Macedonian has led Paul into Greece; Philippi, Thessalonica, Beroea have heard the "good news." Now Paul waits at Athens for disciples Silas and Timothy to rejoin him. The Athens Paul saw was still the center of Greek culture, but decay had long since followed upon the Golden Age. The Epicureans, materialists, had set up pleasure as the highest good; the Stoics, pantheists, esteemed devotion to duty.

This selection from the Acts is taken from Monsignor Ronald A. Knox's translation of the New Testament. Notice how thoroughly modern is the English used by Father Knox.

Those who were escorting Paul on his journey saw him as far as Athens, and then left him, with instructions for Silas and Timothy to rejoin him as soon as possible. And while Paul was waiting for them in Athens, his heart was moved within him to find the city so much given over to idolatry, and he reasoned, not only in the synagogue with Jews and worshippers of the true God, but in the market place, with all he met. He encountered philosophers, Stoics and Epicureans, some of whom asked, What can his drift be, this dabbler? while others said, He would appear to be proclaiming strange gods; because he had preached to them about Jesus and Resurrection. So they took him by the sleeve and led him up to the Areopagus;[1] May we ask, they said, what this new teaching is thou art delivering? Thou dost introduce terms which are strange to our ears; pray let us know what may be the meaning of it. (No townsman of Athens, or stranger visiting it, has time for anything else than saying something new, or hearing it said.)

[1]AREOPAGUS (ăr′ê·ŏp′·à·gŭs)—A high court of Athens which met on a hill west of the Acropolis.

So Paul stood up in full view of the Areopagus, and said, Men of Athens, wherever I look I find you scrupulously religious. Why, in examining your monuments as I passed by them, I found among others an altar which bore the inscription, To the unknown God. And it is this unknown object of your devotion that I am revealing to you. The God who made the world and all that is in it, that God who is Lord of heaven and earth, does not dwell in temples that our hands have made; no human handicraft can do him service, as if he stood in need of anything, he, who gives to all of us life and breath and all we have. It is he who has made, of one single stock, all the nations that were to dwell over the whole face of the earth. And he has given to each the cycles it was to pass through and the fixed limits of its habitation, leaving them to search for God; would they somehow grope their way towards him? Would they find him? And yet, after all, he is not far from any one of us; it is in him that we live, and move, and have our being; thus, some of your own poets have told us, For indeed, we are his children. Why then, if we are the children of God, we must not imagine that the divine nature can be represented in gold, or silver, or stone, carved by man's art and thought. God has shut his eyes to these passing follies of ours; now, he calls upon all men, everywhere, to repent, because he has fixed a day when he will pronounce just judgement on the whole world. And the man whom he has appointed for that end he has accredited to all of us, by raising him up from the dead.

When resurrection from the dead was mentioned, some mocked, while others said, We must hear more from thee about this. So Paul went away from among them. But there were men who attached themselves to him and learned to believe, among them Dionysius the Areopagite; and so did a woman called Damaris, and others with them.

FOR DISCUSSION

1. What evidence have you from the text that St. Paul was familiar with Grecian philosophy and art?

2. If St. Paul stood in Times Square, New York, today and spoke before a representative gathering of the citizens of that city, what might be the contents of his speech?

3. Is the resurrection of the dead still denied by modern thinkers? Why? What is the Communist's philosophy of life?

4. How many converts did St. Paul make on this occasion? Is the modern preacher any more successful?

WORD STUDY

What kind of person is a *dabbler?* What does "to dabble in politics" mean? Give the etymology of the words: *handicraft, cycle, habitation.* What is the relation between *habitation* and *habitat?*

PROJECTS

1. Describe the Athenian market place which met Paul's eyes. Explain the presence of the philosophers there.

2. Compare this passage with that in the Douai-Rheims Version and tell specifically how Monsignor Knox has brought the translation up-to-date.

3. Compare it also with the Kleist-Lilly rendition and discuss which of the two translations more closely catches the tone of English as spoken today.

ELIZABETHAN PROSE

We have already seen that English prose, in its transition from Middle English, developed richly under the masterful pen of Saint Thomas More. The great modern scholar, R. W. Chambers, has written that we must "think of him [More] first in connection with the continuity of English speech, English prose, English literature. . . . To the student of English prose his work is the great link which connects modern prose with the medieval prose of Nicholas Love, Walter Hilton, and Richard Rolle."

Continuing in the scholarly tradition of More and the Christian Humanism of Oxford of which he was a part, Edmund Campion has given us in his *History of Ireland* what Evelyn Waugh has called "a superb piece of literature, comparable in vigour and rhythm to anything written in his day." We know that Campion's future as a man of English letters was cut short by his submission to Rome, his life as a Jesuit priest, and his death as an English martyr. But there is no doubt in the mind of Waugh, the great stylist of modern times, that had Campion continued the life of learning he had planned for himself, "he would have come down in history as one of the great masters of English prose."

Although prose writing lagged far behind the lyrical expression of the period, scores of writers set down in simple English the results of their search in fields of history, travel, navigation, biography, and the like. In spite of the fact that many scholars continued to present their studies in the classic tongue, so many good books in the vernacular appeared that we can only glance at some representative titles.

GEOGRAPHERS AND EXPLORERS

Two English clergymen, Richard Hakluyt and Samuel Purchas, became interested in England's achievements in exploration. They made careful study of the records of men like Drake and Frobisher, checking dates and names and places. Hakluyt published his findings in a three-volume work, *Principal Navigations, Voyages and Discoveries of the English Nation,* issued in 1589, 1598, and 1600. Purchas continued the undertaking after Hakluyt's death with two volumes, *Purchas, His Pilgrimage* in 1616 and *Hakluytus Posthumous, or Purchas, His Pilgrims* in 1625. The books are of interest because they have furnished later writers with accurate information about early English "sea-dogs."

Sir Walter Raleigh and Captain John Smith wrote first-hand accounts of their experiences in the New World, but they were so eager to dazzle the reader with American splendors that their pages were misleading. For some generations, certain Englishmen entertained visions of an American paradise drawn from the accounts in Raleigh's *Discovery of Guiana* or Smith's *Virginia, New England, and the Summer Isles.* While he was in prison, awaiting execution, Sir Walter wrote an ambitious but also untrustworthy *History of the World.* It concludes with a courageous and moving address to Death.

The fervent patriotism of the times aroused an interest in British history. As early as 1578, Holinshed published his *Chronicles of England, Ireland and Scotland,* an important work because it gave Shakespeare some material for *Macbeth* and for his English historical plays. William Camden did a careful piece of historical research which resulted in *Britannia*—an orderly chronicle of English history—and in the *Annals of Queen Elizabeth.* Foxe's *Book of Martyrs* was a favorite of the early Puritans and one of the first books brought to America. John Knox wrote *The History of the Reformation in Scotland.*

The period manifested an interest in the lives of great men of all times. One exceedingly popular book was Thomas North's excellent translation of Plutarch's *Parallel Lives of Greek and Roman Heroes.* This work also furnished Shakespeare with material for some of his tragedies—notably for *Julius Caesar* and *Antony and Cleopatra.*

The books noted above were written, on the whole, in a simple, direct style. Another fashion of prose writing, however, was developed by such men as John Lyly and Sir Philip Sidney. In his *Euphues,* a fictitious account of the experiences of a young Athenian visiting England, Lyly wrote in a bombastic, highly artificial style which later led to the coining of the word *euphuism* to indicate an artificially elegant mode of literary expression. In an attempt to imitate the pastoral romances of the writers of the Italian Renaissance, Sidney wrote his prose romance, *Arcadia.* The work was intended also to react against the euphuistic style of Lyly; however, it too shows a courtly, artificial style, foreign to the direct simplicity of the main stream of English prose.

The Death of Julius Caesar

THE ENGLISH ESSAY MAKES ITS BOW

The most important development in literary prose was the appearance of a form new to English writers—the *essay.* It was Francis Bacon who made the introduction. Over in France, a brilliant writer, Michel de Montaigne, who died in 1592, had been writing down brief impressions of men and human affairs and publishing them as "Essais." Five years later, Bacon, who knew and admired the work of the Frenchman, published ten short prose reflections and called them "Essays." And so the English term was born. Bacon had not rated his papers highly, and he was surprised at their success. His long, serious studies had all been written in Latin, but the essays proved he had a brilliant command of English and an almost poetic prose style. In 1612, he released a second edition, containing twenty-eight additional papers; and in 1625, his final edition, numbering fifty-eight.

Bacon's English is marked by short, pithy sentences, or by longer sentences that break easily into parallel parts. He never loses his way grammatically, and his fondness for balanced structure—phrase with phrase or clause with clause—gives his prose a definite rhythm. It reads well aloud, and it is packed with thought. The best known of all the essays, "Of Studies," appeared in the first edition of his papers. It shows forth his wit, his eloquence, and his intellectual interests. The essays added to the second edition, while he was rising rapidly to power, have a worldy-wise point of view and are coldly calculating in thought. The last twenty, written during retirement after his public disgrace, have a sober moral tone.

The essays reflect to some extent the thoughts and attitudes of the days of Elizabeth and of her successor, James I. More particularly, they reflect the man who wrote them—a man described by a later poet as "the wisest, brightest, meanest of all time."

It is not generally known that another writer of the age added to the store of English essays. We are well acquainted with Ben Jonson the poet and Jonson the dramatist, but Jonson the essayist is less familiar. In the last years of his life, this lusty writer pondered much on men, on books, on learning; and from time to time he jotted down his meditations. Some, like the reminiscence on Bacon, are very short; some are much longer. He grouped them under the name *Timbers,* but they were not published until 1641, four years after his death. Most interesting are his comments on the famous men he knew, such as the one on Shakespeare in which he criticizes the dramatist for writing too much, but in which he also pays a splendid tribute to the man and his work.

OF STUDIES

FRANCIS BACON

"Why do I have to go to school?" is a question that comes up every so often in the average American home. "What good are these things?"—with a contemptuous gesture toward a stack of textbooks—"what good is studying going to do me anyway?"

Well, Francis Bacon, who lived in the days of Shakespeare, has an answer to such questions. Even though it was written almost four centuries ago, it is still a good answer. Briefly, he says that studies add to our profit, to our appearance or personality, and to our fun. Of course, it doesn't take much talking to prove the first point. Some studies are necessary to prepare us to earn a living. And yes, studies do help one "shine" in society. But the high school boy who feels "fed up" with school may balk a bit at the third reason. Yet Bacon considered it so important that he named it first. And isn't he right? Suppose for a moment that you had never gone to school. Suppose you could not read or write. Think of the pleasures you would have to miss. Yes, Bacon is wise to begin by saying, "Studies serve for delight." He is right about most of the other things, too.

Studies serve for delight, for ornament, and for ability. Their chief use for delight is privateness and retiring; for ornament, is in discourse; and for ability, is in the judgement and disposition of business. For expert men[1] can execute and perhaps judge of particulars, one by one; but the general counsels, and the plots and marshaling of affairs, come best from those that are learned. To spend too much time in studies is sloth; to use them too much for ornament is affectation; to make judgment wholly by their rules is the humor[2] of a scholar. They perfect nature, and are perfected by experience; for natural abilities are like natural plants, that need proyning[3] by study; and studies themselves do give forth directions too much at large, except they be bounded in by experience. Crafty men[4] contemn studies; simple men admire them; and wise men use them: for they teach not their own use; but that[5] is a wisdom without them and above them, won by observation. Read not to contradict and confute; nor to believe and take for granted; nor to find talk and discourse; but to weigh and consider. Some books are to be tasted, others to be swallowed, and some few to be chewed and digested: that is, some books are

[1]EXPERT MEN—Specialists who lack general information or culture.

[2]HUMOR—Peculiarity or tendency.

[3]PROYNING—Pruning.

[4]CRAFTY MEN—Laborers; workmen of various crafts or guilds.

[5]THAT—The knowledge of how to use one's learning.

to be read only in parts; others to be read, but not curiously;[6] and some few to be read wholly, and with diligence and attention. Some books also may be read by deputy,[7] and extracts made of them by others; but that would be only in the less important arguments, and the meaner sort of books; else distilled books are like common distilled waters, flashy[8] things. Reading maketh a full man; conference a ready man;[9] and writing an exact man. And therefore, if a man write little, he had need have a great memory; if he confer[10] little, he had need have a present wit; and if he read little, he had need have much cunning, to seem to know that he doth not. Hisories make men wise; poets witty; the mathematics subtile; natural philosophy deep; moral grave; logic and rhetoric able to contend. *Abeunt studia in mores.*[11] Nay, there is no stond or impediment in the wit, but may be wrought out by fit studies:[12] like as diseases of the body may have appropriate exercises. Bowling is good for the stone and reins;[13] shooting for the lungs and breast; gentle walking for the stomach; riding for the head; and the like. So if a man's wit be wandering, let him study the mathematics; for in demonstrations, if his wit be called away never so little, he must begin again: if his wit be not apt to distinguish or find differences, let him study the Schoolmen;[14] for they are *cymini sectores:*[15] if he be not apt to beat over matters, and to call one thing to prove and illustrate another, let him study the lawyers' case: so every defect of the mind may have a special receipt.

[6]CURIOUSLY—With close attention.

[7]READ BY DEPUTY—"Read" through reviews or reports by others.

[8]FLASHY—Flat, tasteless.

[9]CONFERENCE A READY MAN—Conversation (or repartee) makes a man quick-witted.

[10]CONFER—Converse.

[11]*Abeunt studia in mores*—Studies pass into (or grow into) manners.

[12]NO STOND . . . WROUGHT OUT—No lack of mental ability but may be remedied.

[13]STONE AND REINS—Gallstones and similar affections.

[14]SCHOOLMEN—Theologians or philosophers.

[15]*Cymini sectores*—Hairsplitters or quibblers.

FOR DISCUSSION

1. *His Style:* Bacon is a remarkably modern writer. He knows how to use words with economy, and he packs a world of meaning into a single sentence. He is a master of the terse, pithy sentence which makes for an epigrammatical style. His sentences are perfectly *balanced* in structure and in thought. Choose from the selection at least three epigrams and study them for their balanced structure.

2. Think over the opening sentence. Which studies that you are taking serve one or more of these uses of education?

3. In his essay, Bacon is championing the cause of a *liberal* education, that is, an education which teaches us *how* to live, not necessarily how to make a living. Do you agree that a liberal education is a necessary preparation for life? Discuss.

4. To paraphrase means to reword a passage without changing its meaning. As a test of your understanding of the essay, try paraphrasing any three of sentences 2 to 10.

5. What does Bacon say about "digests"? Would he approve of all the "digests" on the market today? Discuss.

6. Give illustrations of the truth of the statement that the chief use of studies "for delight is in privateness and retiring." Is it true, for instance, that an uneducated person is more at a loss for entertainment when he is alone than when he is with others? Do you think that the men in service appreciate the love of good reading which they acquired in school? Why?

7. Apply to the last part of the essay Bacon's precept that we should read "to weigh and consider." Do you think that a man lacking a logical mind can improve it by studying geometry? Or that a slow-witted person may become a clever conversationalist through much practice? Discuss.

WORD STUDY

Be sure you understand the sense in which Bacon used the following words: *affectation, confute, discourse, subtile, contend.* Distinguish between the synonyms: *taste, flavor, tang.*

PROJECTS

1. Memorize the sentences: "Reading maketh a full man; conference a ready man; and writing an exact man." "Some books are to be tasted, others to be swallowed, and some few to be chewed and digested."

2. Take one division of one of the above sentences as a topic sentence and expand it into a paragraph of at least one hundred words.

3. Prepare an oral debate or write a defense of either side of this question: Does a *liberally* educated man give a greater contribution to his age than a specialist without a liberal education? In other words, can an engineer without a liberal education give as great a contribution to society as an engineer with a liberal education?

RELATED READING

Read some other essays of Bacon; for example, "Of Truth" and "Of Friendship." Macaulay was a champion of everything Bacon stood for—especially "progress." Read Macaulay's *Essay on Bacon* and report to the class his general estimate of Bacon's character and his contribution to science.

Francis Bacon

THE DEVELOPMENT OF ENGLISH DRAMA

We have already noted how popular drama had its beginnings in England with the miracle, mystery, and morality plays of Middle English times.

Toward the close of the fifteenth century, there developed another type of play, much shorter than the morality play, known as the *interlude.* The interlude was inserted between the acts of a longer play, or presented between the courses of a banquet. Later, interludes were given on any occasion that called for short entertainment. These playlets were frequently based on some life situation, and so led the way toward the appearance of realistic drama.

The British forerunner of modern drama is usually said to have been born in 1550, when a schoolmaster wrote a crude comedy entitled *Ralph Roister Doister.* In 1561 appeared what is called the first English tragedy, *Gorboduc,* written in blank verse; and in 1566 came another farcical comedy, *Gammer Gurton's Needle,* written by a bishop. These plays showed the influence of the Renaissance in their imitation of classic forms, but the scenes and characters were English, the situations lifelike, and the story with its action held the center of attention.

ELIZABETHAN DRAMA

The culmination toward which the English drama had been developing for centuries came in the days of Elizabeth. Plays became as popular as the movies are in our own. Strolling players armed with scripts and gay costumes set up their temporary stage in the quadrangular court of an inn. Rushes were strewn on the wooden scaffolding; juniper was burned in the yard to purify the air. At three o'clock the flag was run up to announce the beginning of the performance, trumpets blared, and the townsfolk flocked to the innyard. The common folk stood on the ground; the gentry, the burghers, and the dignitaries of the town occupied the galleries. Here the leading lady—whose chin often bristled with a new beard—squeaked her alarm at pasteboard dragons. Here armies had it out with wooden swords. Here "groundlings"—apprentices, serving men, soldiers, colliers, tinkers, and the like—drank ale, cracked nuts, jeered the villain, and hailed the hero.

Nowhere, of course, was the popularity of the play more to be marked than in London, where it early attracted the displeasure of the Puritans who were strong enough in 1574 to secure the enactment of an Order of the Common Council in Restraint of Dramatic Exhibitions. This order led to the building of the first playhouse, called *The Theater,* which was erected by James Burbage in 1576 on a site just north of the city limits where the Order did not apply. For a model he seems to have taken the innyard. It seems probable that the interior of *The Theater* was circular. In this open space, which was called the *pit* or *yard,* on the hard-packed earth stood the groundlings. About the inside walls on the three sides parallel and opposite to the stage were galleries, probably three tiers, after the fashion of the innyards. The best seats were in the galleries. Here sat the "gallery-commoners"—the merchants and gentry. As the picture of *The Fortune* shows, there was also a gallery over

the rear stage. This was the "Lords roome." In the "Lords roome" sat the more aristocratic patrons of the play, both men and women, the latter carefully masked. On the very edge of the stage itself sat the swaggering gallants of the day.

The stage was a raised platform projecting out into the pit. Over the "stage forward" was a "shadow or cover" supported by posts. At the rear and under the "Lords roome" was a kind of recess which might be cut off from the stage forward by a curtain or "arras." Rising above the gallery was a tower which was used for three purposes. Here was flown a flag giving the name of the theater, as *The Theater, The Swan,* or *The Globe.* On days when plays were to be given, a second flag announcing the fact was also hung out. From this tower also the trumpeter sounded the three blasts which announced that the play was about to begin.

There was no scenery such as we know on the Elizabethan stage. It is possible that the curtain or arras at the rear sometimes bore a crude painted picture. It is probable, however,

STAGE SETTINGS

that the setting was generally indicated by no more than a placard or piece of cloth bearing a legend, such as *Macbeth's Castle,* or *A heath.* Although there was little or no scenery, considerable use was made of *properties.* A picture of *The Swan* shows a bench or settle on the stage, and other articles of furniture no doubt were used when required. A document of the time mentions "engines, weapons, and powder used in plays."

One peculiarity of the Elizabethan stage was the absence of actresses. Women's parts were taken by boys, especially trained. This accounts for the fact that Shakespeare frequently has his women characters impersonate men and for the further fact that in all the plays men predominate. Elizabethan actors made little or no attempt to dress according to the time and setting of the play. "Costume," says one writer, "was a means of indicating rank and office more than time or place; it was meant to reveal the characters rather than the setting of the story." The Elizabethan age delighted in extravagant display, especially in clothes.

The actor's life was a strenuous one. Professor Adams in his *A Life of William Shakespeare* writes, "Elizabethan troupes . . . not only performed as a rule every week day, and often on Sundays, but also changed their plays from day to day in a most astonishing fashion. The forenoons of the actors were commonly spent in rehearsals. The afternoons, of course, were occupied with performances before the public, lasting from two or three o'clock until five or six. As to the evenings, not a small share of the time surely had to be devoted to learning new, or refreshing the memory on old plays."

In the reading of Elizabethan plays, we are likely to overlook one of the chief attractions for the audience—the songs and incidental music. Elizabethans were fond of music. And the groundlings and gallants also loved "sound and fury" for its own sake. They liked hurly-burly and commotion. The reader should note the frequency of trumpet calls and fanfares, and other appeals to the ear indicated in the stage directions by *Flourish, Cry within, Thunder and lightning, Drum, Flourish and shout,* and the like. The frequency of *Alarums* in battle scenes no doubt served both to keep the audience on the alert and to stimulate its imagination.

SIDELIGHTS ON THE THEATER

The audience itself was a turbulent and unruly one. Expressions of approval and disapproval were common through applause, noisy laughter, loud spitting, and a whole series of rude guffaws and curses. If the nobles were bored by the play, they interrupted or mimicked the actors or even jumped to the stage and engaged in combat with them.

There remains one thing to say about Elizabethan drama. The dialogue was written in verse. All of Shakespeare's plays—excepting a few comic scenes done in prose—are written in unrhymed iambic pentameter lines. Some scenes for emphasis close with a rhymed couplet. The remarkable thing is that although Shakespeare's characters talk like real men and women, they speak some of the greatest poetry the world has ever known. These mighty lines have power to grip the mind today just as they stilled the boisterous pit and gallery in the days of Elizabeth and James.

By 1616, there were in London at least seven well-established theaters in which plays were regularly given, not to mention certain great inns, such as the Boar's Head, where plays evidently continued.

So great was the demand for plays that not only professional literary men, but scholars and courtiers as well, tried their hand at playmaking. The first men who had taken up dramatic writing as a profession were the so-called "University Wits," so named since they were all university men, who, instead of going into the church or teaching, turned to writing to earn their living. The most conspicuous of the "University Wits" was Christopher Marlowe, who, before his death at twenty-nine, produced four remarkable dramas. Associated with Marlowe are the names of a number of other dramatists, all of whom worked feverishly, often in collaboration, to produce the greatest possible number of dramatic novelties for the stage. In their search for material, they ransacked the past. History, classic myth, legend, medieval romance, and folk tale were all grist to the mill. The situation much resembled that of our own day in which, to meet the insatiable demand for movies and television plays, the literature of the past has been freely used.

UNIVERSITY WITS

Then at the close of the sixteenth century came young William Shakespeare, destined to become the greatest dramatist of England, if not of the entire world. He raised English drama to heights never approached before or since. All the world was his stage, and his zest for life was so great that laughter and tears pulsate in every page of his work. His characters are always dynamic, energetic personalities, from kings like Macbeth to lovers like Romeo and Juliet. There are clowns and cut-purses and drunken porters and fairies and shrews and representatives of practically the whole Elizabethan world.

Perhaps one of the most tangible proofs of Shakespeare's greatness is the fact that after four centuries he is still a Broadway sell-out. The Old Vic Company from London performed *Henry V,* and seats were sold out six months in advance. Laurence Olivier's *Henry V* and *Hamlet* are hailed as the greatest movies of our times. Maurice Evans played *Hamlet* up and down the South Pacific, and the soldiers liked it so much that he has since played the same version to enthusiastic American audiences. Will Shakespeare is the one playwright to whom all concede that final, ultimate adjective—*great!*

Oliver as Hamlet

THE SEVENTEENTH AND EIGHTEENTH CENTURIES

1603-1780

Elizabeth's death in 1603 was properly dramatic. The curtain came down on an ugly old woman in a henna wig calling piteously for a "true mirror" and begging for a good-luck charm to wear around her neck. The new century which she ushered in was to be a hectic one. It would embrace eight different administrations and four major revolutions of government. England would rise up against a king, indict and behead him; shift to a republican commonwealth; restore her monarch; rebel, and finally, without bloodshed, win another foothold in the march towards democracy—the Bill of Rights.

THE STUART INTERVAL (1603-1625)

In literature, the exuberance of Elizabeth's reign carried over into that of James, son of the tragic Queen of Scots, who followed Elizabeth to the throne. Shakespeare produced several of his later plays at James' court, and many of the other Elizabethan writers did some of their best work after the accession of the new monarch. James himself was a literary man and a much more generous patron of letters than his predecessor. The King James Version of the Bible, which was to have such a tremendous influence on the development of English prose, took its name from him. It was James who made Ben Jonson the first poet laureate of England.

The reign of James, however, did not fulfill either politically or in a literary way the national hopes that had sprung up in the days of Elizabeth. Mounting financial and religious difficulties that had been suppressed in her reign owing to the Spanish threat became of more and more concern under James. There were signs of conflict between Parliament and the king which in the next reign became an open revolt. The times were ripe for trouble.

THE PURITAN AGE (1625-1660)

At the death of James I in 1625, Charles I inherited a nightmare. Besides the eternal skirmishing with Scotland, there were unpleasant social conditions at home. The abject poverty of London slums cried out against the gross luxury of upstart lords, fat with the wealth of monastic houses. The newly rich thought nothing of hiring foreign mercenary troops to break up the revolts of the common people. But King Charles' worst headache was Parliament.

Wool, at this time, was the big money-making commodity. The new mercantile aristocracy, looking only toward prizes for itself, was not particular about methods. All sorts of high-pressure tactics were used, and small farms were ruthlessly seized to be turned into grazing lands. Unfortunately for Charles, the moneyed men had powerful representation in Parliament, and the Stuarts were more dependent upon Parliament for revenue than the Tudors had been. Charles had many debts. He was told that if he wanted money, he must grant to certain interests special rights affecting the control of commerce.

Charles was on tenterhooks. A firm believer in the "divine right of kings," he felt a personal responsibility for *all* his subjects. He knew that if he conceded the "rights of enclosure" to the wealthy land-grabbers, it would mean throwing countless poor off their farms and onto the highways as beggars. Hence he refused.

But this is not the whole story of the conflict. The religious situation was even more disturbing. English Protestantism had begun its inevitable process of division. A certain group, almost identical with the newly rich merchant class, had subscribed to the cold, somber, joyless tenets of Calvinism. Though they were shrewd money-makers, they lived sober, abstemious lives. They believed that nature is inherently evil and totally depraved. They mistrusted pleasure; they disapproved of everything beautiful; they were especially opposed to the Catholic Church, which they called "the Scarlet Woman." As the Anglican state church was too "popish" for their taste, they wanted to "purify" it of its worldly formality. And so these straight-laced dissenters came to be known as Puritans.

PROTESTANTS DIVIDED

The tension between Parliament and the king grew ever more serious. The Puritans were violently opposed to Charles on two scores: he refused to make their particular brand of Protestantism the state religion, and he refused to give them a free hand in the matter of enclosures.

There were men who came to the defense of Charles—some because the habit of loyalty is strong; some out of real devotion to their monarch. The king had an attractive personality. When he chose, he could be extremely gracious and generous. His followers—chiefly young men who enjoyed the gay life of the court—were called Cavaliers. The term originally meant "horsemen" or "knights"; but through the seventeenth century, it designated the party loyal to the king. After the fall of the Stuarts, it was replaced by the term Tory.

KING CHARLES I PUT TO DEATH

After three years of civil war, Charles and his Cavaliers were defeated at Naseby. Charles was imprisoned in the Tower of London, accused of high treason against his country, and sentenced to death. On a scaffold in 1649, with surprising dignity, he paid for his kingship with his life. Europe was aghast, and many of the English were horrified. Whatever the uprising meant, it did not mean a victory for democracy nor an emancipation of the poorer classes. There were many who felt that Charles had been their friend and the defender of their rights. Unlike the scenes of frenzied hatred that were to surround the guillotines of the French Revolution, here the silence was broken only by deep groans when the head of the Stuart king rolled in the dust.

A republican commonwealth was organized with Oliver Cromwell at its head. Its purpose was to secure civil freedom to the English people. But many of the leaders were themselves intolerant. The Parliamentary rule went to great extremes. Axes were applied to "idolatrous" statues, "popish pictures," and "the vain show of stained glass windows." But the rule of the Puritans was so confused and mismanaged that Cromwell in disgust finally dismissed Parliament, and with the support of a strong army ruled as absolute dictator. His position was ironic: he who had led the uprising to end the tyranny of the Stuart monarchs had himself become a tyrant.

Oliver Cromwell died in 1658. His son, Richard Cromwell, proved inadequate as a successor, and the Puritan power evaporated. Unrest stirred again. But the period from the accession of Charles in 1625 to the end of the commonwealth in 1660 was important in the field of literature.

CAVALIER POETS

Ben Jonson's influence upon the poets of the early seventeenth century was considerable. Chief among these poets, who because of their admiration and imitation of Jonson were styled "the Tribe of Ben," were Robert Herrick and Thomas Carew. These two, together with Sir John Suckling and Richard Lovelace, have come to be known as "Cavalier Poets," since they were all close followers of King Charles. They wrote contemporaneously with the Metaphysical Group and at times felt that influence. Yet their verse is in a class by itself.

"GATHER YE ROSEBUDS"

It is marked first by a practical, down-to-earth attitude toward "life and love and all things else." They seemed to be waging a "de-bunking" campaign in the field of poetry, especially love poetry. No Cavalier poet believed for one moment that his lady did "in herself contain all this world's riches that may far be found." Beautiful she might be—but so what? Flowers fade and women grow old. One of two conclusions usually followed. The first was altogether worldly and materialistic—"Gather ye rosebuds while ye may!" Make the most of today; you can't escape wrinkles tomorrow! The second conclusion was—seek that loveliness which does not die, *beauty of mind and spirit.* Thus even the gayest Cavalier shows sometimes a serious nature.

There are other characteristics of Cavalier verse. It is keen, clever, sometimes flippant, sometimes delicately, sometimes indelicately sensual and voluptuous. Each poem has a theme and is carefully constructed around it. Sometimes the theme is idealistic, sometimes cynical. But it is there, and well inscribed in an attractive setting. These poets were good craftsmen, and they challenge our thought. Their work is a direct contrast to the Elizabethan lyrics which stir our hearts rather than our minds. Suckling, Herrick, Carew, and Lovelace were brilliant writers, and their verse has the polish and often the hardness of a well-cut gem.

A Song

THOMAS CAREW

Carew's reputation as one of King Charles' Cavaliers was not the most wholesome, but very little of his poetry reflects the excesses of his life at court. Many of his love poems are bitterly cynical, but his "A Song" is a faultless piece of lyrical composition.

Ask me no more where Jove bestows,
When June is past, the fading rose;
For in your beauty's orient deep
These flowers, as in their causes, sleep.

Ask me no more whither do stray
The golden atoms of the day;
For, in pure love, heaven did prepare
Those powders to enrich your hair.

Ask me no more whither doth haste
The nightingale, when May is past;
For in your sweet dividing throat
She winters, and keeps warm her note.

Ask me no more where those stars light
That downwards fall in dead of night;
For in your eyes they sit, and there
Fixèd become, as in their sphere.

Ask me no more if east or west
The Phoenix builds her spicy nest;
For unto you at last she flies,
And in your fragrant bosom dies.

11. DIVIDING—This was a musical term used in Carew's day and refers to singing in harmony or in parts.

18. PHOENIX—The Arabian bird of fable which alternately destroys itself and then rises from its own ashes.

FOR APPRECIATION

1. The subject of this poem is any lady of any time whose lover pays her five distinct compliments. He goes to nature, science, and myth to express these compliments. State the five questions he asks and give the five answers. What, then, is the theme of the poem? Do each of the five answers accentuate and develop the theme? Discuss.

2. Could there be any symbolism in the five stanzas, five compliments, and five fingers which one uses to compose a song on a musical instrument? Discuss.

3. Study the symmetry. Although the poem is written in the couplet form, it is divided into stanzas. Why?

4. In line 3, how many ideas does "orient deep" suggest to you? Show the relationship between "orient deep" and "flowers." Explain how the nightingales winter in "your sweet dividing throat." The poem ends with the word "dies." Is that word to be taken by itself or in connection with the Phoenix? Explain.

To Lucasta, on Going to the Wars

RICHARD LOVELACE

In 1645, Lovelace raised a regiment for service in France through which he hoped to restore Charles II to the throne. His departure to meet his regiment occasioned the following poem. In the poem, the poet is justifying his separation from his loved one. The eminent critic Mark Van Doren has called this poem "one of the briefest masterpieces in the world, and one of the best proofs that poetry can say what nothing else can."

Tell me not, sweet, I am unkind,
  That from the nunnery
Of thy chaste breast and quiet mind
  To war and arms I fly.

True, a new mistress now I chase,
  The first foe in the field;
And with a stronger faith embrace
  A sword, a horse, a shield.

Yet this inconstancy is such
  As you, too, shall adore;
I could not love thee, dear, so much,
  Loved I not honor more.

FOR APPRECIATION

1. How does the first line anticipate the problem to be met and the state of mind of the lady? Discuss. Does "Sweet" both soften the blow and indicate the poet's feeling?

2. In detail explain the beautiful imagery of lines 2 and 3. What does it tell us of the poet's estimate of his lady? Is there an apparent clash between "unkind" of the first line and the second and third lines?

3. Although he knows it would hurt his lady, is the poet honest when he says "a new mistress now I chase"? Explain your answer by carefully reading the rest of the poem. Why does he need a "stronger faith" to embrace "a sword, a horse, a shield"? Is there a clash in thought between "embrace" and the "first foe in the field"? Discuss.

4. Explain the meaning of the word "inconstancy" in line 9. Why must his lady adore this? Is he appealing to her intellect or to her emotions? Discuss.

5. Do you or do you not agree with the thought of the last two lines? Discuss.

To Althea, from Prison

RICHARD LOVELACE

At the age of twenty-four, Lovelace was imprisoned by the Puritans for petitioning the return of Charles. His most famous poem was written there. Although he produced less poetry than the other Cavalier poets, much of it of inferior quality, Lovelace stands assured of lasting fame for the two or three lyrics in which he achieved virtual perfection. Few poems can rival TO ALTHEA, FROM PRISON *for sheer beauty and expression.*

When Love with unconfinèd wings
  Hovers within my gates,
And my divine Althea brings
  To whisper at the grates;
When I lie tangled in her hair
  And fettered to her eye,
The birds that wanton in the air
  Know no such liberty.

When flowing cups run swiftly round
  With no allaying Thames,
Our careless heads with roses bound,
  Our hearts with loyal flames;
When thirsty grief in wine we steep,
  When healths and drafts go free—
Fishes that tipple in the deep
  Know no such liberty.

When, like committed linnets, I
  With shriller throat shall sing
The sweetness, mercy, majesty
  And glories of my King;
When I shall voice aloud how good
  He is, how great should be,
Enlargèd winds, that curl the flood,
  Know no such liberty.

Stone walls do not a prison make,
  Nor iron bars a cage;
Minds innocent and quiet take
  That for an hermitage;
If I have freedom in my love
  And in my soul am free,
Angels alone, that soar above,
  Enjoy such liberty.

7. WANTON—To be extremely merry or gay.
10. WITH NO ALLAYING THAMES—Not diluted by water.
17. COMMITTED LINNETS—Birds which are caged.
23. ENLARGÈD WINDS—Winds which are free.

FOR APPRECIATION

1. Enumerate the comparisons which the poet makes between the liberty of other creatures and his. Is stanza four a logical conclusion from the thought content of the first three? Explain. In stanza four, what two elements must be present if a prison is to be a pleasant hermitage?

2. From reading the poem, how would you know that Lovelace was a loyal Cavalier? What is the significance of "shriller throat" in line 18?

3. Discuss the connotation of such words as *hover, fettered, wanton, steep, tipple, committed linnets, curl the flood.*

To the Virgins

ROBERT HERRICK

Robert Herrick is one of the many paradoxes of this strange age. Although he spent over thirty-five years as an Anglican vicar in Devonshire, he is one of the most prolific love poets of the period. His often quoted "To the Virgins" can be interpreted either as a bit of practical advice to young women or as an expression of the "eat, drink, and be merry" attitude which is to be found in many of the songs of our own day.

Gather ye rosebuds while you may,
  Old Time is still a-flying;
And this same flower that smiles today,
  Tomorrow will be dying.

The glorious lamp of heaven, the sun,
  The higher he's a-getting,
The sooner will his race be run,
  And nearer he's to setting.

That age is best which is the first,
  When youth and blood are warmer;
But being spent, the worse and worst
  Times still succeed the former.

Then be not coy, but use your time;
  And while ye may, go marry;
For, having lost but once your prime,
  You may forever tarry.

FOR APPRECIATION

1. What images does the poet use to contrast youth and old age? Discuss their effectiveness.

2. Do you agree with the thought content of the third stanza?

3. How does the rhyme scheme and the meter produce a lightsome, singing quality in the poem? Does his choice of words also help produce this effect? Discuss.

4. Scan the poem with close attention to the initial and the final feet in each line.

Why So Pale and Wan?

SIR JOHN SUCKLING

In this poem we have the typical Cavalier reaction to the love lyric of the Elizabethans. As a man, Suckling was of rather weak character; he fled from the battlefield during a war with Scotland. His gay and witty poetry, however, is highly rated.

Why so pale and wan, fond lover?
  Prithee, why so pale?
Will, when looking well can't move her,
  Looking ill prevail?
  Prithee, why so pale?

Why so dull and mute, young sinner?
  Prithee, why so mute?
Will, when speaking well can't win her,
  Saying nothing do't?
  Prithee, why so mute?

Quit, quit for shame! This will not move;
  This cannot take her.
If of herself she will not love,
  Nothing can make her:
  The devil take her!

FOR APPRECIATION

1. Point out in detail the characteristics of Cavalier poetry as contained in this lyric. How does it differ from the poems of Lovelace? Discuss.

2. What purpose does the use of the question form serve? Does it make for unity? Do the questions carry the theme to a logical conclusion? Explain. Does the meter change with the abrupt change of thought in the last two lines? Explain.

METAPHYSICAL POETRY

In spite of their beautiful imagery and graceful expression, sonnets and love lyrics, the most popular types of poetry during the Renaissance, were really developing the anti-intellectual theories of the pagan Renaissance. The so-called Metaphysical poets made an effort to stem this pagan development, not primarily because it was pagan, but because it was the artificial product of an essentially Christian culture. They chose to treat the great concerns of man: God, love, sin, suffering, and death—seriously; and to satirize the prevailing ideals and practices. The result is an entirely new kind of lyric poetry. There are serious philosophical truths to be found in most of their poems. The themes are as great as any treated by the great Classical writers. The style attempts to create beauty not by the artificial heaping up of beautiful words or images, but by the perfect expression of man's deepest thoughts and emotions in a rhythm approaching that of natural speech.

The following are some of the elements to be looked for in the study of the Metaphysical poets: 1) dramatic speech; 2) colloquial words and expressions; 3) imagery from science which attempts to find points of similarity in widely differing things; 4) an argumentative approach to the poetic theme and a strict logical structure for the poem; 5) the use of religious imagery for sexual love, and sexual imagery for the expression of religious experience. Sometimes this is done shockingly. More often than not it represents a truer analogy than did the romantic goddesses and pagan myths of the earlier poetry.

The poetry of John Donne, Andrew Marvell, George Herbert, Richard Crashaw, and Henry Vaughan has exercised a tremendous influence upon modern poetry. These poets are much more modern in form and in thought than either the poets of the Renaissance or the Romantic or Victorian poets. Hopkins, T. S. Eliot, and W. H. Auden have written in their tradition. T. S. Eliot has written of Donne, the greatest of the Metaphysical group: "At any time Donne ought to be recognized as one of the few great reformers and preservers of the English tongue."

John Donne

Repentance

JOHN DONNE

Modern poets like T. S. Eliot and W. H. Auden have reawakened interest in the poems of John Donne. Long considered a poet of mere fantastic "metaphysical conceits,"[1] *in recent years he has been discovered as a poet not so much of the external world as of intensely vivid mental experiences. Eliot wrote in his* SELECTED ESSAYS *that "a thought to Donne was an experience." His figures of speech were drawn more from his own learning than from sensuous experience. He had an ear for rugged rhythm which aptly expressed his mode of thought—highly intellectualized, yet suffused with emotion. His sonnet, "Repentance," is taken from his "Divine Poems," written during his years as an Anglican minister.*

At the round earth's imagined corners, blow
Your trumpets, Angels, and arise, arise
From death, you numberless infinities
Of souls, and to your scattered bodies go,
All whom the flood did, and fire shall o'erthrow,
All whom war, dearth, age, agues, tyrannies,
Despair, law, chance, hath slain, and you whose eyes
Shall behold God and never taste death's woe.

But let them sleep, Lord, and me mourn a space,
For if above all these my sins abound,
'Tis late to ask abundance of Thy grace
When we are there; here on this lowly ground,
Teach me how to repent; for that's as good
As if Thou hadst seal'd my pardon with Thy blood.

FOR APPRECIATION

1. Why does the poet say the "round earth's imagined corners"? Is this an example of Johnson's definition of "metaphysical"? Explain.

2. The sonnet paints a picture of the Resurrection of the Dead in the octave and asks, in the sestet, for a longer span of life in which to repent. Is the personal application in the sestet effective?

3. What figure of speech is "numberless infinities"?

4. Explain the meaning of line 8. Is this correct theology?

[1]The word "metaphysical" was first used by William Drummond, a seventeenth-century Scottish poet, to describe Donne's poetry. Dr. Johnson describes such poetry as "a combination of dissimilar images, the discovery of resemblances in things apparently unlike." Johnson said that to write on the plan of the metaphysical poets, "it was necessary to read and think."

Batter My Heart

JOHN DONNE

The theme of this intense, at times violent, expression of the perpetual conflict between fallen human nature and the love of God is found throughout the Epistles of St. Paul, the writings of St. Augustine, and the spiritual autobiographies of the saints. As one reads this sonnet, it is impossible not to experience a sense of agonizing spiritual terror as we listen to the poet call from the depths of his captivity and ask God to break him completely. Here we have the refrain of the later poet Francis Thompson: "My harness piece by piece Thou hast hewn from me. And smitten me to my knee; I am defenseless utterly."

Batter my heart, three-personed God; for you
As yet but knock, breathe, shine, and seek to mend.
That I may rise and stand, o'erthrow me and bend
Your force to break, blow, burn, and make me new.
I, like an usurped town, to another due,
Labor to admit you, but, oh, to no end;
Reason, your viceroy in me, me should defend,
But is captived and proves weak or untrue.

Yet dearly I love you and would be loved fain,
But am betrothed unto your enemy;
Divorce me, untie or break that knot again,
Take me to you, imprison me, for I,
Except you enthrall me, never shall be free,
Nor ever chaste, except you ravish me.

FOR APPRECIATION

1. Note the harsh, almost terrible, thought and diction of the poem, beginning with the opening word *batter.* Discuss the effectiveness of this diction. Contrast and discuss the effectiveness of the diction used in line 2 with that used in line 4.

2. Explain in detail the two metaphors employed in the poem. What is the complete spiritual significance of the phrase *usurped town?* In the light of the thought content of this poem, discuss the Scripture phrase: "The Kingdom of heaven is taken by violence and only the violent bear it away."

3. Note the use of marriage and love terminology. Is this an element of metaphysical poetry? Explain.

4. Explain the paradoxes in the last two lines. Here again we have an example of the metaphysical poet "discovering similarities in differences."

5. Select several other spiritual paradoxes from the Scriptures which express the same thought as that contained in lines 13 and 14.

(FROM) *On The Glorious Assumption of Our Blessed Lady*

RICHARD CRASHAW

Although the dogma of Our Lady's Assumption was not defined until 1950, it has been the subject of art and literature from earliest times. In the opening lines of Crashaw's beautiful tribute to the Blessed Mother, the poet places on the lips of the Holy Spirit a paraphrase of the words of the CANTICLE OF CANTICLES: *"Arise, make haste, my love, my dove, my beautiful one, and come. For winter is now past, the rain is over and gone."*

Hark! she is call'd, the parting hour is come;
Take thy farewell, poor World, Heaven must go home.
A piece of heavenly earth, purer and brighter
Than the chaste stars whose choice lamps come to light her,
While through the crystal orbs clearer than they
She climbs, and makes a far more Milky Way.
She's call'd! Hark, how the dear immortal Dove
Sighs to his silver mate: "Rise up, my love!
Rise up, my fair, my spotless one!
The Winter's past, the rain is gone:
The Spring is come, the flowers appear,
No sweets, but thou, are wanting here.
Come away, my love!
Come away, my dove!
Cast off delay;
The court of Heaven is come
To wait upon thee home;
Come, come away!"

FOR APPRECIATION

1. What is the dominant tone of the poem? Select the details which heighten this tone.

2. Explain the metaphor, the Scriptural allusion, and the Catholic theology implied in the phrase *immortal Dove sighs to his silver mate.* (See lines 7 and 8.)

3. Explain how the varying meter of the poem heightens the effect of the movement and conveys the idea of reluctance, swift ascension, joyful anticipation. For example, compare the meter and the thought expressed in line 2 with the meter and the thought in lines 4, 5, 6.

(FROM) *The Flaming Heart*

RICHARD CRASHAW

Saint Teresa (or Theresa) of Avila, who lived in Spain from 1515-1582, was one of the most remarkable saints of the Church. She was what is known as a mystic; that is, she possessed a rare knowledge of God, of future things, of heavenly joys, and particularly of God's tremendous love for man in all His works. This knowledge was given her by direct visitation of God, and the story of these favors she wrote in a book of personal memoirs. Through this book the young English scholar, Richard Crashaw, came to know Saint Teresa, and by her guidance was brought, first into the Catholic Church, and then to the altar of God as a priest. Father Crashaw wrote a poem in honor of the saint from which the following lines are taken:

O thou undaunted daughter of desires!
By all thy dower lights and fires;
By all the eagle in thee, all the dove;
By all thy lives and deaths of love;
By thy large draughts of intellectual day,
And by thy thirsts of love more large than they;
By all thy brim-fill'd bowls of fierce desire,
By thy last morning's draught of liquid fire;
By the full kingdom of that final kiss
That seized thy parting soul, and seal'd thee His;
By all the Heav'n thou hast in Him
(Fair sister of the seraphim!):
By all of Him we have in thee;
Leave nothing of myself in me.
Let me so read thy life, that I
Unto all life of mine may die!

FOR APPRECIATION

1. If you were asked to write a brief outline of St. Teresa's character, what qualities, tightly packed into this poem, would you attribute to her?

2. Explain the figure and the meaning of lines 3, 8, 11. Is the imitation of the saints contained in line 15? Explain. Discuss the deep spiritual truth contained in lines 15-16.

3. If you wish to know more of one of the greatest of women saints, read *Teresa of Avila* by Thomas Walsh or *Teresa of Avila* by Kate O'Brien. Both authors have done an excellent piece of work.

The Pulley

GEORGE HERBERT

The title of the poem is a symbol of the restlessness which can draw man up to God. The key to the meaning of the poem is in the word "rest." As you read the poem, note the apparent conflict between "rest" and "restlessness," "dispersed" and "contract," "pulley" and "rest," "weariness" and "toss."

When God at first made man,
Having a glasse of blessings standing by,
"Let us," said He, "poure on him all we can;
Let the world's riches, which dispersèd lie,
Contract into a span."

So strength first made a way;
Then beautie flow'd, then wisdome, honour, pleasure;
When almost all was out, God made a stay,
Perceiving that, alone of all His treasure,
Rest in the bottome lay.

10. REST—Note the play on this word in lines 14 and 16.

"For if I should," said He,
"Bestow this jewell also on My creature,
He would adore My gifts in stead of Me,
And rest in Nature, not the God of Nature:
So both should losers be.

"Yet let him keep the rest,
But keep them with repining restlessnesse;
Let him be rich and wearie, that at least,
If goodnesse leade him not, yet wearinesse
May tosse him to My breast."

FOR APPRECIATION

1. Explain the logic of stanza three. Would you say the poem is merely a clever and amusing one, or does it contain a deep spiritual thought? Discuss.

2. Compare this poem in thought and structure with Herbert's "Collar."

RELATED READING

Read Henry Vaughan's "The World" and Andrew Marvell's "Dialogue Between Soul and Body."

PROJECTS

Compare and contrast two or more of the Cavalier poets with two or more of the Metaphysical poets. In a written or oral report, discuss their attitude toward life, love, and religion, as well as their craftsmanship. Which group is more realistic?

Hold a discussion on the subject of "The Elizabethan versus the Metaphysical Poets." State your own preferences and give reasons for your choice. Do you find metaphysical poetry difficult?

PURITAN PROSE AND POETRY

The two outstanding literary figures of the seventeenth century who professed Puritanism in religion and politics were John Milton and John Bunyan.

John Milton, the greatest English poet next to Shakespeare, was born in London in 1608. His father was a Puritan who loved books and music and passed this love on to young John. He received his early education from private tutors and later attended St. Paul's School and Cambridge University.

Young Milton was an avid scholar who spent long hours with the Greek and Roman classics and in the study of several foreign languages. He deliberately chose literature for his vocation and was convinced that he had been called to be a great poet. For several years, he lived in retirement with his father at Horton, near London, where he studied mathematics, music,

JOHN MILTON

history, and the classics. To this early period belong "L'Allegro," "Il Penseroso," "Hymn on the Morning of Christ's Nativity," and "Lycidas." These poems have little or nothing of the Puritan spirit; they breathe a deep love of the beauties of the classics and a deep love of nature.

After leaving retirement at Horton, Milton traveled in Europe. Upon his return, he lived in London, where he took up tutoring and devoted himself to his studies.

During the reign of Cromwell, Milton became the warmest supporter of that dictator and served as Secretary to the Commonwealth. It was during this period that he engaged in controversial writing. In his *Areopagitica*, he opposed censorship of the press, although he denied freedom of press to Catholics. Because of his unhappy first marriage, he wrote a pamphlet advocating divorce.

After ten years of married life, Milton's first wife died. He married a second and a third time. His second wife died after fifteen months of married life.

With the Restoration of the Stuarts in 1660, Milton went into hiding. Although he had advocated regicide, or the killing of the Stuart kings, he was pardoned by Charles II. At forty-five, Milton lost his sight because of the severe eyestrain involved in his work as Secretary of the Commonwealth. But with his youth and politics behind him, he entered upon his most productive literary period—the writing and completion of the great epics *Paradise Lost* and *Paradise Regained,* and his last long poem, *Samson Agonistes.*

John Bunyan

The most astonishingly successful prose piece of the period was *Pilgrim's Progress* by John Bunyan, a fervent evangelist of humble background and scant learning. Written in prison, where Bunyan had been thrown for refusing to submit to Anglicanism under Charles II, *Pilgrim's Progress* presents allegorically the life of a Christian. Containing and continuing the medieval theme of the religious allegory employed by the sermon writers of the Middle Ages and by the authors of the morality plays, *Pilgrim's Progress* is original only in this sense: it gives in a simple, dignified, forceful, dramatic, and concrete manner a Christian's personal religious experience along the stages of life "which lead a man marked out for faith, from the conviction of sin, through despair, temptations, to final peace and blessedness." It may well be called the Protestant lay Bible stripped of all that is not—to a Puritan conscience—the direct teaching of salvation. Perhaps no book in the English language, except the Bible, has been read more widely.

Izaak Walton

One other prose writer of the period deserves special mention—Izaak Walton (1593-1683), whose ninety years spanned the arc of the century. The book that has kept his name alive is his little treatise on fishermen and fishing—*The Compleat Angler.* Modern fishermen still turn its pages with an appreciative smile. It tells no "fish stories." The reader rambles along an English country road, meets a shepherd, hears a milkmaid singing, casts a fly, catches a trout or two, and speculates upon the world and all the pleasant things in it. To day-dreaming anglers, the book seems to have captured the charm of the sport that gives man a chance to "loaf and invite his soul." Walton was not a Puritan. He took no militant part in the struggles of his day. His books have the serenity and sweetness that marked the best prose of his puritanic age.

Many volumes of religious prose found an appreciative audience in the New World as well as the Old during the seventeenth century. Perhaps the most popular of these religious books were Browne's *Religion of a Physician* and Jeremy Taylor's *Holy Living and Holy Dying.*

On His Blindness

JOHN MILTON

From the days of his youth, Milton had felt "called" to write a great religious poem. God had given him a talent which should be devoted to His service. In the mind of the poet, there grew the plan of an epic retelling the story of the fall of man. It would explain the existence of sin in the world and "justify the ways of God to man." But at forty-five, Milton found himself blind, his PARADISE LOST *unwritten—apparently never to be written. After a period of profound dejection, he composed this meditation "On His Blindness."*

When I consider how my light is spent,
Ere half my days in this dark world and wide,
And that one talent which is death to hide
Lodged with me useless, though my soul more bent
To serve therewith my Maker, and present
My true account, lest He returning chide—
"Doth God exact day-labor, light denied?"
I fondly ask.—But Patience, to prevent
That murmur, soon replies, "God doth not need
Either man's work, or His own gifts; who best
Bear His mild yoke, they serve Him best. His state
Is kingly; thousands at His bidding speed
And post o'er land and ocean without rest;
They also serve who only stand and wait."

1. LIGHT—His sight. SPENT—Used up.
3. TALENT—His power to write. Cf. the Parable of the Talents in Matthew 25.
4. BENT—Willing or desirous.
8. FONDLY—Foolishly.

FOR APPRECIATION

1. Milton utters his complaint in the first seven and one-half lines. In a few simple words, give the complete answer of "Patience."

2. Is the doctrine of Divine Providence expressed in the sestet? Explain.

3. Is this strictly an Italian sonnet? Explain. Give the rhyme scheme of the sonnet.

4. Discuss the connection between the words used in the sonnet and the movement of the poem. Does the poet use light, swiftly moving words, or does he use words which are largely monosyllabic, with long vowels? Is the movement of the poem solemn and dignified? Explain.

5. Are both the active and the contemplative life expressed in lines 12, 13, 14? Discuss.

6. Line 14 is famous in literature and rich in suggestion. Do you think the Communist or the modern pagan would agree with the thought of that line? What is the attitude of the non-Christian toward pain and suffering? The Christian attitude? Do shut-ins, incurables, and invalids serve God, country, and fellow man? Discuss in detail.

7. Look up the origin of *post.* What do you mean by *posthaste?*

(FROM) *Paradise Lost*

JOHN MILTON

Throughout Milton's mature years, the great work of his life, his epic, was his first concern. It filled his thoughts for more than twenty years, from its first conception as a possible drama to its completion and perfection as a narrative of epic proportions. He completed his work while the Plague was raging in 1665. Shortly after the outbreak of the Great Fire of 1666, he sent his manuscript to the printer. The payment he received for his masterpiece was a pittance of about ten pounds.

The construction of PARADISE LOST *is upon a vast scale and the result is a unified whole in which every part is logically related to every other part. The action of the twelve books of* PARADISE LOST, *with its setting in hell and in the Garden of Paradise, begins with the fall of Satan and ends with the banishment of Adam and Eve from Paradise. Equally heroic in stature are the characters of Adam and Eve—but Satan is Milton's masterpiece of character portrayal. Only the imagination of a great genius could conceive and execute such a titanic character.*

In some ways, Satan seems to have run away with Milton. Perhaps in Satan's colossal spirit of defiance we see something of the poet's own rebellious nature. Satan is depicted with such grandeur that he is often looked upon as the hero of the epic. In this respect, he is a typical Renaissance character whose "unconquerable will" rebelled against authority and made the creature the master of his own destiny.

PARADISE LOST *is more than "the dream of a Puritan fallen asleep over the first pages of the Bible." Milton was great despite his Puritanism. The glaring weakness of his epic is to be found in its Calvinistic theology with its emphasis upon predestination and its concept of God as drawn from the Old Testament exclusively. The greatness lies in the tremendous sweep of imaginative power, the stately and sonorous rhythms, the grandeur of epic architecture which Milton learned from Virgil and Dante. Many of his lines expressed in "the organ-music of his blank verse" are the essence of vast, rich poetry. Like Shakespeare, he has built word-combinations of universal and immortal appeal.*

There are pages in Milton which cannot be assimilated without the help of an encyclopedia. But in spite of difficult allusions, long sentences, hard words, and extended metaphors, there is that in Milton's poetry which repays the study spent in reading it.

The following selection is taken from Book I of PARADISE LOST.

Of Man's first disobedience, and the fruit
Of that forbidden tree, whose mortal taste
Brought death into the world, and all our woe,
With loss of Eden, till one greater Man
Restore us, and regain the blissful seat,
Sing, heavenly Muse, that on the secret top
Of Oreb, or of Sinai, didst inspire
That shepherd who first taught the chosen seed
In the beginning how the heavens and earth
Rose out of chaos. Or, if Sion hill
Delight thee more, and Siloa's brook that flowed
Fast by the oracle of God, I thence
Invoke thy aid to my adventurous song,
That with no middle flight intends to soar
Above the Aonian mount, while it pursues
Things unattempted yet in prose or rime.
And chiefly thou, O Spirit, that dost prefer
Before all temples the upright heart and pure,
Instruct me, for thou know'st. Thou from the first
Wast present, and with mighty wings outspread,
Dove-like sat'st brooding on the vast abyss,

6. HEAVENLY MUSE—Here not the Greek goddess of song, but the divine inspiration of Moses and the prophets.

7. OREB, SINAI—Twin peaks of mountain where Moses kept his flocks of sheep.

8. CHOSEN SEED—The Jewish people chosen by God in the Old Dispensation to be the nation of the Redeemer.

10. SION HILL—Zion, the city of Jerusalem; here King David sang the famous psalms.

12. ORACLE OF GOD—The Temple in Jerusalem.

15. AONIAN MOUNT—Mount Helicon—represents Greek poetry. Milton means to write on a loftier theme.

17. SPIRIT—Here the Holy Spirit.

And mad'st it pregnant. What in me is dark
Illumine, what is low raise and support;
That to the height of this great argument
I may assert Eternal Providence,
And justify the ways of God to men.

Say first—for heaven hides nothing from thy view,
Nor the deep tract of hell—say first what cause
Moved our grand parents in that happy state
Favored of heaven so highly, to fall off
From their Creator, and transgress his will
For one restraint, lords of the world besides.
Who first seduced them to that foul revolt?
The infernal serpent; he it was whose guile,
Stirred up with envy and revenge, deceived
The mother of mankind, what time his pride
Had cast him out from heaven, with all his host
Of rebel angels, by whose aid, aspiring
To set himself in glory above his peers,
He trusted to have equaled the Most High,
If he opposed; and with ambitious aim
Against the throne and monarchy of God
Raised impious war in heaven, and battle proud,
With vain attempt. Him the Almighty Power
Hurled headlong flaming from the ethereal sky,
With hideous ruin and combustion, down
To bottomless perdition; there to dwell
In adamantine chains and penal fire,
Who durst defy the Omnipotent to arms.

Nine times the space that measures day and night
To mortal men, he with his horrid crew
Lay vanquished, rolling in the fiery gulf,
Confounded, though immortal. But his doom
Reserved him to more wrath; for now the thought
Both of lost happiness and lasting pain
Torments him; round he throws his baleful eyes,
That witnessed huge affliction and dismay,
Mixed with obdurate pride and steadfast hate.
At once, as far as angels ken, he views
The dismal situation waste and wild.
A dungeon horrible on all sides round
As one great furnace flamed; yet from those flames

36. WHAT TIME—When.
59. KEN—Are able to see.

No light; but rather darkness visible
Served only to discover sights of woe,
Regions of sorrow, doleful shades, where peace
And rest can never dwell, hope never comes
That comes to all; but torture without end
Still surges, and a fiery deluge, fed
With ever-burning sulphur unconsumed.
Such place Eternal Justice had prepared
For those rebellious; here their prison ordained
In utter darkness, and their portion set,
As far removed from God and light of heaven
As from the center thrice to the utmost pole.
Oh, how unlike the place from whence they fell!
There the companions of his fall, o'erwhelmed
With floods and whirlwinds of tempestuous fire,
He soon discerns; and weltering by his side,
One next himself in power, and next in crime,
Long after known in Palestine, and named
Beëlzebub. To whom the arch-enemy,
And thence in heaven called Satan, with bold words

74. THE CENTER . . . UTMOST POLE—From the center of the earth to the most distant point in the heavens. Milton here uses for poetic purpose the old theory that the earth was the center of the universe.

Breaking the horrid silence, thus began:
"If thou beëst he—but oh, how fallen! how changed
From him who in the happy realms of light,
Clothed with transcendent brightness, didst outshine
Myriads, though bright!—if he whom mutual league,
United thoughts and counsels, equal hope
And hazard in the glorious enterprise,
Joined with me once, now misery hath joined
In equal ruin—into what pit thou seëst
From what height fallen. So much the stronger proved
He with his thunder; and till then who knew
The force of those dire arms? Yet not for those,
Nor what the potent Victor in his rage
Can else inflict, do I repent, or change,
Though changed in outward luster, that fixed mind,
And high disdain from sense of injured merit,
That with the Mightiest raised me to contend,
And to the fierce contention brought along
Innumerable force of spirits armed
That durst dislike his reign, and me preferring,
His utmost power with adverse power opposed
In dubious battle on the plains of heaven
And shook his throne. What though the field be lost?
All is not lost—the unconquerable will,
And study of revenge, immortal hate,
And courage never to submit or yield;
And what is else not to be overcome;
That glory never shall his wrath or might
Extort from me. To bow and sue for grace
With suppliant knee, and deify his power
Who, from the terror of this arm, so late
Doubted his empire—that were low indeed,
That were an ignominy and shame beneath
This downfall; since by fate the strength of gods
And this empyreal substance cannot fail;
Since, through experience of this great event
In arms not worse, in foresight much advanced,
We may with more successful hope resolve
To wage by force or guile eternal war,
Irreconcilable to our grand Foe,
Who now triumphs, and in the excess of joy
Sole reigning holds the tyranny of heaven."

So spake the apostate angel, though in pain,
Vaunting aloud, but racked with deep despair;

93. HE—God, the Victor.

And thus him answered soon his bold compeer:
"O Prince! O Chief of many thronèd powers
That led the embattled seraphim to war
Under thy conduct, and, in dreadful deeds
Fearless, endangered heaven's perpetual King,
And put to proof his high supremacy,
Whether upheld by strength, or chance, or fate!
Too well I see and rue the dire event
That with sad overthrow and foul defeat
Hath lost us heaven, and all this mighty host
In horrible destruction laid thus low,
As far as gods and heavenly essences
Can perish; for the mind and spirit remains
Invincible, and vigor soon returns,
Though all our glory extinct, and happy state
Here swallowed up in endless misery.
But what if he our Conqueror—whom I now
Of force believe almighty, since no less
Than such could have o'erpowered such force as ours—
Have left us this our spirit and strength entire,
Strongly to suffer and support our pains,
That we may so suffice his vengeful ire;
Or do him mightier service, as his thralls
By right of war, whate'er his business be,
Here in the heart of hell to work in fire,
Or do his errands in the gloomy deep?
What can it then avail, though yet we feel
Strength undiminished, or eternal being
To undergo eternal punishment?"

Whereto with speedy words the archfiend replied:
"Fallen Cherub, to be weak is miserable,
Doing or suffering; but of this be sure—
To do aught good never will be our task,
But ever to do ill our sole delight,
As being the contrary to his high will
Whom we resist. If then his providence
Out of our evil seek to bring forth good,
Our labor must be to pervert that end,
And out of good still to find means of evil;
Which ofttimes may succeed so as perhaps
Shall grieve him, if I fail not, and disturb
His inmost counsels from their destined aim.
But see! the angry Victor hath recalled
His ministers of vengeance and pursuit
Back to the gates of heaven; the sulphurous hail,

Shot after us in storm, o'erblown hath laid
The fiery surge that from the precipice
Of heaven received us falling; and the thunder,
Winged with red lightning and impetuous rage,
Perhaps hath spent his shafts, and ceases now
To bellow through the vast and boundless Deep.
Let us not slip the occasion, whether scorn
Or satiate fury yield it from our Foe.
Seest thou yon dreary plain, forlorn and wild,
The seat of desolation, void of light,
Save what the glimmering of these livid flames
Casts pale and dreadful? Thither let us tend
From off the tossing of these fiery waves;
There rest, if any rest can harbor there;
And, reassembling our afflicted powers
Consult how we may henceforth most offend
Our Enemy, our own loss how repair,
How overcome this dire calamity,
What re-inforcement we may gain from hope;
If not, what resolution from despair."

172. LAID—Calmed.

FOR APPRECIATION

LINES 1-26—THE INVOCATION:

1. In the first five lines, Milton states his theme. Recast the thought in your own words. What is the meaning of "mortal taste," "blissful seat"? Which line is most appealing to you? Does it have sweep and strength?

2. The call for guidance in lines 6-26 is in the classical manner, patterned after the invocations to the Muse in the *Iliad* and the *Aeneid.* To what two sources of inspiration does Milton appeal? Can you select any details which manifest Milton's knowledge of and affection for the Bible?

3. From the invocation, what do you judge the spirit and purpose of this epic to be? Can you identify the account of creation referred to in lines 8-10? Select certain phrases which manifest Milton's seriousness and his ambition to write great poetry. List five lines that you consider worthy of memory because of their happy expression of a worthy thought.

LINES 27-49—SUMMARY OF POEM:

1. What is the subject of the opening verb "say"? Discuss the full meaning of the phrase "lords of the world besides." What is Satan's sin expressed in line 39? Scan line 49; what force is added by the irregularity at the beginning of the line?

2. Why is it important for the author to offer changes from the iambic pentameter? Give a few examples where Milton's thought-phrases break up the over-all rhythm. Discuss what effect this has on the movement of the poem.

LINES 50-191—SCENE IN HELL:

1. Notice the manner in which Milton tells how long the devils have lain vanquished; does this add to the effect? What does Milton gain, in lines 57-58, by allowing us to view hell through Satan's "baleful eyes"? Lines 60-71 give a description of hell; list the details that form

the picture. What does the utter simplicity of line 75 achieve? Is it especially powerful?

2. The opening of Satan's first speech might be compared to the soliloquies in *Macbeth.* Do lines 84-92 make a good sentence? Why or why not? Is the meaning clear? Discuss. How does Satan's mood change after line 92? What is the meaning of "What though the field be lost? All is not lost"? Is the remainder of his speech convincing? Do you think Satan is afraid?

3. What effect does Satan's speech have on Beëlzebub as evidenced in his reply? Is he as strong a character as Satan? What is the spirit of lines 141-42? Is there any trace of repentance in the remainder of his speech? Cite specific lines to prove your point.

4. Do you consider the opening lines of Satan's second speech great poetry? Discuss "to be weak is miserable, doing or suffering." Lines 164-68 give Satan's plan of renewed warfare; they have been applied to an individual case in *The Screwtape Letters* by C. S. Lewis. State this planned campaign simply in your own words.

5. Read aloud the description of the thunder in lines 174-77. How does the last line justify Milton's epithet of organ music? What is the spirit of the concluding lines? Select at least ten outstanding lines in this final section, and read them to the class.

SIGNIFICANT EXPRESSIONS

Study these lines for *(a)* tone color, *(b)* diction, *(c)* thought:

Line 45: "Hurled headlong flaming from the ethereal sky."

Line 126: "Vaunting aloud, but racked with deep despair."

Lines 174-77: ". . . and the thunder
Winged with red lightning and impetuous rage,
Perhaps hath spent his shafts, and ceases now
To bellow through the vast and boundless Deep."

Lines 180-84: ". . . dreary plain, forlorn and wild . . . void of light,
Save what the glimmering of these livid flames
Casts pale and dreadful."

WORD STUDY

Be sure you know the meaning of the following words: *baleful, obdurate, weltering, transcendent, ignominy, empyreal, apostate, compeer, rue, satiate, livid, dire.*

RELATED READING

Your teacher will give you extra credit for reading at least the rest of Book I and all of Book II of this great epic.

THE RESTORATION (1660-1688)

England quickly tired of Cromwell and the Puritan regime. It was like having Ash Wednesday all year long. Lord Macaulay said that the Puritans objected to bear-baiting not because of the pain it caused the animals but because of the pleasure it gave the people. Just to see a play was made a criminal offense. The Londoners had had enough; they sighed for "the good old days," and dreamed romantically of "bonnie Prince Charlie," who had escaped to France.

The son of the dead monarch was living gaily in Paris, surrounded by the Cavaliers who had risked wealth and position, even their lives, for him and his father. In 1660, two years after the death of Cromwell, the time seemed right for him to return to England. The people were wild with joy and crowned him Charles II. Witty, handsome, easy-going, he surrounded himself with a brilliant court. He was prepared to make whatever concessions were necessary for him to keep the throne. His Catholic wife and his own secret Catholicism caused him no end of trouble and embarrassment, for England by this time had become solidly Protestant.

Cromwell Examines the body of Charles I

During the early years of his reign, two calamities struck London—the Plague of 1665, which raged up and down the narrow streets, and the Fire of 1666, which wiped out the heart of the city. Englishmen had to set about rebuilding London, and they were fortunate enough to have Sir Christopher Wren to do the architectural designing. The result may be seen in such magnificent structures as St. Paul's Cathedral and other religious and public buildings in London.

RESTORATION LITERATURE

To mark off and hold to sharp boundaries within short periods of literature is not possible nor advisable. John Dryden, for example, who was to become literary dictator of the Restoration period, began his writing while the Puritans were in control in England. John Milton and John Bunyan produced their greatest works after the Restoration. These discussions of seventeenth and eighteenth century literature, therefore, are based on feelings and attitudes rather than on historical dates. Because Milton and Bunyan reflected the Puritan mind, we call them writers of the Puritan Age. Because Dryden's mature sympathies were with the Restoration, and because his works show the trends of the later period, we think of him as a Restoration writer.

Indeed the works of Dryden reflect all the various phases of the Restoration period. His change from Puritanism to Anglicanism to Catholicism, and his satires describing and defending these changes reflect the conflicting currents of political and religious thought.

The French influence which had come to England with King Charles and his court set a new fashion in literature. It was a frivolous, sophisticated society, and it admired point and wit in letters. The closed couplet was perfectly suited to expressing flashes of irony and keen-edged comment. Dryden took up the form and used it so cleverly that for almost a hundred years it was the ruling verse form in England. His satires in verse are prophetic of the next period in which satire reigns supreme, and he also set the fashion for writing long allegories in verse. These allegories defended his views in politics and religion, ridiculed his opponents at court or his rivals in letters, and delighted or infuriated the social lights of London. Lesser poets adopted the style, and the stage and ballroom moved to the measure of iambic pentameter rhymes.

Dryden was also the most gifted of the Restoration playwrights; he was the first writer to do whole plays in closed couplets. In his position of playwright to the king, he wrote three plays a year for twenty years. His best play was a good comedy written in excellent blank verse—*All for Love.* But even Dryden, with his classical training, bowed to the taste of his audience and wrote scores of the trivial, cheaply immoral plays which were popular at the time.

Modern critics rate John Dryden's prose more important than his verse. One of them even goes so far as to say that Dryden is the "supreme stylist in English prose," possessing "strength, speed, music, continuity, and range." Like most of the interesting prose of the period, his too was written incidentally. In Dryden's case, we find it in the prefaces he wrote

JOHN DRYDEN

SAMUEL PEPYS

for collections of the works of earlier poets like Chaucer and Spenser. These prefaces are really critical essays in which Dryden gives his estimates of the writers and their works, besides expressing his own theories about art and literature. These essays display his strong expressive prose style at its best.

Of greater general interest to the modern reader are the diaries of two men who made no pretense of being writers. One, Samuel Pepys, was an energetic businessman. For his own satisfaction, he kept a diary of the years from 1660-1669; but his pages are so filled with details of events large and small that the reader who samples them feels much at home in seventeenth-century England. It is all there—what people ate and drank, how they dressed, how the little old Queen and the Princesses looked, how business was transacted—everything very frankly and engagingly told.

John Evelyn wrote his diary more carefully and covered a much longer period of time—from 1640-1706. His record lacks the human-interest elements of Pepys' diary, yet makes extremely good reading. Evelyn tried to set down fairly and accurately the important events of the time. Like Pepys, he was a Royalist who rejoiced in the Restoration of the Stuarts. But he did not close his eyes to the shortcomings of his monarchs. In all matters, he tries to weigh carefully both faults and virtues. Both Pepys' and Evelyn's diaries carry accounts of the coronation of Charles II, of the Plague, and of the Great Fire. Together, the works furnish a panoramic picture of England during the Restoration period.

THE AGE OF POPE (1689-1740)

On the death of Charles II in 1685, his brother, James II, took the throne. But James was not happy. Parliament continued to use the king's revenue as a sort of leash to keep His Majesty in check. Should he fail to play along with its leaders, they would simply curtail his allowance as with a naughty schoolboy. To make a delicate situation worse, James was a staunch Catholic and determined to re-establish the Faith in England even if it cost him the crown. And it did. After three years of rule, he had to seek refuge in France.

At the invitation of Parliament, Mary and William of Orange came from the Netherlands to become joint sovereigns of England. This was a triumph for Parliament. It made William sign a Declaration of Rights before he could be proclaimed king. The declaration was incorporated in a Bill of Rights passed by Parliament in 1689. Provisions of the Bill forbade the levying of taxes without the consent of Parliament. This meant that the ministers who constituted the Cabinet would henceforth be responsible, not to the king, but to Parliament. Henceforth, no minister and no cabinet could hold office if Parliament refused its support. It was the document which transformed England into a democratic monarchy.

The results of this change of government had a deep and lasting effect on the literature of the age. Two political parties sprang up, the Whigs and the Tories. In general they represent practically the same differences that have been pointed out between the Cavaliers and the Puritans. The Whigs were usually the dissenters from the Anglican church, the rising merchant citizenry, and the city middle class led by some few aristocrats. The Tories were generally the landowners, the Anglican clergy, and the personal adherents of both. In the next two centuries, the political history of England is the story of the ups and downs of these two parties, and the history of English literature is strongly colored by the conflict between them.

MERCHANTS VS. LANDOWNERS

As a result of several victorious wars during this period, England acquired possessions in India, on the Mediterranean, and in America, which laid the foundation for the British Empire. These new possessions increased trade and enriched the merchant class tremendously, but the heavy war taxes impoverished the lower classes. The smuggling of tea, tobacco, and silk became a profitable enterprise. Buccaneering flourished about the West Indies, and Captain Kidd badgered the Spanish Main. Inside England, agriculture made no advance. Science and education seemed at a standstill. There was cold indifference toward religion. And though everyone talked about prosperity, there was great inequality in the distribution of wealth, and there were sharp distinctions in social classes. The age had a heavy, unventilated atmosphere.

Only the wealthy managed to relish life. The city had become the important center of living. Society flourished. Refinement and the ability to talk in innuendoes counted rather than virtue. Coffee was the favorite drink, and the Coffee Houses became gathering places for writers, politicians, and dandies. Here men could learn the news, transact business, talk politics or art, or gossip. Different groups had their favorite clubs. The literary men gathered at Will's Coffee House where, a generation earlier, John Dryden had ruled.

Men and women donned elaborate dress to match their manners. Women wore extravagant, towering headdresses and billowing brocaded gowns. Men, too, wore powdered wigs, artificial moles, cocked hats, and satin waistcoats. Hogarth satirized the absurd styles and manners of the day in his paintings, while Handel caught the classic precision and formality in his music. As usual, the political and social background of the age determined the characteristics of its literature.

CLASSICISM AND NEO-CLASSICISM

During the years between the Restoration of Charles II and the death of Alexander Pope in 1744, there developed in England a group of writers who came to be known as the Neo-classic School. To understand the spirit of this movement and the literature of the period, one must first understand the meanings of classicism in its true sense.

For centuries, the best Greek and Latin writings were known as *classics,* and the Greek and Latin languages as the *classical languages.* Today the term *classic,* or *classics,* may be applied in three different ways: *(a)* it may designate any piece of art, ancient or modern which is considered a masterpiece—like Dickens' *David Copperfield* or Virgil's *Aeneid*; *(b)* it may designate any Greek or Roman work because it is written in a classic language; *(c)* it may describe all writings that show the qualities that were considered fundamental in the literature of Greece and Rome. It is in the last sense that we use the term *classicism* in distinction from *neo-classicism* and *romanticism.*

JOSEPH ADDISON

RICHARD STEELE

What are these qualities that mark real classicism? In general, they are balance and proportion, restraint, dignity, simplicity, and universality. Classic art tends to be objective and impersonal rather than subjective and personal. It expresses a restrained emotion. It is imaginative, but it does not go into flights of pure fancy. Rather, it uses the imagination to reveal the depth and significance of real experience.

In literature, classicism requires a suitable balance and proportion between expression or wording and the emotion to be expressed. Classic literature is far from lifeless; it does express emotion, but always emotion under control.

It was Aristotle in his famous *Poetics* who most clearly analyzed and formulated the principles of classic art. The Renaissance gave rise in Italy, France, and England to a restudy of the *Poetics* and to a restatement of classic principles. In Elizabethan times, the learned Ben Jonson had come under this influence, and we find him and other playwrights writing new dramas according to the old rules.

COPYING AND IMITATION

A century later, Dryden and Pope established the neo-classic style in England. This pseudo-classic movement grew out of a misinterpretation of Aristotle's, teachings, particularly in respect to imitation. To the school of Dryden and Pope, classicism meant imitating older models of literature and blindly following well-established rules of writing. To Aristotle, *imitation* did not mean copying. In the sense of the *Poetics,* to imitate meant to portray *universal* qualities by presenting *particular* objects, situations, and people. From the artistic portrayal of the joys, sorrows, and aspirations of one man, the reader can recognize

JONATHAN SWIFT

ALEXANDER POPE

in true classicism the joys, sorrows, and aspirations of all men. Through the selective portrayal of the emotion of pity in one particular person in one situation, there may arise the suggestion of the meaning of pity to all men in all times. This is what Aristotle means when he says that through the imitation (that is, *portrayal*) of nature, man expresses the quality of universal truth. To raise a work above the plane of mere photographic representation, to endow it with the power of expressing universal truth, is to express life in the authentically classic spirit.

Yet this is precisely what the pseudo- or neo-classicists failed to do. As we have said, they contented themselves with following rules and copying models. They appreciated the balance and proportion in the *form* of the classics, and these they copied to perfection. But they lacked emotional power and disregarded the importance of creative imagination. The chief doctrines of the neo-classic school may be expressed as follows:

1. Form was more significant than content; manner of expression more important than the truth expressed. It was better to follow tried rules than to attempt the expression of original genius.

2. Cleverness and wit should take the place of emotion, passion, or deep feeling. The poet should remain calm and critical. Display of personal feeling would offend good taste.

3. Poetry should not use commonplace words, but use a special dignified or ornamental vocabulary. Artificial elegance was to be admired.

4. The heroic couplet, with its precision and balance, should be the ideal form of poetic expression.

Although the writers of the Age of Pope are usually called the classic writers of English literature, it was really these neo-classic principles that they followed; and the term "The Classic Age" for the eighteenth century is an established misnomer.

In spite of all their faults, however, we can say that the one contribution of the neo-classic writers was the emphasis they placed on order and care in composition.

NEO-CLASSIC POETRY

In an era of "reason" and "common sense," lyric poetry was impossible. The best medium in which to express the cold literary ideal of the neo-classicists was the rhymed couplet.

Alexander Pope became the virtual dictator in this school of poetry. He was a Catholic poet born in 1688, the year of the "glorious" revolution when Mary and William came to power in England. He had to educate himself because the laws of the land barred Catholics from the universities. He imbibed all the confused ideas of his age to such an extent that one would never guess his Catholicity by reading his many satirical poems. He loved satire, and it is said of him that he purposely estranged his friends in order to have more people to ridicule. He has the distinction of being the first English writer to support himself by his pen alone.

Pope used the heroic couplet like a two-edged sword in his poetic satires. Perhaps the best known of his works is "The Rape of the Lock," a mock epic in which he holds up to ridicule the petty quarrels of court society. His "Dunciad"—the saga of the dunces—is a scathing criticism of the other poets of the time. Pope wrote even letters and essays in verse. His "Essay on Man" and "Essay on Criticism" present in quotable couplets his views on man's place in the world and his views of literary criticism. Pope's most ambitious undertaking was to translate the *Iliad* and the *Odyssey* into rhymed iambic pentameter lines. The venture did nothing to increase Homer's prestige as a poet, but it made a fortune for Mr. Pope.

The emphasis of the neo-classicists was on the importance of man. Pope put it this way, "The proper study of mankind is man." But without the Christian idea of the worth and dignity of each individual, some writers of the period presented a sorry picture of the human race. In his "Essay on Man," Pope emphasizes the puniness and insignificance of the human individual, and Jonathan Swift, the great prose satirist, in his last works reveals a terrible hatred for "that creature man."

(FROM) *An Essay on Criticism*

ALEXANDER POPE

Pope's ESSAY ON CRITICISM *might well be called the commonplace book of eighteenth-century criticism. In his witty and pointed epigrams, Pope has expressed the current views of his day: follow "nature" (by which he means human conduct in the best cultivated society); model your writings on the classical authors; adhere closely to the standard rules; cultivate good taste and restraint.*

The subject matter of the poem seems to be better suited to prose than poetry, but Pope considered the function of verse to instruct the intellect rather than to arouse the emotions.

After reading the selection below, we will understand how Pope's terse, epigrammatic couplets have made him the most often quoted source in the language, with the exception of the Bible and Shakespeare.

FROM PART I

'Tis hard to say, if greater want of skill
Appear in writing or in judging ill;
But, of the two, less dangerous is th' offence
To tire our patience, than mislead our sense.

Some few in that, but numbers err in this,
Ten censure wrong for one who writes amiss;
A fool might once himself alone expose,
Now one in verse makes many more in prose.
'Tis with our judgments as our watches, none
Go just alike, yet each believes his own.
In poets as true genius is but rare,
True taste as seldom is the critic's share;
Both must alike from Heaven derive their light,
These born to judge, as well as those to write.
Let such teach others who themselves excel,
And censure freely who have written well.
Authors are partial to their wit, 'tis true,
But are not critics to their judgment too?

FROM PART II

True wit is nature to advantage dressed,
What oft was thought, but ne'er so well expressed:
Something, whose truth convinced at sight we find.
That gives us back the image of our mind.
As shades more sweetly recommend the light,
So modest plainness sets off sprightly wit.
For works may have more wit than does 'em good,
As bodies perish through excess of blood.
Others for language all their care express,
And value books, as women men, for dress;
Their praise is still—the style is excellent;
The sense they humbly take upon content.
Words are like leaves; where they most abound,
Much fruit of sense beneath is rarely found.
False eloquence, like the prismatic glass,
Its gaudy colors spreads on every place.
The face of nature we no more survey;
All glares alike, without distinction gay;
But true expression, like the unchanging sun,
Clears and improves whate'er it shines upon;
It gilds all objects, but it alters none.

5. SOME FEW IN THAT—Some few (err) in that.

8. NOW ONE IN VERSE, etc.—For one poor poet are many foolish critics.

11. IN POETS, etc.—True genius is rare among poets.

17. PARTIAL—Biased, in favor of.

17-18. AUTHORS ARE PARTIAL, etc.—The meaning is that authors have as much right to think their work is good as the critics have to think their criticisms are right.

1. WIT—Used in the meaning of writing.

9. LANGUAGE—Style.

12. CONTENT—Trust.

Expression is the dress of thought, and still
Appears more decent, as more suitable;
A vile conceit in pompous words expressed
Is like a clown in regal purple dressed;
For different styles with different subjects sort,
As several garbs with country, town and court.
Some by old words to fame have made pretense,
Ancients in phrase, mere moderns in their sense;
Such labored nothings, in so strange a style,
Amaze the unlearned, and make the learnèd smile.
Unlucky, as Fungoso in the play,
These sparks with awkward vanity display
What the fine gentleman wore yesterday;
And but so mimic ancients wits at best,
As apes our grandsires, in their doublets dressed.
In words, as fashions, the same rule will hold,
Alike fantastic, if too new, or old:
Be not the first by whom the new is tried,
Nor yet the last to lay the old aside.

. . . .

True ease in writing comes from art, not chance,
As those move easiest who have learned to dance.
'Tis not enough no harshness gives offense,
The sound must seem an echo to the sense.

23. DECENT—Attractive.
24. VILE CONCEIT—An unnatural expression.
32. FUNGOSO—A character in Ben Jonson's play, *Every Man Out of His Humour.*

FOR DISCUSSION

1. According to Pope, what qualities should a critic possess? Do you agree with him? Discuss.

2. Interpret lines 1-6 of Part II in the light of what you have learned of the spirit of neo-classicism.

3. Do lines 13-25 express a sound theory of writing and speaking? Explain your answer.

4. Are lines 28-36 a criticism of the very things Pope stands for? Discuss.

5. Memorize at least three couplets which you consider worth remembering.

RELATED READING

If you like Pope's polished and sophisticated verse, you will enjoy reading "The Rape of the Lock."

NEO-CLASSIC PROSE

At its best, neo-classic prose is clear, forceful, and direct—lighted sometimes by wit but only occasionally mellow with humor. At its worst, it is heavy, cumbersome, overloaded with long hard words and round-about expressions. It served as a vehicle for almost every possible kind of writing—satire, fantasy, argument, biography, letters, memoirs, essays, oratory, history, and fiction. Adequate mention cannot be made of all the kinds of writing turned out by the tireless scholars of the eighteenth century. And a disproportionately small number of works proved great enough to live. These we shall discuss briefly.

THE ESSAY

When the Frenchman, Montaigne, published the first two books of his *Essais* in 1580, a new kind of prose literature was born. *Essais* in French (*essays* in English) at that time meant *trials* or *attempts.* Montaigne had chosen the term as the title for his short prose pieces because they were attempts to present in no formal style his views on a variety of subjects.

In 1603 Florio translated Montaigne's essays into English, and immediately they became popular reading. Francis Bacon admired them greatly, and hastened to try out the new form. His essay, "Of Studies," which you have read, is an example of his success. To Bacon, an essay meant a first trial in the exposition of a subject, and so his works in the form seem like compact sentence outlines of thoughts that could be more fully developed. Later writers discovered many possibilities in the form.

Loosely, the essay may be defined as a piece of prose literature written to give a personal exposition of a subject. That is, in any essay the author is trying to explain his views or to express his thoughts and opinions. The viewpoint of the writer and the expression of his personality is of first importance. According to the author's special intention and method, essays are classified as (1) *formal,* and (2) *informal,* or *familiar.* In formal essays, like those written by Bacon, the personality of the writer is expressed indirectly. In the familiar essay, it is revealed more directly.

The primary purpose of the formal essay is to explain and instruct. Such an essay follows a unified plan in an orderly development of thought. It treats serious subjects in a serious and dignified manner. Formal essays may be *didactic* or *critical.* A *didactic* essay gives information on such matters as biography, history, science, politics, and philosophy. A *critical* essay presents a study and appraisal of some work in music or art or literature. We think of a formal essay as something to be read by a mature person or by an earnest student in search of enlightenment.

The informal or familiar essay may be compared in some respects to a lyric poem. Although it is written in prose, it is short; it presents an author's personal impressions; it draws the attention of the reader to the author's relation to his subject, rather than to the subject itself. The familiar essay is written for entertainment, primarily. But since one can never write much without expressing in some way his philosophy of life, even informal essays often serve a serious purpose. The subject matter may be deep or trivial, but the style is marked by originality of treatment, by geniality or humor, and by ease of manner. The informal essay allows great freedom in form. Whereas the formal essay may remind one of a structure in classical architecture, the familiar essay reminds one of a pleasant rambling dwelling. It is the sort of thing one reads lounging in a favorite chair beside a comfortable fire.

ESSAYS FOR ENTERTAINMENT

The first English essayists—Bacon, Jonson, and Dryden—were formal in style. It remained for Addison and Steele to introduce the informal essay. They did so in a new kind of periodical, a forerunner of the magazine.

As early as 1622, there had been weekly newspapers in England, but it was not until 1702 that there was a regular daily paper. Daniel Defoe was one of the earliest journalists, and one of the best. To him is given the credit for writing the first "interview" and of featuring the "leading editorial." Moreover, he contributed thousands of essays to his paper, the *Review,* over a nine-year period. Here was the germ of an idea upon which Richard Steele seized. Borrowing Swift's pen-name of "Isaac Bickerstaff" and Defoe's trick of dressing up a paper with literary contributions, Steele issued his *Tatler.*

The *Tatler* was a gossipy paper that was issued three times a week. Each number featured a polished essay. But the paper was for entertainment rather than for spreading the news, and the essays became its most delightful feature. In that early day, it served much the purpose of the modern magazine. It became immensely popular. Joseph Addison came in as a co-writer, and the paper ran for two years. After it was discontinued, the two friends issued a new publication, the *Spectator,* which became even more popular. Thereafter, the light periodical featuring a familiar essay became a habit of eighteenth-century English life. Nearly every writer tried his hand at writing one.

The essays were usually amusing rather than instructive. They presented serio-comic character studies, commented on fashions, or discussed in a semi-serious way philosophy and morals. The writers did not escape entirely the impersonal spirit of the age. In the essays of the *Tatler* and *Spectator* papers, the person who does the talking is the fictitious Mr. Bickerstaff. It is ostensibly his opinions—not Addison's or Steele's—that are expressed. Nonetheless, the essays proved so popular that many of them were collected and bound in book form. Those that enjoyed the widest reading were the *Spectator Papers,* and the special group from them called the "Sir Roger de Coverley Papers."

THE SATIRES

Dryden and Pope had set a fashion for satire in verse which spilled over into prose. Individuals and institutions alike were victims. Education, history, government, religion—nothing was safe from the barbed words with double meaning.

Jonathan Swift was the most powerful of the prose satirists. In his hands, satire became a political weapon. Pamphlets ridiculing leaders and policies were distributed like handbills about the streets of the city. Since Swift had a brilliant imagination and a kind of perverted genius, he was employed by the party in power, first by the Whigs and then by the Tories, to demolish their rivals. Two of his longer satires were allegories—*The Battle of the Books,* on the advantages of classic learning over "modern" learning; and *The Tale of a Tub,* intended to support the Church of England as opposed to the Dissenters and the Catholics. Swift overshot his mark and succeeded only in antagonizing all three churches.

The most surprising of all Swift's works was *Gulliver's Travels,* written to vent his spite against all men everywhere. It tells of Gulliver's adventures in four imaginary countries: Lilliput, or the land of tiny folk; Brobdingnag, or the land of the giants; Laputa, or the floating island of the scientists; and the land of the Houyhnhnms, where degraded human beings called Yahoos were the servants of fine, intelligent horses. Swift's venom grows devastating as the book progresses, so that the last two voyages prove unpleasant reading. But the direct, realistic style in which the first two voyages have been related has made them popular with young readers, who care nothing at all about the ironic purpose underlying them. They have become Swift's most enduring work.

The popular team of Joseph Addison and Sir Richard Steele used satire skillfully. Such essays as "The Coquette's Heart," "Fan Drill," and the "Sir Roger de Coverley Papers" show English classic prose at its best. They deal with polite society; they reflect the polish and sophistication of the age; they are lightly satiric and delicately impersonal; they are gracefully written and smooth. There is an important difference between their kind of satire and that of Swift or Pope. The essays are pleasant reading because their fun is never aimed at individuals. They ridicule types and fashions but not some certain man or woman. When Pope's "The Rape of the Lock" came out, everyone knew the name of the girl and the incident that inspired it. Society tittered at the real Sir Plume of the "round, unthinking face." There was spite behind the work. But the Beau and Coquette of whom Steele and Addison wrote are no more nor less real than Skeezix and Nina of the Gasoline Alley comic strip. The mark of a gentleman is kindness, and being gentlemen, Steele and Addison never stepped beyond the bounds of courtesy. One other point should be made about their work. It was their admitted intention, through satire, to make vice unattractive and virtue popular. Thus it is only the silly, trashy weaknesses of men that are held up to ridicule. And even in such an eccentric character as Sir Roger, there are fundamental human virtues of kindness and honor that endear him to the reader.

SIR ROGER AT CHURCH

JOSEPH ADDISON, WITH RICHARD STEELE

One of the most lovable figures moving through the pages of English literature is the country gentleman. He is always delightful, and somehow very typically British. But at no time is he more lovable than in the person of Sir Roger de Coverley—an eccentric, good-hearted eighteenth-century landlord.

Steele introduced him in the second number of the SPECTATOR, *and he quickly became the feature of the paper. His ardent, if timorous, devotion to the widow was followed with as much eager suspense as are comic-strip love-adventures of modern heroes. When the co-author let him die, readers of the* SPECTATOR *protested their loss and were not at all consoled by the magnificence of his funeral.*

But here is the good squire alive, and very much himself!

SIR ROGER HIMSELF

The first of our society is a gentleman of Worcestershire, of ancient descent, a baronet, his name Sir Roger de Coverley. His great grandfather was inventor of that famous country-dance which is called after him. All who know that shire, are very well acquainted with the parts and merits of Sir Roger. He is a gentleman that is very singular in his behavior, but his singularities proceed from his good sense, and are contradictions to the manners of the world, only as he thinks the world is in the wrong. However, this humor creates him no enemies, for he does nothing with sourness or obstinacy; and his being unconfined to modes and forms, makes him but the readier and more capable to please and oblige all who know him. When he is in town, he lives in Soho-square.[1] It is said, he keeps himself a bachelor by reason he was crossed in love by a perverse beautiful widow of the next county to him. Before this disappointment, Sir Roger was what you call a fine gentleman, had often supped with Lord Rochester and Sir George Etherege, fought a duel upon his first coming to town, and kicked Bully Dawson[2] in a public coffeehouse for calling him youngster. But being ill used by the above mentioned widow, he was very serious for a year and a half; and though, his temper being naturally jovial, he at last got over it, he grew careless of himself, and never dressed[3] afterwards. He continues to wear a coat and doublet of the same cut that were in fashion at the time of his repulse, which, in his merry humors, he

[1] SOHO-SQUARE—A square in London.

[2] LORD ROCHESTER, SIR GEORGE ETHEREGE, BULLY DAWSON—The first, John Wilmot, an English poet and courtier of Charles II; the second, an English dramatist; the third, a notorious London swindler. These three are typical of the dissolute gentlemen prominent in London society in the closing years of the reign of Charles II.

[3] DRESSED—Dressed up.

tells us, has been in and out[4] twelve times since he first wore it. He is now in his fifty-sixth year, cheerful, gay, and hearty; keeps a good house both in town and country; a great lover of mankind; but there is such a mirthful cast in his behavior, that he is rather beloved than esteemed; his tenants grow rich, his servants look satisfied; all the young women profess love to him, and the young men are glad of his company: when he comes into a house, he calls the servants by their names, and talks all the way upstairs to a visit. I must not omit, that Sir Roger is a justice of the quorum;[5] that he fills the chair at a quarter-session[6] with great abilities, and three months ago gained universal applause by explaining a passage in the game act.

SIR ROGER AT CHURCH

I am always very well pleased with a country Sunday, and think, if keeping holy the seventh day were only a human institution, it would be the best method that could have been thought of for the polishing and civilizing of mankind. It is certain the country people would soon degenerate into a kind of savages and barbarians, were there not such frequent returns of a stated time, in which the whole village meet together with their best faces, and in their cleanliest habits,[1] to converse with one another upon indifferent subjects, hear their duties explained to them, and join together in adoration of the Supreme Being. Sunday clears away the rust of the whole week, not only as it refreshes in their minds the notions of religion, but as it puts both the sexes upon appearing in their most agreeable forms, and exerting all such qualities as are apt to give them a figure in the eye of the village. A country fellow distinguishes himself as much in the churchyard, as a citizen does upon the 'Change, the whole parish-politics being generally discussed in that place either after sermon or before the bell rings.

My friend Sir Roger, being a good churchman, has beautified the inside of his church with several texts of his own choosing. He has likewise given a handsome pulpit-cloth, and railed in the communion-table at his own expense. He has often told me, that at his coming to his estate he found his parishioners very irregular; and that in order to make them kneel and join in the responses, he gave every one of them a hassock and a common prayer book; and at the same time employed an itinerant singing-master, who goes about the country for that purpose, to instruct them rightly in the tunes of the psalms:[2] upon which they now very much value themselves, and indeed outdo most of the country churches that I have ever heard.

As Sir Roger is landlord to the whole congregation, he keeps them in very good order, and will suffer nobody to sleep in it besides himself; for if by chance he has been surprised into a short nap at sermon, upon recovering out of it he stands up and looks about him, and if he sees anybody else nodding, either wakes them himself, or sends his servant to them. Several other of the old knight's peculiarities break out upon these occasions. Sometimes he will be lengthening out a verse in the singing psalms, half a minute after the rest of the congregation have done with it; sometimes when he is pleased with the matter of his

[4] IN AND OUT—In and out of fashion.

[5] JUSTICE OF THE QUARUM—Justice of the peace.

[6] QUARTER SESSION—A court held four times a year, trying many petty offences.

[1] HABITS—Clothes.

[2] PSALMS—The earliest church hymns were paraphrases of the Psalms set to music.

devotion, he pronounces Amen three or four times to the same prayer: and sometimes stands up when everybody else is upon their knees, to count the congregation, or see if any of his tenants are missing.

I was yesterday very much surprised to hear my old friend in the midst of the service calling out to one John Matthews to mind what he was about, and not disturb the congregation. This John Matthews it seems is remarkable for being an idle fellow, and at that time was kicking his heels for his diversion. This authority of the knight, though exerted in that odd manner which accompanies him in all circumstances of life, has a very good effect upon the parish, who are not polite[3] enough to see anything ridiculous in his behavior; besides that the general good sense and worthiness of his character make his friends observe these little singularities as foils that rather set off than blemish his good qualities.

As soon as the sermon is finished, nobody presumes to stir till Sir Roger is gone out of the church. The knight walks down from his seat in the chancel between a double row of his tenants, that stand bowing to him on each side: and every now and then inquires how such an one's wife, or mother, or son, or father do, whom he does not see at church; which is understood as a secret reprimand to the person that is absent.

The chaplain[4] has often told me, that upon a catechising day, when Sir Roger has been pleased with a boy that answers well, he has ordered a Bible to be given him next day for his encouragement: and sometimes accompanies it with a flitch of bacon to his mother. Sir Roger has likewise added five pounds a year to the clerk's place; and, that he may encourage the young fellows to make themselves perfect in the church service, has promised upon the death of the present incumbent, who is very old, to bestow it according to merit.

The fair understanding between Sir Roger and his chaplain, and their mutual concurrence in doing good, is the more remarkable, because the very next village is famous for the differences and contentions that rise between the parson and the squire, who live in a perpetual state of war. The parson is always preaching at the squire; and the squire, to be revenged on the parson, never comes to church. The squire has made all his tenants atheists and tithe-stealers; while the parson instructs them every Sunday in the dignity of his order, and insinuates to them almost in every sermon that he is a better man than his patron. In short, matters are come to such an extremity, that the squire has not said his prayers either in public or private this half year; and that the parson threatens him, if he does not mend his manners, to pray for him in the face of the whole congregation.

Feuds of this nature, though too frequent in the country, are very fatal to the ordinary people; who are so used to be dazzled with riches, that they pay as much deference to the understanding of a man of an estate, as of a man of learning; and are very hardly brought to regard any truth, how important soever it may be that is preached to them, when they know there are several men of five hundred a year[5] who do not believe it.

[3] POLITE—Here, sophisticated.

[4] CHAPLAIN—Here, a resident clergyman.

[5] FIVE HUNDRED A YEAR—Five hundred pounds a year.

FOR DISCUSSION

1. The *Tatler* and the *Spectator* might be called gossipy periodicals. Do you know any modern magazines similar to them? Addison and Steele were men-about-town in the eighteenth-century journalistic world. Mention some of their modern counterparts.

2. How do the styles of Bacon and Addison differ? Explain.

3. What sorts of people are likely to be "rather beloved than esteemed"? What kind of people may be both beloved and esteemed? Discuss, with illustrations.

4. Explain the meaning of the last sentence in the first paragraph of "Sir Roger at Church." Is the statement still true? Why or why not?

5. What parts of the essay are a satire on Sir Roger himself? Which parts are a satire on English society or upon any special classes of people? Discuss.

6. Does the reader feel scornful of Sir Roger in the end, or sympathetic towards him? Why?

7. Show that the two selections possess the qualities of an informal essay.

WORD STUDY

From what sport is *foils* taken? Explain its usage in the sentence: "His friends observe these little singularities as foils that rather set off than blemish his good qualities." What is the difference in meaning between *itinerant* and *itinerary?* Look up the origin of the word, and explain why a man in office is called the present *incumbent.* Give the origin of *tithe.* What part of the church is the *chancel*? Give two synonyms for *insinuate.*

A PROJECT

One of the most interesting features of the *Reader's Digest* is the monthly portrayal of the "Most Interesting Character I Have Ever Met." Choose some interesting character you have known and try writing a pleasantly whimsical character sketch of him or her, modeled after the *Spectator* sketch of Sir Roger.

RELATED READING

Read other famous accounts of country squires such as those in Washington Irving's "Christmas Sketches" in *The Sketch Book* and in *Bracebridge Hall,* or the picture of Squire Cass in *Silas Marner.* Read "Sir Roger Goes A-Hunting" in the "Sir Roger de Coverley Papers."

A Country Gentleman

THE AGE OF JOHNSON (1740-1780)

By 1745, classicism had almost played "its hour upon the stage"; the satyrs, fauns, goddesses were ready to retire to the musty regions where old literary props are stored. But then the great, uncouth, Falstaffian figure of Dr. Samuel Johnson waddled from the wings—the last and most celebrated of the classic Titans. He gathered about him a group of artists, essayists, and poets which included such outstanding figures as Sir Joshua Reynolds, David Garrick, Oliver Goldsmith, Edmund Burke, and Edward Gibbon, and founded the famous Literary Club. It was here that the great minds of the day drank in the sage wisdom of the greatest conversationalist of all time. Happily, one of that group, James Boswell, was a born hero-worshiper, and his famous biography of Johnson has preserved for posterity the vigorous talk and wise comment of his hero.

Johnson's writings, which include his *Lives of the Poets* and the essays he wrote for his two magazines *The Rambler* and *The Idler,* show almost all the characteristics of eighteenth-century classicism: its wit, its interest in men and manners, its good sense, its love of the town, and its indifference to nature. It seems strange today that books of English literature usually contain more literature about Samuel Johnson than by him. The great literary dictator was ponderous in every respect: in body, in thought, in style. Few modern readers will have the patience to struggle with his Ciceronic sentences laden with heavy Latinisms and filled with erudite allusions to universal knowledge. His intimate friend and Club member, Goldsmith, once said of him that if Johnson wrote a fable about little fishes, he would have the fishes talk like whales. Johnson's great work is his *Dictionary,* upon which he spent seven years. Despite its real scholarship, the author frequently obscured rather than clarified the meanings of words by involved definitions. Thus he actually did define "network" as "any thing reticulated or decussated, at equal distances, with the interstices between the intersections." Also, in many instances he allowed his personal prejudices to color his definitions. With his traditional hatred of Scotland, he defined "oats" as "a grain which in England is generally given to horses, but in Scotland supports the people."

DR. JOHNSON'S WRITING STYLE

Johnson, however, is more important for the inspiration and encouragement he gave others than for his writing. There is hardly a single contemporary writer who did not owe something to this dynamic man. Johnson was also remarkable for his simple and sincere piety in an age when religion was at a very low ebb.

His infectious vigor also effected a revival of interest in the theater. One of his circle was the madcap Irishman, Richard Sheridan, who, at twenty, fell in love with a singer, defied parental opposition, indulged in wild escapades, and fought two duels. His famous plays *The Rivals* and *The School for Scandal* are as dashing and spirited as himself. Oliver Goldsmith was a second friend of Johnson's to make history with a play: his famous comedy, *She Stoops to Conquer.*

Another writer of the Johnsonian school was the statesman, Edmund Burke. Though Americans know Burke chiefly through his speech, *On Conciliation with the American Colonies,* his collected works fill fourteen volumes. Well trained in the classics, he filled his speeches with references to the ancients. His style is rhetorical—filled with adjectives and dressed-up, round-about expressions. He used words precisely, and his orderly mind demanded logical development.

With the exception of Edward Gibbon, late eighteenth-century English prose writers composed in the heavy style of Johnson. But Gibbon, in his *Decline and Fall of the Roman Empire,* wrote flawless prose in the best neo-classic tradition. His history, however, is extremely bigoted and anti-Catholic.

THE NOVEL

There was one other important development in the literature of the period—the emergence of the novel. Our best sellers in their flaming jackets—our murder mysteries, our twenty-first-century romances, our historical novels—all trace their genealogy back to this period. There had been long prose romances in English before this time, but it was this age which first produced stories with definite plot development.

To Samuel Richardson's *Pamela* is usually awarded the title of "the first English novel." Other well known novels of this period are: *Tom Jones* by Henry Fielding, *Peregrine Pickle* by Tobias Smollet, and *The Vicar of Wakefield* by Oliver Goldsmith. When Horace Walpole wrote his *Castle of Otranto* in 1764, he introduced the mystery story into the English novel.

(FROM) **LIFE OF JOHNSON**

JAMES BOSWELL

It is no exaggeration to say that Dr. Johnson, the most celebrated figure of the eighteenth century and the Great Dictator of London's literary circles, lives today not so much by what he wrote as by what James Boswell wrote of him. For almost twenty years, this hero-worshiping little Scotsman carefully observed and made notes on what the "Great Bear of Literature" said and did. As a result, we have one of the most famous, unprejudiced, and readable biographies in the English language, written in a style both clear and flexible. John Kieran, of "Information Please" fame, has named Boswell's LIFE OF JOHNSON *as his third choice (after the Bible and Shakespeare) for a companion on a desert island. The excerpts below will give us a brief glimpse into the diverse characters of Johnson and his biographer.*

JOHNSON AT SCHOOL

He was first taught to read English by Dame Oliver, a widow, who kept a school for young children in Lichfield. He told me she could read black letter,[1] and asked him to borrow for her, from his father, a Bible in that character. When he was going to Oxford, she came to take leave of him, brought him, in the simplicity of her kindness, a present of gingerbread, and said he was the best scholar she ever had. He delighted in mentioning this early compliment: adding, with a smile, that "this was as high a proof of his merit as he could conceive." His next instructor in English was a master, whom, when he spoke of him to me, he familiarly called Tom Brown, who, said he, "published a spelling-book and dedicated it to the Universe; but I fear no copy of it can now be had."

He began to learn Latin with Mr. Hawkins, usher, or undermaster, of Lichfield school—"a man" (said he) "very skilful in his little way." With him he continued two years, and then rose to be under the care of Mr. Hunter, the head master, who according to his account, "was severe and wrong-headedly severe. He used" (said he) "to beat us unmercifully; and he did not distinguish between ignorance and negligence; for he would beat a boy equally for not knowing a thing, as for neglecting to know it. He would ask a boy a question, and if he did not answer it, he would beat him, without considering whether he had an opportunity of knowing how to answer it. For instance, he would call up a boy and ask him Latin for a candlestick, which the boy could not expect to be asked. Now, Sir, if a boy could answer every question, there would be no need of a master to teach him."

However, Johnson was very sensible how much he owed to Mr. Hunter. Mr. Langton[2] one day asked him how he had acquired so accurate a knowledge of Latin, in which I believe he was exceeded by no man of his time; he said, "My master whipped me very well. Without that, Sir, I should have done nothing." He told Mr. Langton that while Hunter was flogging his boys unmercifully, he used to say, "And this I do to save you from the gallows." Johnson, upon all occasions, expressed his approbation of enforcing instruction by means of the rod. "I would rather" (said he) "have the rod to be the general terror to all, to make them learn, than to tell a child, if you do thus, or thus, you will be more esteemed than your brothers or sisters. The rod produces an effect which terminates in itself. A child is afraid of being whipped, and gets his task, and there's an end on't: whereas, by exciting emulation and comparisons of superiority, you lay the foundation of lasting mischief; you make brothers and sisters hate each other."

[1] BLACK LETTER—Old English letters.

[2] MR. LANGTON—Member of the Literary Club, famous Greek Scholar.

That superiority over his fellows, which he maintained with so much dignity in his march through life, was not assumed from vanity and ostentation, but was the natural and constant effect of those extraordinary powers of mind, of which he could not but be conscious by comparison; the intellectual difference, which in other cases of comparison of characters, is often a matter of undecided contest, being as clear in his case as the superiority of stature in some men above others. Johnson did not strut or stand on tiptoe; he only did not stoop. From his earliest years, his superiority was perceived and acknowledged. He was from the beginning *anax andron,* a king of men. His schoolfellow, Mr. Hector, has obligingly furnished me with many particulars of his boyish days; and assured me that he never knew him corrected at school but for talking and diverting other boys from their business. He seemed to learn by intuition; for though indolence and procrastination were inherent in his constitution, whenever he made an exertion he did more than any one else. In short, he is a memorable instance of what has been observed, that the boy is the man in miniature; and that the distinguishing characteristics of each individual are the same through the whole course of life. His favourites used to receive very liberal assistance from him; and such was the submission and deference with which he was treated, such the desire to obtain his regard that three of the boys, of whom Mr. Hector was sometimes one, used to come in the morning as his humble attendants, and carry him to school. One in the middle stooped while he sat upon his back, and one on each side supported him, and thus he was borne triumphant. Such a proof of the early predominance of intellectual vigour is very remarkable and does honour to human nature.

JOHNSON AND BOSWELL MEET

(1763) This is to me a memorable year; for in it I had the happiness to obtain the acquaintance of that extraordinary man whose memoirs I am now writing, an acquaintance which I shall ever esteem as one of the most fortunate circumstances in my life. Though then but two-and-twenty I had for several years read his works with delight and instruction, and had the reverence for their author, which had grown up in my fancy into a kind of mysterious veneration by figuring to myself a state of solemn, elevated abstraction, in which I supposed him to live in the immense metropolis of London. Mr. Gentleman, a native of Ireland, who passed some years in Scotland as a player, and as an instructor in the English language, a man whose talents and worth were de pressed by misfortunes, had given me a representation of the figure and manner of "Dictionary Johnson," as he was then called; and during my first visit to London, which was for three months in 1760, Mr. Derrick, the poet, who was Gentleman's friend and countryman, flattered me with hopes that he would introduce me to Johnson. But he never found an opportunity, which made me doubt that he had promised to do what was not in his power; till Johnson some years afterwards told me, "Derrick, sir, might very well have introduced you. I had a kindness for Derrick, and am sorry he is dead."

Mr. Thomas Davies, the actor, who then kept a bookseller's shop in Russell Street, Covent Garden, told me that Johnson came frequently to his house, where he more than once invited me to meet him; but by some unlucky accident or other he was prevented from coming to us.

Mr. Davies recollected several of Johnson's remarkable sayings, and was one of the best of the many imitators of his voice and manner while relating them. He increased my impatience more and more to see the extraordinary man whose works I highly valued, and whose conversation was reported to be excellent.

At last, on Monday the 16th of May, when I was sitting in Mr. Davies' back parlor, after having drunk tea with him and Mrs. Davies, Johnson unexpectedly came into the shop; and Mr. Davies having perceived him through the glass door in the room in which we were sitting, advancing toward us—he announced his awful approach to me, somewhat in the manner of an actor in the part of Horatio when he addresses Hamlet on the appearance of his father's ghost, "Look, my Lord, it comes." I found that I had a perfect idea of Johnson's figure, from the portrait of him painted by Sir Joshua Reynolds soon after he had published his *Dictionary,* in the attitude of sitting in his easy chair in deep meditation. Mr. Davies mentioned my name, and respectfully introduced me to him; I was much agitated, and recollecting his prejudice against the Scotch, of which I had heard much, I said to Davies, "Don't tell him where I come from."—"From Scotland," cried Davies, roguishly. "Mr. Johnson," said I, "I do indeed come from Scotland, but I cannot help it."

I am willing to flatter myself that I meant this as light pleasantry to soothe and conciliate him, and not as an humiliating abasement at the expense of my country.

But however that might be, this speech was somewhat unlucky, for he seized the expression "come from Scotland," and retorted, "That, sir, I find, is what a great many of your countrymen cannot help." This stroke stunned me a good deal, and when we had sat down, I felt myself not a little embarrassed, and apprehensive of what might come next. He then addressed himself to Davies: "What do you think of Garrick?[3] He refused me an order for the play for Miss Williams, because he knows the house will be full, and that an order would be worth three shillings." Eager to take any opening to get into the conversation with him, I ventured to say, "Oh, sir, I cannot think Mr. Garrick would grudge such a trifle to you." "Sir," said he, with a stern look, "I have known David Garrick longer than you have done, and I know no right you have to talk to me on the subject." Perhaps I deserved this check, for it was rather presumptuous in me, an entire stranger, to express any doubt of the justice of his animadversion upon his old acquaintance and pupil. I now felt myself much mortified, and began to think that the hope which I had long indulged of obtaining his acquaintance was blasted. And, in truth, had not my ardor been uncommonly strong, and my resolution uncommonly persevering, so rough a reception might have deferred me forever from making any further attempts. Fortunately, however, I remained upon the field not wholly discomfited, and was soon rewarded by hearing some of his conversation.

AN EVENING AT THE MITRE TAVERN

On Wednesday, July 6, he was engaged to sup with me at my lodgings in Downing Street, Westminster. But on the preceding night, my landlord having behaved very rudely to me and some company who were with me, I had resolved not to remain another night in his house. I was exceedingly uneasy at the awkward appearance I supposed I should make to Johnson and the other gentlemen whom I had invited, not being able to receive them at home, and being obliged to order supper at the Mitre, I went to Johnson in the morning, and talked of it as of a serious distress. He laughed and said, "Consider, sir, how insignificant this will appear a twelve-month hence. There is nothing," continued he, "in this mighty misfortune; nay, we shall be better at the Mitre." I told him that I had been at Sir John Fielding's[4] office, complaining of my landlord, and had been informed that though I had taken my lodgings for a year, I might upon proof of his bad behavior, quit them when I pleased, without being under an obligation to pay rent for any longer time than while I possessed them. The fertility of Johnson's mind could show itself even upon so small a matter as this. "Why, sir," said he, "I suppose this must be the law since you have been told so in Bow Street.[5] But if your landlord could hold you to your bargain, and the lodgings should be yours for a year, you may certainly use them as you think fit. So, sir, you may quarter two life-guardsmen upon him, or you may send the greatest scoundrel you can find into your apartments, or you may say that you want to make some experiments in natural

[3]GARRICK—One of the greatest Shakespearean actors of all time and co-manager of the Drury Lane Theater in Covent Garden. A movie of some years ago, *The Great Garrick,* was well done.

[4]SIR JOHN FIELDING—A half-brother of Henry Fielding, classical novelist and author of *Tom Jones.*

[5]BOW STREET—The principal police court of London is situated there. A fashionable site in the eighteenth century where Will's Coffee House was situated.

philosophy, and may burn a large quantity of asafetida[6] in his house."

I had as my guests, this evening at the Mitre Tavern, Dr. Johnson, Dr. Goldsmith, Mr. Thomas Davies, Mr. Eccles, an Irish gentleman, for whose agreeable company I was obliged to Mr. Davies, and the Reverend Mr. John Ogilvie.

Mr. Ogilvie was unlucky enough to choose for the topic of his conversation the praises of his native country. He began with saying that there was very rich land around Edinburgh. Goldsmith, who had studied physics there, contradicted this, very untruly, with a sneering laugh. Disconcerted a little by this, Mr. Ogilvie then took a new ground, where I suppose, he thought himself perfectly safe, for he observed that Scotland had a great many noble wild prospects. JOHNSON. "I believe, sir, you have a great many. Norway, too, has noble, wild prospects, and Lapland is remarkable for prodigious, noble, wild prospects. But sir, let me tell you, the noblest prospect which a Scotchman ever sees is the high road that leads him to England!" This unexpected and pointed sally produced a roar of applause. After all, however, those who admire the rude grandeur of nature cannot deny it to Caledonia.

On Saturday, July 9, I found Johnson surrounded with a numerous levee, but have not preserved any part of his conversation. On the 14TH we had another evening by ourselves at the Mitre. It happening to be a very rainy night, I made some commonplace observations on the relaxation of nerves and depression of spirits which such weather occasioned, adding, however, that it was good for the vegetable creation. Johnson, who denied that the temperature of the air had any influence on the human frame, answered, with a smile of ridicule, "Why, yes, sir, it is good for vegetables, and for the animals who eat those vegetables, and, for the animals who eat those animals." This observation of his aptly enough introduced a good supper, and I soon forgot, in Johnson's company, the influence of a moist atmosphere.

[6]ASAFETIDA (ăs′a·fĕt′ĭ·da)—A fetid smelling medicine.

FOR DISCUSSION

1. What traits of character are discovered in the selections just read? Is your impression of Johnson favorable?

2. Discuss Boswell's personality and character as revealed in the selections.

3. Explain what Boswell meant when he wrote: "The boy is the man in miniature." Wordsworth wrote that "the child is father of the man."

4. Boswell had lodgings in Downing Street. What English official resides at No. 10 Downing Street today?

5. Discuss the following quotations of Johnson:

"If man does not make new acquaintance as he advances through life, he will soon find himself left alone. A man, Sir, should keep his friendships in constant repair."

"What we read with inclination makes a much stronger impression. If we read without inclination half the mind is employed in fixing the attention; so there is but one half to be employed on what we read."

"A man of sense and education should meet a suitable companion in a wife. It is a miserable thing when the conversation can only be such as, whether the mutton should be broiled or roasted, and probably a dispute about that."

WORD STUDY

By comparison, Boswell's diction is much lighter than that of Johnson, which makes for a much more flexible style. Remarkable for eighteenth-century prose, there are not more Latin words in his biography than one would find in a modern writer. Learn the definitions of *emulate, ostentatious, intuition, tremulous, lurking, impute, animadversion.* Rewrite the following in simple words: "procrastination was inherent in his constitution." Note that the English add a *u* to words ending in *-or;* for example, *favour, colour, honour,* and *dolour.*

PROJECTS

1. The Literary Club was founded by Johnson and Sir Joshua Reynolds in 1764. It met at Turk's Head Tavern every week and in later years numbered thirty-five members. Besides Johnson and Boswell, some of the famous members were Sir Joshua Reynolds, Oliver Goldsmith, David Garrick, Edmund Burke, and Richard Sheridan. Prepare a brief written or oral report on each of these men.

2. Select some outstanding twentieth-century Catholic writers for an imaginary Literary Club. From your knowledge of their interests and their views on certain subjects, write an imaginary conversation between them which could be used as a radio or television script.

3. Have the ghosts of the famous Club members return to life and comment on life and letters in this modern age.

RELATED READING

In the Victorian Age, Macaulay wrote a famous biographical essay on Johnson. Acquaint yourself with this essay. A hasty or a leisured reading of Boswell's *Johnson* in any abridged edition should be the ambition of every high school senior.

SAMUEL JOHNSON

JAMES BOSWELL

THE TRANSITION FROM CLASSICISM TO ROMANTICISM (1780-1798)

As early as Pope's time, a reaction against the neo-classic standards was evident among a group of poets living in isolated rural areas who wrote about nature, solitude, and death. Far removed from the sophistication of London life, they wrote about the things which surrounded them: about nature and the familiar objects of everyday life. They discarded satire and criticism and attempted ballads and simple tales. Convinced that by entirely suppressing their natural feelings and appealing only to cold, formal logic, they were missing a great deal in life, these poets began to use "the language of the heart" in odes, lyrics, and elegies. Some of these poems, which were written with sincerity and in good taste, possessed real literary merit. Others, however, reflected a morbid and almost unnatural interest in death; they contained long descriptions of cemeteries at night replete with phantoms, owls, newly dug graves, and crumbling ivy walls. So mawkish and melancholy were many of these poems that their authors were designated as the "Graveyard School."

A renewed interest in the poetry of the Elizabethans led the way to the adoption of new poetic interests and a return to a simpler diction. We see this influence partly at work in Gray's "Elegy," whose thought was definitely influenced by the "Graveyard School" and whose diction manifested a partial, though not complete, veering away from the stock diction of the neo-classic. The best examples of the work of this new school of "sentiment and return to nature" are Thomson's "Seasons," William Collins' "Ode to Evening," and Cowper's "Olney Hymns." Reflective poems of this type were written in blank verse, similar to Milton's, instead of in conventional couplets.

A reawakened interest in man as a human being and in democratic living found expression in Oliver Goldsmith's poem, "The Deserted Village" and in such poems of Robert Burns as "The Cotter's Saturday Night." Both voice a protest against the encroachments of a growing capitalistic economy and its oppression of the poor. In Burns, the purest lyricist of Scotland, with his incomparable songs of highland life and love, we find the most important forerunner of the Romantic Movement. The simple lyrics and mystical fancies of William Blake also show a complete turning away from the formality of eighteenth-century classicism.

Such a sweeping century of achievement proves in review to have left surprisingly little that is of intrinsic interest. The "classical" writers overestimated the value of their work. Much of it is of historic significance; little is still read. The student will remember it best for the vogue of classicism in literature; for the wit of Alexander Pope (one of the most quoted writers in the English tongue); for the satire of Swift; for the literary elegance and healthful influence of Addison and Steele; for the strange power wielded by Dr. Johnson; for a revival of the drama; for the emergence of three new literary forms: the newspaper, the magazine, and the novel.

Elegy Written in a Country Churchyard

THOMAS GRAY

A country burying-ground—especially an old one—has a curious fascination for anyone of imaginative mind. In England the churchyard cemeteries are very old. One knows that the people buried in them were humble; for according to European custom, persons of rank were buried within the churches, or in vaults or crypts beneath the floors.

At Stoke Poges in Buckinghamshire lies an old churchyard, once the haunt of a dreamy poet, Thomas Gray. Gray liked to wander among the graves, looking at the simple monuments and deciphering the inscriptions. Poorly worded, almost ludicrous in their awkwardness, the epitaphs told of the poverty of the neighborhood. As Gray tried to repicture the simple lives remembered there, he wondered what difference it might have made had these folks had the privileges of education and contact with public affairs. Did this spot hold the remains of some possible genius, forever hidden from the world? Fired by such fancies, Gray wrote an elegy to celebrate the "unhonored dead." His tribute has become one of the best known poems in the English language. To it, in conclusion, he added the lines that he chose for his own epitaph when he should be laid to rest in some such quiet spot.

The curfew tolls the knell of parting day;
    The lowing herd winds slowly o'er the lea;
The plowman homeward plods his weary way,
    And leaves the world to darkness and to me.

Now fades the glimmering landscape on the sight,
    And all the air a solemn stillness holds,
Save where the beetle wheels his droning flight,
    And drowsy tinklings lull the distant folds;

Save that from yonder ivy-mantled tow'r
    The moping owl does to the moon complain
Of such as, wandering near her secret bow'r,
    Molest her ancient solitary reign.

Beneath those rugged elms, that yew-tree's shade,
    Where heaves the turf in many a mold'ring heap,
Each in his narrow cell forever laid,
    The rude forefathers of the hamlet sleep.

The breezy call of incense-breathing Morn,
    The swallow twitt'ring from the straw-built shed,
The cock's shrill clarion, or the echoing horn,
    No more shall rouse them from their lowly bed.

For them no more the blazing hearth shall burn,
    Or busy housewife ply her evening care;
No children run to lisp their sire's return,
    Or climb his knees the envied kiss to share.

Oft did the harvest to their sickle yield,
    Their furrow oft the stubborn glebe has broke;
How jocund did they drive their team a-field!
    How bowed the woods beneath their sturdy stroke!

Let not Ambition mock their useful toil,
    Their homely joys and destiny obscure;
Nor Grandeur hear with a disdainful smile
    The short and simple annals of the poor.

The boast of heraldry, the pomp of pow'r,
    And all that beauty, all that wealth e'er gave,
Awaits alike the inevitable hour:
    The paths of glory lead but to the grave.

Nor you, ye proud, impute to these the fault,
    If Memory o'er their tomb no trophies raise,
Where, through the long-drawn aisle and fretted vault,
    The pealing anthem swells the note of praise.

26. GLEBE—Turf, sward.

29. AMBITION—Those who have made it their purpose to achieve power, fame, wealth, and the like. Similarly *Grandeur,* in line 31, refers to those who have such wealth and power.

33. BOAST OF HERALDRY—Family pride; inherited rank, indicated by family coats-of-arms.

Can storied urn or animated bust
    Back to its mansion call the fleeting breath?
Can Honor's voice provoke the silent dust,
    Or Flatt'ry soothe the dull, cold ear of Death?

Perhaps in this neglected spot is laid
    Some heart once pregnant with celestial fire;
Hands that the rod of empire might have swayed,
    Or waked to ecstasy the living lyre.

But Knowledge to their eyes her ample page,
    Rich with the spoils of time, did ne'er unroll;
Chill Penury repressed their noble rage,
    And froze the genial current of their soul.

Full many a gem of purest ray serene
    The dark unfathomed caves of ocean bear;
Full many a flower is born to blush unseen,
    And waste its sweetness on the desert air.

Some village-Hampden that with dauntless breast
    The little tyrant of his fields withstood,
Some mute inglorious Milton, here may rest,
    Some Cromwell guiltless of his country's blood.

Th' applause of list'ning senates to command,
    The threats of pain and ruin to despise,
To scatter plenty o'er a smiling land,
    And read their hist'ry in a nation's eyes,

Their lot forbade: nor circumscribed alone,
    Their growing virtues, but their crimes confined;
Forbade to wade through slaughter to a throne,
    And shut the gates of mercy on mankind;

41. STORIED URN—Burial urns inscribed with records of achievements and honors.

41. ANIMATED—Lifelike.

43. PROVOKE—Arouse, awaken.

46. PREGNANT WITH CELESTIAL FIRE—Filled with heaven-sent genius.

51. PENURY REPRESSED THEIR NOBLE RAGE—Poverty stifled or smothered their talents.

52. FROZE THE GENIAL CURRENT OF THEIR SOUL—Prevented them from following their natural bents.

57. HAMPDEN—An English squire who refused to pay the "tax of ship money," thus starting the argument which led to the Puritan Revolution.

58. LITTLE TYRANT OF HIS FIELDS—His landlord.

61-64. Notice the punctuation in this stanza, which must be read together with the following stanza. *Lot (l. 65)* is the subject of the main clause; *forbade* is the verb; and the infinitives *to command, to despise, to scatter,* and *read* are the objects.

65. CIRCUMSCRIBED—Set limits to. The thought is that if their lot prevented them from being benefactors of mankind, it may also have prevented them from causing widespread pain and suffering. It thus "confined their crimes."

The struggling pangs of conscious truth to hide,
    To quench the blushes of ingenuous shame,
Or heap the shrine of Luxury and Pride
    With incense kindled at the Muse's flame.

Far from the madding crowd's ignoble strife,
    Their sober wishes never learned to stray;
Along the cool sequestered vale of life
    They kept the noiseless tenor of their way.

Yet e'en these bones from insult to protect,
    Some frail memorial still erected nigh,
With uncouth rhymes and shapeless sculpture decked,
    Implores the passing tribute of a sigh.

Their name, their years, spelt by th' unlettered Muse,
    The place of fame and elegy supply;
And many a holy text around she strews,
    That teach the rustic moralist to die.

69-72. This stanza must be read in connection with the preceding one. The infinitives *to hide, to quench,* and *heap* are the objects of *forbade* in line 67. Gray is here referring to the practice of patronage under which an author would dedicate his work to a wealthy or influential person expecting to receive money or favors in return.

81. UNLETTERED MUSE—Uneducated poet or rhymster.

84. TEACH THE RUSTIC MORALIST TO DIE—Texts intended to give comfort in the face of death.

For who, to dumb Forgetfulness a prey,
    This pleasing, anxious being e'er resigned,
Left the warm precincts of the cheerful day,
    Nor cast one longing, ling'ring look behind?

On some fond breast the parting soul relies,
    Some pious drops the closing eye requires;
E'en from the tomb the voice of nature cries,
    E'en in our ashes live their wonted fires.

For thee who, mindful of th' unhonored dead,
    Dost in these lines their artless tale relate,
If chance, by lonely Contemplation led,
    Some kindred spirit shall inquire thy fate,

Haply some hoary-headed swain may say,
    "Oft have we seen him at the peep of dawn,
Brushing with hasty steps the dews away,
    To meet the sun upon the upland lawn.

"There, at the foot of yonder nodding beech
    That wreathes its old fantastic roots so high,
His listless length at noontide would he stretch,
    And pore upon the brook that babbles by.

"Hard by yon wood, now smiling as in scorn,
    Mutt'ring his wayward fancies, he would rove;
Now drooping, woeful—wan, like one forlorn
    Or crazed with care or crossed in hopeless love.

"One morn I missed him from the customed hill,
    Along the heath, and near his fav'rite tree.
Another came, nor yet beside the rill,
    Nor up the lawn, nor at the wood was he;

"The next, with dirges due, in sad array,
    Slow through the churchway path we saw him borne:
Approach and read (for thou canst read) the lay
    Graved on the stone beneath yon aged thorn."

THE EPITAPH

Here rests his head upon the lap of Earth,
    A youth to Fortune and to Fame unknown:
Fair Science frowned not on his humble birth,
    And Melancholy marked him for her own.

Large was his bounty, and his soul sincere;
Heaven did a recompense as largely send:
He gave to Mis'ry (all he had) a tear,
He gained from Heav'n ('twas all he wished) a friend.

No farther seek his merits to disclose,
Or draw his frailties from their dread abode,
(There they alike in trembling hope repose),
The bosom of his Father and his God.

FOR APPRECIATION

Although Gray has chosen a simple subject for his "Elegy," he has kept the long words of classic poetry. Yet so popular was the poem with our parents and grandparents that many of its lines have passed into common speech *in quotation.*

1. The first three stanzas are introductory, planned to set the mood for the poem. What things does the reader see? What does he hear? What does he feel? Choose three adjectives of your own to describe the kind of mood or feeling set by the first twelve lines.

2. Which stanza describes the cemetery? What kinds of trees grew there? What was the "narrow cell"?

3. Which three stanzas present imaginary scenes from the daily lives of those now lying in the churchyard? Are the pictures happy or sad?

4. What is the general thought of lines 29-36? What is the connection—expressed or implied—between the humble villagers of the churchyard and the "paths of glory"? Windsor Castle is situated just across the valley from Stoke Poges. Does this fact make the thought content of lines 33-44 more meaningful? Explain.

5. Quote the lines in the succeeding stanzas which express the following thoughts:

a. The absence of suitable markers or memorials does not mean necessarily that the men were unworthy.

b. Splendid monuments cannot alter the fact of death.

Quote the lines which indicate that England's "honored dead" are buried within the churches. Which English church holds the tombs of her greatest men? Where is it located?

6. Restate in simple prose the meaning of lines 45 and 46. Quote a later stanza which says that the same sort of thing happens often in the realm of nature.

7. In lines 45-60 what undeveloped talents does Gray suggest may have been buried in that "neglected spot"? Do you think that Gray approved or disapproved of the Puritan Revolution of the seventeenth century? How can you tell how he felt?

8. In which stanzas does Gray say that lack of opportunity may have prevented great misfortunes or unhappiness at the same time that it robbed men of fame and success? Do you think that Gray is right? In your discussion follow some of these thoughts to a conclusion:

a. Name some men in history who "waded through a slaughter to a throne." Were they all men from privileged circumstances? Do you think they would have become famous no matter what their original circumstances were?

b. Can you name some men or women of humble origin who have been the cause of great human suffering? How were they able to win or wield power?

9. Do you think Gray's ideas as presented in the first 72 lines are an argument for or against the principle that there should be equal opportunities for all persons? Discuss.

10. Which lines say that even these simple graves bear markers of some sort? Which lines say that it is a common trait of human nature to want to be missed and mourned?

11. How can the reader tell that Gray is writing of himself in lines 93-96? What do we learn about Gray's habits, in the stanzas that follow? What was he doing when he acted like one "crazed with care or crossed in hopeless love"? Was Gray excitable?

12. What does the parenthetical expression, "for thou canst read," imply about the educational status of the cornmunity?

13. It is customary in an epitaph to mention the virtues of the one remembered. What virtues does Gray claim in his epitaph?

14. How does the "Elegy" prove that Gray was interested in ordinary men and women? Which passages in it show the most effective use of poetic imagination?

15. Why do you think this poem became a favorite in Gray's time and for many succeeding generations? Make a list of lines or expressions from it which you have heard quoted. Which passages from it do you consider most worthy of memorization? Why?

John Anderson, My Jo

ROBERT BURNS

Most of Robert Burns' poetry is written in Scotch brogue. The poet used dialect deliberately. It was not that he knew no better. You will notice that when it pleased him, he could turn out stanzas in pure English as polished and smooth as those of any classic poet.

Burns used dialect because—however well educated a Scotsman may be—when he is with those he loves and trusts, he drops naturally into brogue. It is the cozy, familiar speech of the home. John Muir, the Scottish-born American naturalist, has said that no matter how hot a Scotch argument waxed, so long as the men used dialect, you could know that all was friendly beneath; but if one man "put his English on"—then look out! Burns, writing for his neighbors and cronies, uses the daily speech, homelike and comfortable as their old clothes. He "puts his English on" only when he wants dignity for a dedication, as in the first stanza of "The Cotter's Saturday Night," or when he turns aside to moralize a bit.

Familiar songs like "Auld Lang Syne" and "Comin' Through the Rye" have given us some practice with Burns' speech. Try reading some of the following lines aloud until you can get them smoothly.

John Anderson, my jo, John,
  When we were first acquent,
Your locks were like the raven,
  Your bonie brow was brent;
But now your brow is beld, John,
  Your locks are like the snaw;
But blessings on your frosty pow,
  John Anderson, my jo!

1. JO—Sweetheart.
4. BRENT—Smooth, unwrinkled.
5. BELD—Bald.
8. POW—Head.

John Anderson, my jo, John,
  We clamb the hill thegither;
And mony a canty day, John
  We've had wi' ane anither;
Now we maun totter down, John,
  And hand in hand we'll go,
And sleep thegither at the foot,
  John Anderson, my jo!

11. CANTY—Happy.
13. MAUN—Must.

FOR APPRECIATION

1. Show how this poem is a beautiful "love lyric" of old age and a tribute to the fulfillment of marriage vows.

2. Find in the poem the secret of the old couple's happiness together.

3. Name at least two familiar American or English songs which express the same sentiment expressed in the poem. How many old couples do you know to whom this poem might be applied? Perhaps they can inspire you to write a lyric poem or prose tribute to one of them.

4. Compare the thought content of this poem with Shakespeare's Sonnet LXXIII.

A Man's a Man for A' That

ROBERT BURNS

In the late years of the eighteenth century, the British Isles hummed with democratic doctrines. Revolutions, first in America and then in France, had started Britishers thinking about "the rights of man." Ardent in his sympathies for poor men everywhere, Burns poured his articles of faith into what might be called the THEME-POEM *of Democracy—"A Man's a Man for A' That." The "a' that" of the poem stands for all the external differences between men—dress, rank, manners, and the like. But for all that, says Burns, it's the Man himself that counts.*

Is there for honest Poverty
  That hings his head, an' a' that;
The coward slave—we pass him by,
  We dare be poor for a' that!
For a' that, an' a' that,
  Our toils obscure an' a' that,
The rank is but the guinea's stamp,
  The Man's the gowd for a' that.

What though on hamely fare we dine,
  Wear hoddin greay, an' a' that;
Gie fools their silks, and knaves their wine,
  A Man's a Man for a' that:
For a' that, and a' that,
  Their tinsel show, an' a' that;
The honest man, tho' e'er sae poor,
  Is king o' men for a' that.

Ye see yon birkie ca'd a lord,
  Wha struts, an' stares, an' a' that;
Tho' hundreds worship at his word,
  He's but a coof for a' that:
For a' that, an' a' that,
  His ribband, star, an' a' that:
The man o' independent mind
  He looks an' laughs at a' that.

A prince can mak a belted knight,
  A marquis, duke, an' a' that;
But an honest man's aboon his might,
  Gude faith, he maunna fa' that!
For a' that, an' a' that,
  Their dignities an' a' that;
The pith o' sense, an' pride o' worth,
  Are higher rank than a' that.

Then let us pray that come it may,
  (As come it will for a' that,)
That Sense and Worth, o'er a' the earth,
  Shall bear the gree, an' a' that.
For a' that, an' a' that,
  It's coming yet for a' that,
That Man to Man, the world o'er,
  Shall brothers be for a' that.

2. HINGS—Hangs.
7. GUINEA—An English gold coin worth about \$5.11.
8. GOWD—Gold. Burns meant that it is the gold, not the mark, or stamp, which makes the coin valuable.
9. HAMELY—Common; coarse.
10. HODDIN GREAY—Coarse grey woolen.
17. BIRKIE—Conceited fellow.
20. COOF—Dull fellow; dolt; ninny.
22. RIBBAND, STAR—Symbols of orders of nobility.
27. ABOON—Above.
28. MAUNNA FA'—Must not claim that.
36. —Have the first place.

FOR APPRECIATION

1. Does Burns mean in the first three lines that all poor men are "coward slaves"? Under what conditions dare a man be poor and proud?

2. Explain the meaning of the figure of speech which Burns uses in lines 7 and 8.

3. What kind of differences between men is the poet referring to in the second stanza? What are some of the things in life that might be classed as "tinsel show"?

4. What other poet, or poets, have expressed thoughts similar to the one in lines 15 and 16?

5. What kind of differences between men is the poet referring to in the third stanza? Do such distinctions exist even in America? Discuss.

6. Quote lines written by one of Burns' contemporaries which express a thought the same as that in lines 25-29. What does the poet say really indicates rank?

7. Since Burns wrote this poem, there have been several civil wars and two World Wars. Do you think the world is any closer today to the ideal expressed in the last stanza than it was in the poet's day? What nation or nations have come the closest to realizing these ideals?

8. Enumerate and discuss the definite Catholic principles which men and nations must follow if there is to be a universal brotherhood.

(FROM) *Auguries of Innocence*

WILLIAM BLAKE

Can you do the things suggested in the four lines below? If so, you may count yourself wise. Blake says that they are "signs of innocence." Of course, philosophers and poets have long said that the innocent are the truly wise, and that if we would understand the Kingdom of Heaven we must become as little children. Blake firmly believed this.

To see a world in a grain of sand,
And a heaven in a wild flower;
Hold infinity in the palm of your hand,
And eternity in an hour.

FOR APPRECIATION

1. Is there the same mystery involved in accounting for the existence of a single grain of sand that there is in accounting for the existence of a world? Discuss.

2. What element not present in sand or earth characterizes a plant or flower? What does a flower bear or produce? Why have flowers been used so often as the symbol of immortality? How can one "see a heaven in a wild flower"? Explain.

3. Is the bit of space that may be measured by the palm of one's hand *really* separated from the infinity of space that surrounds us? Discuss.

4. Are the limits that men set upon time *real*? Does time actually have a beginning and ending? In what respect is an "hour" a part of the eternity of time?

The Tiger

WILLIAM BLAKE

Man stands in bewilderment before the contrasts of nature. On the one hand we see the uplifting freshness of trees and flowers; on the other hand, the destructive fury of the hurricane. There are volcanos, and there are snowflakes. And behind these paradoxes—what? What creative mind and force? "The Tiger" expresses man's bafflement over the problem.

Tiger! Tiger! burning bright
In the forests of the night,
What immortal hand or eye
Could frame thy fearful symmetry?

In what distant deeps or skies
Burnt the fire of thine eyes?
On what wings dare he aspire?
What the hand dare seize the fire?

And what shoulder, and what art,
Could twist the sinews of thy heart?
When thy heart began to beat,
What dread hand forged thy dread feet?

What the hammer? What the chain?
In what furnace was thy brain?
What the anvil? What dread grasp
Dared its deadly terrors clasp?

When the stars threw down their spears,
And watered heaven with their tears,
Did He smile His work to see?
Did He who made the Lamb make thee?

Tiger, Tiger, burning bright
In the forests of the night,
What immortal hand or eye
Dare frame thy fearful symmetry?

FOR APPRECIATION

1. Why do you think Blake chose the Tiger as especially symbolic of the mysteries of creation? Discuss. If you are not sure of the answer now, come back to it after you have considered the following questions.

2. Is there foundation in fact for Blake's poetic fancy which sees the tiger *"burning bright* in the forests of the *night"?* Explain.

3. What does *symmetry* mean? Is there symmetry in all living creatures? Why is the tiger well described as a "fearful symmetry"?

4. What characteristics peculiar to the tiger are implied in the following expressions: *(a)* the fire of thine eyes? *(b)* the sinews of thy heart? *(c)* thy dread feet? *(d)* the deadly terrors of thy brain?

5. With what matching expressions does Blake suggest the Power that could create a tiger? List at least four.

6. What do you think was Blake's intention in writing the first two lines of the fifth stanza? What deeper question lies behind line 19? What deeper question lies behind line 20?

7. Does Blake answer his questions in the last stanza?

8. What kind of thoughts or feelings does this poem excite in the reader? Can you see any reasons why some critics have considered this short lyric to be the most truly poetic verse written in the eighteenth century? Would you agree? Why or why not?

The Little Black Boy

WILLIAM BLAKE

In this childlike yet profound poem all the arguments against the inequality of races are swept away. The profundity of the arguments is clothed in the sweet simplicity and innocence of a child retelling a lesson which he learned at his mother's knee.

My mother bore me in the southern wild,
And I am black, but O! my soul is white;
White as an angel is the English child,
But I am black, as if bereaved of light.

My mother taught me underneath a tree,
And, sitting down before the heat of day,
She took me in her lap and kissèd me,
And, pointing to the east, began to say:

"Look on the rising sun: there God does live,
And gives His light, and gives His heat away;
And flowers and trees and beasts and men receive
Comfort in morning, joy in the noonday.

"And we are put on earth a little space,
That we may learn to bear the beams of love;
And these black bodies and this sunburnt face
Is but a cloud, and like a shady grove.

"For when our souls have learned the heat to bear,
The cloud will vanish; we shall hear His voice,
Saying: 'Come out from the grove, my Love and care,
And round My golden tent like lambs rejoice.' "

Thus did my mother say, and kissèd me;
And thus I say to little English boy:
When I from black and he from white cloud free,
And round the tent of God like lambs we joy,

I'll shade him from the heat, till he can bear
To lean in joy upon our Father's knee;
And then I'll stand and stroke his silver hair,
And be like him, and he will then love me.

FOR APPRECIATION

1. What is the thought expressed in stanza 1? Is there implied in it both a sense of spiritual equality and social inferiority? Discuss.

2. Point out in detail how the mother teaches her son the important spiritual lesson of equality before God. Discuss the use of the image of the rising sun as referred to God. Is this image used throughout the poem? Of what advantage is the "cloud" of black upon earth? In Heaven?

3. Discuss the thought content of stanza 3. Explain in detail the meaning of lines 19-20 and lines 25-26.

4. Would you say that the spiritual strength of the poem lies in this: the black boy will be able to stand the intense rays of God's love because while on earth he has borne the lack of understanding and sympathy from his white brothers? Discuss.

5. Scan line 12. Does this line break the iambic meter of the previous lines? Discuss the reason for this change.

Further Readings
The Seventeenth and Eighteenth Centuries

THE SEVENTEENTH CENTURY

*Atteridge, Helen, *At the Sign of the Silver Cup* (fiction)

*Belloc, Hilaire, *James I; Charles II; Milton; Cromwell* (biographical studies)

Defoe, Daniel, *Journal of the Plague Year*

*Hollis, Christopher, *Dryden* (biographical study)

Macaulay, Thomas B., *Essay on Milton*

Sabatini, Raphael, *Fortune's Fool* (fiction)

*Yeo, Margaret, *King of Shadows* (fiction)

THE AGE OF POPE

Aitken, G. A., *Steele* (biography)

*Chesterton, G.K., *Essay on Pope*

Dobson, Austin, *Eighteenth Century Vignettes* (essays)

Fitch, Clyde, *Beau Brummell* (drama)

*Leslie, Shane, *The Skull of Swift* (biographical study)

Scott, Walter, *Rob Roy; Waverly* (fiction)

Sheridan, Richard Brinsley, *The Rivals; School for Scandal* (dramas)

Tarkington, booth, *Monsieur Beaucaire* (fiction)

* Thorton, Francis B., *Alexander Pope* (biography)

Thackeray, William M., *Henry Esmond, Virginians* (fiction)

Van Doren, Carl, *Swift* (biographical study)

THE AGE OF JOHNSON

Balderston, J. L., *Berkeley Square* (drama)

Carlyle, Thomas, *Essay on Burns*

*Chesterton, G. K., *The Judgment of Dr. Johnson* (biographical study)

Daichies, David, *Robert Burns* (critical study)

Dickens, Charles, *Barnaby Rudge* (fiction)

Goldsmith, Oliver, *She Stoops to Conquer* (drama); *The Deserted Village* (poetry)

*Hollis, Christopher, *Doctor Johnson* (biographical study)

Krutch, Joseph Wood, *Samuel Johnson* (biography)

Moore, L.L., *The Jessamy Bride* (fiction)

Williamson, Claude, *Writers of Three Centuries*

THE AGE OF ROMANTICISM

1780 - 1840

There were many indications that the old formal world of classicism was "as dead as a coffin-nail." A new spirit was blowing through the land. England's complacency had been shaken by the American Revolution. In 1783, Sir William Pitt, a liberal, had become Prime Minister. Wisely, he adopted a generous policy toward the remaining colonies of the Crown. And as English trade expanded, wealth increased and the country prospered.

But across the channel there was trouble. When the French Revolution broke out, Englishmen in general were in sympathy with the desperate peasant classes. Young idealists hurried abroad to do what they could to help. "Liberty! Fraternity! Equality!" was the war slogan of the day. Jean Jacques Rousseau proposed the idea that man left to himself is entirely good; that all evils to which flesh is heir have come from civilization; that "primitive man," the "noble savage," is naturally good. The idea of the French radicals was to destroy the artificial culture bred by the court and to start over.

But as the movement became more and more violent and the guillotine became the symbol of a Reign of Terror, English sympathy cooled. The terrorist measures of frenzied republican leaders alarmed the rest of Europe; and by 1793 English sympathy was no longer with the new Republic. The wild-eyed young Bonaparte had everyone on edge. Ambition was on the march, and no one knew where it would end. England was forced into defense. There was no peace until the Battle of Waterloo, fought in 1815 upon the fields of Belgium, disposed of Napoleon and his dreams of world conquest. Then the great powers met in Vienna to settle the peace of Europe. England emerged from the wars more powerful than before. She had gained new territory and new respect. The victory of Lord Nelson at Trafalgar in 1805 had reaffirmed her supremacy on the sea, and she was generally conceded to be the most powerful of existing empires.

THE DEFEAT OF NAPOLEON

But Rousseau had made an impression. Men had grown tired of the classical ideal with its emphasis on reason. Perhaps the new philosophy of feeling and emotion might contribute more to the happiness they were seeking.

False as Rousseau's ideas were—he claimed that man was an *emotional animal* rather than a rational being—they did have several good effects on English literature. The suggestion that "primitive men" led a happier and nobler life than those "spoiled" by civilization prompted several poets to seek inspiration in humble people, instead of in urbane society. Nature, also, began to look good to them. Impelled by Rousseau's exaltation of the emotions, these poets became more interested in their own feelings and reactions to beauty than in the consecrated descriptions of classical authors. They looked at this magic planet, the earth, and at the wonder-change of seasons, as if they were seeing them for the first time. At times, they approached the true Catholic attitude which sees the beauty of God shining forth from every corner of the universe. The fresh contact with nature and the new emphasis on emotion, imagination, and personal feeling created the right atmosphere for lyric poetry. At no other point in the history of English literature do we find such a joyous outburst of lyric melodies.

Renewed interest in the life and literature of the Middle Ages was also an important factor of the movement. A certain Bishop Percy had made a collection of medieval ballads and romances back in 1765. They had been read and imitated by a few writers at that time, but in this new century when young poets were rejecting the restrictions and rules of the classicists, the old ballads became immensely popular. The variety of verse forms and the sense of mystery and wonder that pervaded them became features of the new poetry. The ballads were the more eagerly taken over because the new writers preferred the simplicity of "primitive" medieval folk literature to the stiff, artificial forms of the classicists. And since these early nineteenth-century poets were trying to bring some of the freshness of the old romances into their own poetry, they came to be known as romanticists.

THE REDISCOVERY OF OLD BALLADS

Romanticism stresses the personal feelings of the writer; therefore, no two romantic poets are alike. Wordsworth concerned himself with the simple, humble phases of nature which he met in the secluded Lake District. Coleridge gave voice to the mysterious and strange in such poems as "The Ancient Mariner." Keats captured the rich, sensuous beauty of nature and perpetuated it in his immortal odes. Byron and Shelley were in revolt against all law, not so much because they felt individual laws were unjust as because they believed that all law hampers personal liberty. This sense of rebellion is expressed passionately in their verse.

The accentuation of personal feeling also had its effect in the prose writing of the times. The personal essay, under the pen of Charles Lamb, achieved new charm. Addison and Steele had written delightful light essays. But Lamb added the personal note that made him the first great familiar essayist in our language. Under the influence of *Blackwood's Magazine* and the *London Magazine,* which furnished a ready market for the familiar essays of Lamb, Hazlitt, Hunt, and De Quincey, the personal essay attained a grace and perfection which have seldom been excelled. Few essayists have matched the charm of Lamb. He wrote not to instruct, but to share with his readers the humor, the pathos, and the beauty which he discovered in the common adventure of living.

ROMANTICISM AND EXAGGERATED ROMANTICISM

In any discussion of art, whether it be music, architecture, poetry, or literature, this question will always be asked—Is the work classical or romantic? Today, for example, we hear much about the preference, in music, for the classicism of Bach to the romanticism of Wagner.

The history of arts and letters has shown that the tempo and spirit of each age have emphasized either the romantic or the classical tradition. We say emphasized, since no age has seen the complete absence of either spirit. In fact, in the great masterpieces of world literature the two traditions have been fused harmoniously. Thus, in Sophocles as in Virgil, in Shakespeare as in Milton, there is a wedding of the two spirits, with the classical element predominant in Virgil and the romantic triumphing in Shakespeare's dramas.

In our study of neo-classic literature we discussed the differences between real classicism and the exaggerated form of pseudo-classicists. Before beginning the study of the great romantic poets, we shall do well to understand what romanticism as opposed to classicism means, and to discuss the exaggerated romanticism which colored many of the writings of the romantic movement.

Someone has defined romanticism as "strangeness wedded to beauty." It is an attitude of the mind which views the world under the guise of the strange, the fanciful, the mysterious, and the wondrous. The artistic expression of this romantic spirit fills the beholder with awe and wonder. Romanticism symbolizes the restless pursuit of adventure, of the extraordinary, of the search for an ideal. This romantic spirit belongs to all ages. It is found in Homer's *Odyssey* and in Spenser's *Faerie Queene.* But in the Middle Ages it was predominant. The Gothic cathedral—the contribution of the Middle Ages to architecture—symbolizes the fusion of the romantic spirit and Christianity. The gargoyles, the flying buttresses, the myriad details of its decorative devices all produce a sense of strangeness and wonder, the very opposite of the simplicity and repose of the classical temple. The arched columns and the Gothic spires reaching into the heavens represent the upward striving of man away from earth and his yearning for the *Summum Bonum,* God. In the medieval romances, especially those dealing with the quest of the Holy Grail, we have the perfect illustration of the romantic spirit in pursuit of idealistic adventure.

Strong as was the classical tradition in the writings of the great Elizabethans, the romantic elements triumphed. The romantic spirit was even kept alive throughout the neo-classical era, but it was in the Romantic Movement proper that the themes of extravagant love, heroism, and adventure came back into English literature. We have seen that the ballad literature was rediscovered and the Middle Ages explored, not for the faith which the Middle Ages possessed but for the romantic spirit which that faith had supernaturalized.

But with the dawn of the Romantic Movement a number of new qualities were added to the old spirit of romanticism. Hence the Romantic Movement, as an epoch in English art, is a mixture of old and new characteristics. Noteworthy among the new elements were a rebellion against the restraining influence of neo-classic rules and an insistence upon spontaneity in artistic expression; a rediscovery of the Middle Ages, resulting in a renewal of interest in the themes of chivalrous love, heroism, and adventure; a rediscovery of the classical spirit as opposed to the neo-classical. Some of the poets looked beyond the Middle Ages to be influenced by the spirit of Greece and Rome. Hence we have in the odes of Keats a manifestation of a sane classicism—a suggestion of universal truth from particular images.

REVOLT AGAINST ARTIFICIALITY

ROBERT BURNS

WILLIAM WORDSWORTH

SAMUEL COLERIDGE

WALTER SCOTT

LORD BYRON

PERCY BYSSHE SHELLEY

JOHN KEATS

CHARLES LAMB

All the above tendencies were healthy and wholesome and of themselves would have produced masterpieces in the spirit of the medieval romances and of Shakespeare. But the great romantic poets, now almost completely cut off from the Catholic tradition and Christian philosophy, lost their way in the new and pagan doctrines of Rousseau. It is a far cry from the romantic poets of the Elizabethan era, who were consciously or unconsciously still fed upon the Christian orthodoxy of Thomas Aquinas, and the great romantic geniuses who inherited a Christianity stripped of the supernatural, the moral law stripped of everything but convention, and the human heart stripped of Divine Love and left alone to contemplate its morbidly sad, empty, and naked self.

It is little wonder that many dangerous elements entered into the authentic romantic spirit and created what we shall term an *exaggerated romanticism*. The most destructive of these elements were, first, a contempt for restraint which led to the glorification of unrestrained emotions and the expression of the poet's subjective feelings with an exaggerated intensity; and secondly, a misinterpretation of the place of nature in the eternal scheme of things; the romantics looked upon nature as an end rather than a stepping-stone to the Ultimate Good. For them nature was not a sacrament, a symbol of the beauty, power, and goodness of the Divine Creator, above and apart from the physical universe as it is for the Christian philosopher and poet. For the romanticists, nature constituted the ultimate with which they endeavored to become physically identified. Guided by a misty sort of pantheism, they wanted to come into an emotional communion with the "world soul." Religion for them became an emotional contemplation of the universe, and the poet became the high priest of a hazy nature worship. They failed to recognize the distinction between the natural and the supernatural and often confused the ideal with the real and the spiritual with the earthy.

NATURE AND THE ETERNAL

Moreover, this extreme subjectivity led to an inevitable disillusionment and the disease of romantic melancholy. An unhealthy self-pity inspired the romanticists to picture themselves as sensitive and superior beings neglected and misunderstood by the common herd. This morbid brooding, this parading of the wounded, bleeding heart before the world intensified their egoism and made them revel in their own melancholy. Such exaggerated introspection influenced their poetry and greatly minimized the universal appeal and the objectivity which every truth artistically expressed should contain.

Hence, the major weakness of the romantic poets was that they gave free rein to the expression of personal moods and distorted fancies rather than to the utterance of universal truths and emotions common to mankind.

This exaggerated romanticism paved the way for the naturalism and ultra-realism which have plagued English and American literature to the present day. Nor is it difficult to see the connection between modern surrealism[1] and that type of romanticism which overestimated

[1] SURREALISM—An artistic movement which tries to express subconscious mental activities in disconnected and dreamlike images.

the place of sensation, feeling, imagination, and emotion to the disregard of reason and objective truth, and which paraded for public dissection the intimate secrets of the poets' introspective selves.

She Dwelt Among the Untrodden Ways

WILLIAM WORDSWORTH

When Wordsworth was twenty-nine years old, he wrote a group of five poems sometimes known as the "Lucy lyrics." There is no way of knowing who Lucy was. But the poems about her breathe a sense of reality. In the following "Lucy lyric," there is an authentic expression of the emotion of grief that avoids sentimentality. The poem tells its story so simply and clearly that it needs no explanation.

She dwelt among the untrodden ways
  Beside the springs of Dove;
A maid whom there were none to praise,
  And very few to love.

A violet by a mossy stone
  Half hidden from the eye;
Fair as a star, when only one
  Is shining in the sky.

She lived unknown, and few could know
  When Lucy ceased to be;
But she is in her grave, and oh
  The difference to me!

FOR APPRECIATION

1. Point out the different ways in which the poet suggests that Lucy lived in a remote, lonely place. Do you have any idea where it was?

2. Discuss the aptness of the figures in stanza 2. What do they tell us of the character of Lucy? Is this the poetic, or artistic, way of expressing a reality? Discuss.

3. How does the third stanza convey the impression of sincere emotion? Would the feeling of grief be stronger if the poet said more about it? Why or why not?

She Was a Phantom of Delight

WILLIAM WORDSWORTH

The following lines are a beautiful tribute, "written from the heart," to Mrs. Wordsworth. Note the use of everyday language in the poem—an example of Wordsworth's theory that in treating of everyday realities, commonplace and simple language should be used.

She was a phantom of delight
When first she gleamed upon my sight;
A lovely apparition, sent
To be a moment's ornament;
Her eyes as stars of twilight fair;
Like twilight's, too, her dusky hair;
But all things else about her drawn
From Maytime and the cheerful dawn;
A dancing shape, an image gay,
To haunt, to startle, and waylay.

I saw her upon nearer view,
A spirit, yet a woman too!
Her household motions light and free,
And steps of virgin liberty;
A countenance in which did meet
Sweet records, promises as sweet;
A creature not too bright or good
For human nature's daily food;
For transient sorrows, simple wiles,
Praise, blame, love, kisses, tears, and smiles.

And now I see with eye serene
The very pulse of the machine;
A being breathing thoughtful breath,
A traveler between life and death;
The reason firm, the temperate will,
Endurance, foresight, strength, and skill;
A perfect woman, nobly planned,
To warn, to comfort, and command;
And yet a spirit still, and bright
With something of angelic light.

22. MACHINE—Body.

FOR APPRECIATION

1. Sketch in a few sentences the character portrait of Mrs. Wordsworth as suggested by Wordsworth in the poem. Does the poet give us a picture of a person with one predominant characteristic, or is the portrait a series of equally important physical and spiritual qualities? Discuss.

2. Select various metaphors from the poem and state simply what physical or spiritual quality each metaphor describes. Discuss and memorize lines 27-28.

3. Compare and contrast this poem with any one or several of Elizabethan, Cavalier, or Metaphysical love poems. Which type do you prefer? Explain. Do not fail to compare and contrast both the diction and the imagery in the Romantics and the poets of the seventeenth century.

The Tables Turned

WILLIAM WORDSWORTH

The title of the poem indicates a rebuttal. And so it is. The poem is Wordsworth's answer to a critic who accused him of making nature his sole preoccupation to the neglect of formal study. The poem contains in germ what Wordsworth taught throughout his poetry: nature is a great moral teacher. We shall meet this theory again in "Tintern Abbey." In a certain sense, nature can be a moral teacher, but not to the exclusion of those sacred and profane studies which contain the truths of Divine Wisdom made known to man through the light of reason and Revelation. The poem contains some truth, but exaggerates nature's importance.

Up! up! my Friend, and quit your books;
Or surely you'll grow double.
Up! up! my Friend, and clear your looks;
Why all this toil and trouble?

The sun, above the mountain's head,
A freshening lustre mellow
Through all the long green fields has spread,
His first sweet evening yellow.

Books! 'tis a dull and endless strife;
Come, hear the woodland linnet,
How sweet his music! on my life,
There's more of wisdom in it.

And hark! how blithe the throstle sings!
He, too, is no mean preacher;
Come forth into the light of things,
Let Nature be your teacher.

She has a world of ready wealth,
Our minds and hearts to bless—
Spontaneous wisdom breathed by health,
Truth breathed by cheerfulness.

One impulse from a vernal wood
May teach you more of man,
Of moral evil and of good,
Than all the sages can.

Sweet is the lore which Nature brings;
Our meddling intellect
Misshapes the beauteous forms of things—
We murder to dissect.

Enough of Science and of Art;
Close up those barren leaves;
Come forth, and bring with you a heart
That watches and receives.

FOR APPRECIATION

1. Discuss in detail the meter and the rhyme of the poem in its relationship to a) the poet's attitude toward his critic b) the poet's attitude toward nature. Do you think that there is a disparity between the subject matter and the rhythm employed? Or do you think that

the author deliberately varied his rhythms to express both his attitude toward the critic and his attitude toward nature? Compare, e.g., the thought and movement in stanza 3 with the thought and movement in stanza 6.

2. Would you consider the poem in its entirety to be a light and flippant reply to the critic, or do you think that at times Wordsworth is deadly serious when he says that Nature is more effective than study? Discuss.

3. Discuss the individual manifestations of Nature which the poet selects to contrast the place of Nature and of books in man's life.

4. Do you agree with the thought content of lines 25-29? Explain what the poet means in lines 29-32.

Lines Written in Early Spring

WILLIAM WORDSWORTH

This poem illustrates both the subjectivism of lyric poetry and the heightened subjectivism of the poetry of the Romantics. A mood is created in this poem not by the objective consideration of nature in the springtime, but by the attitude or the mood which the poet brings to the subject. For Wordsworth, the joyous manifestations of nature only intensify his lament of "what man has made of man." In the third and fourth lines, he gives us the key to the mood of the poem in a typical expression of Romantic melancholy.

I heard a thousand blended notes
While in a grove I sate reclined,
In that sweet mood when pleasant thoughts
Bring sad thoughts to the mind.

To her fair works did Nature link
The human soul that through me ran;
And much it grieved my heart to think
What man has made of man.

Through primrose tufts, in that green bower,
The periwinkle trailed its wreaths;
And 'tis my faith that every flower
Enjoys the air it breathes.

The birds around me hopped and played,
Their thoughts I cannot measure:—
But the least motion which they made,
It seemed a thrill of pleasure.

The budding twigs spread out their fan,
To catch the breezy air;
And I must think, do all I can,
That there was pleasure there.

If this belief from heaven be sent,
If such be Nature's holy plan,
Have I not reason to lament
What man has made of man?

10. PERIWINKLE—A trailing evergreen herb with blue or white flowers.

FOR APPRECIATION

1. Discuss in detail how the poet develops the tone of "sweet mood" and "sad thoughts" throughout the poem.

2. Which is predominant in the poem, the intellectual or the emotional element? Is the emotion expressed overdone? Do you think that it borders upon the sentimental? Discuss the meaning of "What man has made of man."

3. What is your opinion of both the intellectual and the poetic value of lines 11-12? Lines 19-20?

The Solitary Reaper

WILLIAM WORDSWORTH

In this famous poem we have an illustration of how a chance line of casual reading can give birth to an immortal poem. It was while reading a sentence about a solitary girl in Wilkinson's TOURS OF SCOTLAND *that Wordsworth received the inspiration to write the poem. Wordsworth loved solitude, and perhaps the solitude of the girl had an immediate appeal to him. At any rate, solitude is the theme of the first stanza and the overtone of the entire poem. In the first stanza, which is by far the best, note how many words the poet uses to attain the effect of solitude.*

Behold her, single in the field,
You solitary highland lass!
Reaping and singing by herself;
Stop here, or gently pass!
Alone she cuts and binds the grain,
And sings a melancholy strain;
O listen! for the vale profound
Is overflowing with the sound.

No nightingale did ever chaunt
More welcome notes to weary bands
Of travelers in some shady haunt,
Among Arabian sands;
A voice so thrilling ne'er was heard
In springtime from the cuckoo-bird,
Breaking the silence of the seas
Among the farthest Hebrides.

Will no one tell me what she sings?
Perhaps the plaintive numbers flow
For old, unhappy, far-off things,
And battles long ago;
Or is it some more humble lay,
Familiar matter of today?
Some natural sorrow, loss, or pain,
That has been, and may be again!

Whate'er the theme, the maiden sang
As if her song could have no ending;
I saw her singing at her work,
And o'er the sickle bending—
I listened, motionless and still;
And, as I mounted up the hill,
The music in my heart I bore
Long after it was heard no more.

16. HEBRIDES (hĕb´rĭ·dēz)—A group of islands off the coast of Scotland.

FOR APPRECIATION

1. Explain the two figures of speech used in stanza 2 to suggest the quality of the girl's song. Explain the meaning of lines 15-16.

2. What kind of song is suggested in stanza 3? What would the mood of such a song be? Why? Discuss the place of the imagination in Romantic poetry as suggested by the stanza. Is it healthy?

3. How does this poem illustrate the meaning of Wordsworth's statement that "poetry is a powerful emotion recollected in tranquility"? Do lines 31-32 give the key to your answer? Explain.

4. Reread the poem and follow carefully the comparison between the girl and the birds. How does the song of the girl resemble the song of the birds?

Composed Upon Westminster Bridge

WILLIAM WORDSWORTH

There is something about the silence of an unawakened city in the early morning hours that is awe-inspiring. From Westminster Bridge, Wordsworth watched London, born anew with the dawn, and saw the city almost as if it were some great object of nature.

Earth has not anything to show more fair:
Dull would he be of soul who could pass by
A sight so touching in its majesty:
This City now doth, like a garment, wear
The beauty of the morning; silent, bare,
Ships, towers, domes, theatres, and temples lie
Open unto the fields, and to the sky;
All bright and glittering in the smokeless air.
Never did sun more beautifully steep
In his first splendour, valley, rock, or hill;
Ne'er saw I, never felt, a calm so deep!
The river glideth at his own sweet will:
Dear God! the very houses seem asleep;
And all that mighty heart is lying still!

FOR APPRECIATION

1. The subject of this sonnet is a city at sunrise. Is this the ordinary subject matter of Wordsworth's poetry? What precise quality of the city so appealed to the poet that he was forced to state: "Dull would he be of soul, etc."? Do you think that Wordsworth proved his statement of line 1? Discuss.

2. State the central thought of the poem. What details did the poet select to develop this thought?

3. What is the predominant mood of the poem? Show how the meter and the choice of words help to attain this mood.

4. Discuss the effectiveness of the imagery; e.g., *wear the beauty of the morning; sun . . . steeps; mighty heart is lying still.*

5. Would Wordsworth's description be true of modern London? Of any modern city in early morning? Discuss.

PROJECTS

1. Read the interesting description of Westminster Bridge in E. V. Lucas' *Introducing London and London Afresh.*

2. Place yourself in reality or in imagination on some spot where you can view your city or town in panorama. Write a prose description or attempt a sonnet.

The World Is Too Much With Us

WILLIAM WORDSWORTH

Since the Industrial Revolution ushered in the dawn of our mechanistic era, men have been tempted to think of success in terms of bank accounts, and to measure progress in the number of gadgets which clutter up our highways, offices, and homes. Men are so busy making a living that they have forgotten the art of how to live. The industrial world is so much with us that too often we have neither the time nor the inclination to enjoy the beauty of the universe or the beauty of the human mind. This is the lesson of Wordsworth's poem. But we need not be "a pagan suckled in a creed outworn" to appreciate God's handiwork. Christian philosophy gives the true perspective to time and eternity. As you read the poem, notice the special beauty of the sonnet form with its carefully woven rhyme scheme.

The world is too much with us; late and soon,
Getting and spending, we lay waste our powers;
Little we see in Nature that is ours;
We have given our hearts away, a sordid boon!
The sea that bares her bosom to the moon;
The winds that will be howling at all hours,
And are upgathered now like sleeping flowers;
For this, for everything, we are out of tune;
It moves us not.—Great God! I'd rather be
A pagan suckled in a creed outworn;
So might I, standing on this pleasant lea,
Have glimpses that would make me less forlorn;
Have sight of Proteus rising from the sea;
Or hear old Triton blow his wreathèd horn.

11. SO MIGHT I—If then I might.

13. PROTEUS—A lesser sea-god under Neptune who could transform himself into any shape that pleased him.

14. TRITON—The son of Poseidon or Neptune who blew upon a seashell trumpet to raise or calm the seas. Both gods are here used as symbolic of the great love of nature which the pagan Greeks and Romans had. Those who have studied the *Aeneid* are acquainted with both the sea-gods.

FOR APPRECIATION

1. Explain the meaning of "world" in line 1. Do lines 3 and 4 help us to obtain the right meaning? Explain fully line 4.

2. What is the figure of speech in lines 6 and 7?

3. Do you think that Wordsworth means literally that he would like to return to heathen beliefs? If not, what do the last six lines of his sonnet mean? Discuss.

A PROJECT

Write an editorial on the theme of this poem, or discuss in a written paper your reactions to the thoughts contained in the introduction to this poem.

Westminister Bridge today.

Xanadu

Kubla Khan

SAMUEL TAYLOR COLERIDGE

In the summer of 1797, Coleridge, who was in ill health, went to a farm house near Porlock, England, hoping the rest would cure him. One morning as he sat reading Purchas's Pilgrimage *he fell asleep in his chair. The last words he read were: "In Xanadu did Cublai Can build a stately Palace, encompassing sixteene miles of plaine ground with a wall, wherein are fertile Medowes, pleasant Springs, delightfull Streames, and all sorts of beasts of chase and game, and in the middest thereof a sumptuous house of pleasure." He said upon awakening that he had composed during his sleep about three hundred lines telling of magnificent scenes of oriental splendor. He immediately began writing them down and had completed fifty-four lines when he was interrupted by a visitor who stayed an hour. Coleridge was never able to remember any more of the dream.*

In Xanadu did Kubla Khan
A stately pleasure-dome decree,
Where Alph, the sacred river, ran
Through caverns measureless to man
Down to a sunless sea.
So twice five miles of fertile ground
With walls and towers were girdled round;
And here were gardens bright with sinuous rills,
Where blossomed many an incense-bearing tree;
And here were forests ancient as the hills,
Enfolding sunny spots of greenery.

But O that deep romantic chasm which slanted
Down the green hill athwart a cedarn cover!
A savage place! as holy and enchanted
As e'er beneath a waning moon was haunted
By woman wailing for her demon-lover!
And from this chasm, with ceaseless turmoil seething,
As if this earth in fast thick pants were breathing,
A mighty fountain momently was forced;
Amid whose swift half-intermitted burst,
Huge fragments vaulted like rebounding hail,
Or chaffy grain beneath the thresher's flail;
And 'mid these dancing rocks at once and ever
It flung up momently the sacred river.
Five miles meandering with a mazy motion,
Through wood and dale the sacred river ran,
Then reached the caverns measureless to man,
And sank in tumult to a lifeless ocean;
And 'mid this tumult Kubla heard from far
Ancestral voices prophesying war!

The shadow of the dome of pleasure
Floated midway on the waves;
Where was heard the mingled measure
From the fountain and the caves.
It was a miracle of rare device,
A sunny pleasure-dome with caves of ice!
A damsel with a dulcimer
In a vision once I saw;
It was an Abyssinian maid,
And on her dulcimer she played,

1. XANADU (zăn´a·dōō)—A region of Tartary.

1. KHAN—Khan means king or emperor. Kubla (or Kublai) Khan was the rich and powerful founder of the Mongol dynasty of China. He lived from 1216(?) to 1294. Medieval travelers have written of the splendors of his court.

3. ALPH—Probably an imaginary name suggested by the Alpheus, a river of southern Greece which plunges underground and flows under the sea, emerging in Sicily.

Singing of Mount Abora.
Could I revive within me
Her symphony and song,
To such a deep delight 't would win me,
That with music loud and long
I would build that dome in air,
That sunny dome! those caves of ice!
And all who heard should see them there,
And all should cry, "Beware! beware!
His flashing eyes, his floating hair!
Weave a circle round him thrice,
And close your eyes with holy dread,
For he on honey-dew hath fed,
And drunk the milk of Paradise."

FOR APPRECIATION

1. The chief beauty of this uncompleted poem is in its music. Read aloud the poem, with a care for the cadences caused by the sentence structure. Can you suggest a reason for the changes in meter?

2. Where does the river have its source? How long does it run? Which is the better description of its end—"sunless sea" or "lifeless ocean"? Why?

3. Does line 30 give a hint as to how the thought might have been developed? Suggest a complete plot.

4. What does "the damsel with a dulcimer" have to do with the pleasure dome? What do lines 45-47 mean?

5. Who is the subject of the description in lines 50-55? What is suggested as the effect of feeding on *honey-dew* and drinking the *milk of Paradise?*

Ave Maria

WALTER SCOTT

To understand fully the sentiments expressed in this lovely song, it is important to know its setting in the romantic tale, THE LADY OF THE LAKE. *Ellen Douglas, a chieftain's daughter, is the heroine of the tale. Her home is in the midst of the wild Scottish highlands, far up in a mountain glade. Two powerful Scottish clansmen seek her hand in marriage; these two young warriors have met and quarrelled but have been suddenly called to gather their clans to defend Scotland. In the peril of the impending battle, Ellen's father, who must join in the fray, hides her away in a lonely, fearsome glen with only an old bard, Allan-Bane, for protector. As night falls, the girl becomes frightened and lonely. Then it is that she turns like a little child to the Mother she had learned to love when she was but a baby.*

Ave Maria! Maiden mild!
Listen to a maiden's prayer!
Thou canst hear though from the wild,
Thou canst save amid despair.
Safe may we sleep beneath thy care,
Though banished, outcast and reviled—
Maiden, hear a maiden's prayer;
Mother, hear a suppliant child.
Ave Maria!

Ave Maria! Undefiled!
The flinty couch we now must share
Shall seem with down of eider piled,
If thy protection hover there.
The murky cavern's heavy air
Shall breathe of balm, if thou hast smiled;
Then, Maiden, hear a maiden's prayer;
Mother, list a suppliant child!
Ave Maria!

Ave Maria! Stainless styled!
Foul demons of the earth and air,
From this their wonted haunt exiled,
Shall flee before thy presence fair.
We bow us to our lot of care,
Beneath thy guidance reconciled;
Hear for a maid a maiden's prayer;
And for a father hear a child.
Ave Maria!

FOR APPRECIATION

1. Which words of the song tell in what kind of place the maid is singing? What is her mood?

2. Is this really a prayer? Explain. Explain how Walter Scott, a non-Catholic, came to write a beautiful tribute to Mary.

3. Explain the meaning of the following phrases: *flinty couch; down of eider; breathe of balm; stainless styled; wonted haunt.*

4. What is the effect of the repeated invocation "Ave Maria"? What stanza do you like the best? Why?

5. If you have read *The Lady of the Lake,* recall the story and some of the characters.

(FROM) CHILDE HAROLD'S PILGRIMAGE

GEORGE GORDON, LORD BYRON

When Byron published the first two cantos of *Childe Harold's Pilgrimage* in 1812, he became famous overnight. In these cantos, Byron takes "Harold" through Spain, Portugal, and Greece. The last two cantos, published later, cover his journey through Belgium, Switzerland, and Italy. In its entirety, the poem is a long, descriptive narrative bound together by the endearing hero, "Childe Harold," who is Byron himself. In this indirect manner, Byron gave England a poetic personal travelogue in which he combines lyrical passages with romantic scenes and sentimental situations. Through the poem, he also expresses his revolt against the conventions of English society, as well as his own enthusiasms, his disillusionments, and his romantic melancholy.

Poetry seems to have come more naturally to Byron than normal speech. Almost all of *Childe Harold* is written in the Spenserian stanza. Its best passages have always found an admiring audience.

The Eve of Waterloo

A particularly vivid passage from the third canto of Byron's CHILDE HAROLD *is the description of the eve of Waterloo—a contrast of Brussels just before the battle, with the events that were to follow; carefree revelry, with horror and death. As you read, notice how effectively Byron has used the last line of each stanza to point out and emphasize the thought.*

It is true that there was a holiday spirit abroad in Brussels on the evening before the famous battle. Thackeray in his novel, VANITY FAIR, *has given us a similar picture in his description of Crawley's visit to Brussels, for the husbands of both Becky and Amelia were with the British forces. The same sort of scene has been enacted too often in human history, most notably—in recent times—when the Japanese during World War II stormed Singapore amidst the revelry in fashionable ball rooms, and when Rommel's German army thundered at the back door of Alexandria while the gaiety of the night life in the city was at its height.*

There was a sound of revelry by night,
And Belgium's capital had gather'd then
Her Beauty and her Chivalry, and bright
The lamps shone o'er fair women and brave men;
A thousand hearts beat happily; and when
Music arose with its voluptuous swell,
Soft eyes looked love to eyes which spake again,
And all went merry as a marriage bell;
But hush! hark! a deep sound strikes like a rising knell!

Did ye not hear it?—No; 'twas but the wind,
Or the car rattling o'er the stony street;
On with the dance! Let joy be unconfined;
No sleep till morn, when Youth and Pleasure meet
To chase the glowing Hours with flying feet.—
But hark! that heavy sound breaks in once more,
As if the clouds its echo would repeat:
And nearer, clearer, deadlier than before!
Arm! Arm! it is—it is—the cannon's opening roar!

Within a window'd niche of that high hall
Sate Brunswick's fated chieftain; he did hear
That sound the first amidst the festival,
And caught its tone with Death's prophetic ear,
And when they smiled because he deemed it near,
His heart more truly knew that peal too well
Which stretched his father on a bloody bier,
And roused the vengeance blood alone could quell:
He rushed into the field, and, foremost fighting, fell.

Ah! then and there was hurrying to and fro,
And gathering tears, and tremblings of distress,
And cheeks all pale, which but an hour ago
Blush'd at the praise of their own loveliness;
And there were sudden partings, such as press
The life from out young hearts, and choking sighs
Which ne'er might be repeated: who could guess
If ever more should meet those mutual eyes,
Since upon night so sweet such awful morn could rise!

1. REVELRY BY NIGHT—On the evening of the Battle of Quatre Bras, which preceded the Battle of Waterloo, the Countess of Richmond gave a ball in Brussels.

20. BRUNSWICK'S FATED CHIEFTAIN—The Duke of Brunswick, Frederick William, who was slain on the battlefield the next day.

And there was mounting in hot haste: the steed,
The mustering squadron, and the clattering car,
Went pouring forward with impetuous speed,
And swiftly forming in the ranks of war;
And the deep thunder, peal on peal afar;
And near, the beat of the alarming drum
Roused up the soldier ere the morning star;
While thronged the citizens with terror dumb,
Or whispering with white lips—"The foe! They come! they come!"

And wild and high the "Cameron's Gathering" rose!
The war-note of Lochiel, which Albyn's hills
Have heard, and heard, too, have her Saxon foes:—
How in the noon of night that pibroch thrills,
Savage and shrill! But with the breath which fills
Their mountain pipe, so fill the mountaineers
With the fierce native daring which instils
The stirring memory of a thousand years,
And Evan's, Donald's, fame rings in each clansman's ears!

The Ardennes waves above them her green leaves,
Dewy with Nature's tear-drops, as they pass,
Grieving, if aught inanimate e'er grieves,
Over the unreturning brave,—alas!
Ere evening to be trodden like the grass
Which now beneath them, but above shall grow
In its next verdure, when this fiery mass
Of living valour, rolling on the foe,
And burning with high hope, shall moulder cold and low.

Last noon beheld them full of lusty life,
Last eve in Beauty's circle proudly gay;
The midnight brought the signal-sound of strife,
The morn the marshalling in arms—the day
Battle's magnificently-stern array!
The thunder-clouds close o'er it, which when rent,
The earth is covered thick with other clay,
Which her own clay shall cover, heaped and pent,
Rider and horse—friend, foe—in one red burial blent!

49. PIBROCH (pē´brŏk)—A Scottish bagpipe.

54. EVAN'S . . . DONALD'S—The poet is here referring to Donald Cameron and his ancestor, Evan Cameron. In the preceding lines he describes the spirit of the Scottish soldiers in the English army.

55. THE ARDENNES—Situated in northern France. Byron is here using the wooded forests, associated with peace, for contrast with the marching army. These historic forests have been deluged with the blood of two World Wars. What part did they play in World War II?

FOR APPRECIATION

1. Select and study the passages which illustrate the contrast between the spirit of revelry and the spirit of war.

2. Line 12 is famous. What does it mean here in its context? Explain the figure in lines 13-14. The whole selection contains many famous lines. Make a list of those that you have heard quoted.

3. To how many kinds of sudden catastrophes could the description in stanza 4 apply? Discuss.

4. What differences in sound are indicated by stanzas six and seven?

5. Explain the meaning of the following phrases: *Death's prophetic ear; Albyn's hills and Saxon foes; noon of night; the stirring memory of a thousand years; covered thick with other clay.*

The Coliseum

This selection is taken from Canto IV of CHILDE HAROLD. *Omitted from the selection are forty-five lines of Byron's introduction which contain some of the most boastful and arrogant passages in English literature. In the selection given below, Byron uses the ruins of the Coliseum as a medium for lyrical outburst of emotional eloquence. In it are contained his fierce pride and his hatred for, and resentment of, society.*

And here the buzz of eager nations ran,
In murmured pity or loud-roared applause,
As man was slaughtered by his fellow man.
And wherefore slaughtered? Wherefore, but because
Such were the bloody Circus' *genial* laws,
And the imperial pleasure.—Wherefore not?
What matters where we fall to fill the maws
Of worms—on battle-plains or listed spot?
Both are but theaters where the chief actors rot.

I see before me the Gladiator lie:
He leans upon his hand—his manly brow
Consents to death, but conquers agony,
And his drooped head sinks gradually low—
And through his side the last drops, ebbing slow
From the red gash, fall heavy, one by one,
Like the first of a thunder-shower; and now
The arena swims around him—he is gone,
Ere ceased the inhuman shout which hailed the wretch who won.

5. CIRCUS—The Roman amphitheatre. During the corruption of the last years of the Empire, "bread and circuses" were given to the populace to keep them from revolting.

He heard it, but he heeded not—his eyes
Were with his heart, and that was far away;
He recked not of the life he lost, nor prize,
But where his rude hut by the Danube lay;
There were his young barbarians all at play,
There was their Dacian mother—he, their sire,
Butchered to make a Roman holiday—
All this rushed with his blood.—Shall he expire
And unavenged?—Arise! ye Goths, and glut your ire!

But here, where Murder breathed her bloody steam;
And here, where buzzing nations choked the ways,
And roared or murmured like a mountain stream
Dashing or winding as its torrent strays;
Here, where the Roman millions' blame or praise
Was death or life, the playthings of a crowd,
My voice sounds much, the fall the stars' faint rays
On the arena void—seats crushed—walls bowed—
And galleries, where my steps seem echoes strangely loud.

A ruin—yet what ruin! From its mass,
Walls, palaces, half-cities have been reared;
Yet oft the enormous skeleton ye pass,
And marvel where the spoil could have appeared.
Hath it indeed been plundered, or but cleared?
Alas! developed, opens the decay,
When the colossal fabric's form is neared.
It will not bear the brightness of the day,
Which streams too much on all years man have reft away.

But when the rising moon begins to climb
Its topmost arch, and gently pauses there;
When the stars twinkle through the loops of time,
And the low night-breeze waves along the air
The garland forest, which the gray walls wear
Like laurels on the bald first Caesar's head;
When the light shines serene but doth not glare,
Then in this magic circle raise the dead:
Heroes have trod this spot—'tis on their dust ye tread.

24. DACIAN—Dacia was a province of the Roman Empire.
27. GOTHS—The Goths, together with the other Teutonic tribes, eventually overran the Roman Empire.

"While stands the Coliseum, Rome shall stand;
When falls the Coliseum, Rome shall fall;
And when Rome falls—the World!" From our own land
Thus spake the pilgrims o'er this mighty wall
In Saxon times, which we are wont to call
Ancient; and these three mortal things are still
On their foundations, and unaltered all;
Rome and her Ruin past Redemption's skill,
The World, the same wide den—of thieves, or what ye will.

55. These lines have been ascribed to Venerable Bede.

FOR APPRECIATION

1. Point out in detail how the selection lacks the objectivity of a narrative poem. Explain how it is a good example of Romantic poetry. Begin your study with an analysis of lines 10-27. In these lines, does Byron give the feelings of the gladiator, or his own feelings?

2. Study in detail the imagery of lines 46-54. Can you visualize it?

3. There is a great deal of objective truth in the entire passage. Discuss the Coliseum as a symbol of the decay of the Roman Empire.

4. Explain the meaning of lines 5-9; lines 60-64. Do you agree with the thought content of these lines? Explain. Does the place of Rome in the world today justify Byron's remark? Explain.

The Destruction of Sennacherib

GEORGE GORDON, LORD BYRON

Remarkable for the swing of its rhythm and the vividness of its imagery, "The Destruction of Sennacherib" (sĕ·năk´ĕr·ĭb) *is a descriptive version of the Old Testament story found in* 4 *Kings,* 19. *The scene is the besieging of Jerusalem by Sennacherib, king of the Assyrians, in* 703 *B.C.*

The Assyrian came down like a wolf on the fold,
And his cohorts were gleaming in purple and gold;
And the sheen of their spears was like stars on the sea,
When the blue wave rolls nightly on deep Galilee.

2. HIS COHORTS—His troops of soldiers.

Like the leaves of the forest when Summer is green,
That host with their banners at sunset were seen:
Like the leaves of the forest when Autumn hath blown,
That host on the morrow lay withered and strown.

For the Angel of Death spread his wings on the blast,
And breathed in the face of the foe as he passed;
And the eyes of the sleepers waxed deadly and chill,
And their hearts but once heaved, and forever grew still!

And there lay the steed with his nostril all wide,
But through it there rolled not the breath of his pride,
And the foam of his gasping lay white on the turf,
And cold as the spray of the rock-beating surf.

And there lay the rider distorted and pale,
With the dew on his brow and the rust on his mail;
And the tents were all silent, the banners alone,
The lances unlifted, the trumpet unblown.

And the widows of Ashur are loud in their wail,
And the idols are broke in the temple of Baal;
And the might of the Gentile, unsmote by the sword,
Hath melted like snow in the glance of the Lord!

8. STROWN—Scattered.
21. ASHUR—Assyria.
22. BAAL—A heathen god which the Assyrians worshiped.
23. GENTILE—One not of the Jewish faith. Here, Sennacherib.

FOR APPRECIATION

1. Pick out the similes which describe the Assyrians in the first two stanzas.

2. What idea does the comparison in the first line give you about the Assyrians?

3. What two related comparisons does the poet use to contrast the Assryians in life with the Assyrians in death?

4. Was Sennacherib's army a large one? How do you know? Were they well equipped and clothed? Point out the lines which prove your answer.

5. Who or what was the Angel of Death?

6. Read the story in the last part of 4 Kings, 19, and point out what Byron omitted or added. On what particular verse in the Old Testament does this poem seem to be based?

She Walks in Beauty

GEORGE GORDON, LORD BYRON

It is a beautiful and charming woman whom Byron pictures here. She partakes of all the finest things of earth and yet is wound about with a soft, ethereal light that constitutes "the nameless grace which waves in every raven tress, or softly lightens o'er her face."

She walks in beauty, like the night
  Of cloudless climes and starry skies;
And all that's best of dark and bright
  Meet in her aspect and her eyes:
Thus mellowed to that tender light
  Which heaven to gaudy day denies.

One shade the more, one ray the less,
  Had half impaired the nameless grace
Which waves in every raven tress,
  Or softly lightens o'er her face;
Where thoughts serenely sweet express
  How pure, how dear, their dwelling-place.

And on that cheek, and o'er that brow,
  So soft, so calm, yet eloquent,
The smiles that win, the tints that glow,
  But tell of days in goodness spent,
A mind at peace with all below,
  A heart whose love is innocent!

FOR APPRECIATION

1. Although the poem appears in Byron's works under the heading "Hebrew Melodies," its inspiration is said to have been Mrs. Wilmot, the poet's cousin by marriage, who appeared at a ball in a black gown covered with spangles. What lines of the poem would lead you to suppose she wore that kind of dress?

2. In what sense is the term "beauty" used throughout the poem? Discuss. Could the lady described here be taken as an ideal of a lovely woman? Explain.

3. Could "aristocracy of character" be attributed to her? Enumerate the various qualities in the portrayal which you would desire in the ideal Catholic woman. Are there any qualities lacking? Discuss.

Ozymandias

PERCY BYSSHE SHELLEY

Shelley composed this well-known poem after he had read an account of a huge statue which had been found lying deserted in Egyptian sands. The inscription on the statue read: "I am Ozymandias, king of kings."

I met a traveler from an antique land
Who said: Two vast and trunkless legs of stone
Stand in the desert. Near them, on the sand,
Half sunk, a shattered visage lies, whose frown,
And wrinkled lip, and sneer of cold command,
Tell that its sculptor well those passions read
Which yet survive, stamped on these lifeless things,
The hand that mocked them, and the heart that fed;
And on the pedestal these words appear:
"My name is Ozymandias, king of kings:
Look on my works, ye Mighty, and despair!"
Nothing beside remains. Round the decay
Of that colossal wreck, boundless and bare
The lone and level sands stretch far away.

1. ANTIQUE LAND—Egypt.
7. YET SURVIVE—As seen in the face of the statue.
8. THEM—The passions.
8. HEART—The heart of the king.

FOR APPRECIATION

1. State in a sentence the theme of the poem. Might the theme be contained in line 11? Does it constitute a warning?

2. Discuss the effect of lines 12-14 in their relationship to the previous lines.

3. Discuss the structure of the poem.

4. Compare the thought content of this with Shakespeare's Sonnet LV.

The Cloud

PERCY BYSSHE SHELLEY

While boating on the Thames one afternoon, Shelley lay back in the boat to watch the constantly reshaping cloud masses and their gradual progress across the skies. The experience led him to compose the following poem which, because of the brilliancy of its individual pictures and the facile handling of its rhythm, has become one of his most popular.

A thoughtful reading of the poem discloses the fact that in it Shelley has his cloud take on all the shapes and forms that may ever be seen in the sky, at any time of day or night, in any season. He also suggests what the scientist would call the "function" of the cloud—that is, all the changes in weather and atmosphere that accompany various cloud formations. And lastly, he touches upon the strange nature of the cloud—its unending cycle.

I bring fresh showers for the thirsting flowers,
 From the seas and the streams;
I bear light shade for the leaves when laid
 In their noonday dreams.
From my wings are shaken the dews that waken
 The sweet buds every one,
When rocked to rest on their mother's breast,
 As she dances about the sun.
I wield the flail of the lashing hail,
 And whiten the green plain under,
And then again I dissolve it in rain,
 And laugh as I pass in thunder.
I sift the snow on the mountains below,
 And their great pines groan aghast
And all the night 'tis my pillow white,
 While I sleep in the arms of the blast.
Sublime on the towers of my skyey bowers,
 Lightning my pilot sits;
In a cavern under is fettered the thunder,
 It struggles and howls at fits;
Over earth and ocean, with gentle motion,
 This pilot is guiding me,
Lured by the love of the genii that move
 In the depths of the purple sea;
Over the rills, and the crags, and the hills,
 Over the lakes and the plains,
Wherever he dream, under mountain or stream,
 The Spirit he loves remains;
And I all the while bask in heaven's blue smile,
 Whilst he is dissolving in rains.

The sanguine Sunrise, with his meteor eyes,

31. SANGUINE—Red, like blood.

And his burning plumes outspread,
Leaps on the back of my sailing rack,
When the morning star shines dead,
As on the jag of a mountain crag,
Which an earthquake rocks and swings,
An eagle alit one moment may sit
In the light of its golden wings.
And when sunset may breathe, from the lit sea beneath,
Its ardors of rest and of love,
And the crimson pall of eve may fall
From the depth of heaven above,
With wings folded I rest, on mine airy nest,
As still as a brooding dove.

That orbèd maiden with white fire laden,
Whom mortals call the Moon,
Glides glimmering o'er my fleece-like floor,
By the midnight breezes strewn;
And wherever the beat of her unseen feet,
Which only the angels hear,
May have broken the woof of my tent's thin roof,
The stars peep behind her and peer;
And I laugh to see them whirl and flee,
Like a swarm of golden bees,
When I widen the rent in my wind-built tent,
Till the calm rivers, lakes, and seas,
Like strips of the sky fallen through me on high,
Are each paved with the moon and these.

I bind the Sun's throne with a burning zone,
And the Moon's with a girdle of pearl;
The volcanoes are dim, and the stars reel and swim,
When the whirlwinds my banner unfurl.
From cape to cape, with a bridge-like shape,
Over a torrent sea,
Sunbeam-proof, I hang like a roof—
The mountains its columns be.
The triumphal arch through which I march
With hurricane, fire, and snow,
When the Powers of the air are chained to my chair,
Is the million-colored bow;
The sphere-fire above its soft colors wove,
While the moist earth was laughing below.

I am the daughter of Earth and Water,
And the nursling of the Sky;
I pass through the pores of the ocean and shores;
I change, but I cannot die.
For after the rain when with never a stain
The pavilion of heaven is bare,
And the winds and sunbeams with their convex gleams,
Build up the blue dome of air,
I silently laugh at my own cenotaph,
And out of the caverns of rain,
Like a child from the womb, like a ghost from the tomb,
I arise and unbuild it again.

33. RACK—Thin, floating, broken clouds.
59. ZONE—Girdle; belt.
67. TRIUMPHAL ARCH—The rainbow.
81. CENOTAPH (sěn´ô·tăf)—An empty tomb.

FOR APPRECIATION

1. What meters does Shelley employ to achieve both the swift and majestic movement in the poem? Point out examples of internal rhyme. What effect does the habitual use of liquid sounds have upon the movement of the poem? Explain.

2. What time of year does the first stanza suggest? What kind of clouds? What kind of weather? What is meant by "their mother's breast" (line 7)? How and when does she "dance about the sun"?

3. What time of year do lines 13-16 suggest? Does the rest of the stanza keep the same picture? How can you tell? Who is the *pilot* of the cloud? Through how many lines is this figure continued? What cloud shapes do you see as you read this second stanza? Describe them. If you have read Virgil's *Aeneid,* you will recall an expression similar to that of lines 19-20.

4. Which lines in the third stanza describe the effect of the sunrise on the cloud? Which lines describe the sunset? Explain the different meanings of the word *sanguine.* What is the meaning of the word in line 31? What does *pall* mean? What are the two sources of color for the cloud in lines 39-44? Describe the difference between the sunrise and the sunset clouds. A Homeric simile is a long simile in which a series of details are compared. Explain the Homeric simile in lines 31-38.

5. What time of year is suggested in the fourth stanza? Which words give that impression? What new and different picture does Shelley use for the moon? What does he call the cloud-form? Why? Draw a rough sketch of the picture described in the fourth stanza.

6. Does the fifth stanza present one picture or a series of pictures? Explain. What do you think is the "burning zone" of line 59? What is the meaning of the expression, "When the Powers of the *air are chained to my chair"?* Show how lines 71-72 describe the conditions that cause a rainbow.

7. In what sense is the cloud a "daughter of *earth* and *water"?* As a scientist, do you agree with Shelley's explanation of why the sky is *blue?* Show how the word *cenotaph* gives the key to the meaning of lines 81-84.

To a Skylark

PERCY BYSSHE SHELLEY

Andre Maurois, the French biographer, wrote a life of Shelley entitled ARIEL—*a name which has a two-fold connotation, both meanings being applicable to Shelley. In medieval folklore, Ariel was a light, graceful spirit of the air; in Milton's* PARADISE LOST, *Ariel was one of the rebel angels.*

Shelley, in his subject matter as well as in his treatment of it, shows both natures. His works have an ethereal, intangible quality—an evidence of his yearning to escape from the conventional, earthy things in this material world. He shows himself also a rebel against the rules and shackles of society. He saw himself as a prophet, a liberator who would free mankind from enslavement to a conventional morality and bring to the world a clear white vision of the "ideal"—an ideal which, sadly, had no counterpart in reality. Thus he wrote in his famous Defence of Poetry, *"What were virtues of hope, love, . . . if Poetry did not ascend to bring light and fire from those eternal regions where the owl-winged faculty of calculation did not soar?"*

Hail to thee, blithe spirit!
Bird thou never Overt,
That from heaven, or near it,
Pourest thy full heart
In profuse strains of unpremeditated
art.

Higher still and higher
From the earth thou springest
Like a cloud of fire;
The blue deep thou wingest,
And singing still dost soar, and soaring
ever singest.

In the golden lightning
Of the sunken sun,
O'er which clouds are brightening,
Thou dost float and run,
Like an unbodied joy whose race is just
begun.

The pale purple even
Melts around thy flight;
Like a star of heaven,
In the broad daylight
Thou art unseen, but yet I hear thy shrill
delight,

Keen as are the arrows
Of that silver sphere,
Whose intense lamp narrows
In the white dawn clear,
Until we hardly see, we feel that it is
there.

All the earth and air
With thy voice is loud,
As, when night is bare,
From one lonely cloud
The moon rains out her beams, and
heaven is overflowed.

What thou art we know not;
What is most like thee?
From rainbow clouds there flow not
Drops so bright to see
As from thy presence showers a rain of
melody.

Like a poet hidden
In the light of thought,
Singing hymns unbidden,
Till the world is wrought
To sympathy with hopes and fears it
heeded not;

Like a high-born maiden
In a palace tower,
Soothing her love-laden
Soul in secret hour
With music sweet as love, which over-
flows her bower;

Like a glowworm golden
In a dell of dew,
Scattering unbeholden
Its aërial hue
Among the flowers and grass, which
screen it from the view;

Like a rose embowered
In its own green leaves,
By warm winds deflowered,
Till the scent it gives
Makes faint with too much sweet those
heavy-winged thieves.

Sound of vernal showers
  On the twinkling grass,
Rain-awakened flowers,
  All that ever was
Joyous, and clear, and fresh, thy music
    doth surpass.

Teach us, sprite or bird,
  What sweet thoughts are thine;
I have never heard
  Praise of love or wine
That panted forth a flood of rapture so
    divine.

Chorus Hymeneal
  Or triumphal chaunt
Matched with thine, would be all
  But an empty vaunt—
A thing wherein we feel there is some
    hidden want.

What objects are the fountains
  Of thy happy strain?
What fields, or waves, or mountains?
  What shapes of sky or plain?
What love of thine own kind? what
    ignorance of pain?

With thy clear keen joyance
  Languor cannot be;
Shadow of annoyance
  Never came near thee;
Thou lovest—but ne'er knew love's sad
    satiety.

Waking or asleep
  Thou of death must deem
Things more true and deep
  Than we mortals dream,
Or how could thy notes flow in such a
    crystal stream?

We look before and after,
  And pine for what is not;
Our sincerest laughter
  With some pain is fraught;
Our sweetest songs are those that tell of
    saddest thought.

Yet if we could scorn
  Hate, and pride, and fear;
If we were things born
  Not to shed a tear,
I know not how thy joy we ever should
    come near.

66. CHORUS HYMENEAL (hī′mĕ·nē′al)—Wedding music; from Hymen, the god of marriage.

Better than all measures
  Of delightful sound,
Better than all treasures
  That in books are found,
Thy skill to poet were, thou scorner of
    the ground!

Teach me half the gladness
  That thy brain must know,
Such harmonious madness
  From my lips would flow,
The world should listen then, as I am
    listening now.

FOR APPRECIATION

1. Keeping in mind Shelley's theory about the function of the poet, we can see his skylark as a symbol of the poet-seer who ascends to the realm of the ideal to get his inspiration and then from those invisible realms sheds his music—and message—on the earth below. Exploring this point of view, re-read the poem, referring frequently to the following outline.

STANZA I:

An address to the lark as more than bird, as symbol of the poet's "unpremeditated art."

STANZAS II-VII:

A series of similes showing the lark's song as symbolic of the poet's song:

(a) inspiring like fire
(b) joyous
(c) invisibly inspired
(d) mysterious
(e) poignant, keen, intense, moving
(f) flooding all earth and air

STANZAS VIII-XII:

A series of similes showing that the source of inspiration is hidden:

(a) like the source of a poet's song
(b) like the light of a glowworm (sight)
(c) like the fragrance of a rose (scent)
(d) like the sound and sight of raindrops on the grass

STANZAS XII-XXI:

An apostrophe to the skylark as the spirit of inspiration, with the poet asking that his work may have the joyousness of the lark's song.

2. Show how the last phrase of line 100, "scorner of the ground" may be used to identify the skylark with the poet Shelley. Point out the passages in the poem which show the lark as a scorner of the ground. Point out examples from Shelley's poetry (his subjects and his treatment of them) that show the poet also as a scorner of the ground.

3. What is the meaning of the words, "love's sad satiety"? What were the circumstances in Shelley's life that make us feel that he had experienced that "sad satiety"? Select specific lines which express the strain of "romantic melancholy" running throughout the poem.

4. Quote the lines in stanza 8 that express the purpose and effect of a poet's work. Check the thought of this stanza with the explanation of the function of a poet as explained in the introduction to this poem.

5. What lines of the poem imply Shelley's personal conviction that he is to bring a "new gospel" to the universe? Discuss. Compare these lines with the last stanza of the "Ode to the West Wind," on which begins the following page.

6. What modern English playwright took the title for one of his plays from the first line of the poem?

7. Do you or do you not agree with the thought content of stanza 17? Prove your answer from your knowledge of literature and music.

8. Select at least ten striking figures of speech and analyze their poetic imagery.

Ode to the West Wind

PERCY BYSSHE SHELLEY

Shelley has told us that his "Ode to the West Wind" was "conceived and chiefly written in a wood that skirts the Arno, near Florence, Italy." It was a day when the wind was gathering clouds for the beginning of the autumn rains. By sunset the rains came with a tempest of hail and with "that magnificent thunder and lightning peculiar to the . . . regions."

To appreciate the beauty of the poem, the reader should be aware of its design, which is based upon various sets of threes. The wind acts upon three things—the dead leaves of earth (Stanza I), the clouds of heaven (Stanza II), and the waves of the sea (Stanza III). The fourth stanza gathers together the three pictures, and in it and the last stanza the poet presents this "wild west wind" as a symbol of himself—"tameless and swift and proud." The stanzas, like sonnets, have fourteen lines, except that they are broken into sets of threes and a couplet, and that the interlocking rhyming words (all but the first group in each stanza) appear in sets of threes. As you read, notice the exquisite blending of thought and design.

I

O wild West Wind, thou breath of Autumn's being,
Thou, from whose unseen presence the leaves dead
Are driven, like ghosts from an enchanter fleeing,

Yellow, and black, and pale, and hectic red,
Pestilence-stricken multitudes; O thou,
Who chariotest to their dark wintry bed

The wingèd seeds, where they lie cold and low,
Each like a corpse within its grave, until
Thine azure sister of the spring shall blow

Her clarion o'er the dreaming earth, and fill
(Driving sweet buds like flocks to feed in air)
With living hues and odors plain and hill;

Wild Spirit, which art moving everywhere;
Destroyer and preserver; hear, O hear!

9. AZURE SISTER—The mild west wind of spring as contrasted to the wild west wind of autumn.

II

Thou on whose stream, 'mid the steep sky's commotion,
Loose clouds like earth's decaying leaves are shed,
Shook from the tangled boughs of heaven and ocean,

Angels of rain and lightning; there are spread
On the blue surface of thine airy surge,
Like the bright hair uplifted from the head

Of some fierce Maenad, even from the dim verge
Of the horizon to the zenith's height,
The locks of the approaching storm. Thou dirge

Of the dying year, to which the closing night
Will be the dome of a vast sepulcher,
Vaulted with all thy congregated might

Of vapors, from whose solid atmosphere
Black rain, and fire, and hail will burst; O hear!

III

Thou who didst waken from his summer dreams
The blue Mediterranean, where he lay,
Lulled by the coil of his crystalline streams,

Beside a pumice isle in Baiae's bay,
And saw in sleep old palaces and towers
Quivering within the wave's intenser day,

All overgrown with azure moss and flowers
So sweet, the sense faints picturing them! thou
For whose path the Atlantic's level powers

Cleave themselves into chasms, while far below
The sea-blooms and the oozy woods which wear
The sapless foliage of the ocean, know

Thy voice, and suddenly grow gray with fear,
And tremble and despoil themselves; O hear!

21. MAENAD (mē´năd)—A frenzied priestess of Bacchus, the god of wine.

32. BAIAE (bī´ē)—A site of many ruins of ancient luxury near Naples. The region is volcanic, hence "pumice" or volcanic isle.

39-42. The explanation of these lines is to be found in Shelley's notes as follows: "The phenomenon alluded to at the conclusion of the third stanza is well known to naturalists. The vegetation at the bottom of the sea, of rivers, and of lakes, sympathizes with that of the land in the change of seasons, and is consequently influenced by the winds which announce it."

IV

If I were a dead leaf thou mightest bear;
If I were a swift cloud to fly with thee;
A wave to pant beneath thy power, and share

The impulse of thy strength, only less free
Than thou, O uncontrollable! If even
I were as in my boyhood, and could be

The comrade of thy wanderings over heaven,
As then, when to outstrip thy skyey speed
Scarce seemed a vision, I would ne'er have striven

As thus with thee in prayer in my sore need.
O lift me as a wave, a leaf, a cloud!
I fall upon the thorns of life! I bleed!

A heavy weight of hours has chained and bowed
One too like thee—tameless, and swift, and proud.

V

Make me thy lyre, even as the forest is;
What if my leaves are falling like its own!
The tumult of thy mighty harmonies

Will take from both a deep, autumnal tone,
Sweet though in sadness. Be thou, spirit fierce,
My spirit! Be thou me, impetuous one!

Drive my dead thoughts over the universe
Like withered leaves to quicken a new birth!
And, by the incantation of this verse,

Scatter, as from an unextinguished hearth
Ashes and sparks, my words among mankind!
Be through my lips to unawakened earth

The trumpet of a prophecy! O Wind,
If winter comes, can spring be far behind?

FOR APPRECIATION

1. In line 14, Shelley summarizes the twofold function of the west wind. Enumerate in detail how the west wind is both a destroyer and preserver.

2. Note the difference in tone quality, the harsh, staccato movement and the liquid cadence, between lines 1-8 and lines 9-12. Explain how the contrast is accomplished.

3. In stanza II, Shelley uses at least four figurative representations of the cloud. Point out each of these four similes or metaphors. Which one links this stanza with the preceding one? Show how the last line of the second stanza describes part of the experience which inspired the poem.

4. What effect does the west wind of fall have on the Mediterranean? Explain the meaning of lines 33-34. Note carefully how, by the use of liquid sounds, Shelley achieves the languid movement in lines 29-31.

5. Show how the opening lines of the fourth stanza tie together the imagery of the first three stanzas. In what respects does Shelley resemble the west wind?

6. Reread carefully the introduction to Shelley's "To a Skylark." Then explain in detail the lines in this poem which portray Shelley's aspirations as a social reformer.

7. Shelley usually chose as the subject matter of his poetry the intangible and ethereal. Explain how "Ode to the West Wind" illustrates this fact.

8. Why are the last two lines of the poem famous in literature?

9. Explain the rich imagery of the following phrases: *ghosts from an enchanter fleeing; pestilence-striken multitudes; clarion o'er the dreaming earth; dirge of the dying year; incantation of this verse.*

PROJECTS

1. Some critics have found elements of exaggerated romanticism in this poem, such as intensity of subjective feelings, a suggestion of pantheism, an unhealthy self-pity, revolt against convention. Select the lines in the poem which might justify the claim of the critics.

2. Discuss in detail why or why not this poem is intellectually satisfying to a Catholic.

On First Looking into Chapman's Homer

JOHN KEATS

Keats himself was not able to read Greek. A friend, however, brought him a copy of George Chapman's translation of Homer, and the two stayed up all night reading the book, "Keats shouting with delight as some passage of special energy struck his imagination." Fired by the splendors of the Greek culture thus opened to him, Keats composed the following sonnet after his friend had left, and presented it to him the next morning. It is considered one of the best sonnets in English literature.

Much have I traveled in the realms of gold
And many goodly states and kingdoms seen;
Round many western islands have I been
Which bards in fealty to Apollo hold.
Oft of one wide expanse had I been told
That deep-browed Homer ruled as his demesne;
Yet did I never breathe its pure serene
Till I heard Chapman speak out loud and bold.
Then felt I like some watcher of the skies
When a new planet swims into his ken;
Or like stout Cortez, when with eagle eyes
He stared at the Pacific—and all his men
Looked at each other with a wild surmise—
Silent, upon a peak in Darien.

1. REALMS OF GOLD—Great literature.
3-4. That is, I have read much poetry by English writers. "Western islands" refers to the British Isles. "Bards in fealty to Apollo" means "poets who have kept faith with Apollo, the god of song and music."
6. DEMESNE (dē·mān´)—Domain.
8. CHAPMAN—George Chapman (1559-1634), whose translation of Homer gives him a high place in English literature.
11. CORTEZ—Balboa, not Cortez, was discoverer of the Pacific Ocean.
14. DARIEN—A district covering the eastern part of the Isthmus of Panama joining Central and South America

FOR APPRECIATION

1. Put the thought of the first four lines into a few simple prose sentences. Such an exercise will show you the difference between the approach of prose and poetry to a subject.

2. What is the wide expanse that Homer "ruled"? Mention several other great Greek writers.

3. The sestet summarizes Keats' reaction to his discovery of Greek literature. He gives us two figures to help make this experience real. Explain them. Try to appreciate his feelings. Perhaps you have had a similar experience in your own life. Portray your reactions in several similes.

4. Line 14 is very famous in English literature. Why? To what kind of human experiences can this line be applied?

5. What noun is understood after "serene" in line 7? Look up the origin of the words: *fealty; ken; demesne.*

6. Scan the sonnet. Is it Italian in form? Explain.

PROJECTS

1. Read Keats' sonnet, "When I Have Fears that I May Cease To Be."

2. Attempt a paper on the place of Greek culture in our present civilization.

Ode to a Nightingale

JOHN KEATS

In the spring of 1819, the spirits of John Keats were weighed down by the remembrance of the recent death of his brother, and by the knowledge that he himself had only a short time left to live. His contemplated marriage with Fanny Brawne, thus, would now be impossible. It was in this mood that Keats wrote his "Ode to a Nightingale." The poem opens with a description of Keats' experience of both joy and pain as he listens to the song of the nightingale. His desire to avoid pain leads him to dream about the pleasures of wine, but he finally determines to escape the pain of life by living in his imagination with the nightingale he hears singing. This imaginary life is found to carry with it great beauty as symbolized by the poet's description of the flowers surrounding him. In such beauty Keats finds that it would be pleasant to die. But the thought of death leads him to consider that the nightingale is, in a sense, deathless, and that the song of the nightingale has been present not only during his own sorrow but in the sorrow of all human beings as symbolized in the story of Ruth, a figure from the Old Testament. In Ruth, then, Keats sees that sorrow as well as joy is a thing of beauty, and he is led to accept without rebellion the human lot of pain as well as happiness. The use of the word "forlorn" serves to end the poet's musings on the pain of life, and with the flight of the nightingale he becomes uncertain whether his acceptance of the beauty of suffering was real or not. A Catholic, with his appreciation of suffering and pain derived from an understanding of Calvary, should be able to follow the poet's reasoning easily.

My heart aches, and a drowsy numbness pains
    My sense, as though of hemlock I had drunk,
Or emptied some dull opiate to the drains
    One minute past, and Lethe-wards had sunk
'Tis not through envy of thy happy lot,
    But being too happy in thine happiness—

2. HEMLOCK—A drug made from hemlock, a poisonous herb.
4. LETHE-WARDS—Lethe is a river in Hades, whose water when drunk would cause one to forget the past. "Lethe-wards" of course means "toward" or "in the direction of Lethe."

That thou, light-wingèd Dryad of the trees,
In some melodious plot
Of beechen green, and shadows numberless,
Singest of summer in full-throated ease.

O, for a draught of vintage! that hath been
Cooled a long age in the deep-delvèd earth,
Tasting of Flora and the country green,
Dance, and Provencal song, and sun-burnt mirth!
O for a beaker full of the warm South,
Full of the true, the blushful Hippocrene,
With beaded bubbles winking at the brim,
And purple-stainèd mouth;
That I might drink, and leave the world unseen,
And with thee fade away into the forest dim,

Fade far away, dissolve, and quite forget
What thou among the leaves hast never known,
The weariness, the fever, and the fret
Here, where men sit and hear each other groan;
Where palsy shakes a few, sad, last gray hairs;
Where youth grows pale, and specter-thin and dies
Where but to think is to be full of sorrow
And leaden-eyed despairs;
Where Beauty cannot keep her lustrous eyes
Or new Love pine at them beyond tomorrow.

Away! away! for I will fly to thee,
Not charioted by Bacchus and his pards,
But on the viewless wings of Poesy,
Though the dull brain perplexes and retards
Already with thee! tender is the night,
And haply the Queen-Moon is on her throne,
Clustered around by all her starry Fays;
But here there is no light,
Save what from heaven is with the breezes blown
Through verdurous glooms and winding mossy ways.

7. DRYAD—Wood nymph.
13. FLORA—Goddess of flowers and the spring.
14. PROVENCAL SONG—Songs of the troubadours of Provencal in southern France.
16. HIPPOCRENE—A spring sacred to the goddesses who presided over poetry, art, and sciences (the Muses).
32. BACCHUS—God of wine. His chariot is often represented as being drawn by two leopards (pards).
37. FAYS—Fairies.

I cannot see what flowers are at my feet,
 Nor what soft incense hangs upon the boughs,
But, in embalmèd darkness, guess each sweet
 Wherewith the seasonable month endows
The grass, the thicket, and the fruit-tree wild;
 White hawthorne, and the pastoral eglantine;
Fast fading violets covered up in leaves;
 And mid-May's eldest child,
The coming musk-rose, full of dewy wine,
 The murmurous haunt of flies on summer eves.

Darkling I listen; and, for many a time
 I have been half in love with easeful Death,
Called him soft names in many a musèd rhyme,
 To take into the air my quiet breath;
Now more than ever seems it rich to die,
 To cease upon the midnight with no pain,
While thou art pouring forth thy soul abroad
 In such an ecstasy!
Still wouldst thou sing, and I have ears in vain—
 To thy high requiem become a sod.

Thou wast not born for death, immortal Bird!
 No hungry generations tread thee down;
The voice I hear this passing night was heard
 In ancient days by emperor and clown;
Perhaps the self-same song that found a path
 Through the sad heart of Ruth, when, sick for home,
She stood in tears amid the alien corn;
 The same that oft-times hath
Charmed magic casements, opening on the foam
 Of perilous seas, in faëry lands forlorn.

Forlorn! the very word is like a bell
 To toll me back from thee to my sole self!
Adieu! the fancy cannot cheat so well
 As she is famed to do, deceiving elf.
Adieu! adieu! thy plaintive anthem fades
 Past the near meadows, over the still stream,
Up the hill-side; and now 'tis buried deep
 In the next valley-glades.
Was it a vision, or a waking dream?
 Fled is that music:—Do I wake or sleep?

64. CLOWN—Peasant.
66. RUTH—See the Book of Ruth in the Bible. With her mother-in-law, Naomi, Ruth left her home and went to Bethlehem.

FOR APPRECIATION

1. What mood does the song of the nightingale arouse in the poet? What words in the first stanza suggest the place and the time of year?

2. In the second stanza, do you think that the poet really wants to be overcome with wine, or is he just daydreaming about the qualities associated with wine? Discuss. What connotation do you suppose "vintage" has that leads Keats to choose it rather than the word "wine"? What effect does the inclusion of the proper words *Flora, Provençal, Hippocrene* have? What associations do they carry with them to add to the effect of the stanza?

3. What word connects the thought of the third stanza with the thought of the second stanza? How is the poetic summary of the sorrows of life associated with the nightingale? Keep in mind that Keats himself was very ill.

4. The wish of the second stanza is now rejected. What new means of sharing the happiness of the nightingale is proposed? What common word would we use to express the idea "the viewless wings of Poesy"?

5. The impossibility of sight connects the fifth stanza with the previous one. Why does the poet use the phrase "embalmèd darkness"? Do you think line 50 is a successful line of poetry? Why or why not?

6. What words in the fifth stanza suggest the subject of death which the sixth stanza treats? What is the poet's attitude toward death in this stanza?

7. Why does Keats call the nightingale immortal? Is the nightingale's immortality similar to that implied by Shelley in the last stanza of "The Cloud"? Why did Keats refer to the story of Ruth in this passage? Lines 69-70 are often chosen as two of the most poetical lines of English literature. Do you agree with such a selection? Why or why not?

8. How is the poet called back to actual life in the last stanza? What is the fault found with fancy in lines 73-74? Explain the significance of the last half-line, "Do I wake or sleep?"

Ode on a Grecian Urn

JOHN KEATS

The eternal freshness and the perennial quality of art—this might well summarize the theme of Keats' beautiful "Ode on a Grecian Urn." The poet's youthful life was dedicated to the search for beauty, an ideal beauty which would transcend the transient human joys and earthly beauties. He saw that art makes permanent what life destroys, another way of expressing the belief that runs throughout his poetry that "a thing of beauty is a joy forever."

One day, Keats made a visit to the British Museum shortly after the famous collection of Elgin marbles had been brought from the Parthenon in Athens.

One marble vase had a decorative band which showed a group of men and women going to offer a sacrifice. They were playing various instruments and dancing as they went—a happy scene. The vase inspired Keats to compose an ode which has made the beauty of one Greek vase in the British Museum full of meaning to readers of poetry all through the world.

Thou still unravished bride of quietness,
  Thou foster-child of silence and slow time,
Sylvan historian, who canst thus express
  A flowery tale more sweetly than our rhyme:
What leaf-fringed legend haunts about thy shape
  Of deities or mortals, or of both,
    In Tempe or the dales of Arcady?
What men or gods are these? What maidens loth?
  What mad pursuit? What struggle to escape?
    What pipes and timbrels? What wild ecstasy?

Heard melodies are sweet, but those unheard
  Are sweeter; therefore, ye soft pipes, play on;
Not to the sensual ear, but, more endeared,
  Pipe to the spirit ditties of no tone.
Fair youth, beneath the trees, thou canst not leave
  Thy song, nor ever can those trees be bare;
    Bold Lover, never, never canst thou kiss,
Though winning near the goal—yet, do not grieve;
  She cannot fade, though thou hast not thy bliss,
    Forever wilt thou love, and she be fair!

Ah, happy, happy boughs! that cannot shed
  Your leaves, nor ever bid the Spring adieu;
And, happy melodist, unwearièd,
  Forever piping songs forever new;
More happy love! more happy, happy love!
  Forever warm and still to be enjoyed,
    Forever panting, and forever young;
All breathing human passion far above,
  That leaves a heart high-sorrowful and cloyed,
    A burning forehead, and a parching tongue.

1. Because undisturbed and unmolested, the urn has retained its original beauty and purity.
2. So-called because it has been preserved by silence and time.
3. SYLVAN HISTORIAN—Historian of rural scenes.
7. TEMPE—A valley in Greece, famed for its beauty and sacred to Apollo, the sun god.
7. ARCADY—A district of Greece inhabited by simple, contented people. It has become a symbol of peace and happiness.

Who are these coming to the sacrifice?
  To what green altar, O mysterious priest,
Lead'st thou that heifer lowing at the skies,
  And all her silken flanks with garlands dressed?
What little town by river or sea shore,
  Or mountain-built with peaceful citadel,
    Is emptied of this folk, this pious morn?
And, little town, thy streets for evermore
  Will silent be; and not a soul to tell
    Why thou art desolate, can e'er return.

O Attic shape! Fair attitude! with brede
  Of marble men and maidens overwrought,
With forest branches and the trodden weed;
  Thou, silent form, dost tease us out of thought
As doth eternity. Cold Pastoral!
  When old age shall this generation waste,
    Thou shalt remain, in midst of other woe
Than ours, a friend to man, to whom thou say'st,
  "Beauty is truth, truth beauty,"—that is all
    Ye know on earth, and all ye need to know.

41. ATTIC SHAPE—The urn. "Attic" means "Athenian." Attic sculpture is marked by its simplicity and purity.
41. BREDE—Decoration.
45. PASTORAL—That which pictures rural life and scenes.

FOR APPRECIATION

1. Why is the vase called an "unravished bride," "a foster-child of silence and slow time," "a sylvan historian"?

2. Do you think the vase really expresses a "flowery tale more sweetly" than the poet's rhyme? That is, do you think you could read as much into the vase as the poet did? Discuss.

3. Explain fully the meaning of lines 11-14. Why will the key to your explanation be the power of the imagination? Discuss.

4. In the last lines of stanza 2, why does the poet say the fair youth will forever love and the maiden be forever fair? Is there a permanence about art? Explain.

5. Explain fully the meaning of line 24. Explain the moral truth contained in lines 29-30. Do they aptly express the difference between spiritual and purely sensual love? Discuss.

6. In stanza 4, why will the little town be forever empty? Is there something significant in the fact that the holiday is also a holy day? Explain.

7. In what sense is the word *attitude* used in line 41? What likeness is there in the thoughts inspired by this centuries-old vase and by eternity (lines 44-45)? What *generation* does Keats mean in line 46? Explain the meaning of the next four lines. Do you agree with them? Why or why not?

8. We have seen that the imagination played a great part in the poetic theory of the Romantic poets. Keats is *par excellence* the poet of the imagination. Show in detail how this statement is exemplified in the "Ode on a Grecian Urn."

9. Compare the thought of this ode with stanza 15 of Shelly's "To a Skylark." Does any part of this ode express a similar thought? Is there any similarity in treatment? Discuss.

Bright Star! Would I Were Steadfast as Thou Art

JOHN KEATS

This last sonnet of Keats is a piercing cry of grief wrung from the young poet already dying of tuberculosis. While sailing from England to Italy in 1820, he was particularly struck one evening by the radiance of the evening star. He felt that he would never return to England nor see again his sweetheart, Fanny Brawne. In a moment of intense sadness, he composed this beautiful lyric.

Bright Star! would I were steadfast as thou art—
Not in lone splendour hung aloft the night,
And watching, with eternal lids apart,
Like Nature's patient sleepless Eremite,
The moving waters at their priestlike task
Of pure ablution round earth's human shores,
Or gazing on the new soft fallen mask
Of snow upon the mountains and the moors:—
No—yet still steadfast, still unchangeable,
Pillow'd upon my fair love's ripening breast,
To feel forever its soft fall and swell,
Awake forever in a sweet unrest,
Still, still to hear her tender-taken breath,
And so live ever—or else swoon to death.

4. EREMITE—Hermit.

FOR APPRECIATION

1. Explain in detail the imagery in lines 3-6. What is the relationship between "priestlike task" and "ablution"? What is the precise meaning of "No" in line 9?

2. Explain the relationship between line 11 and the moving waters of line 5.

3. Discuss the emotion expressed in lines 12-14. Is it a pure or a mixed emotion? Explain the phrase *sweet unrest.*

PROJECTS

1. Write a paper or prepare an oral discussion comparing Keats and Shelley as Romantic poets. Which do you prefer and why? Which poet is more objective? What are the differences in their subject matters and their treatment of them? Are the elements of exaggerated romanticism present in one or the other, or both?

2. Compare and contrast the lyric poetry of the Romantic poets with that of the Elizabethan or seventeenth-century poets.

RELATED READINGS

Wordsworth's "Ode on Intimations of Immortality" and "Michael"; Coleridge's "Christabel"; Byron's "Prisoner of Chilion"; Shelley's "Indian Serenade" and, for the very mature student, "Adonais"; Keats' "To Autumn" and "The Eve of St. Agnes."

WORD STUDY—ROMANTIC POETRY

The following words have been selected from the poems which you have studied. Endeavor to make them a part of your active vocabulary.

1. Give antonyms for: *transient; spontaneous; serene; sordid; unblemished; colossal; unpremeditated.*

2. What mood do the following words convey? *blithe; plaintive; fretful; hectic.*

3. What particular sensation is suggested by each of the following? *seething; meandering; sinuous; glut; satiety; fettered; sportive; meddling; lure.*

4. Make sure you know the meaning of: *recompense; matured; maws.*

The Defeat of Sennacherib

THE VICTORIAN ERA

1840-1900

When the eighteen-year-old Victoria became queen in 1837, England was confronted with the economic and social problems brought on by the industrial revolution. Feudalism was a thing of the past. The largely agricultural economy of the sixteenth and seventeenth centuries was being replaced by a new order. Cloth and pottery making, once carried on in the home, were being transferred to the factory. The family, as a closely-bound social and economic unit, was being disrupted by the necessity for finding work in the new industrial centers.

CHANGING ENGLAND

Within less than a century, the whole pattern of English life was changed. The invention of the steam engine, the flying shuttle, the spinning jenny, the spinning mule, and the power loom untied the bonds of English energy. Industry moved from the home, and hamlets, often within a generation, grew into cities. The resulting expansion of trade served to widen the gulf between the few rich and the many poor. Factory production brought on an evil time of human exploitation, child labor, and mass misery.

During this time of great industrial development, living and working conditions were very bad for the many lowly paid workers. Women often worked fourteen and sixteen hours a day in the coal mines, crawling on their hands and knees in the narrow passages, like beasts of burden, drawing their loaded cars. The price of food, kept high by a protective tariff on some staple products, attained levels almost beyond the reach of many families. Living quarters were wretched and unsanitary, as were the factories in which the people labored.

These were the first bitter fruits of the new industrial expansion. Times were ripe for revolt, but unlike the French Revolution which had been a battle of swords, the English revolution became a battle of books and legislation.

The social reforms which began in the middle years of the reign of Victoria have been continuing under varying leadership through the twentieth and twenty-first centuries. Restrictions in voting and holding public office were removed from Roman Catholics in 1829 and from Jews in 1839. In 1846, the Corn Laws were repealed. By 1833, slavery had been abolished in the colonies of West India, and in the same year was inaugurated the first important Factory Law, regulating child labor. Trade unionism was legalized in 1864, min 1867, the vote was extended to laboring classes, and by 1885, the third Reform Bill gave complete manhood suffrage to England. A post office system was adopted in 1839. Almost fifty years later—due largely to the efforts of William Gladstone—a system of universal state education was established, and religious tests were dropped from the entrance requirements of Oxford and Cambridge. Tariff laws that had kept up the price of essential foods had been repealed. Little by little, at the insistence of an aroused public, conditions in charity schools, prisons, hospitals, and asylums were improved.

DEMOCRACY ON THE MARCH

THE VICTORIAN WRITERS

The period was a prolific one for writers. Carlyle, Ruskin, Elizabeth Browning, Tennyson, Dickens, Thackeray—these were among the first Victorian writers to condemn the social injustices and the attendant moral degradation of their times. They threw the weight of their talents and prestige into the task of re-educating England to the rights and moral worth of every human individual, to the fact that these are higher values than those measured in terms of money. Carlyle rebuked the English for their smug materialism, crude tastes, and weekly genuflection condescending to God. Ruskin and Arnold urged their contemporaries to pick up once again the continuity of Western thought and culture which had been broken by the industrial revolution. But they relied on art, literature, and culture to produce virtuous living and felt that poetry was an adequate substitute for grace and revealed truth. Dickens, Eliot, and Elizabeth Gaskell tried to make men conscious of the bond of brotherhood among the poor, while Thackeray held up to ridicule the follies and extravagances of the wealthy class. But prose and poetry alike reflected the spiritual uncertainty, the economic ills, the ethical and moral problems of the day.

While the non-fiction prose of Macaulay, Newman, Ruskin, Carlyle, and Huxley reached a new "high" in expression, Victorian England achieved its greatest distinction in the development of the novel. The men and women who walked out of the pages of the Victorian novel—Micawber, Becky Sharp, Madame DeFarge, Jane Eyre, Hetty Sorrel—have become as well known to the world as the great folks in history. The last years of the century also saw the short story make a beginning in Britain.

OUTSTANDING POETS

Tennyson and Browning were the two great poets of the period. Nothing ever seemed to cloud Browning's happy outlook on life or disturb his faith in the ultimate goodness of the world and its Maker. He was sincere, matter of fact, and healthily happy. Tennyson had his periods of distress and doubt, expressed in the poems written in the middle period of his life, but he worked them through to a triumphant assurance. He was sensitive to the changing conditions about him; thus, his thoughtful work over a long lifetime reflects unusually well all that was most significant in the days of Queen Victoria.

The works of the lesser poets reflect several varying phases or aspects of Victorian England. Elizabeth Barrett Browning began writing occasional verse, then became a crusader in the interests of social reform, and after her marriage produced her finest work in a cycle of love sonnets. The poetry of Matthew Arnold reveals moments of disillusionment and uncertainty about God and external reality. He constantly thought to find serenity but had to conclude that serenity was impossible in the Victorian life he saw about him with "its sick hurry, its divided aims." There was also the group, during the closing years of the century, known as the "Pre-Raphaelites"—men who found inspiration in the simple, imaginative, but primitive art of the days before Raphael. Their poetry was melodious, often medieval in subject, and symbolic rather than realistic. They glorified the ballad form, making of the once-simple folk song a highly artistic, though quite artificial, form of storytelling. Their work may be studied in the poems of William Morris and the two Rossettis, Dante Gabriel and Christina. Algernon Charles Swinburne was greatly admired for the musical effects of his lyrics but is now seldom read because of the general lack of substance in his work. And there was the versatile Robert Louis Stevenson, whom some readers remember for his delightful *Child's Garden of Verses* and a few simple songs like "Requiem" rather than for his more pretentious works.

THE SHORT STORY APPEARS IN ENGLAND

The English short story may be said to have begun with Robert Louis Stevenson, when in 1877, he published "A Lodging for the Night." Stevenson was a born storyteller, and to give his talent proper expression, he developed a polished style. He has described his method. He studied other great writers, and in self-imposed exercises he painstakingly imitated them. He was a close student of Hawthorne particularly, and most of his stories—like the American's—inquire into the moral nature of man. He was of course also familiar with Poe's technique and theories, with his emphasis upon tone and mood. But Stevenson had his own genius, too—a knack of telling an absorbing story, and a liking for adventure tempered by a knowledge of life and an understanding of people. This combination gives a sense of reality even to a story like "Markheim," removing it from the whimsical fantasy that Hawthorne delighted in and also from the exaggerated distortions of Poe. Stevenson, moreover, had a wide range of interests and a mastery of many styles so that he appeals to readers of various tastes. "Markheim" represents the peak of his work in the short story.

Almost at the same time that Stevenson's stories were winning readers, three other Englishmen began experimenting in the field—Kipling, Barrie, and Hardy; but because all three lived on well into the next century, it is customary to group them with the modern writers. Kipling did most of his work in his early years, and his Victorian period introduced a new scene to English letters—the scene of the British colonial empire, especially India. He sounded a vigorous new note, and his productivity, together with the promise of Hardy and Barrie, meant that the short story was at home in England by the end of the century.

VICTORIAN DRAMA

In the nineteenth century, the theater became so anemic that it was not until the last decade of the Victorian Era that one could be sure it was still breathing. Chief interest lay in revivals of earlier plays. This period has often been called the "age of actors." It was the name on the billboard that mattered, not the play.

In the last years of the century, there arose a new interest in light opera, awakened by the tuneful, hilariously satirical comedies of Sir Arthur Sullivan and Sir William S. Gilbert.

ALFRED TENNYSON

ROBERT BROWNING

JOHN NEWMAN

MATTHEW ARNOLD

DANTE GABRIEL ROSSETTI

FRANCIS THOMPSON

ALICE MEYNELL

RUDYARD KIPLING

Revivals of their operas *The Mikado, Trial by Jury,* and *The Pirates of Penzance* bring perennial delight to American and British audiences.

The three British playwrights chiefly responsible for bringing the English stage back into relationship with contemporary life were Pinero, Jones, and Wilde, who began to write social plays of truly dramatic power.

Sir Arthur Pinero (1855-1934) is probably best known for his tragedy, *The Second Mrs. Tanqueray.* Some of his other works are *The Magistrate, Trelawney of the Wells, Iris,* and *The Enchanted Cottage.*

Henry Arthur Jones (1851-1929), a contemporary of Pinero, first won recognition through *The Silver King.* Then a succession of plays including *The Liars, Mary Goes First,* and *Saints and Sinners* showed a developing power of characterization which placed him among the first-rank dramatists.

Oscar Wilde (1855-1900) also won consideration among the successful modern dramatists with his two plays, *The Importance of Being Earnest* and *Lady Windermere's Fan.* Both of these plays enjoy periodical revivals on the legitimate stages of England and the United States. *The Importance of Being Earnest* is considered by many critics to be the finest farce in the English language. With its crisp dialogue and its travesty on respectability, it conveys a dramatic protest against Victorian smugness.

Joan of Arc

POPE FRANCIS

(FROM) RANKE'S HISTORY OF THE POPES

THOMAS BABINGTON MACAULAY

In 1840, Macaulay reviewed Ranke's HISTORY OF THE POPES *for the* EDINBURGH REVIEW. *In the introductory pages of this lengthy review, Macaulay wrote a tribute to the Catholic Church which has been quoted innumerable times since its publication. In this passage we see Macaulay's style at its best. Outside of its context in the Essay, his tribute to the Catholic Church is a glowing panegyric. Taken in its context, it is a fine example of how Macaulay, in spite of anti-Catholic prejudice, finds in the Church a splendid subject for his eloquent prose. The remainder of the Essay on Ranke's* HISTORY *evidences, in many places, both an ignorance and a lack of understanding of the history and position of the Catholic Church.*

The subject of this book has always appeared to us singularly interesting. How it was that Protestantism did so much, yet did no more, how it was that the Church of Rome, having lost a large part of Europe, not only ceased to lose, but actually regained nearly half of what she had lost, is certainly a most curious and important question; and on this question Professor Ranke has thrown far more light than any other person who has written on it.

There is not, and there never was on this earth, a work of human policy so well deserving of examination as the Roman Catholic Church. The history of that Church joins together the two great ages of human civilization. No other institution is left standing which carries the mind back to the times when the smoke of sacrifice rose from the Pantheon, and when camelopards and tigers bounded in the Flavian amphitheatre. The proudest royal houses are but of yesterday, when compared with the line of the Supreme Pontiffs. That line we trace back in an unbroken series, from the Pope who crowned Napoleon in the nineteenth century to the Pope who crowned Pepin in the eighth; and far beyond the time of Pepin the august dynasty extends, till it is lost in the twilight of fable. The republic of Venice came next in antiquity. But the republic of Venice was modern when compared with the Papacy; and the republic of Venice is gone, and the Papacy remains. The Papacy remains, not in decay, not a mere antique, but full of life and youthful vigor. The Catholic Church is still sending forth to the farthest ends of the world, missionaries as zealous as those who landed in Kent with Augustine, and still confronting hostile kings with the same spirit with which she confronted Attila. The number of her children is greater than in any former age. Her acquisitions in the New World have more than compensated her for what she has lost in the Old. Her spiritual ascendency extends over the vast countries which lie between the plains of the Missouri and Cape Horn, countries which, a century hence, may not improbably contain a population as large as that which now inhabits Europe. The members of her communion are certainly not fewer than a hundred and fifty millions; and it will be difficult to show that all other Christian sects united amount to a hundred and twenty millions. Nor do we see any sign which indicates that the term of her long dominion is approaching. She saw the commencement of all the governments and of all the ecclesiastical establishments that now exist in the world; and we feel no assurance that she is not destined to see the end of them all. She was great and respected before the Saxon had set foot on Britain, before the Frank had passed the Rhine, when Grecian eloquence still flourished in Antioch, when idols were still worshipped in the temple of Mecca. And she may still exist in undiminished vigor when some traveller from New Zealand shall, in the midst of a vast solitude, take his stand on a broken arch of London Bridge to sketch the ruins of St. Paul's.

We often hear it said that the world is constantly becoming more and more enlightened, and that this enlightening must be favorable to Protestantism and unfavorable to Catholicism. We wish that we could think so. But we see great reason to doubt whether this be a well-founded expectation. We see that during the last two hundred and fifty years the human mind has been in the highest degree active, that it has made great advances in every branch of natural philosophy, that it has produced innumerable inventions tending to promote the convenience of life, that medicine, surgery, chemistry, engineering, have been very greatly improved, though not to so great an extent as the physical sciences. Yet we see that, during these two hundred and fifty years, Protestantism has made no conquests worth speaking of. Nay, we believe that, as far as there has been a change, that change has, on the whole, been in favor of the Church of Rome. We cannot, therefore, feel confident that the progress of knowledge will necessarily be fatal to a system which has, to say the least, stood its ground in spite of the immense progress made by the human race in knowledge since the days of Queen Elizabeth.

FOR DISCUSSION

1. Select and analyze two or more sentences of the essay for 1) their perfectly balanced structure, 2) their pictorial appeal, 3) their historical allusions.

2. In what definite sense was this passage from Macaulay prophetic? Discuss. Discuss the thought expressed in the last sentence.

PROJECTS

Make an oral report or hold a class discussion on the growth of the Catholic Church in the United States since 1840.

In Macaulay's time it was the popular notion that all progress, cultural, scientific, or economic, was a result of the Reformation. In such books as *Europe and the Faith, Survivals and New Arrivals* by Hilaire Belloc, and *Progress and Religion* by Christopher Dawson this thesis has been challenged. You may want to read selections from these books and hold a class discussion on the subject of the relationship between Western civilization and Catholicism.

THE STORMING OF THE BASTILLE

THOMAS CARLYLE

In this exciting selection, Carlyle reminds us of a twentieth-century news reporter as he pours forth his almost incoherent account of the French Revolution. He is a glorified radio announcer, standing, as it were, at the ringside of the battle of the century—the tumultuous eighteenth century. Though the battle was fought and won six years before Carlyle was born, it comes to us hot from his pages as if, instead, he were being borne by the crowd through the streets of Paris, microphone to his lips, shouting to the world the blow-by-blow description of the fall of the Bastille.

"And now, friends, we switch you over to our announcer, Mr. Thomas Carlyle, who will pick up the story. Here we are—"

The Bastille[1] is besieged!

On, then, all Frenchmen that have hearts in your bodies! Roar with all your throats of cartilage and metal, ye sons of liberty; stir spasmodically whatsoever of utmost faculty is in you, soul, body, or spirit, for it is the hour! Smite thou, Louis Tournay, cartwright of the Marais, old soldier of the Regiment Dauphine;[2] smite at that outer drawbridge chain, though the fiery hail whistles around thee! Never, over nave or felloe,[3] did thy axe strike such a stroke. Down with it, man; down with it to Orcus;[4] let the whole accursed edifice sink thither, and tyranny be swallowed up forever. Mounted, some say, on the roof of the guard-room, some "on bayonets stuck into joints of the wall," Louis Tournay smites, brave Aubin Bonnemère (also an old soldier) seconding him. The chain yields, breaks; the huge drawbridge slams down, thundering. Glorious! and yet, alas! it is still but the outworks. The eight grim towers with their invalide musketry,[5] their paving-stone and cannon-mouths still soar aloft intact; ditch yawning impassable, stone-faced; the inner drawbridge with its back toward us; the Bastille is still to take!

To describe this siege of the Bastille (thought to be one of the most important in history) perhaps transcends the talent of mortals ... Paris, wholly,[6] has got to the acme of its frenzy, whirled all ways by panic madness. At every street-barricade there whirls, simmering a minor whirlpool, strengthening the barricade, since God knows what is coming; and all minor whirlpools play distractedly into that grand fire-maelstrom which is lashing round the Bastille.

And so it lashes and roars. Cholat, the wine-merchant, has become an im promptu cannoneer. See Georget, of the marine service, fresh from Brest,[7] play the King of Siam's cannon. Singular (if we were not used to the like). Georget lay last night taking his ease at his inn; the King of Siam's cannon also lay, knowing nothing of *him* for a hundred years; yet now, at the right instant, they have got together, and discourse eloquent music; for, hearing what was toward, Georget sprang from the Brest diligence,[8] and ran. Gardes Francaises,[9] also, will be here with real artillery. Were not the walls so thick! Upward from the esplanade, horizontally from all neighboring roofs and windows, flashes one irregular deluge of musketry, without effect. The invalides lie flat, firing comparatively at their ease from behind stone; hardly through port-holes show the tip of a nose. We fall, shot, and make no impression!

Let conflagration rage of whatsoever is combustible! Guard rooms are burnt, invalides mess-rooms. A distracted "peruke-maker with two fiery torches" is burning "the saltpeters of the arsenal," had not a woman run screaming, had not a patriot,

[1]BASTILLE (băs·tēl´)—The former state-prison of France, begun in 1370, one of the strongest fortresses and most dreaded prisons of Europe. On July 14, 1789, the mobs of Paris stormed the fortress and demanded its surrender. The governor of the prison pretended to comply, then had his soldiers fire into the mob and the fight was on.

[2]REGIMENT DAUPHINE—Regiment of the prince.

[3]NAVE OR FELLOE—Parts of a wooden wheel.

[4]ORCUS—In Roman mythology, the underworld, the abode of the dead.

[5]INVALIDE MUSKETRY—The handful of soldiers defending the Bastille; *invalide* meaning originally a wounded soldier, later, any veteran.

[6]PARIS, WHOLLY—A mob of about 12,000 citizens, armed with whatever they could lay hands on.

[7]BREST—A French seaport.

[8]DILIGENCE—A stagecoach.

[9]GARDES FRANCAISES—French guards.

with some tincture of natural philosophy, instantly struck the wind out of him (butt of musket on pit of stomach), overturned barrels, and stayed the devouring element. A young, beautiful lady seized, escaping, in these outer courts, and thought, falsely, to be De Launay's[10] daughter, shall be burnt in De Launay's sight; she lies, swooned, on a paillasse;[11] but, again, a patriot—it is brave Aubin Bonnemère, the old soldier—dashes in, and rescues her. Straw is burnt; three cartloads of it, hauled hither, go up in white smoke, almost to the choking of patriotism itself; so that Elie had, with singed brows, to drag back one cart, and Reole, the "gigantic haberdasher," another. Smoke as of Tophet,[12] confusion as of Babel,[13] noise as of the crack of doom!

Blood flows, the aliment of new madness. The wounded are carried into houses of the Rue Cerisaie,[14] the dying leave their last mandate not to yield till the accursed stronghold fall. And yet, alas! how fall? The walls are so thick! Deputations, three in number, arrive from the Hôtel-de-Ville.[15]... These wave their town flag in the arched gateway, and stand, rolling their drum, but to no purpose. In such crack of doom De Launay cannot hear them, dare not believe them; they return, with justified rage, the whew of lead still singing in their ears. What to do? The firemen are here, squirting with their fire-pumps on the invalides cannon to wet the touch-holes; they unfortunately cannot squirt so high, but produce only clouds of spray. Individuals of classical

[10] DE LAUNAY—The governor of the prison. He was killed by the mob.

[11] PAILLASSE—Bed of straw.

[12] TOPHET (tō´fĕt)—Part of a valley near Jerusalem, used for burning refuse; hence, hell.

[13] BABEL (bā'bĕl)—The tower described in Genesis 11:9; hence, confusion of sound, tumult.

[14] RUE CERISAIE—A neighboring street.

[15] HÔTEL-DE-VILLE—Town-house, guild-hall.

knowledge propose *catapults.* Santerre, the sonorous brewer of the suburb Saint-Antoine, advises rather that the place be fired by "a mixture of phosphorous and oil of turpentine spouted up through forcing-pumps." O Spinola-Santerre,[16] hast thou the mixture *ready?* Every man his own engineer! And still the fire-deluge abates not; even women are firing, and Turks—at least one woman (with her sweetheart) and one Turk. Gardes Francaises have come; real cannon, real cannoneers. Usher Maillard is busy; half-pay Elie, half-pay Hulin, rage in the midst of thousands.

How the great Bastille clock ticks (inaudible) to its inner court, there, at its ease, hour after hour; as if nothing special, for it or the world, were passing! It tolled one when the firing began, and is now pointing toward five, and still the firing slakes not. Far down in their vaults, the seven prisoners hear muffled din as of earthquakes; their turnkeys answer vaguely.

Woe to thee, De Launay, with thy poor hundred invalides! ...

What shall De Launay do? One thing only De Launay could have done—what he said he would do. Fancy him sitting, from the first, with lighted taper, within arm's-length of the powder-magazine; motionless, like an old Roman senator, or bronze lamp-holder; coldly apprising Thuriot,[17] and all men, by a slight motion of his eye, what his resolution was. Harmless he sat there, while unharmed; but the king's fortress, meanwhile, could, might, would, or should in nowise be surrendered, save to the king's messenger; one old man's life is worthless, so it be lost with honor; but think, ye brawling *canaille,*[18] how will it be when a whole Bastille springs skyward? In such statuesque, taper-holding attitude, one fancies De Launay might have left Thuriot, the red clerks of the Basoche,[19] cure of St. Stephen, and all the tagrag and bobtail of the world, to work their will.

And yet, withal, he could not do it. Hast thou considered how each man's heart is so tremulously responsive to the hearts of all men? Hast thou noted how omnipotent is the very sound of many men? How their shriek of indignation palsies the strong soul? Their howl of contumely withers with unfelt pangs? ... Great is the combined voice of men, the utterance of their *instincts,* which are truer than their *thoughts;* it is the greatest a man encounters, among the sounds and shadows which make up this world of time. He who can resist that, has his footing somewhere *beyond* time. Distracted he hovers between two—hopes in the middle of despair; surrenders not his fortress; declares that he will blow it up, seizes torches to blow it up, and does not blow it. Unhappy old De Launay, it is the death agony of the Bastille and thee! Jail, jailoring, and jailor, all three, such as they may have been, must finish.

For four hours now has the world-bedlam roared; call it the world-chimera,[20] blowing fire! The poor invalides have sunk under their battlements, or rise only with reversed muskets; they have made a white flag of napkins, go beating the chamade,[21] or seeming to beat, for one can hear nothing.

[16]SPINOLA-SANTERRE—Santerre was a leader of the mob; Spinola was an Italian general in the early seventeenth century.

[17]THURIOT—A revolutionary leader.

[18]*Canaille*—Mob.

[19]RED CLERKS OF BASOCHE—The revolutionaries.

[20]CHIMERA—One of the mythical fire-breathing monsters.

[21]CHAMADE—Drum signal for a conference.

The very Swiss[22] at the portcullis look weary of firing, disheartened in the fire-deluge; a port-hole at the drawbridge is opened, as by one that would speak. See Huissier Maillard, the shifty man! On his plank, swinging over the abyss of that stoned ditch, plank resting on parapet, balanced by weight of patriots, he hovers perilous—such a dove toward such an ark! Deftly, thou shifty ushers; one man already fell and lies smashed, far down there against the masonry! Usher Maillard falls not; deftly, unerringly, he walks, with outspread palm. The Swiss holds a paper through the port-hole; the shifty usher snatches it and returns. Terms of surrender: Pardon, immunity to all! Are they accepted? "*Foi d' officier* (on the word of an officer)," answers half-pay Hulin, or half-pay Elie—for men do not agree on it—"they are!" Sinks the drawbridge, Usher Maillard bolting it when down; rushes in the living deluge; the Bastille is fallen!

Victoire! La Bastille est prise![23]

[22]SWISS—Swiss mercenary soldiers hired by the French government.

[23]*Victoire! La Bastille est prise*—Victory! The Bastille is taken.

FOR DISCUSSION

1. How would you summarize Carlyle's style? Compare it with that of Macaulay. Which do you prefer? Why? Do you think reading Carlyle might grow monotonous after a while? Explain.

2. Note the scarcity of adjectives and adverbs in the narrative. Why? List ten vivid nouns and ten expressive verbs from the passage.

3. Where do Carlyle's sympathies lie—with the mob or with the defenders of the prison? How do you know? Should De Launay have blown up the prison?

WORD STUDY

Many French words are used in the passage. If there are pupils in the class who have studied French, let them list all the French names and words on the blackboard, give the correct pronunciation, and if possible, translate them. Carlyle also uses a number of words used in war terminology. Make a list of them. Give the word history of *maelstrom, bedlam, chimera.* Be sure you know the meaning of *esplanade, aliment, portcullis.* Give synonyms for *slake* and *immunity.*

PROJECTS

1. Consult a standard encyclopedia for a short history of the Bastille to be given before the class.

2. Charles Dickens used *The French Revolution* as a principal source for *A Tale of Two Cities.* Compare his description of the storming of the Bastille with that of Carlyle. Which do you prefer? Why?

3. Write an editorial on the significance of July 14 in present-day France.

RELATED READINGS

Carlyle has written a biographical and critical essay on his fellow countryman, Robert Burns, which you may use for a book report.

Break, Break, Break

ALFRED TENNYSON

When Tennyson was in Trinity College, Cambridge, he formed a deep and sincere friendship with a fellow student, Arthur Hallam. During college and in later years, the men were constantly together, and Hallam's sudden death in 1833 *left Tennyson heartbroken. "Break, Break, Break" was Tennyson's first cry of sadness at the loss of his friend.*

Break, break, break,
  On thy cold gray stones, O Sea!
And I would that my tongue could utter
  The thoughts that arise in me.

O, well for the fisherman's boy,
  That he shouts with his sister at play!
O, well for the sailor lad,
  That he sings in his boat on the bay!

And the stately ships go on
  To their haven under the hill;
But O for the touch of a vanish'd hand,
  And the sound of a voice that is still!

Break, break, break,
  At the foot of thy crags, O Sea!
But the tender grace of a day that is dead
  Will never come back to me.

Ulysses and the Sirens

FOR APPRECIATION

1. Can this simple lyric be called an elegy? If so, why?

2. What universal emotion does it express? What details does the poet use to express it? Enumerate. Is the emotion intensified by the use of contrast? Explain. Would you say the author displays a *classical restraint* in the expression of the emotion? Discuss.

3. Lines 11 and 12 are frequently quoted. Can you suggest why? Explain the meaning of "haven under the hill." What is the thought of the last two lines?

4. The rhythm plays an important part in the poem. Why? Scan the first stanza carefully.

(FROM) *In Memoriam*

ALFRED TENNYSON

Arthur Hallam, the friend and confidant of Tennyson's young manhood, died in 1833. The event made an unusual impression on the poet because, added to the sense of personal grief, came perplexing questions concerning what had been his fundamental faiths. Why, if there was Divine Justice, should a gifted and good young man die? Were the new philosophers right who denied a God with any personal interest in human beings? Was there indeed a human immortality? For years, Tennyson wrestled with these and similar questions. And throughout that time he wrote down his thoughts in lyrics—some very short, others of many stanzas. Those that were in any way the outgrowth of his affection for Hallam, he kept together, using for them a special stanza form.

In 1850, there were one hundred and thirty lyrics which he published together under the title of IN MEMORIAM. *They show a growth in vision and understanding. The early poems reflect mostly the bewilderment of his grief—*

"O life as futile, then, as frail!
O for thy voice to soothe and bless!
What hope of answer, or redress?
Behind the veil, behind the veil."

In the later ones, he sets his personal experience against the background of universal life and of eternity. And in the end, there grows within him a faith larger and stronger than that of his youth, a belief in

"That God, which ever lives and loves,
One God, one law, one element,
And one far-off divine event,
To which the whole creation moves."

The separate lyrics are designated merely by number. They are of many moods, and concern many incidental themes. The following selections will introduce you to some of the finest thoughtful poetry of the nineteenth century.

LYRIC 27

If you had to be a prisoner, would you wish that you had never known freedom? Is the animal better off than man because it has no sense of right or wrong? Is it better never to love than to have to suffer separation from a dear one? Tennyson gives his answers to these questions in the following stanzas.

I envy not in any moods
The captive void of noble rage,
The linnet born within the cage,
That never knew the summer woods;

I envy not the beast that takes
His license in the field of time,
Unfetter'd by the sense of crime,
To whom a conscience never wakes;

Nor, what may count itself as blest,
The heart that never plighted troth
But stagnates in the weeds of sloth;
Nor any want-begotten rest.

I hold it true, whate'er befall;
I feel it, when I sorrow most;
'T is better to have loved and lost
Than never to have loved at all.

3. LINNETT—A singing bird, caged in England as we cage canaries.

12. NOR ANY WANT-BEGOTTEN REST—Rest or contentedness which is the result of never having known a high desire.

LYRIC 54

Is there really a divine and growing purpose guiding the destiny of the ages? Is there a meaning to the sin and the waste and the losses of life? When the following lines were written, the poet hoped, but he was not confident in his hope.

O, yet we trust that somehow good
Will be the final goal of ill,
To pangs of nature, sins of will,
Defects of doubt, and taints of blood;

That nothing walks with aimless feet;
That not one life shall be destroy'd,
Or cast as rubbish to the void,
When God hath made the pile complete;

That not a worm is cloven in vain;
  That not a moth with vain desire
  Is shrivell'd in a fruitless fire,
Or but subserves another's gain.

Behold, we know not anything;
  I can but trust that good shall fall
  At last—far off—at last, to all,
And every winter change to spring.

So runs my dream; but what am I?
  An infant crying in the night;
  An infant crying for the light,
And with no language but a cry.

LYRICS 126 AND 127

Again Tennyson shows himself to have a touch of prophetic insight. In lyrics 126 *and* 127, *which really belong together, it is almost as if he were seeing through a crystal ball the fury of two World Wars and their accompanying changes. Some of the thrones did topple in World War I. But "social justice" was by no means established. Is ours the great aeon that must "sink in blood"? Was World War II the predicted conflict? Is there comfort in the faith that believes the outcome will be a new order in which "All is well"?*

The first of these two lyrics serves merely as an introduction to the stanzas of the second. Tennyson pictures the spirit of his friend as now "living in God" and thus being able to see human affairs with the understanding of eternal values.

LYRIC 126

Love is and was my lord and king,
  And in his presence I attend
  To hear the tidings of my friend,
Which every hour his couriers bring.

Love is and was my king and lord,
  And will be, tho' as yet I keep
  Within the court on earth, and sleep
Encompass'd by his faithful guard,

And hear at times a sentinel
  Who moves about from place to place,
  And whispers to the worlds of space,
In the deep night that all is well.

1. LOVE—Tennyson's faith is in a God of love. He made love a guiding principle of his life. This lyric expresses the poet's belief that his friend's spirit lives and forms a bond between this world and eternity.

LYRIC 127

And all is well, tho' faith and form
Be sunder'd in the night of fear;
Well roars the storm to those that hear
A deeper voice across the storm,

Proclaiming social truth shall spread,
And justice, even tho' thrice again
The red fool-fury of the Seine
Should pile her barricades with dead.

But ill for him that wears a crown,
And him, the lazar, in his rags!
They tremble, the sustaining crags;
The spires of ice are toppled down,

And molten up, and roar in flood;
The fortress crashes from on high,
The brute earth lightens to the sky,
And the great Æon sinks in blood

And compass'd by the fires of hell;
While thou, dear spirit, happy star,
O'erlook'st the tumult from afar,
And smilest, knowing all is well.

16. STORMS—The social disturbances of Tennyson's day.

22. LAZAR—Beggar. The two extremes of social injustice are represented by the crowned head on one hand and the beggar on the other.

24. SPIRES OF ICE—The artificial distinctions of society—of class, of caste, of race, etc.—which allow a small proportion of men to enrich themselves at the cost of the impoverished masses.

FOR APPRECIATION

LYRIC 27

1. How would you answer the first question in the introduction to this lyric? Would the bird hatched in a cage be happier than the one caught and brought from the woods to captivity? Is a pet singing canary *really* happy? Discuss.

2. Do you agree with the poet that it is better to be a man knowing what *good* is, though often falling short of it, than to be like a beast with no sense of right and wrong? Why or why not?

3. In what respect is the man who has seen and lost his eyesight *richer* than the man who has never seen at all?—What things can the person born deaf not even *imagine?* In what sense was Tennyson's life richer after Hallam's death than if he had never known the man? Do you agree with the poet in the thought of the closing lines of the lyric?

LYRIC 54

1. Is it true that a long view of events *often* shows that what looked like misfortunes proved to be blessings? Cite at least one example from history. Cite one example, if possible, from your own life or from the life of someone you know. Is the reverse situation sometimes true?

2. Express in your own words the theme of the first three stanzas. Quote, if you can, a sentence from some other book or piece of literature which expresses the same thought.

3. Lines 14-16 echo a thought expressed by what other poet whose works you have recently studied? What feeling does the poet suggest in lines 13-20?

LYRICS 126 AND 127

1. To understand the meaning of the three stanzas of Lyric 126, one must study the metaphor in which it is expressed. The key is contained in the first line. *Who* or *what* is the

king? Who "waits in the presence" of the king? Why? What do you think could be meant by the *couriers* of the king? What is meant by keeping "within the court on earth"? Who is the *faithful guard?* Who do you think is the *sentinel?*

2. Explain the relationship in thought between the third stanza of lyric 126 and the last stanza of lyric 127.

3. Mention briefly some of the political, economic, and social disturbances in England during the nineteenth century.

4. At what times before 1850 had heaps of dead reddened the waters of the Seine? To which occasion do you think Tennyson is referring in his "red fool-fury" (l. 19)? How many times since 1850 has the Seine been the scene of war?

5. What reforms does the poet say need to be accomplished? Why does the beggar need to tremble? How does Tennyson think those reforms will come about? Quote the lines with which the poet says the reforms will come.

6. To what extent has history in the last one hundred years proved the poet correct in his prophecies? For example, what *crowns* have fallen since 1850? When did most of them go? Are we any closer to achieving *social justice* today?

7. Why does the "spirit" over-looking the conflict *smile?* How does the underlying thought of this lyric differ in spirit from lyric 54, which was written years earlier? Do you see any indication of growth or maturity in the poet? Discuss.

Ulysses

ALFRED TENNYSON

The average reader lays aside the ODYSSEY *of Homer with some misgivings at its conclusion. Could Ulysses after twenty years of warfare and of wandering settle down to peaceful domesticity? Would the faithful Penelope remain so charming after all those years of waiting? Somehow, the usually accepted "happily-ever-after" ending is threatened in this instance with a number of possible snags. Tennyson, with poetic insight, saw the greatest hazard to retirement in the restless nature of Ulysses. And so this more realistic poet has written a new ending to an old story—or rather he carries on where the older poet stopped. Ulysses is speaking as the poem opens.*

It little profits that an idle king,
By this still hearth, among these barren crags,
Matched with an aged wife, I mete and dole
Unequal laws unto a savage race,

3. METE AND DOLE—Measure and give out.

That hoard, and sleep, and feed, and know not me.
I cannot rest from travel; I will drink
Life to the lees. All times I have enjoyed
Greatly, have suffered greatly, both with those
That loved me, and alone; on shore, and when
Through scudding drifts the rainy Hyades
Vext the dim sea. I am become a name;
For always roaming with a hungry heart,
Much have I seen and known; cities of men
And manners, climates, councils, governments,
Myself not least, but honored of them all;
And drunk delight of battle with my peers,
Far on the ringing plains of windy Troy.
I am a part of all that I have met;
Yet all experience is an arch wherethrough
Gleams that untraveled world whose margin fades
Forever and forever when I move.
How dull it is to pause, to make an end,
To rust unburnished, not to shine in use!
As though to breathe were life! Life piled on life
Were all too little, and of one to me
Little remains; but every hour is saved
From that eternal silence, something more,
A bringer of new things; and vile it were
For some three suns to store and hoard myself,
And this gray spirit yearning in desire
To follow knowledge like a sinking star,
Beyond the utmost bound of human thought.

This is my son, my own Telemachus,
To whom I leave the scepter and the isle—
Well-loved of me, discerning to fulfill
This labor, by slow prudence to make mild
A rugged people, and through soft degrees
Subdue them to the useful and the good.
Most blameless is he, centered in the sphere
Of common duties, decent not to fail
In offices of tenderness, and pay
Meet adoration to my household gods,
When I am gone. He works his work, I mine.

There lies the port; the vessel puffs her sail;
There gloom the dark, broad seas. My mariners,
Souls that have toiled, and wrought, and thought with me—
That ever with a frolic welcome took

10. HYADES (hī´ȧ·dēz)—Rain nymphs, placed in the sky by Jupiter.
33. TELEMACHUS—Pronounced tê-lĕm´a·kŭs.

The thunder and the sunshine, and opposed
Free hearts, free foreheads—you and I are old;
Old age hath yet his honor and his toil.
Death closes all; but something ere the end,
Some work of noble note, may yet be done,
Not unbecoming men that strove with gods.
The lights begin to twinkle from the rocks;
The long day wanes; the slow moon climbs; the deep
Moans round with many voices. Come, my friends,
'Tis not too late to seek a newer world.
Push off, and sitting well in order smite
The sounding furrows; for my purpose holds
To sail beyond the sunset, and the baths
Of all the western stars, until I die.
It may be that the gulfs will wash us down;
It may be we shall touch the Happy Isles,
And see the great Achilles, whom we knew.
Though much is taken, much abides; and though
We are not now that strength which in old days
Moved earth and heaven, that which we are, we are—
One equal temper of heroic hearts,
Made weak by time and fate, but strong in will
To strive, to seek, to find, and not to yield.

58-59. SMITE THE SOUNDING FURROWS—ROW.

63. HAPPY ISLES—The Islands of the Blest, sometimes confused with the Elysian Fields, the home of heroes after death.

FOR APPRECIATION

1. Tennyson said that the poem "was written sometime after Hallam's death and gave my feeling about going forward in the struggle of life more simply perhaps than anything in *In Memoriam."* In the light of this statement, can the poem be looked upon as an *allegory* depicting life as a great adventure? Discuss.

2. Tennyson was a young man when he wrote this poem. Do you think the poet has interpreted old age from a young man's viewpoint? Discuss your opinion.

3. According to Tennyson, what has Ulysses been doing since his return? Is he fitted for this kind of work? Explain. With what feelings does he look back on his years of wandering? Read aloud the lines that give the answer.

4. How does Ulysses think old age should be spent? What lines tell what he hoped to do?

5. To whom is Ulysses speaking from line 45 to the end of the poem? What picture of declining years does he present? Quote the lines with which Ulysses expresses his purpose. Does he have some definite goal in mind? Discuss. With what lines does the poet sum up the spirit of Ulysses? Do you think Ulysses has an admirable character?

6. What do you think is the theme of the poem? Can you find the line or lines that state it?

7. Explain the figures and the imagery in lines 6-7; lines 15-16; lines 18-21; lines 22-23; lines 50-53, lines 60-61, line 70.

8. Select the lines which have been frequently quoted and that could serve as mottoes. Discuss some venerable old men of our present age who hold high positions and carry on in the spirit of "Ulysses."

Locksley Hall

ALFRED TENNYSON

"Locksley Hall," one of the earlier poems of Tennyson, is well-known today for the startling prophecies it contains about the scientific, social, and political progress of a future age. Tennyson puts on the lips of a young man—who is disappointed in love and has turned for inspiration to "the large excitement that the coming years will yield"—his own convictions of a better and braver world.

The excerpt given below was often quoted by ex-President Truman during those days when the United Nations Assembly was being established and the vision of peace in "One World" seemed to be a reality.

Men, my brothers, men the workers, ever reaping something new:
That which they have done but earnest of the things that they shall do.

For I dipt into the future, far as human eye could see,
Saw the Vision of the world, and all the wonder that would be;

Saw the heavens fill with commerce, argosies of magic sails,
Pilots of the purple twilight, dropping down with costly bales;

Heard the heavens fill with shouting, and there rain'd a ghastly dew
From the nations' airy navies grappling in the central blue;

Far along the world-wide whisper of the south-wind rushing warm,
With the standards of the peoples plunging thro' the thunder-storm;

Till the war-drum throbb'd no longer, and the battle-flags were furl'd
In the Parliament of man, the Federation of the world.

There the common sense of most shall hold a fretful realm in awe,
And the kindly earth shall slumber, lapt in universal law.

5. AREGOSIES—Fleets of ships filled with great riches.
14. LAPT—Wrapped.

FOR APPRECIATION

1. Enumerate and discuss the prophecies in the poem which have become realities.

2. Discuss the thought expressed in lines 11-14 and apply them to the situation of our own world.

3. Scan the poem for its meter and rhyme scheme.

The Year's at the Spring

ROBERT BROWNING

In his dramatic poem, "Pippa Passes," Browning presents a little Italian girl from a silk factory, singing as she enjoys her one holiday of the year. Her path crosses those of four persons, each facing a great crisis, and each is helped by the unknowing singer. "The Year's at the Spring" is the song with which Pippa began her day.

The year's at the spring,
And day's at the morn;
Morning's at seven;
The hillside's dew-pearled;
The lark's on the wing;
The snail's on the thorn;
God's in His heaven—
All's right with the world.

FOR APPRECIATION

1. What is the dominant mood of the poem? Select the details which show it.

2. Scan the poem. What is the effect of the change of meter within each line?

3. The last two lines sum up Browning's spirit of optimism. They are famous. In what sense are they true and in what sense false? Explain.

Home Thoughts from Abroad

ROBERT BROWNING

Homesickness strikes suddenly sometimes. A sudden fragrance on the wind, a hint of rain in the air—and our hearts are miles away! Browning found rare happiness in Italy and in another poem, "De Gustibus," expresses a preference for his southern home. But once on an April day, his thoughts flew to England—England in the spring!

Oh, to be in England
Now that April's there,
And whoever wakes in England
Sees, some morning, unaware,
That the lowest boughs and the brushwood sheaf
Round the elm tree bole are in tiny leaf,
While the chaffinch sings on the orchard bough
In England—now!

And after April, when May follows,
And the whitethroat builds, and all the swallows!
Hark, where my blossomed pear tree in the hedge
Leans to the field and scatters on the clover
Blossoms and dewdrops—at the bent spray's edge—
That's the wise thrush; he sings each song twice over,
Lest you should think he never could recapture
The first fine careless rapture!
And though the fields look rough with hoary dew,
All will be gay when noontide wakes anew
The buttercups, the little children's dower
—Far brighter than this gaudy melon flower!

FOR APPRECIATION

1. It is the little details in a picture—whether on canvas or in the memory—that give the touch of reality. Mention the details that make Browning's description of spring in England sound real. What birds does he name? What trees? What flowers? What unexpected bits of detail?

2. What makes the blossoming pear tree lean to the edge of the field with one bent spray? What do you learn in lines 14-16 about the way a thrush sings?

3. How does spring in England compare with spring in your home state? Discuss.

4. With what feelings would an English soldier on duty in Africa or Australia read this poem? Discuss.

(FROM) *Rabbi Ben Ezra*

ROBERT BROWNING

What is failure? How do you gauge it or success? You will find the answers in your Catholic philosophy. This poem of Browning's, put into the mouth of a famous Jewish philosopher and poet of the twelfth century, contains some of the most often quoted expressions of Browning's faith in life and in immortality.

The poem is full of a healthy optimism; its central theme is: Look forward triumphantly, for aspiration means more than accomplishment, and the apparent failure may be really high success. The most striking feature of the poem, however, is its estimate of old age; the human soul is immortal, and the climax and fruition of this life on earth are reached not in youth or middle age but in old age. Read Browning slowly, and you will find his expression not too difficult and his thought inspiring.

Grow old along with me!
The best is yet to be,
The last of life, for which the first was made;
Our times are in His hand
Who saith, "A whole I planned;
Youth shows but half; trust God, see all, nor be afraid!"...

Then, welcome each rebuff
That turns earth's smoothness rough,
Each sting that bids nor sit nor stand but go!
Be our joys three parts pain!
Strive, and hold cheap the strain;
Learn, nor account the pang; dare, never grudge the throe! . . .

Fool! All that is, at all,
Lasts ever, past recall;
Earth changes, but thy soul and God stand sure;
What entered into thee,
THAT was, is, and shall be;
Time's wheel runs back or stops; Potter and clay endure. . . .

So, take and use Thy work;
Amend what flaws may lurk,
What strain o' the stuff, what warpings past the aim!
My times be in Thy hand!
Perfect the cup as planned!
Let age approve of youth, and death complete the same!

FOR APPRECIATION

1. How would you scan the first stanza? What is the rhyme scheme?

2. In the first three lines, what relationship is expressed between youth and old age?

3. To whom does the pronoun "His" in the fourth line refer? What is the tenor of His message?

4. What attitude towards difficulties and trouble does Browning express in the second stanza? What is the value of these "rebuffs," these strivings, in their effect upon character?

5. Browning has developed at some length the metaphor of the Potter's wheel: man, affixed to the wheel of Life, is the clay which God molds to His designs. Explain in your own words the poet's message in this third stanza. How are the experiences we undergo, the "things that enter us," given a kind of immortality?

6. In the next to the last stanza, the poet has addressed himself to God, stating his own need of Him "Who moldest men." In the concluding stanza, as given here, what is the poet's prayer? What lines express the poet's yielding to God's Will?

7. How does Browning's attitude compare with that of Herrick in "Advice to Maidens?"

Prospice (Look Ahead!)

ROBERT BROWNING

"Faces front!" The crisp command suggests Browning's attitude toward death. His thoughts about it were expressed in the following poem written in the first year after Mrs. Browning had died. The poet admits the instinctive fear men have of this last experience, but he finds in it a challenge to be met face forward, strongly, gladly, in expectation of what lies ahead.

Twenty-five years passed before Browning's call came. He met it just as he had looked forward to it—a momentary paying of "glad life's arrears."

Fear death?—to feel the fog in my throat,
 The mist in my face,
When the snows begin, and the blasts denote
 I am nearing the place,
The power of the night, the press of the storm,
 The post of the foe;
Where he stands, the Arch Fear in a visible form,
 Yet the strong man must go:
For the journey is done and the summit attained,
 And the barriers fall,
Though a battle's to fight ere the guerdon be gained,
 The reward of it all.
I was ever a fighter, so—one fight more,
 The best and the last!
I would hate that death bandaged my eyes, and forbore,
 And bade me creep past.
No! let me taste the whole of it, fare like my peers
 The heroes of old,
Bear the brunt, in a minute pay glad life's arrears
 Of pain, darkness and cold.
For sudden, the worst turns the best to the brave,
 The black minute's at end,
And the elements' rage, the fiend-voices that rave,
 Shall dwindle, shall blend,
Shall change, shall become first a peace out of pain,
 Then a light, then thy breast,
O thou soul of my soul! I shall clasp thee again,
 And with God be the rest!

FOR APPRECIATION

1. Browning compares the experience of dying to a mountain citadel to be stormed. Enumerate each detail which develops this metaphor.

2. Is the "guerdon" to be gained in line 11 described in lines 27-28? Explain. Discuss the meaning of lines 15 and 16.

3. Explain fully "glad life's arrears" in line 19. Would you conclude from these words that Browning's life had been a happy one? Explain. Can you cite any examples where the "worst" may turn into the "best" for someone not afraid to face an experience?

4. Note the change of movement in lines 24-25 and 26-27. By the use of what poetical devices is this change brought about? Does the change in movement correspond to the change in thought? Discuss.

5. What lines express Browning's love for his wife? Compare the conclusion of this poem with the conclusion of Mrs. Browning's "How Do I Love Thee" on pg. 282.

My Last Duchess

ROBERT BROWNING

This poem is a dramatic monologue. The speaker is the Duke of Ferrara. The setting is his ducal palace in Italy during the Renaissance. Read the poem aloud in a conversational tone of voice, as if you were the Duke himself; pay careful attention to the punctuation marks, for the ends of the sentences seldom coincide with the line-endings. The business negotiations for a marriage between the Duke and the daughter of a neighboring Count have just been concluded. Now, about to descend the stairs with the ambassador, the Duke pauses to draw aside the curtain which hangs before the portrait of his latest wife, the last Duchess of Ferrara.

That's my last Duchess painted on the wall,
Looking as if she were alive. I call
That piece a wonder, now: Frà Pandolf's hands
Worked busily a day, and there she stands.
Will 't please you sit and look at her? I said
"Fra Pandolf" by design, for never read

3. FRÀ—Italian for brother. Many of the Italian painters of the Renaissance were friars.
5. The Duke offers the ambassador a chair.
6. BY DESIGN—That is, for the purpose of concealing the name of the real painter. Frà Pandolf is evidently a fictitious name.

Strangers like you that pictured countenance,
The depth and passion of its earnest glance,
But to myself they turned (since none puts by
The curtain I have drawn for you, but I)
And seemed as they would ask me, if they durst,
How such a glance came there; so, not the first
Are you to turn and ask thus. Sir, 'twas not
Her husband's presence only, called that spot
Of joy into the Duchess' cheek: perhaps
Frà Pandolf chanced to say, "Her mantle laps
Over my lady's wrist too much," or "Paint
Must never hope to reproduce the faint
Half flush that dies along her throat"; such stuff
Was courtesy, she thought, and cause enough
For calling up that spot of joy. She had
A heart—how shall I say?—too soon made glad,
Too easily impressed: she liked whate'er
She looked on, and her looks went everywhere.
Sir, 'twas all one! My favor at her breast,
The dropping of the daylight in the west,
The bough of cherries some officious fool

16-19. The Duke throws out as an explanation for the "spot of joy" the tactful compliments to the Duchess' beauty in the remarks of the painter. He implies his contempt for a woman in the Duchess' position who would be affected by the compliments of such an ordinary person as a portrait painter. See lines 19-20.

23-31. The Duke describes an eager soul that delighted in life.

27. OFFICIOUS—Impertinent, one who should have minded his own business.

Broke in the orchard for her, the white mule
She rode with round the terrace—all and each
Would draw from her alike the approving speech,
Or blush, at least. She thanked men—good! but thanked
Somehow—I know not how—as if she ranked
My gift of a nine-hundred-years-old name
With anybody's gift. Who'd stoop to blame
This sort of trifling? Even had you skill
In speech—(which I have not)—to make your will
Quite clear to such an one, and say, "Just this
Or that in you disgusts me; here you miss,
Or there exceed the mark"—and if she let
Herself be lessoned so, nor plainly set
Her wits to yours, forsooth, and made excuse
—E'en then would be some stooping; and I choose
Never to stoop. Oh, sir, she smiled, no doubt,
Whene'er I passed her; but who passed without
Much the same smile? This grew; I gave commands;
Then all smiles stopped together. There she stands
As if alive. Will 't please you rise? We'll meet
The company below, then. I repeat,
The Count your master's known munificence
Is ample warrant that no just pretence
Of mine for dowry will be disallowed;
Though his fair daughter's self, as I avowed
At starting, is my object. Nay, we'll go
Together down, sir. Notice Neptune, though,
Taming a sea horse, thought a rarity,
Which Claus of Innsbruck cast in bronze for me!

34. WHO'D . . . TRIFLING—That is, who would lower himself to explain to such a person that her conduct was vulgar?

40. SET HER WITS—That is, argued.

45. I GAVE COMMANDS—Hiram Corson once asked Browning if he meant that the Duke gave commands that the Duchess be put to death. "Yes," Browning said, "I meant that the commands were that she should be put to death," and then he added after a pause, "or he might have had her shut up in a convent."

47. The Duke intimates that the ambassador has looked at the picture long enough.

48-53. The Duke says that knowing the Count's reputation for doing things in a magnificent way, he has no fear that the latter will refuse the dowry which he, the Duke, wishes, and then he adds that it is, of course, not the wedding gift which he wants but the Count's fair daughter. Do you believe him?

53. The ambassador has stepped back to let the Duke precede him, but the latter condescends to treat him as an equal.

54. NEPTUNE—That is, a statue of Neptune, the ancient god of the sea.

56. CLAUS OF INNSBRUCK—An imaginary artist.

FOR APPRECIATION

1. No description of the Duke is given us, yet in his speech his character is completely revealed. What general notion did you receive?

2. What is the outstanding quality of the picture which causes comment? What feeling on the part of the Duke is suggested in lines 14-15?

3. List the qualities of the Duchess which are commented upon in lines 22–23, 29–34. Does his attitude towards these qualities also characterize the Duke?

4. What do you learn of the Duke in lines 22–26, 43–46, 48–53?

5. The section of Italy known as Ferrara produces a famous marble. Can you now attach any significance to the word "Ferrara" used in connection with the title of the poem?

6. Explain the meaning of the following expressions: *thought a rarity, too soon made glad, let herself be lessoned so.*

7. Throughout the poem, Browning has implied that there was a contrast of wills between the proud Duke of Ferrara and his young wife. Unable to dominate her while alive, his sense of possessive tyranny is satisfied by placing her portrait among his collections. In the light of the above statement, can you explain the almost casual remark at the conclusion of the poem: "Notice Neptune, . . ."?

How Do I Love Thee

ELIZABETH BARRETT BROWNING

"The face of all the world is changed, I think,
Since first I heard the footsteps of thy soul
Move still, oh still, beside me as they stole
Betwixt me and the dreadful outer brink
Of obvious death, where I, who thought to sink,
Was caught up into love, and taught the whole
Of life in a new rhythm."

There is no over-statement in these lines from the seventh of the "Sonnets from the Portuguese." When Robert Browning first came to see her, Elizabeth Barrett had been given only a few months to live. She had almost stopped writing, and had reconciled all her thoughts to death. Forty-four sonnets tell the story of the transformation that Browning's love brought into her life. The poems were intended for him alone to read. But he believed that they were truly great and should be published. It was a gesture toward disguising their personal meaning that gave them the printed title, "Sonnets from the Portuguese."

One needs to read the whole cycle to learn the story. But one sonnet—the forty-third—is a perfect summing-up of Elizabeth's love. Indeed, it is a question whether anything in literature has surpassed these fourteen lines in defining the love that may exist between man and woman.

How do I love thee? Let me count the ways.
I love thee to the depth and breadth and height
My soul can reach, when feeling out of sight
For the ends of being and ideal Grace.
I love thee to the level of every day's
Most quiet need, by sun and candlelight.
I love thee freely, as men strive for right;
I love thee purely, as they turn from praise,
I love thee with the passion put to use
In my old griefs, and with my childhood's faith.
I love thee with a love I seemed to lose
With my lost saints—I love thee with the breath,
Smiles, tears, of all my life! and, if God choose,
I shall but love thee better after death.

FOR APPRECIATION

1. In order to see the full meaning of the sonnet, you must be sure to understand some of the expressions in it, considering it first line by line. What is the meaning implied in the expression, "when feeling out of sight for the *ends of being* and *ideal Grace*"? What word usually covers this human experience? Why is the word *freely* good to use in connection with men's striving for *right?* What is the thought suggested in the line, "I love thee *purely,* as they *turn from praise*"? Do all men and women turn away from praise? What kind of motives do we usually find in people who are not interested in winning honor or praise? Are the emotions of children usually more intense than those of grown-ups? What kind of faith do children give to their beliefs? Is it a true and strong faith?

2. Considering the sonnet as a whole, which lines express the *idealism* that is a part of true love? Which lines express love's kindness and consideration in everyday living? Which lines express the intensity of love? The unquestioning assurance of love? Which lines sum up the range of Elizabeth's love? Which lines express the deathlessness of love?

3. Reread Shakespeare's Sonnet CXVI beginning "Let me not to the marriage of true minds." Note that Mrs. Browning's sonnet appeals to the emotional sense; Shakespeare's has a reasoning appeal. Which do you prefer?

4. For further study of the romance between the Brownings, read *Flush* by Virginia Woolf and *The Barretts of Wimpole Street* by Rudolph Besier.

Dover Beach

MATTHEW ARNOLD

In "Dover Beach" we have an example of the reflective or meditative lyric—a poem in which the writer presents a chain of thoughts that have come to him while contemplating some familiar object, some natural scene. In this instance, the scene shows a strip of moonlit beach and beyond it the sea. The sound of the waves breaking upon the sands has brought in "an eternal note of sadness" which sets the mood of the poem. The sea, at ebb tide, turns the thought of the poet from a contemplation of its own melancholy beauty to a consideration of the "sea of faith" which was "once too at the full" and this in turn leads him to reflections on the condition of the world and his own relationships with it.

The lyric is typical of Arnold's poetry, which is touched with romantic melancholy. Such melancholy, when not morbid, may be beautifully expressed; and there is much beauty in this poem. The emotion here is one of almost universal sadness, wrung from the depth of a human heart. It is not a dramatic show of feeling like that—for instance—of Byron, whom Arnold characterized as bearing through Europe "the pageant of a bleeding heart." In "Dover Beach" Arnold is voicing the cry of every person—Victorian or modern—who has lost his way in the profound gloom of spiritual confusion, doubt, and flight from reality. It is the agonizing cry of one who has lost the key to the riddle of human existence and whose heart cannot be satisfied until it discovers the End of all living.

The sea is calm tonight.
The tide is full, the moon lies fair
Upon the straits; on the French coast the light
Gleams and is gone; the cliffs of England stand,
Glimmering and vast, out in the tranquil bay.
Come to the window, sweet is the night-air!
Only, from the long line of spray
Where the sea meets the moon-blanched land,
Listen! you hear the grating roar
Of pebbles which the waves draw back, and fling,
At their return, up the high strand,
Begin, and cease, and then again begin,
With tremulous cadence slow, and bring
The eternal note of sadness in.

Sophocles long ago
Heard it on the Ægean, and it brought
Into his mind the turbid ebb and flow
Of human misery; we
Find also in the sound a thought,
Hearing it by this distant northern sea.
The sea of faith
Was once, too, at the full, and round earth's shore
Lay like the folds of a bright girdle furled.
But now I only hear
Its melancholy, long, withdrawing roar,
Retreating, to the breath
Of the night-wind, down the vast edges drear
And naked shingles of the world.

Ah, love, let us be true
To one another! for the world which seems
To lie before us like a land of dreams,
So various, so beautiful, so new,
Hath really neither joy, nor love, nor light,
Nor certitude, nor peace, nor help for pain;
And we are here as on a darkling plain
Swept with confused alarms of struggle and flight,
Where ignorant armies clash by night.

15. SOPHOCLES (sŏf′ō·klēz)—One of the great tragic poets of Greece.
16. AEGEAN (ė·jē′ăn)—The sea lying between Greece and Asia Minor.

28. SHINGLES—Pebbled shores.

FOR APPRECIATION

1. Lines 1-6 paint a vivid picture. From what position is the poet viewing the scene? If you were to use this section for a scene in a movie, give the details of the setting.

2. How do the rhythm and the sense pauses in lines 7-14 convey the movement of the sea and the mood of the poem? Have you ever had a similar experience as you stood by the seashore? How did it affect you?

3. In what lines are we told that the sea had a similar effect on Sophocles?

4. Lines 21-23 contain a beautiful simile. Explain it. At what precise age in history was "the sea of faith" full? Why and how was the "bright girdle" broken?

5. Lines 25-28 contain a fine example of poetic imagination. Why? Does the opinion poetically expressed there describe the condition of faith in the Victorian era? Discuss.

6. Is devoted love the only solution for lack of faith? What is the attitude of Arnold in lines 30-34? What is the reason for the contrast of "the world which seems" and the actual? Criticize the thought expressed in these lines.

7. Could lines 35-37 be applied in any sense to the historical events of the past twenty years? Discuss.

8. Explain fully the meaning of the following phrases: *moon-blanched land; line of spray; tremulous cadence; turbid ebb and flow; vast edges drear; darkling plain.*

Lost Days

DANTE GABRIEL ROSSETTI

Time is a table of measurement by which we gauge the glory of life really lived, or by which we are judged before the grim accusation of life lived in vain. Our poet faces the specters of lost days as they spring up suddenly before him . . .

The lost days of my life until today,
What were they, could I see them on the street
Lie as they fell? Would they be ears of wheat
Sown once for food but trodden into clay?
Or golden coins squandered and still to pay?
Or drops of blood dabbling the guilty feet?
Or such spilt water as in dreams must cheat
The undying throats of Hell, athirst alway?
I do not see them here: but after death
God knows I know the faces I shall see,
Each one a murdered self, with low last breath.
"I am thyself,—what hast thou done to me?"
"And I—and I—thyself" (lo! each one saith),
"And thou thyself to all eternity!"

FOR APPRECIATION

1. What different ways of wasting or misusing time are suggested in the first eight lines by:

a. The trampled ears of wheat?
b. The squandered coins?
c. The drops of blood on *guilty* feet?
d. The spilt water?

From what you know about Rossetti's life, did he *lose* some of his days?

2. In what sense is it true that each wasted day is a "murdered self"? What, on the other hand, may be said of past days that have been wisely used? Can you think of a good figure for a poet to use in representing such days?

3. What, according to Rossetti, will be the saddest reproach for wasted time as each soul reaches eternity? Do you waste much time yourself?

Up-Hill

CHRISTINA ROSSETTI

Christina Rossetti's "Up-Hill" is a question-and-answer poem. We hear each swift question, then listen to the steady reply. Isn't it always true that the beginner is eager, though fearful, and that the one who has found the way is confident?

Does the road wind up-hill all the way?
  Yes, to the very end.
Will the day's journey take the whole long day?
  From morn to night, my friend.

But is there for the night a resting-place?
  A roof for when the slow dark hours begin.
May not the darkness hide it from my face?
  You cannot miss that inn.

Shall I meet other wayfarers at night?
  Those who have gone before.
Then must I knock, or call when just in sight?
  They will not keep you standing at that door.

Shall I find comfort, travel-sore and weak?
  Of labour you shall find the sum.
Will there be beds for me and all who seek?
  Yea, beds for all who come.

FOR APPRECIATION

1. What is the full meaning of "up-hill" as it is used in this poem? What is the "road"? Are the words here used in a universal sense? Explain.

2. What is the traveler really asking? What gives us the impression that it is a young traveler who asks the questions? What does Experience—or Knowledge—reply? Try to express the theme or central thought of this beautiful poem in your own words.

3. Show how the dialogue of the poem might be applied to a young Catholic graduate about to start out in his new life. Of whom might he be asking his questions? How might it be applied to a prospective convert seeking the Faith? Discuss.

Gunga Din

RUDYARD KIPLING

A veteran British soldier, who has seen service in India, tells or possibly sings this ballad to a group of buddies gathered in the barracks at Aldershot, a famous military camp near London. The dialect is cockney.

You may talk o' gin and beer
When you're quartered safe out 'ere,
An' you're sent to penny-fights an' Aldershot it;
But when it comes to slaughter
You will do your work on water,
An' you'll lick the bloomin' boots of 'im that's got it.
Now in Injia's sunny clime,
Where I used to spend my time
A-servin' of 'Er Majesty the Queen,
Of all them blackfaced crew
The finest man I knew
Was our regimental *bhisti,* Gunga Din.
He was "Din! Din! Din!
You limping lump o' brick-dust, Gunga Din!
Hi! *slippy hitherao!*
Water! get it! *Panee lao!*
You squidgy-nosed old idol, Gunga Din."

The uniform 'e wore
Was nothin' much before,
An' rather less than 'arf o' that be'ind,
For a piece o' twisty rag
An' a goatskin water-bag
Was all the field-equipment 'e could find.
When the sweatin' troop-train lay
In a sidin' through the day,
Where the 'eat would make your bloomin' eyebrows crawl,
We shouted *"Harry By!"*
Till our throats were bricky-dry,
Then wopped 'im cause 'e couldn't serve us all.
It was "Din! Din! Din!
You 'eathen, where the mischief 'ave you been?
You put some *juldee* in it
Or I'll marrow you this minute
If you don't fill up my helmet, Gunga Din!"
'E would dot an' carry one
Till the longest day was done;
An' 'e didn't seem to know the use 'o fear.
If we charged or broke or cut,
You could bet your bloomin' nut,
'E'd be waitin' fifty paces right flank rear.
With 'is *mussick* on 'is back
'E would skip with our attack,

"Gunga Din" from *Departmental Ditties and Ballads and Barrack-Room Ballads* by Rudyard Kipling, reprinted by permission of Mrs. George Bambridge and Doubleday & Company, Inc.; also by permission of A. P. Watt & Son, London, and The Macmillan Company of Canada, Ltd., Toronto.

2. QUARTERED SAFE OUT 'ERE—Quartered at Aldershot, near London.
3. PENNY-FIGHTS—Sham battles.
6. IT—Water. That is, you will do anything, no matter how servile, for a drink of water.
12. *Bhisti*—Water-carrier.
15. *Slippy hitherao*—Slide here quickly.
16. *Panee lao*—Bring water swiftly.
27. *"Harry By"*—"Oh, brother!"
32. *Juldee*—Speed.
33. *Marrow*—Hit.
41. *Mussick*—Water bag made of skin.

An' watch us till the bugles made "Retire,"
An' for all 'is dirty 'ide
'E was white, clear white, inside
When 'e went to tend the wounded under fire!
It was "Din! Din! Din!"
With the bullets kickin' dust-spots on the green,
When the cartridges ran out,
You could hear the front-files shout,
"Hi! ammunition-mules an' Gunga Din!"

I shan't forgit the night
When I dropped be'ind the fight
With a bullet where my belt-plate should 'a' been.
I was chokin', mad with thirst,
An' the man that spied me first
Was our good old grinnin', gruntin' Gunga Din.
'E lifted up my 'ead,
An' he plugged me where I bled,
An' 'e guv me 'arf-a-pint o' water—green;
It was crawlin' and it stunk,
But of all the drinks I've drunk,
I'm gratefullest to one from Gunga Din.
It was "Din! Din! Din!
'Ere's a beggar with a bullet through 'is spleen,
'E's chawin' up the ground,
An' 'e's kickin' all around:
For Gawd's sake git the water, Gunga Din!"

'E carried me away
To where a *dooli* lay,
An' a bullet come an' drilled the beggar clean.
'E put me safe inside,
An' just before 'e died:
"I hope you liked your drink," sez Gunga Din.
So I'll meet 'im later on
At the place where 'e is gone—

70. *Dooli*—A litter for the wounded.

Where it's always double drill and no
 canteen;
'E'll be squattin' on the coals,
Givin' drink to poor damned souls,
An' I'll get a swig in hell from Gunga
 Din!
 Yes, Din! Din! Din!
 You Lazarushian-leather Gunga Din!
Though I've belted you and flayed you,
By the livin' Gawd that made you,
You're a better man than I am, Gunga
 Din!

82. LAZARUSHIAN—From Lazarus, a kindly beggar.

FOR APPRECIATION

1. What line indicates the subject of the soldiers' talk before this poem begins? What contrast is brought out in line 5?

2. Who is the "blackfaced crew"? What is the figure of speech in line 26? Is it a good one? Does the comparison in line 28 convey the idea of thirst? What does line 45 mean?

3. What were the virtues of Gunga Din? Did the soldiers like him? How do you know? What do you think of the way they talked to him?

4. Do you think the soldier really means what he says in the last stanza, or do you think it is just a way an old soldier would talk?

5. Why is Gunga Din a better man than the soldier? Do you think so? Why or why not?

6. What is the principal emotion of this poem?

7. This poem is a barrack-room ballad. Can you discover any ballad characteristics in it? Compare it with some of the old ballads. Which do you prefer? Why?

Recessional

RUDYARD KIPLING

The Diamond Jubilee which marked Queen Victoria's sixty years of sovereignty was held in England in 1897. The power of England, her imperial possessions, her wealth were all subjects of song and story. It remained for Kipling in his now famous "Recessional" to write a prayer for moderation and humility. The two-line refrain at the conclusion of each stanza has become immortal. The poem has been set to music and is frequently heard today.

God of our fathers, known of old,
 Lord of our far-flung battle-line,
Beneath whose awful hand we hold
 Dominion over palm and pine—
Lord God of Hosts, be with us yet,
 Lest we forget—lest we forget!

"Recessional" from *The Five Nations* by Rudyard Kipling, reprinted by permission of Mrs. George Bambridge and Doubleday & Company, Inc.; also by permission of A. P. Watt & Son, London, and The Macmillan Company of Canada, Ltd., Toronto.

4. PALM AND PINE—Representative of the extent of the British colonies.

The tumult and the shouting dies;
The Captains and the Kings depart:
Still stands Thine ancient sacrifice,
An humble and a contrite heart.
Lord God of Hosts, be with us yet,
Lest we forget—lest we forget!

Far-called our navies melt away;
On dune and headland sinks the fire;
Lo, all our pomp of yesterday
Is one with Nineveh and Tyre!
Judge of the nations, spare us yet,
Lest we forget—lest we forget!

If, drunk with sight of power, we loose
Wild tongues that have not Thee in
awe,
Such boasting as the Gentiles use
Or lesser breeds without the Law—
Lord God of Hosts, be with us yet,
Lest we forget—lest we forget!

For heathen heart that puts her trust
In reeking tube and iron shard,
All valiant dust that builds on dust,
And guarding calls not Thee to guard,
For frantic boast and foolish word—
Thy mercy on Thy people, Lord!

16. NINEVEH (nĭn'ĕ·vĕ) AND TYRE (tīr)—The Assyrian empire, after existing as a great power for more than twelve centuries, came to an end with the fall of Nineveh. Tyre was a splendid Phoenician city which was captured by Alexander the Great in 332 B.C. and never recovered its greatness.

21. GENTILES—Kipling thinks of the English as being God's chosen people of modern times—the Israelites. Hence, the Gentiles would be other nations, outside or "without" God's Law.

26. TUBE AND IRON SHARD—Cannon and bombshell.

FOR APPRECIATION

1. As Chesterton has pointed out, there is definitely a note of "jingoism" or exaggerated nationalism in the poem. This is developed by borrowing from Old Testament terminology. Point out specific examples of exaggerated nationalism in the poem.

2. In stanza 1, what figures does Kipling use to tell us the extent of the British Empire? In stanzas 2 and 3, how does he tell us the celebration is over? Explain fully.

3. In lines 9 and 10, there is a reference to the Psalm "Miserere." What sentiment does Kipling wish to express in the midst of national exaltation? Discuss.

4. To what leaders of today and the past decade could lines 19 and 20 be applied? Has World War II verified the deep truth of lines 25-29? Discuss.

5. Could every American make the refrain of the poem a real prayer? Discuss your answer.

THE OXFORD MOVEMENT AND THE CATHOLIC REVIVAL

It was natural that for many unthinking persons, the Victorian era with its numerous reform bills, national prosperity, scientific discoveries, expansion of trade, and gradual development of the English imperialistic policy, should seem to mark the "golden age" of progress. It was largely through the influence of such optimistic rationalists as James Mill and T. R. Malthus that there grew up the belief that every day in every way man was getting better and better. This belief was reinforced by the "findings" of Darwin and the theory of evolutionary perfectibility.

Most of the great writers of the period realized what was amiss—the loss of a spiritual basis for life. Instead of prescribing the only remedy that would be effective, however, they seemed willing to accept any other substitute. But, as Maritain says:

> "Poetry is a spiritual nourishment, but the savour of it is created and insufficient. There is only one eternal nourishment. Unhappy you who think yourselves ambitious, if you whet your appetites for anything less than the three divine Persons and the humanity of Christ."—*Art and Scholasticism*

Man, who had unwisely sought to repair the seamless Robe of Christ by cutting it, now found that he no longer possessed a robe but countless unassorted pieces of cloth. One by one, the great doctrines of Revelation had become vague, or had been discarded altogether.

THE "VICTORIAN COMPROMISE"

Outside of Catholicism and the devoted followers of Wesley's Methodism, the Deism of the eighteenth century had left very little faith in England. It was typical of the "Victorian Compromise" that it was possible to be a Deist with no belief in the supernatural and an Anglican in good standing. The Fundamentalists, the religious group who based their beliefs on the literal interpretation of the Bible, had, in their sincere zeal for reform in government and personal life, done much to awaken men to the need for God in their lives. The "broad churchmen" or Latitudinarians, following the *laissez faire* theory in religious thought, held conflicting opinions but were one in maintaining that what one believed was not so important as how one lived. Finally, the Established Church or "high church" Anglicanism had itself tended to become a tool of the government.

To some, this decline of Anglicanism was a matter of grave concern. One such individual was John Henry Newman, who in 1833 sailed back from Sicily where he had barely escaped death from the fever. He was convinced that God had spared him to fight the dry rot of liberalism and rationalism that was eating away the heart of the Church of England. So obsessed was he with his mission that even his close friends, Keble, Froude, and Pusey, failed to recognize the shy don they had known at Oxford. Newman's zeal was infectious and soon all three were writing against those who wanted to whittle down revealed truths to pure naturalism. Convinced that the Anglican church was the reformed stock of Christ's Apostolic Community, the Oxford group set out to restate the doctrinal content of early Christianity. A feeling of almost unbearable nostalgia filled the souls of these men when they contrasted the religion and life of the Primitive Church with the church of nineteenth-century England. It was their conviction that these glories might be resurrected and used as a kind of spiritual blood transfusion for the languishing faith.

John Keble's sermon on "National Apostasy" was the match that set off enough spiritual fireworks to startle even the complaisant Victorian conscience. The preaching of this rousing indictment on July 14, 1833, was considered the beginning of the Oxford Movement. The immediate occasion was the famous Reform Bill and its aftermath. The Whigs, or Liberal Party, were riding roughshod over religion. Their latest venture had been abolishing the ten Anglican bishoprics in Ireland. This was the state of things Keble opposed, protesting that the Anglican church derived authority not from the secular state but from the Apostles. Here is the recurrence of that age-old battle between church and state which cost the lives of Thomas à Becket, Thomas More, John Fisher, and Edmund Campion.

THE CHURCH CHALLENGED BY THE STATE

In a series of famous tracts, the leaders of the movement endeavored to show that "authority" was not in the individual nor in the Bible, but in the "undivided Catholic Church" of the early centuries of Christianity. They claimed that since the Anglican church enjoyed "Apostolic succession" it should be Catholic as well as Protestant. They called their position the *via media.*

But for some, like Newman, this "middle way" was hard to find and keep, and after ten years of leadership, he abandoned the Oxford Movement. It was while engaged in the study of the heretical Arians of the fourth century that the brilliant Oxford scholar came to believe that the Anglican church stood in the same heretical position towards Rome as had the Arians of the fourth century. He saw that a rebirth of religion in England was not primarily a matter of renewing contact with the past at all. It was primarily a matter of re-establishing contact with the authentic source *in the present.* There was no other road left for him to take but the road that leads to Rome. In his famous *Apologia pro Vita Sua,* he tells how on a rainy night at Littlemore, in 1845, he was received into the Catholic Church. Years later he was to become one of her Princes.

John Henry Newman's acceptance of the ancient Faith of Britain marks the "second spring" of Catholic letters. His conversion was the beginning of an era of great converts to Catholicism, foremost of whom were Henry Manning, later to become archbishop of Westminster and primate of England; William George Ward; and Frederick William Faber. Although Newman did not consciously form a literary movement, he did supply the impetus and inspiration to other artist-converts like DeVere, Patmore, Hopkins, and Alice Meynell to turn their search for beauty and truth towards the English Catholic heritage.

Victorian Catholic letters reached its impressive renaissance under the influence and leadership of the brilliant Alice Meynell. She brought together and inspired such Catholic writers as Francis Thompson, "the poet of the return to God"; Coventry Patmore, the poet of wedded love; Lionel Johnson; and Katharine Tynan. Of Mrs. Meynell, Calvert Alexander writes in his *Catholic Literary Revival,* "In her vision the Catholic tradition stood not apart, but in the center of things, in intimate contact with the glories of the European past and the really valuable tendencies of the present, engaged in the work of carrying forward the main stream of Catholic letters. This mark of hers may be seen in the Revival today."

(FROM) APOLOGIA PRO VITA SUA

JOHN HENRY NEWMAN

Newman's APOLOGIA *is one of the greatest autobiographies in the English language and, next to St. Augustine's* CONFESSIONS, *one of the best known spiritual autobiographies of world literature.*

All but the last chapter of the APOLOGIA *are concerned with a detailed history of Newman's mind during his long journey from Anglicanism to Roman Catholicism in* 1845. *In the last chapter, Newman answers the difficulties to some of the Catholic dogmas misunderstood by his contemporaries. In the passage which you will read, he endeavors to prove from reason that only a religious body invested with the prerogative of infallibility could save Christianity from the deluge of agnosticism, atheism, and moral decay. With prophetic vision, he predicted the almost total collapse of the religious and moral structure of the modern world.*

From the time that I became a Catholic, of course I have no further history of my religious opinions to narrate. In saying this, I do not mean to say that my mind has been idle, or that I have given up thinking on theological subjects; but that I have had no variations to record, and have had no anxiety of heart whatever. I have been in perfect peace and contentment; I never have had one doubt. I was not conscious to myself, on my conversion, of any change, intellectual or moral, wrought in my mind. I was not conscious of firmer faith in the fundamental truths of Revelation, or of more self-command; I had not more fervour; but it was like coming into port after a rough sea; and my happiness on that score remains to this day without interruption.

Nor had I any trouble about receiving those additional articles, which are not found in the Anglican Creed. Some of them I believed already, but not any one of them was a trial to me. I made a profession of them upon my reception with the greatest ease, and I have the same ease in believing them now. I am far of course from denying that every article of the Christian Creed, whether as held by Catholics or by Protestants, is beset with intellectual difficulties; and it is simple fact, that, for myself, I cannot answer those difficulties. Many persons are very sensitive of the difficulties of Religion: I am as sensitive of them as any one; but I have never been able to see a connexion between apprehending those difficulties, however keenly, and multiplying them to any extent, and on the other hand doubting the doctrines to which they are attached. Ten thousand difficulties do not make one doubt, as I understand the subject; difficulty and doubt are incommensurate. A man may be annoyed that he cannot work out a mathematical problem, of which the answer is or is not given to him, without doubting that it admits of an answer, or that a certain particular answer is the true one.

People say that the doctrine of Transubstantiation is difficult to believe; I did not believe the doctrine till I was a Catholic. I had no difficulty in believing it, as soon as I believed that the Catholic Roman Church was the oracle of God, and that she had declared this doctrine to be part of the original revelation. It is difficult, impossible, to imagine, I grant;—but how is it difficult to believe? Yet Macaulay thought it so difficult to believe, that he had need of a believer in it of talents as eminent as Sir Thomas More, before he could bring himself to conceive that the Catholics of an enlightened age could resist "the overwhelming force of the argument against it."

"Sir Thomas More," he says, "is one of the choice specimens of wisdom and virtue; and the doctrine of Transubstantiation is a kind of proof charge. A faith which stands that test, will stand any test." But for myself, I cannot indeed prove it, I cannot tell *how* it is; but I say, "Why should it not be? What's to hinder it? And, in like manner, of that majestic Article of the Anglican as well as of the Catholic Creed,—the doctrine of the Trinity in Unity. What do I know of the Essence of the Divine Being? I know that my abstract idea of three is simply incompatible with my idea of one; but when I come to the question of concrete fact, I have no means of proving that there is not a sense in which one and three can equally be predicated of the Incommunicable God.

Starting then with the being of a God (which, as I have said, is as certain to me as the certainty of my own existence, though when I try to put the grounds of that certainty into logical shape I find a difficulty in doing so in mood and figure to my satisfaction,) I look out of myself into the world of men, and there I see a sight which fills me with unspeakable distress. The world seems simply to give the lie to that great truth, of which my whole being is so full; and the effect upon me is, in consequence, as confusing as if it denied that I am in existence myself. If I looked into a mirror, and did not see my face, I should have the sort of feeling which actually comes upon me, when I look into this living busy world, and see no reflexion of its Creator. This is, to me, one of those great difficulties of this absolute primary truth, to which I referred just now.

To consider the world in its length and breadth, its various history, the many races of man, their starts, their fortunes, their mutual alienation, their conflicts; the greatness and littleness of man, his far-reaching aims, his short duration, the curtain hung over his futurity, the disappointments of life, the defeat of good, the success of evil, physical pain, mental anguish, the prevalence and intensity of sin, the prevading idolatries, the corruptions, the dreary hopeless irreligion, that condition of the whole race, so fearfully yet exactly described in the Apostle's words, "having no hope and without God in the world,"—all this is a vision to dizzy and appal: and inflicts upon the mind the sense of a profound mystery, which is absolutely beyond human solution.

And in these latter days, in like manner, outside the Catholic Church things are tending,—with far greater rapidity than in that old time from the circumstance of the age,—to atheism in one shape or other. What a scene, what a prospect, does the whole of Europe present at this day! and not only Europe, but every government and every civilization through the world, which is under the influence of the European mind! Especially, for it most concerns us, how sorrowful, in the view of religion, even taken in its most elementary, most attenuated form, is the spectacle presented to us by the educated intellect of England, France, and Germany!

What shall be said to this heart-piercing, reason-bewildering fact? I can only answer, that either there is no Creator, or this living society of men is in a true sense discarded from His presence. Did I see a boy of good make and mind, with the tokens on him of a refined nature, cast upon the world without provision, unable to say whence he came, his birthplace or his family connexions, I should conclude that there was some mystery connected with his history, and that he was one, of whom, from one cause or other, his parents were ashamed. Thus only should I be able to account for the contrast between the promise and the condition of

his being. And so I argue about the world; —*if* there be a God, *since* there is a God, the human race is implicated in some terrible aboriginal calamity. It is out of joint with the purposes of its Creator. This is a fact, a fact as true as the fact of its existence; and thus the doctrine of what is theologically called original sin becomes to me almost as certain as that the world exists, and as the existence of God.

And now, supposing it were the blessed and loving Will of the Creator to interfere in this anarchical condition of things, what are we to suppose would be the methods which might be necessarily or naturally involved in His purpose of mercy? Since the world is in so abnormal a state, surely it would be no surprise to me, if the interposition were of necessity equally extraordinary—or what is called miraculous. The necessity of some form of religion for the interests of humanity, has been generally acknowledged; but where was the concrete representative of things invisible, which would have the force and the toughness necessary to be a breakwater against the deluge? Three centuries ago the establishment of religion, material, legal, and social, was generally adopted as the best expedient for the purpose, in those countries which separated from the Catholic Church; and for a long time it was successful; but now the crevices of those establishments are admitting the enemy. Thirty years ago, education was relied upon: ten years ago there was a hope that wars would cease for ever, under the influence of commercial enterprise and the reign of the useful and fine arts; but will any one venture to say that there is any thing any where on this earth, which will afford a fulcrum for us, whereby to keep the earth from moving onwards?

Supposing then it to be the Will of the Creator to interfere in human affairs, and to make provisions for retaining in the world a knowledge of Himself, so definite and distinct as to be proof against the energy of human scepticism, in such a case,—I am far from saying that there was no other way,—but there is nothing to surprise the mind, if He should think fit to introduce a power into the world, invested with the prerogative of infallibility in religious matters. Such a provision would be a direct, immediate, active, and prompt means of withstanding the difficulty; it would be an instrument suited to the need; and, when I find that this is the very claim of the Catholic Church, not only do I feel no difficulty in admitting the idea, but there is a fitness in it, which recommends it to my mind. And thus I am brought to speak of the Church's infallibility, as a provision, adapted by the mercy of the Creator, to preserve religion in the world, and to restrain that freedom of thought, which of course in itself is one of the greatest of our natural gifts, and to rescue it from its own suicidal excesses.

WORD STUDY AND STYLE

Is the diction used by Newman predominantly of Latin or Anglo-Saxon origin? Could you explain the reason for Newman's choice of words? Are the words, for the most part, denotative or connotative? Again, can you defend Newman's choice?

Give the definition of *incompatible* and *attenuated.* Also, define *prerogative* and *infallibility*.

Give three adjectives which would best describe Newman's style. Illustrate your choice of adjectives from one passage of the autobiography.

FOR DISCUSSION

1. What were Newman's reactions upon becoming a Roman Catholic? Would his reactions differ, perhaps, from those of a converted atheist? Discuss.

2. Discuss Newman's statement: "Ten thousand difficulties do not make a doubt . . . Difficulty and doubt are incommensurate." Discuss the application of the above statement to his treatment of the difficulty of Transubstantiation.

3. Outline the points which Newman puts forward to prove the fact of "some terrible aboriginal calamity," or Original Sin.

4. Outline the arguments which he proposes to prove the necessity of a "power invested with the prerogative of infallibility in religious matters."

5. Could the thoughts expressed in paragraph 6 be well applied to our present day world? Explain.

(FROM) THE IDEA OF A UNIVERSITY

Newman's *The Idea of a University* belongs "to the literature of all time." In his lucidly logical style of liquid rhythms and stately balanced expressions, Newman proposed his theory of education which, in his own day, was an answer to the growing utilitarian concept of education; which was to serve as the ideal of the Catholic University of Ireland which he was invited to establish; and which, in our own day, still serves as a blueprint for a liberal education.

His *Idea* is expressed in the published lectures given at the Irish university. Newman's ambition was to produce an intelligent Irish laity, such as he had outlined on a previous occasion in his *The Present Position of Catholics in England.* He said: "I want a laity, not arrogant, not rash in speech, not disputatious, but men who know their religion, who enter into it, who know just where they stand, who know what they hold, and what they do not, who know their creed so well, that they can give an account of it, who know so much of history that they can defend it. I want an intelligent, well-instructed laity."

Newman could not envisage a university in which religion, science, and literature did not flourish side by side. He insisted that a university was not a university which did not teach theology and religion. Since a university is supposed to teach universal knowledge, its curriculum must include theology, because theology gives "unity and coherence to all our knowledge in the light of ultimate ends." Newman was opposed to purely secular education for the simple fact that it was not complete education. Knowledge of the whole truth is the primary aim of education, but we cannot know the *whole* truth unless we also know revealed truths.

Newman, however, was certainly opposed to making a university into a "glorified theological school" or seminary. He insisted that all his students be acquainted with secular literature and science for, as he states in his essay on "Literature and Life," "we educate . . . to prepare for the world."

Newman's concept of education differs radically from that of educators who see little value in the mental discipline of the traditional subjects, and who would make the primary end of education *social adjustment* or the direct preparation for life. Newman would certainly deny that the prime object of education is "educating for freedom" or "making enlightened citizens for Democracy." He certainly held that "good citizenship" would be a natural by-product of any sound program of liberal education.

For Newman, education was not "the loading of the memory with a mass of undigested facts"; it was not "a smattering in a dozen branches of study"; it was not "learning without exertion, without attention, and without toil." Education was not "dancing and fencing," "stuffing birds or playing string instruments." In the final analysis, Newman held that, although education can help, its prime purpose is not the making of saints. An education is not "a guarantee of sanctity . . . it makes not the Christian, not the Catholic, but the gentleman."

Excerpts from *The Idea of a University* are given below: the first is taken from his lecture "Knowledge and Professional Skill" and the second from "Duties of the Church Towards Knowledge."

THE PURPOSE OF A LIBERAL EDUCATION

JOHN HENRY NEWMAN

Today I have confined myself to saying that that training of the intellect, which is best for the individual himself, best enables him to discharge his duties to society. The Philosopher, indeed, and the man of the world differ in their very notion, but the methods, by which they are respectively formed, are pretty much the same. The Philosopher has the same command of matters of thought, which the true citizen and gentleman has of matters of business and conduct. If then a practical end must be assigned to a University course, I say it is that of training good members of society. Its art is the art of social life, and its end is fitness for the world. It neither confines its views to particular professions on the one hand, nor creates heroes or inspires genius on the other. Works indeed of genius fall under no art; heroic minds come under no rule; a University is not a birthplace of poets or of immortal authors, of founders of schools, leaders of colonies, or conquerors of nations. It does not promise a generation of Aristotles or Newtons, or Napoleons or Washingtons, of Raphaels or Shakespeares, though such miracles of nature it has before now contained within its precincts. Nor is it content on the other hand with forming the critic or the experimentalist, the economist or the engineer, though such too it includes within its scope. But a University training is the great ordinary means to a great but ordinary end; it aims at raising the intellectual tone of society, at cultivating the public mind, at purifying the national taste, at supplying true principles to popular enthusiasm and fixed aims to popular aspiration, at giving enlargement and sobriety to the ideas of the age, at facilitating the exercise of political power, and refining the intercourse of private life. It is the education which gives a man a clear conscious view of his own opinions and judgments, a truth in developing them, an eloquence in expressing them, and a force in urging them. It teaches him to see things as they are, to go right to the point, to disentangle a skein of thought, to detect what is sophistical, and to discard what is irrelevant. It prepares him to fill any post with credit, and to master any subject with facility. It shows him how to accommodate himself to others, how to throw himself into their state of mind, how to bring before them his own, how to influence them, how to come to an understanding with them, how to bear with them. He is at home in any society, he has common ground with every class; he knows when to speak and when to be silent; he is able to converse, he is able to listen; he can ask a question pertinently, and gain a lesson seasonably, when he has nothing to impart himself; he is ever ready, yet never in the way; he is a pleasant companion, and a comrade you can depend upon; he knows when to be serious and when to trifle, and he has a sure tact which enables him to trifle with gracefulness and to be serious with effect. He has the repose of a mind which lives in itself, while it lives in the world, and which has resources for its happiness at home when it cannot go abroad. He has a gift which serves him in public, and supports him in retirement, without which good fortune is but vulgar, and with which failure and disappointment have a charm. The art which tends to make a man all this, is in the object which it pursues as useful as the art of wealth or the art of health, though it is less susceptible of method, and less tangible, less certain, less complete in its result.

FOR DISCUSSION

1. According to Newman, what is the practical end of a liberal education? Enumerate the specific advantages of a liberal education as given by Newman to develop this statement: "A University training is the great ordinary means to a great but ordinary end."

2. Do you agree with any or all of these purposes? Discuss. Do you think that they are important in the world today?

LITERATURE AND LIFE

JOHN HENRY NEWMAN

Literature stands related to Man as Science stands to Nature; it is his history. Man is a being of genius, passion, intellect, conscience, power. He exercises these various gifts in various ways, in great deeds, in great thoughts, in heroic acts, in hateful crimes. He founds states, he fights battles, he builds cities, he ploughs the forest, he subdues the elements, he rules his kind. He creates vast ideas, and influences many generations. Literature records them all.

He pours out his fervid soul in poetry; he soars, he dives in his restless speculations; he touches the canvas and it glows with beauty; he sweeps the strings, and they thrill with ecstatic meaning. He looks back into himself, and he reads his own thoughts, and notes them down. All this constitutes his life; of all this Literature is the expression; so that Literature is to man in some sort what autobiography is to the individual; it is his Life and Remains.

Man will never continue in a mere state of innocence; he is sure to sin, and his literature will be the expression of his sin, and this whether he be heathen or Christian. It is a contradiction in terms to attempt a sinless Literature of sinful man. You may gather together something very great and very high; something higher than any Literature ever was; and when you have done so, you will find that it is not Literature at all. You will simply have left the delineation of man, as such, and have substituted for it, as far as you have had anything to substitute, that of man, as he is or might be, under certain special advantages. Not till the whole human race is made new will its literature be pure and true. Possible of course it is in idea, for nature, inspired by heavenly grace, to exhibit itself on a large scale, in an originality of thought or action, even far beyond what the world's literature has recorded or exemplified; but, if you would in fact have a literature of saints, first of all have a nation of them. If then by Literature is meant the manifestation of human nature in human language, you will seek for it in vain except in the world. Put up with it, as it is, or do not pretend to cultivate it; take things as they are, not as you could wish them.

Nay, I am obliged to go further still; even if we could, still we should be shrinking from our plain duty, Gentlemen, did we leave out Literature from Education. For why do we educate, except to prepare for the world? Why do we cultivate the intellect of the many beyond the first elements of knowledge, except for this world? Will it be much matter in the world to come whether our bodily health or whether our intellectual strength was more or less, except of course as this world is in all its circumstances a trial for the next? If then a University is a direct preparation for this world, let it be what it professes. It is not a Convent, it is not a Seminary; it is a place to fit men of the world for the world. We cannot possibly keep them from plunging into the world, with all its ways and principles and maxims, when their time comes; but we can prepare them against what is inevitable; and it is not the way to learn to swim in troubled waters, never to have gone into them. Proscribe (I do not merely say particular authors, particular works, particular passages) but Secular Literature as such; cut out from your class books all broad manifestations of the natural man; and those manifestations are waiting for your pupil's benefit at the very doors of your lecture room in living and breathing substance. They will meet him there in all the charm of novelty, and all the fascination of genius or of amiableness. Today a pupil, tomorrow a member of the great world: today confined to the Lives of the Saints, tomorrow thrown upon Babel;—thrown on Babel, without the honest indulgence of wit and humour and imagination having ever been permitted to him, without any fastidiousness of taste wrought into him, without any rule given him for discriminating "the precious from the vile," beauty from sin, the truth from the sophistry of nature, what is innocent from what is poison. You have refused him the masters of human thought who would in some sense have educated him, because of their incidental corruption: you have shut up from him those whose thoughts strike home to our hearts, whose words are proverbs, whose names are indigenous to all the world, who are the standard of their mother tongue, and the pride and boast of their countrymen, Homer, Ariosto, Cervantes, Shakespeare, because the old Adam smelt rank in them; and for what have you reserved him? You have given him, "a liberty unto" the multitudinous blasphemy of his day; you have made him free of its newspapers, its reviews, its magazines, its novels, its controversial pamphlets, of its Parliamentary debates, its law proceedings, its platform speeches, its songs, its drama, its theatre, of its enveloping, stifling atmosphere of death. You have succeeded but in this,—in making the world his University.

FOR DISCUSSION

1. In what specific ways is Literature man's "Life and Remains"? Could we have civilization without literature? Or literature without civilization?

2. What reasons does Newman give to prove that you cannot have a "sinless Literature of sinful man"? Do you think the human race will ever be free of sin?

3. Outline Newman's arguments for the necessity of the study of secular literature in a Catholic school. Do you think his arguments are valid ones? Explain.

4. What is your opinion of studying Catholic authors and works exclusively in a Catholic high school? Would it give you a balanced education?

WORD STUDY AND STYLE

Does the style in Newman's *Idea of a University* differ from that of the *Apologia*? Discuss in detail.

What kind of diction does Newman use in his lectures? Are the words denotative or connotative? Abstract or concrete? Illustrate by examples.

By selecting examples from the two essays, show that Newman's style is "lucidly logical with liquid rhythms and stately balanced expressions."

Give the origin of the following words: *tangible; sophisticated; sobriety.* Could you select one *maxim* from Newman's writing? What is the difference between *proscribe* and *prescribe?* Describe a *fastidious* person. Define *indigenous.*

THE TWENTIETH CENTURY

The diamond Jubilee of Queen Victoria in 1897 symbolized the full tide of English glory. It marked the occasion when the world paid homage to England as the wealthiest, the most secure, the most liberal, and the most powerful nation of the world. At the turn of the century, the ordinary middle-class Victorian, steeped in the heritage of material well-being which the liberal reforms of the democratic Gladstone and the confident imperialism of Disraeli had bequeathed him, considered himself a part of an integral and fixed society. Amidst the rumblings of international, political, social, and industrial unrest, the horizons of the new-born twentieth century heralded the vision of "a brave, new world" which would far surpass the "golden age" of Victoria.

The England of today is a far cry from the birth of "the brave, new world" of 1900. Within the space of a half-century, two colossal World Wars, political upheaval, national strikes, and a paralyzing depression have left England deeply in debt, her vast Empire disintegrating, and her world leadership in question, as she faces the intricately complex problems of the Atomic Age.

POLITICAL AND SOCIAL CHANGES

By the time of Queen Victoria's death in 1901, it was apparent that Parliament, much more than the king or queen, was the real ruler of the English people. The English monarch now has no direct power, but stands above and outside political parties as a symbol of national unity. In the first decades of the twentieth century, Parliament became more completely representative of the people. The English have kept their House of Lords just as they have kept their monarch, but the Parliament Bill of 1911 took away the Lords' power of veto. The supreme governmental power is the House of Commons, which is an elected body. Electoral reforms finally extended the vote to nearly all male adults in England. In 1918, women won the right to vote. Both Parliament and the municipal governments made strenuous efforts to help the poorer classes and to provide equal opportunities for all members of society. Free public education was improved and extended, and unemployment insurance, health insurance, and old age pensions were established.

Beginning in the 1920s, a new party emerged powerfully upon the English political scene. The Labor Party, under the guidance of labor union officials, was strong enough at the conclusion of World War II to dethrone Winston Churchill and his liberal Conservatives by winning a sweeping victory in the general elections. The new administration enacted a series of laws designed to benefit the small wage-earners, at the same time laying heavier taxes on merchants and manufacturers. Among the more controversial measures were free medical care for the entire population and the taking over of the coal mining industry by the government. The Labor Party aroused much antagonism. It was charged with being too extreme and with being destructive of private initiative. It was defended with equal vigor, but by 1951 public opinion had shifted

THE RISE OF THE LABOR PARTY

sufficiently to bring Churchill, Anthony Eden, and his liberal Conservatives back to office. The two parties have been vying for control of parliament ever since.

England is no longer the proprietor of a vast empire. Canada, Australia, and New Zealand, which were formerly colonial possessions, have long been self-governing nations. India and Pakistan have had the same status since 1947. All these nations are members of the loosely organized "British Commonwealth." No doubt some of these nations would come to the aid of the mother country in case of war—but the days of England's military superiority over the rest of the world are gone.

In World War I (1914-1918), England came dangerously near being defeated by Germany under Kaiser Wilhelm II. She was saved when, angered by German submarine attacks on neutral ships, America entered the war with fresh troops in 1917. In World War II (1939-45), England faced a still greater ordeal. Again the chief enemy was Germany, this time under the Nazi regime of Adolf Hitler. Hitler and his generals were confident of victory. In the second year of the war, the Nazis swept over France and drove the British troops off the continent. During the next few months there was mass bombing of London and other English cities. This "Battle of Britain" was halted only by heroic attacks on German planes by the outnumbered Royal Air Force. The United States was brought into the war in 1941 by Japan's bombing of Pearl Harbor. American troops and equipment were sent to England until the whole island was one great fortress. American and British armies together invaded the continent in 1944, and after a year of bitter fighting, Germany surrendered.

ENGLAND SUFFERED FROM WORLD WARS

England suffered terribly from both World Wars. The weapons of war developed by modern science devastated her cities and industrial plants, and while England was busy fighting, she lost her foreign markets. The country also suffered peacetime reverses. The world depression of the 1930s drained her of her wealth. Today she finds it difficult to compete with America in most kinds of manufacturing, and nations all over the world are building up their own industries rather than buying from Britain.

But "there will ever be an England." England has survived and will survive because there is inherent in the British character that insatiable love of the homeland and the British soil, and that indomitable fire of liberty and thirst for freedom. In the English character there is a conservatism which has effected revolutions without bloodshed, and a strong faith in the stability and enduring quality of her centuries-old Christian culture. English reverence for the past showed itself again in the pageantry of Queen Elizabeth's coronation in 1953, when the nation was thrilled by ceremonies and traditions which had their roots in the Catholic Middle Ages.

LITERATURE REFLECTS COMPLEXITY OF THE AGE

As is to be expected, the literature of the twentieth century is as complex and diverse as the age that produced it. It varies in its interpretation of life in proportion to the writers' reaction to the "Victorian Compromise," and to the twentieth century upheaval in which they lived.

Writers of the generation before and shortly after World War I rebelled against the "Victorian Compromise." They noted with cynical eyes the contradiction of church attendance on Sunday with the widespread injustices against the laboring classes, and with the adoration and service of materialism six days a week. The result was a loss of faith in tradition, an intellectual and spiritual decline, a lowering of moral standards, and a general attitude of world-weariness and disillusionment. Some of the writers of the age simply mirrored this despair. Others, with a strong social and religious consciousness, attempted to expose the social injustices and the absence of traditional values. Some others attempted an escape from reality by losing themselves in the substitution of the subconscious and the experience of sex for moral and religious values.

THE CATHOLIC REVIVAL

The revival of Catholic letters and life, which began over a century ago with the conversion of Newman and other leaders of the Oxford Movement to the Faith, grew steadily during the twentieth century. It is no exaggeration to say that Catholic men and women of letters have and are contributing works of distinction to every field of English literature. The contemporary intellectual and literary leadership of Catholicism in England was due largely to two men, Hilaire Belloc and G. K. Chesterton. The plan of these two men was to reawaken England to the glories of the Catholic heritage and to redirect English life and letters into the main stream of English Catholic culture, with a re-emphasis on man's free will and his supernatural destiny.

In the wake, and oftentimes under the influence of Belloc and Chesterton, there emerged many other Catholic writers, mostly converts: writers like Christopher Dawson, with his erudition and precise scholarship; Monsignor Ronald Knox, a leader of British thought for both Catholic and non-Catholic youth; Arnold Lunn and Christopher Hollis, who continued the work of Belloc in the revaluation of English history; and the brilliant fiction writers, Sheila Kaye-Smith, Bruce Marshall, Evelyn Waugh, and Graham Greene.

Closely allied to the Catholic resurgence in England, there has risen an Anglo-Catholic literary awakening under the leadership of T. S. Eliot and C. S. Lewis. Both have exerted a profound influence on contemporary England and have helped in the redirection of English thought toward a complete Christian thinking. Eliot has traveled far from his early unbelief to his firm belief in Anglo-Catholic theology. C. S. Lewis, in his skillful allegories, deals frankly with the doctrines of grace, Hell, the Trinity, and the spiritual life of the soul. W. H. Auden, who began his literary career as an intellectual radical with Leftist leanings, within recent

JOHN MASEFIELD

WILLIAM BUTLER YEATS

T. S. ELIOT

DYLAN THOMAS

EVELYN WAUGH

GRAHAM GREENE

G. K. CHESTERTON

HILAIRE BELLOC

years has aligned himself with Belloc, Dawson, and the great French philosopher, Maritain, in diagnosing the decline of culture and predicting the death of Western civilization unless the world returns to the true sources of life. Auden is now an American citizen.

THE SHORT STORY

In the accelerated tempo of the twentieth century, it is not surprising that there has been a rich development of the short story. But the traditional pattern of Poe's short story structure has lost favor. Poe, with his insistence upon "a certain unique or single effect," was the first to make a distinction between the short story and the novel. In 1885, Brander Matthews pointed out that "a true short story differs from the novel chiefly in its essential unity of impression . . . A short story deals with a single character, a single event, a single emotion, or the series of emotions called forth by a single situation . . . Thus the short story has what the novel cannot have, the effect of 'totality' as Poe called it, the unity of impression." In the old type of short story, the author must introduce his characters and set his scene briefly, vividly. In the body of the story, the reader sees the characters perform and the plot rise step by step to a climax. This climax has to come near the end of the story with the untangling of the problem.

Beginning in the early twentieth century, partly because of the influence of the brilliant Russian writer, Anton Chekhov, the rules governing short story writing were much relaxed.

SHORT STORIES OF TODAY

Perhaps the only requirement for writing a short story is that there must be some opposition or struggle involved (external or internal) and that the story leave one definite impression. The modern technique is usually terse and direct, and the subject matter is limited to what the character sees, hears, feels, and does. There is little description, and the reader must supply the details of time, place, and situation. We judge the character indirectly—by what he says and does.

Many present day stories might be called "narrative essays"—portraying some seemingly ordinary situation, but doing it in such a way as to express an idea or a mood of the author's, or to reveal some interesting character trait. Outwardly nothing remarkable happens in the story.

Both the older and the newer types of short stories are written in great numbers today. Both kinds, at their best, are more subtle and penetrating than the stories created by earlier writers. They are fine works of literary art in which every sentence, almost every word, plays its part in creating the effect the author wants to achieve.

Most of the twentieth-century English novelists have succeeded in writing good short stories. Among these we can number Joseph Conrad, John Galsworthy, Conan Doyle, Somerset Maugham, Elizabeth Bowen, E. M. Forster, and the great Catholic writers G. K. Chesterton, Bruce Marshall, Evelyn Waugh, and Graham Greene.

Among the best exponents of the modern technique is Katherine Mansfield. Eric Knight, Llewelyn Rhys, and H. H. Munro (who wrote under the pen name of "Saki") have all successfully written in her tradition.

Perhaps the best short story writing in recent times was done by Irish Catholic writers. Oustanding among this group are Bryan MacMahon, Michael McLaverty, and Sean O'Faolain.

SHERLOCK HOLMES!

"The Hound of the Baskervilles,"

ANOTHER ADVENTURE OF

Sherlock Holmes

BY

A. CONAN DOYLE.

THIS Adventure of the great Detective, whose reappearance has so long been hoped for, will be found equal, if not superior, in vivid and thrilling interest to the best of those which first made his name celebrated all over the world.

"The Hound of the Baskervilles"

COMMENCES IN THE STRAND MAGAZINE

For AUGUST, 1901, AND IS CONTINUED FOR SEVERAL MONTHS.

Sherlock Holmes stories appeared in the Strand Magazine.

THE HINT OF AN EXPLANATION

GRAHAM GREENE

In his essay, "The Lost Childhood," Graham Greene discussed the influence of his childhood reading upon his life and writings. Speaking of Marjorie Bowen's Viper Of Milan, *he wrote: "Anyway she had given me my pattern—perfect evil walking the world where perfect goodness can never walk again, and only the pendulum ensures that after all in the end justice will be done . . . Goodness has only once found a perfect incarnation in a human body and never will again, but evil can always find a home there. Human nature is not black and white but black and grey."*

Throughout Greene's works we find the constant theme of the problem of evil and grace. The visible world of external events is not the great reality but the symbol of the internal struggle of characters who have souls to be saved or lost. If sin is an obsession with Greene, he sees it as the frightful calamity resulting from man's free refusal to accept Love.

With that classical economy of style which has made him the outstanding master craftsman of modern English prose, Greene gives us in "The Hint of an Explanation" a short story of incarnate evil—starkly realistic and almost terrifying in its emotional impact. Here is Catholic literature at its very best.

A long train journey on a late December evening, in this new version of peace, is a dreary experience. I suppose that my fellow traveller and I could consider ourselves lucky to have a compartment to ourselves, even though the heating apparatus was not working, even though the lights went out entirely in the frequent Pennine tunnels and were too dim anyway for us to read our books without straining our eyes, and though there was no restaurant car to give at least a change of scene. It was when we were trying simultaneously to chew the same kind of dry bun bought at the same station buffet that my companion and I came together. Before that we had sat at opposite ends of the carriage, both muffled to the chin in overcoats, both bent low over type we could barely make out, but as I threw the remains of my cake under the seat our eyes met, and he laid his book down.

By the time we were half-way to Bedwell Junction we had found an enormous range of subjects for discussion; starting with buns and the weather, we had gone on to politics, the government, foreign affairs, the atom bomb, and, by an inevitable progression, God. We had not, however, become either shrill or acid. My companion, who now sat opposite me, leaning a little forward, so that our knees nearly touched, gave such an impression of serenity that it would have been impossible to quarrel with him, however much our views differed, and differ they did profoundly.

I had soon realized I was speaking to a Catholic, to someone who believed—how do they put it?—in an omnipotent and omniscient Deity, while I was what is loosely called an Agnostic. I have a certain intuition (which I do not trust, founded as it may well be on childish experiences and needs) that a God exists, and I am surprised occasionally into belief by the extraordinary coincidences that beset our path like the traps set for leopards in the jungle, but intellectually I am revolted at the whole notion of such a God who can so abandon his creatures to enormities of Free Will. I found myself expressing this view to my companion, who listened quietly and with respect. He made no attempt to interrupt: he showed none of the impatience or the intellectual arrogance I have grown to expect from Catholics; when the lights of a wayside station flashed across his face that had escaped hitherto the rays of the one globe working in the compartment, I caught a glimpse suddenly of—what? I stopped speaking, so strong was the impression. I was carried back ten years, to the other side of the great useless conflict, to a small town, Gisors in Normandy. I was again, for a moment, walking on the ancient battlements and looking down across the grey roofs, until my eyes for some reason lit on one grey stony "back" out of the many, where the face of a middle-aged man was pressed against a windowpane (I suppose that face has ceased to exist now, just as I believe the whole town with its medieval memories has been reduced to rubble). I remember saying to myself with astonishment, "That man is happy—completely happy." I looked across the compartment at my fellow traveller, but his face was already again in shadow. I said weakly, "When you think what God—if there is a God—allows. It's not merely the physical agonies, but think of the corruption, even of children. . . "

He said, "Our view is so limited," and I was disappointed at the conventionality of his reply. He must have been aware of my disappointment (it was as though our thoughts were huddled as closely as ourselves for warmth), for he went on, "Of course there is no answer here. We catch hints..." and then the train roared into another tunnel and the lights again went out. It was the longest tunnel yet; we went rocking down it, and the cold seemed to become more intense with the darkness like an icy fog (perhaps when one sense—of sight—is robbed of sensation, the others grow more sensitive). When we emerged into the mere grey of night and the globe lit up once more, I could see that my companion was leaning back on his seat.

I repeated his last words as a question, "Hints?"

"Oh, they mean very little in cold print—or cold speech," he said, shivering in his overcoat. "And they mean nothing at all to a human being other than the man who catches them. They are not scientific evidence—or evidence at all for that matter. Events that don't, somehow, turn out as they were intended—by the human actors I mean, or by the thing behind the human actors."

"The thing?"

"The word Satan is so anthropomorphic."[1]

I had to lean forward now: I wanted to hear what he had to say. I am—I really am, God knows—open to conviction.

He said, "One's words are so crude, but I sometimes feel pity for that thing. It is so continually finding the right weapon to use against its Enemy and the weapon breaks in its own breast. It sometimes seems to me so—powerless. You said something just now about the corruption of children. It reminded me of something in my own childhood. You are the first person—except for one—that I have thought of telling it to, perhaps because you are anonymous. It's not a very long story, and in a way it's relevant."

I said, "I'd like to hear it."

"You mustn't expect too much meaning. But to me there seems to be a hint. That's all. A hint."

He went slowly on, turning his face to the pane, though he could have seen nothing real in the whirling world outside except an occasional signal lamp, a light in a window, a small country station torn backwards by our rush, picking his words with precision. He said, "When I was a child they taught me to serve at Mass. The church was a small one, for there were very few Catholics where I lived. It was a market town in East Anglia, surrounded by flat, chalky fields and ditches—so many ditches. I don't suppose there were fifty Catholics all told, and for some reason there was a tradition of hostility to us. Perhaps it went back to the burning of a Protestant martyr in the sixteenth century—there was a stone marking the place near where the meat stalls stood on Wednesdays. I was only half aware of the enmity, though I knew that my school nickname of Popey Martin had something to do with my religion, and I had heard that my father was nearly excluded from the Constitutional Club when he first came to the town.

"Every Sunday I had to dress up in my surplice and serve Mass. I hated it—I have always hated dressing up in any way (which is funny when you come to think of it), and I never ceased to be afraid of losing my place in the service and doing something which would put me to ridicule. Our services were at a different hour from the Anglican, and as our small, far-from-select band trudged out of the hideous chapel the whole of the townsfolk seemed to be on the way past to the proper church—I always thought of it as the proper church. We had to pass the parade of their eyes, indifferent, supercilious, mocking; you can't imagine how seriously religion can be taken in a small town, if only for social reasons.

"There was one man in particular; he was one of the two bakers in the town, the one my family did not patronize. I don't think any of the Catholics patronized him because he was called a freethinker—an odd title, for, poor man, no one's thoughts were less free than his. He was hemmed in

[1]ANTHROPOMORPHIC (ăn´thrô·pô·môr´fĭc)—From two Greek words meaning to represent a non-mortal with human attributes. The narrator's companion says that "The Thing" is a better expression than "Satan," since the word "Satan" makes him too much like a human being.

by his hatred—his hatred of us. He was very ugly to look at, with one wall-eye and a head the shape of a turnip, with the hair gone on the crown, and he was unmarried. He had no interests, apparently, but his baking and his hatred, though now that I am older I begin to see other sides to his nature—it did contain, perhaps, a certain furtive love. One would come across him suddenly sometimes on a country walk, especially if one were alone and it was Sunday. It was as if he rose from the ditches, and the smear of chalk on his clothes reminded one of the flour on his working overalls. He would have a stick in his hand and stab at the hedges, and if his mood were very black he would call out after one strange abrupt words like a foreign tongue—I know the meaning of those words, of course, now. Once the police went to his house because of what a boy said he'd seen, but nothing came of it except that the hate shackled him closer. His name was Blacker and he terrified me.

"I think he had a particular hatred of my father—I don't know why. My father was manager of the Midland Bank, and it's possible that at sometime Blacker may have had unsatisfactory dealings with the bank; my father was a very cautious man who suffered all his life from anxiety about money—his own and other people's. If I try and picture Blacker now I see him walking along a narrowing path between high windowless walls, and at the end of the path stands a small boy of ten—me. I don't know whether it's a symbolic picture or the memory of one of our encounters—our encounters somehow got more and more frequent. You talked just now about the corruption of children. That poor man was preparing to revenge himself on everything he hated—my father, the Catholics, the God whom people persisted in crediting—and that by corrupting me. He had evolved a horrible and ingenious plan.

"I remember the first time I had a friendly word from him. I was passing his shop as rapidly as I could when I heard his voice call out with a kind of sly subservience as though he were an under servant. 'Master David,' he called, 'Master David,' and I hurried on. But the next time I passed that way he was at his door (he must have seen me coming) with one of those curly cakes in his hand that we called Chelsea buns. I didn't want to take it, but he made me, and then I couldn't be other than polite when he asked me to come into his parlour behind the shop and see something very special.

"It was a small electric railway—a rare sight in those days, and he insisted on showing me how it worked. He made me turn the switches and stop and start it, and he told me that I could come in any morning and have a game with it. He used the word 'game' as though it were something secret, and it's true that I never told my family of this invitation and of how, perhaps twice a week those holidays, the desire to control that little railway became overpowering, and looking up and down the street to see if I were observed, I would dive into the shop."

Our larger, dirtier, adult train drove into a tunnel and the light went out. We sat in darkness and silence, with the noise of the train blocking our ears like wax. When we were through we didn't speak at once and I had to prick him into continuing. "An elaborate seduction," I said.

"Don't think his plans were as simple as that," my companion said, "or as crude. There was much more hate than love, poor man, in his make-up. Can you hate

something you don't believe in? And yet he called himself a free-thinker. What an impossible paradox, to be free and to be so obsessed. Day by day all through those holidays his obsession must have grown, but he kept a grip; he bided his time. Perhaps that thing I spoke of gave him the strength and the wisdom. It was only a week from the end of the holidays that he spoke to me on what concerned him so deeply.

"I heard him behind me as I knelt on the floor, coupling two coaches. He said, 'You won't be able to do this, Master David, when school starts.' It wasn't a sentence that needed any comment from me any more than the one that followed. 'You ought to have it for your own, you ought,' but how skillfully and unemphatically he had sowed the longing, the idea of a possibility. . . . I was coming to his parlour every day now; you see, I had to cram every opportunity in before the hated term started again, and I suppose I was becoming accustomed to Blacker, to that wall-eye, that turnip head, that nauseating subservience. The Pope, you know, describes himself as 'the servant of the servants of God,' and Blacker—I sometimes think that Blacker was 'The servant of the servants of . . . ,' well, let it be.

"The very next day, standing in the doorway watching me play, he began to talk to me about religion. He said, with what untruth even I recognized, how much he admired the Catholics; he wished he could believe like that, but how could a baker believe? He accented 'a baker' as one might say a biologist, and the tiny train spun round the gauge O track. He said, 'I can bake the things you eat just as well as any Catholic can,' and disappeared into his shop. I hadn't the faintest idea what he meant. Presently he emerged again, holding in his hand a little wafer. 'Here,' he said, 'eat that and tell me . . .' When I put it in my mouth I could tell that it was made in the same way as our wafers for communion—he had got the shape a little wrong, that was all—and I felt guilty and irrationally scared. 'Tell me,' he said, 'what's the difference?'

" 'Difference?' I asked.

" 'Isn't that just the same as you eat in church?'

"I said smugly, 'It hasn't been consecrated.'

"He said, 'Do you think, if I put the two of them under a microscope, you could tell the difference?'

"But even at ten I had the answer to that question. 'No,' I said, 'the—accidents don't change,' stumbling a little on the word 'accidents' which had suddenly conveyed to me the idea of death and wounds.

"Blacker said with sudden intensity, 'How I'd like to get one of your ones in my mouth—just to see. . . .'

"It may seem odd to you, but this was the first time that the idea of transubstantiation really lodged in my mind. I had learned it all by rote; I had grown up with the idea. The Mass was as lifeless to me as the sentences in *De Bello Gallico*; communion a routine like drill in the school-yard, but here suddenly I was in the presence of a man who took it seriously, as seriously as the priest whom naturally one didn't count—it was his job. I felt more scared than ever.

"He said, 'It's all nonsense, but I'd just like to have it in my mouth.'

" 'You could if you were a Catholic,' I said naively.

"He gazed at me with his one good eye, like a Cyclops.[2] He said, 'You serve at Mass, don't you? It would be easy for you to get at one of those things. I tell you what I'd do—I'd swap this electric train for one of your wafers—consecrated, mind. It's got to be consecrated.'

" 'I could get you one out of the box,' I said. I think I still imagined that his interest was a baker's interest—to see how they were made.

" 'Oh, no,' he said, 'I want to see what your God tastes like.'

" 'I couldn't do that.'

" 'Not for a whole electric train, just for yourself? You wouldn't have any trouble at home. I'd pack it up and put a label inside that your dad could see: "For my bank manager's little boy from a grateful client." He'd be pleased as punch with that.'

"Now that we are grown men it seems a trivial temptation, doesn't it? But try to think back to your own childhood. There was a whole circuit of rails there on the floor at our feet, straight rails and curved, and a little station with porters and passengers, a tunnel, a footbridge, a level crossing, two signals, buffers, of course—and, above all, a turntable. The tears of longing came into my eyes when I looked at the turntable. It was my favorite piece—it looked so ugly and practical and true. I said weakly, 'I wouldn't know how.'

"How carefully he had been studying the ground! He must have slipped several times into Mass at the back of the church. It would have been no good, you understand, in a little town like that, presenting himself for communion. Everybody there knew him for what he was. He said to me, 'When you've been given communion you could just put it under your tongue a moment. He serves you and the other boy first, and I saw you once go

[2]CYCLOPS (sī´klŏps)—One-eyed giant of Grecian mythology.

out behind the curtain straight afterwards. You'd forgotten one of those little bottles.'

" 'The cruet,' I said.

" 'Pepper and salt.' He grinned at me jovially, and I—well, I looked at the little railway which I could no longer come and play with when term started. I said, 'You'd just swallow it, wouldn't you?'

" 'Oh, yes,' he said, 'I'd just swallow it.'

"Somehow I didn't want to play with the train any more that day. I got up and made for the door, but he detained me, gripping my lapel. He said, 'This will be a secret between you and me. Tomorrow's Sunday. You come along here in the afternoon. Put it in an envelope and post it to me. Monday morning the train will be delivered bright and early.'

" 'Not tomorrow,' I implored him.

" 'I'm not interested in any other Sunday,' he said. 'It's your only chance.' He shook me gently backwards and forwards. 'It will always have to be a secret between you and me,' he said. 'Why, if anyone knew they'd take away the train and there'd be me to reckon with. I'd bleed you something awful. You know how I'm always about on Sunday walks. You can't avoid a man like me. I crop up. You wouldn't ever be safe in your own house. I know ways to get into houses when people are asleep.' He pulled me into the shop after him and opened a drawer. In the drawer was an odd looking key and a cut-throat razor. He said, 'That's a master key that opens all locks and that—that's what I bleed people with.' Then he patted my cheek with his plump floury fingers and said, 'Forget it. You and me are friends.'

"That Sunday Mass stays in my head, every detail of it, as though it had happened only a week ago. From the moment of the Confession to the moment of Consecration it had a terrible importance; only one other Mass has ever been so important to me—perhaps not even one, for this was a solitary Mass which would never happen again. It seemed as final as the last Sacrament when the priest bent down and put the wafer in my mouth where I knelt before the altar with my fellow server.

"I suppose I had made up my mind to commit this awful act—for, you know, to us it must always seem an awful act—from the moment when I saw Blacker watching from the back of the church. He had put on his best black Sunday clothes, and, as though he could never quite escape the smear of his profession, he had a dab of dried talcum on his cheek, which he had presumably applied after using that cut-throat of his. He was watching me closely all the time, and I think it was fear—fear of that terrible undefined thing called bleeding—as much as covetousness that drove me to carry out my instructions.

"My fellow server got briskly up and, taking the paten, preceded Father Carey to the altar rail where the other communicants knelt. I had the Host lodged under my tongue; it felt like a blister. I got up and made for the curtain to get the cruet that I had purposely left in the sacristy. When I was there I looked quickly round for a hiding place and saw an old copy of the *Universe* lying on a chair. I took the Host from my mouth and inserted it between two sheets—a little damp mess of pulp. Then I thought: perhaps Father Carey has put out the paper for a particular purpose and he will find the Host before I have time to remove it, and the enormity of my act began to come home to me when I tried to imagine what punishment I should incur. Murder is sufficiently trivial to have its appropriate punishment, but for this act the mind boggled at the thought of any retribution at all. I tried to remove the Host, but it stuck clammily between the pages, and in desperation I tore out a piece of the newspaper and, screwing the whole thing up, stuck it in my trousers pocket. When I came back through the curtain carrying the cruet my eyes met Blacker's. He gave me a grin of encouragement and unhappiness—yes, I am sure, unhappiness. Was it perhaps that the poor man was all the time seeking something incorruptible?

"I can remember little more of that day. I think my mind was shocked and stunned, and I was caught up too in the family bustle of Sunday. Sunday in a provincial town is the day for relations. All the family are at home, and unfamiliar cousins and uncles are apt to arrive, packed in the back seats of other people's cars. I remember that some crowd of the kind descended on us and pushed Blacker temporarily out of the foreground of my mind. There was somebody called Aunt Lucy, with a loud hollow laugh that filled the house with mechanical merriment like the sound of recorded laughter from inside a hall of mirrors, and I had no opportunity to go out alone even if I had wished to. When six o'clock came and Aunt Lucy and the cousins departed and peace returned, it was too late to go to Blacker's, and at eight it was my own bed-time.

"I think I had half forgotten what I had in my pocket. As I emptied my pocket the little screw of newspaper brought quickly back the Mass, the priest bending over me, Blacker's grin. I laid the packet on the chair by my bed and tried to go to sleep, but I was haunted by the shadows on the wall where the curtains blew, the squeak of furniture, the rustle in the chimney, haunted by the presence of God there on the chair. The Host had always been to me—well the Host. I knew theoretically, as I have said, what I had to believe, but suddenly, as someone whistled in the road outside, whistled secretively, knowingly, to me, I knew that this which I had beside my bed was something of infinite value—something a man would pay for with his whole peace of mind, something that was so hated one could love it as one loves an outcast or a bullied child. These are adult words, and it was a child of ten who lay scared in bed, listening to the whistle from the road, Blacker's whistle, but I think he felt fairly clearly what I am describing now. That is what I meant when I said this Thing, whatever it is, that seizes every possible weapon against God, is always, everywhere, disappointed at the moment of success. It must have felt as certain of me as Blacker did. It must have felt certain too of Blacker. But I wonder, if one knew what happened later to that poor man, whether one would not find again that the weapon had been turned against its own breast.

"At last I couldn't bear that whistle any more and got out of bed. I opened the curtains a little way, and there right under my window, the moonlight on his face, was Blacker. If I had stretched my hand down, his fingers reaching up could almost have touched mine. He looked up at me, flashing the one good eye, with hunger—I realize now that near-success must have developed his obsession almost to the point of madness. Desperation had driven him to the house. He whispered up at me. 'David, where is it?'

"I jerked my head back at the room. 'Give it me,' he said. 'Quick. You shall have the train in the morning.'

"I shook my head. He said, 'I've got the bleeder here, and the key. You'd better toss it down.'

" 'Go away,' I said, but I could hardly speak for fear.

" 'I'll bleed you first and then I'll have it just the same.'

" 'Oh, no, you won't,' I said. I went to the chair and picked it—Him—up. There was only one place where He was safe. I couldn't separate the Host from the paper, so I swallowed both. The newsprint stuck like a prune skin to the back of my throat, but I rinsed it down with water from the ewer. Then I went back to the window and looked down at Blacker. He began to wheedle me. 'What have you done with it, David? What's the fuss? It's only a bit of bread,' looking so longingly and pleadingly up at me that even as a child I wondered whether he could really think that, and yet desire it so much.

" 'I swallowed it,' I said.

" 'Swallowed it?'

" 'Yes,' I said. 'Go away.'

"Then something happened which seems to me now more terrible than his desire to corrupt or my thoughtless act: he began to weep—the tears ran lopsidedly out of the one good eye and his shoulders shook. I only saw his face for a moment before he bent his head and strode off, the bald turnip head shaking, into the dark. When I think of it now, it's almost as if I had seen that Thing weeping for its inevitable defeat. It had tried to use me as a weapon, and now I had broken in its hands and it wept its hopeless tears through one of Blacker's eyes."

The black furnaces of Bedwell Junction gathered around the line. The points switched and we were tossed from one set of rails to another. A spray of sparks, a signal light changing to red, tall chimneys jetting into the gray night sky, the fumes of steam from stationary engines—half the cold journey was over, and now remained the long wait for the slow cross-country train. I said, "It's an interesting story. I think I should have given Blacker what he wanted. I wonder what he would have done with it."

"I really believe," my companion said, "that he would first of all have put it under his microscope—before he did all the other things I expect he had planned."

"And the hints," I said, "I don't quite see what you mean by that."

"Oh, well," he said vaguely, "you know for me it was an odd beginning, that affair, when you come to think of it," but I never should have known what he meant had not his coat, when he rose to take his bag from the rack, come open and disclosed the collar of a priest.

I said, "I suppose you think you owe a lot to Blacker."

"Yes," he said, "you see, I am a very happy man."

WORD STUDY AND STYLE

Does Greene's style appeal primarily to the imagination or to the intellect? Select examples from the story to prove your point.

Some or all of the following adjectives might characterize Greene's style. List these adjectives in the order of their importance and select at least one sentence which each adjective might describe: *compact, concise, controlled, restrained, economical, austere, classical, graphic.*

Is there any difference between *intuition* and *reasoning?* When is some fact *relevant* to an argument? What kind of glance would a *furtive* glance be? Describe a *supercilious smirk.*

FOR DISCUSSION

1. Which is greater in the story—the external or internal action? Could this story be called a psychological study? Discuss in detail.

2. Show in detail how the word "Hint" in the title carries the theme throughout the story. Just what is "hinted"?

3. "Serenity" is the key word to describe the character of the narrator's companion. Discuss in detail how the narrator's companion arrived at this "serenity." Explain the relationship between "serenity," "the thing," "the hint," and Blacker.

4. Enumerate the details of the "elaborate seduction" of the child. What particular human weaknesses of the child and what external circumstances made him so susceptible to the temptation of Blacker? Are these temptations described realistically? Is there a great deal of "Satanic psychology" contained in them? Explain.

5. Describe in a few words the climax of the story. What is the predominant effect which the short story produces upon the reader? Explain.

6. Briefly describe the physical appearance of Blacker. Why is his name an appropriate one?

7. What was the narrator's great obstacle to a belief in a personal God? Does this argument introduce the story proper? Explain.

8. Do you consider this story to be a good piece of Christian propaganda? Why or why not?

9. Reread the statements of Greene quoted in the introduction to this story. Apply these statements to the short story.

10. Explain: 1) the general meaning of the following statements; 2) their meaning in their context in the story:

a. "...intellectual arrogance I have grown to expect from Catholics."

b. "I sometimes feel pity for this thing. It is continually finding the right weapon to use against its Enemy and the weapon breaks in its own breast."

c. "Can you hate something you don't believe in? And yet he called himself a free-thinker. What an impossible paradox to be free and to be so obsessed."

d. "The Mass was as lifeless to me as the sentences in *De Bello Gallico;* communion a routine like a drill in the school-yard."

e. "This Thing . . . that seizes every sensible weapon against God is always, everywhere, disappointed at the moment of success."

THE MODERN NOVEL

Because of its multiplicity and variety, the twentieth century novel is extremely difficult to classify. In the years before and shortly after World War I, such names as Conrad, H. G. Wells, Galsworthy, and Arnold Bennett loomed large in the field of fiction.

JOSEPH CONRAD: WRITER OF MEN AND THE SEA

Joseph Conrad, a Pole by birth, did not learn English until he was twenty-one; yet he lived to become one of the great masters of English prose. In a preface to his *The Nigger of the Narcissus,* which he regarded as his best literary work, he wrote: "My task which I am trying to achieve is by the power of the written word, to make you hear, to make you feel—above all, to make you *see*." There is no doubt that Conrad succeeded in his aim. As a novelist who spent more than twenty years at sea, he portrayed individuals who must fight the forces of nature. *Lord Jim* is typical of his brooding tales about men and ships in lonely tropical seas. Conrad specialized in exploring the inner workings of his characters' minds. But he did not isolate character from the outside world. For him "the perfection of individual conduct" was the theme of all his novels, but this conduct resulted from following objective moral standards.

Because science fiction is so extremely popular today, we might falsely conclude that this kind of writing is something very new. But at the beginning of the century, H. G. Wells was writing about mechanical devices that would carry man into the future as far ahead as the year 802,701, and of the invasion of the earth by the Martians. These possibilities he discussed in *The Time Machine* and *The War of the Worlds*.

Later, Wells turned from the study of physical science to the study of human society. *Tono-Bungay* he regarded as his masterpiece. Tono-Bungay was a worthless patent medicine which the hero of the novel and his uncle manufactured, and which they sold to the public through high-pressure advertising. Wells used this patent medicine as a symbol of a disintegrating society.

War, religion, and education formed the themes of Wells' other works. In *Mr. Britling Sees It Through,* a novel of World War I, he announced his discovery of God. But the God which Wells described was a very vague and finite god—the captain of those great souls who fight for a better world. A modern critic has said that the typical Wells hero is either a scientist or a man of affairs who is determined to better the world in which he lives; however, such a hero is liable to succumb at any time to the temptation of private profit. The pet theories of Wells about social reform, religion, and history—all of which excluded the spiritual and absolute moral concepts—were the frequent targets for the literary barbs of such men as Chesterton and Belloc.

Arnold Bennett is famous for the *Old Wives' Tale* and *The Clayhanger Trilogy,* a series of novels about the people who lived in Staffordshire, the pottery-manufacturing center of England. Bennett gave infinite care to the physical details of his stories—clothes, food, dwellings—and traced the effects of economic and social trends in his characters' personal lives. He describes his characters through environment. Bennet's basic weakness was that his realism focused attention on the lowest elements of life. He failed to describe the good man from within.

One year before he died in 1933, John Galsworthy was awarded the Nobel Prize for literature. Galsworthy is most famous for his *Forsyte Saga,* a trilogy. It is a family novel with Soames Forsyte as the hero. In picturing the "Forsyte age and the Forsyte way of life," Galsworthy viewed the transformation that was taking place in every aspect of English life in the first years of the century, changes in the concept of property, manners, and morals. As a somewhat detached critic of life, Galsworthy was not too reliable. He rejected all religious authority and believed that "life was a mess and that we should be kind." Summing up his own philosophy, he wrote: "Life for those who still have vital instinct in them is good enough in itself even if it lead to nothing, and we have only ourselves to blame if we, alone among animals, so live that we lose the love of life for *itself.*"

CHANGING TIMES AS SEEN BY JOHN GALSWORTHY

In the 1920s, James Joyce, the rebellious, ex-Catholic Irishman, and Virginia Woolf gave impetus to the stream of consciousness technique. Miss Woolf turned her attention away from the outside world to the mind of man as it *knows* and *feels* the outside world. She recorded the involuntary movements of the mind, and portrayed character through the description of impressions which are fragmentary and disconnected. Her descriptions of sensations as they flow through the mind were sensitive. She turned her prose into a lyrical instrument which recorded sensations in the process of change. As a result, she did not portray a complete personality, but only the sum total of disconnected sensations. *To the Lighthouse, Mrs. Dalloway,* and *The Waves* brilliantly exemplify this type of writing.

Joyce explored the vague and chaotic area of the subconscious mind in his *Ulysses,* a novel that exhausts seven hundred pages about the events of a single day in Dublin. In the novels of Joyce, D. H. Lawrence, and Somerset Maugham, we have realism which has degenerated into naturalism and, at times, pure animalism. In too many of their novels, hatred, lust, and the uninhibited and unprincipled activity of the imagination are all described with minute fidelity. In Maugham, Aldous Huxley, and other realistic novelists, we have competent writing and fine technique, but all their writings are suffused with a materialism which finds no lasting significance in life.

Most of the realism of the twentieth-century non-Catholic novelists is, paradoxically, not realism at all, but an escape from reality. Viewing man as a helpless victim of social environment or blind fate is not realism. Nor is morbid self-analysis, or the portrayal of the objective world through disconnected and subconscious images, true realism. A return to primitive animalism in which the exaltation of sex is substituted for religion and objective morality can hardly be called viewing life realistically. All of these novelists have failed artistically because they have not recreated life in its *totality.* They have been lacking in an understanding of man's *total nature* because they have deliberately cut themselves off from the spiritual, moral, and cultural traditions of the past.

NON-CATHOLIC "REALISM"

Although it is not the purpose of fiction to deal with philosophy or the causes of things, but only with things themselves, still it is impossible to know life and artistically re-create it unless one can see the relationships between life and the ultimate meaning of life. Unfortunately, many modern novelists tell only half-truths, or they mistake disordered and chaotic impressions for reality. They consciously or unconsciously fail to portray man as a moral and religious creature. All great literature is profoundly religious. It is ever haunted by the memory of a lost paradise and a deep sense of humility which represents man neither as an animal nor as a god—but as a rational being ever conscious of his tremendous freedom. This freedom, which implies a moral responsibility to himself and to society, man can abuse and thus become the tragic hero; or he can, against all odds, accept his responsibility and his place in the scheme of Divine Providence, and thus play a superb role in the Divine Comedy.

The twentieth-century Catholic novelists have helped to preserve the human and supernatural values in a world dedicated to materialism and imbued with a sense of disillusionment. Aware of man's insecurity and the ease with which he falls prey to the naturalistic viewpoint, the Catholic fiction writer has provided a means by which an ordinary man may see life in its totality.

In many ways this task was accomplished in the twentieth century, whether it was through the subtle and indirect approach of the satires of Evelyn Waugh and Bruce Marshall; or through the stark and, at times, startling presentation of the conflict between man's lower nature and grace in the realistic novels of Graham Greene; or in the more subdued character study of the historical novels of Sheila Kaye-Smith. Writing in the Catholic tradition (although not a Catholic) is H. F. M. Prescott, whose historical chronicle, *The Man on the Donkey,* is unquestionably one of the classics of the twentieth century. Prescott's *The Unhurrying Chase* was published in 1955.

No survey of English Catholic novelists would be complete that did not include such names as: A. J. Cronin, Compton MacKenzie, Philip Gibbs, Maurice Baring, Robert Spaight, and the Irish Catholic fiction writers Kate O'Brien and Michael McLaverty.

NONFICTION: BIOGRAPHY

A new trend in the writing of biographies appeared in the 1920s. A modern biographer sets himself the task of *interpreting and explaining* the man he is writing about, of re-creating him as a complex and interesting human being.

The older biographers, following a strict chronological order, plodded along through a mass of fact, until they concluded with their subject's death and burial. They did not distinguish between important and less important facts, and failed to emphasize the personality of the subject about whom they were writing. The modern biographer will record his hero's weaknesses and prejudices along with his achievements. He sifts all his source material in such a way as to present a sharply defined character-portrait or a dramatic life story. This kind of biography at its best rivals fiction in vividness, color, and drama. But in the hands of cynical writers intent on finding all bad and no good in the record of a human life, it is dangerous and destructive of objective truth.

Outstanding among the English non-Catholic biographers of this new school are Lytton Strachey, Philip Guedalla, and Hesketh Pearson. Any enumeration of British Catholic biographers must include Hilaire Belloc, G. K. Chesterton, Christopher Hollis, and Evelyn Waugh. All of these use the new biographical techniques to present vivid analytical and dramatic interpretations of important historic and literary personages. In another sense, however, they are biographical essayists, since they utilize both the subject of the biography and the period background as mediums for reinterpreting an historical age and for restating the Catholic position.

Under the impetus and the influence of the great French Catholic writer, Henri Gheon, much has been done by modern biographers of saints to present them as human beings of flesh and blood. Father C. C. Martindale was one of the first who succeeded in making hagiography, or the biographies of saintly people, both a literary accomplishment and an inspiration to the average Christian. This method has been enthusiastically followed by Margaret Yeo and Christopher Hollis. Father James Brodrick should be mentioned as an historical biographer of the first rank, who satisfies the high demand of both art and scholarship.

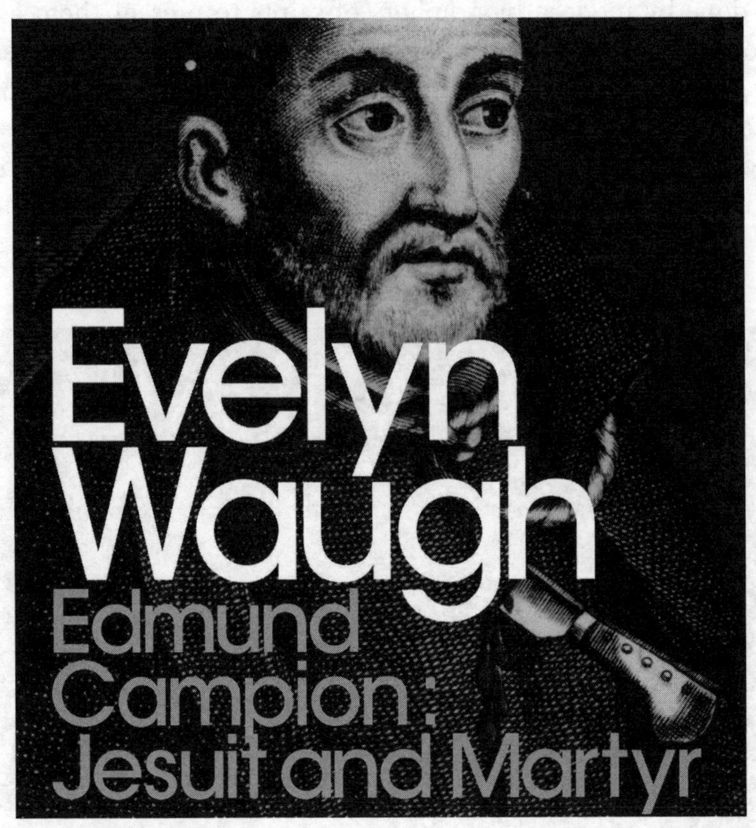

(FROM) EDMUND CAMPION

EVELYN WAUGH

The publication of any book by Evelyn Waugh is a literary landmark. It was not surprising, then, that TIME *magazine and the* SATURDAY REVIEW OF LITERATURE *gave generous space to their reviews of his* CAMPION *when the American edition appeared in 1946.* CAMPION, *written in the sparkling brilliance of the purest modern prose, first appeared in England in 1935 as Waugh's tribute to the English faith and to Father Martin D'Arcy, gifted Jesuit and Master of Campion House at Oxford, who converted Waugh to Catholicism. The biography won for Waugh the Hawthornden Prize in 1936.*

The word "fabulous" has been attributed to Campion by both his biographer and recent reviewers, and the epithet best summarizes the underground of the bloody and tragic days of Elizabethan persecution.

As a young Oxford scholar, Campion caught the fancy of Queen Elizabeth by his learning and his charm. He might have enjoyed a rich career as an ecclesiastic in the Church of England, but clear logic and a correct conscience persuaded him from playing the hypocrite. He left England for Douai to study for the priesthood and shortly afterward joined the new Jesuit Order. After spending several years as a brilliant orator and professor at Prague, in 1580 he received the summons to return to England and martyrdom; for Elizabeth's government had made it high treason to act as a Roman Catholic priest in England. For a full year, Campion journeyed up and down England, eluding Topcliffe and his pursuivants, saying Mass in "priest-holes," instructing, inspiring, and consoling English Catholics whose hopes for their beloved religion were slowly dying. He issued his famous BRAG *which he had published for distribution in the event of his arrest, but which was circulated by fellow Catholics immediately. In the following selection, Waugh gives us an account of his reception and his labors in England following the publication of the* BRAG.

Campion was eventually arrested, imprisoned, racked, and finally dragged through the rain to Tyburn where he was hanged and quartered. After you have been introduced to Campion the Hero in the following selection, you will want to complete this brilliant book about a brilliant martyr, written by a brilliant Catholic.

The result, both for good and ill, was a vast augmentation of Campion's fame. This, obscured now by his long absence abroad, had, even in the old days before his exile, been local and limited; he was known at the Universities and at Court, among scholars, men of affairs and men of fashion, but it is improbable that his name had ever reached the market towns and remote manors, where now it became fabulous.

Both sides now looked upon him as the leader and spokesman of the new mission; his membership in the Society of Jesus cast over him a peculiar glamour, for, it must be remembered, the Society had, so far, no place in the English tradition. Many Englishmen could remember the day when the great estates were religious property; when friars tramped the roads from village to village, and monks, tonsured and habited, drove their animals to market and dispensed alms and hospitality to the destitute; many had their earliest lessons from Dominican or Benedictine in the drowsy village schools; the desolate monuments of the old orders stood in every county; their names were familiar and their memory still sweet with the gentleness and dignity of a lost age. But "Jesuit" was a new word, alien and modern.

To the Protestants it meant conspiracy. The countryman knew for himself the virtues and defects of the old monks; he had seen the methods by which the Royal Commissioners obtained their evidence, and he understood their motives perfectly; but of the Jesuits he knew nothing, except distorted and monstrous reports; that their founder was a Spaniard[1] and they were sworn to another allegiance than the Queen's. Stories of Spanish atrocities were eagerly devoured; the Jesuits were the vanguard of Spanish invasion; their business was to murder the Queen and the Council, and set the country in anarchy so that Philip[2] could march in with the tortures of the Inquisition. Preposterous tales obtained credence of the Jesuits' rule and training and the enormous crimes daily committed behind their walls. The news that disguised Jesuits were now at large in the English countryside caused indignation and alarm, and those who had been apathetic in helping the authorities when the quarry was a Marian[3] priest, now joined fiercely in the hunt.

To the Catholics, too, it meant something new, the restless, uncompromising zeal of the Counter-Reformation.[4] The Queen's Government had taken away from them the priest that their fathers had known; the simple, unambitious figure who had pottered about the parish, lived among his flock, christened them and married them and buried them; prayed for their souls and blessed their crops; whose attainments were to sacrifice and absolve and apply a few rule-of-thumb precepts of canon law; whose occasional lapses from virtue were expected and condoned; with whom they squabbled over their tithes, about whom they grumbled and gossiped; whom they consulted on every occasion; who had seemed, a generation back, something inalienable from the soil of England, as much a part of their lives as the succession of the seasons—he had been stolen from them, and in his place the Holy Father was sending them, in their dark hour, men of new light, equipped in every Continental art, armed against every frailty, bringing a new kind of intellect, new knowledge, new holiness. Campion and Persons found themselves travelling in a world that was already tremulous with expectation.

We have few details of this expedition. The two priests separated at Hoxton and met again three months later at Uxbridge; in the intervening time Persons had passed through Gloucester, Hereford, Worcester, and up into Derbyshire; Campion had been in Berkshire, Oxfordshire, and Northamptonshire. Both they and their hosts were careful to leave no record of their visits, and the letters in which the Jesuits reported progress to their superiors maintain strict anonymity for their converts; edifying anecdotes are related of *"a certain noble lady"* who was offered her liberty on the condition of once walking through a Protestant church, but indignantly refused; of *"a young lady of sixteen"* who was flung into the public prison for prostitutes on account of her courageous answers to the *"sham Bishop of London"*; of a *"boy of, I believe, twelve years"* who was inveigled

[1]SPANIARD—Ignatius of Loyola, who founded the Jesuits.

[2]PHILIP—Philip II of Spain who sent the Armada of 1588 against the English.

[3]MARIAN—The native English clergyman who served under Queen Mary Tudor, 1553-58.

[2]PHILIP—Philip II of Spain who sent the Armada of 1588 against the English.

[4]COUNTER-REFORMATION—The bold counter movement of the Catholic Church against the reformers, planned by the Council of Trent and assisted by the activities of the new Jesuit Order.

into acting as page at a Protestant wedding, was inconsolable with shame until he was able to make his confession to a priest—but nothing is said to identify the protagonists. The only names that can be given with any certainty as Campion's hosts during this journey are Sir William Catesby of Ashby St. Leger, Lord Vaux of Harrowden, and Sir Thomas Tresham, a man of exceptional character, eventually brought to ruin for his faith, whose singular and brilliant taste in architecture may still be seen in the exquisite, unfinished mansion at Lyveden and the unique, triangular pavilion, planned and intricately decorated in honour of the Trinity, which stands, concealed and forlorn, among the trees that border the park at Rushton. It is possible, however, to form a tolerably clear, general impression of the journey from the letters already mentioned and the numerous sources of information about Elizabethan conditions.

He travelled in fair comfort, mounted and equipped as befitted a gentleman of moderate means. He was attended by his servant, and more often than not by one or more of the younger members of the household where he had last stayed, but it was his habit for the most of the way to ride in silence at some little distance from his companions, praying and meditating as he had done on the road to Rheims. Changes of horse and clothing were provided for him at different stages; he was constantly on the move, rarely, for fear of the pursuivants, stopping anywhere for more than one night. He must in this way have visited fifty or more houses during the three months.

Along the road the scenes were familiar enough, but he was seeing them with new eyes; the scars of the Tudor revolution[5] were still fresh and livid; the great houses of the new ruling class were building, and in sharp contrast to their magnificence stood the empty homesteads of the yeomen, evicted to make way for the "grey-faced sheep" or degraded to day-labour on what had once been their common land; the village churches were empty shells, their altars torn out and their ornaments defaced; while here and there throughout his journey he passed, as with a different heart, he had often passed before, the buildings of the old monasteries, their roofs stripped of lead and their walls a quarry for the new contractors.[6] The ruins were not yet picturesque; moss and ivy had barely begun their work, and age had not softened the stark lines of change. Many generations of orderly living, much gentle association, were needed before, under another Queen, the State Church should assume the venerable style of *Barchester Towers.*[7] But if the emotions of the Journey were shame and regret, hope and pride waited for him at the end of the day. Wherever they went the priests found an eager reception. Sometimes they stayed in houses where only a few were Catholic. There was constant coming and going in the vast ramshackle households of the day, and an elaborate hierarchy in the great retinues;

[5]TUDOR REVOLUTION—The destruction of the Catholic monasteries, churches, and Catholic estates begun by Henry VIII.

[6]THE GREAT HOUSES...QUARRY FOR THE NEW CONTRACTORS—Here the author refers to the historical fact that the "new rich" became so through the enclosures of the common lands when wool-growing became a monopoly, through the destruction of the Church and monasteries, the precious metals of which were given to those who supported Henry in his revolt against Rome. Shakespeare is apparently summarizing this condition when he writes in his sonnet: "Bare ruined choirs where late the sweet birds sang."

[7]*Barchester Towers*—Made famous in Trollope's Victorian novel, *Barchester Towers.*

there were galleries where the master never penetrated. It was natural enough that any respectable wayfarer should put up there for the night, whether or no he had any acquaintance with his host. . . .

At Catholic houses they found themselves guests of the highest honour, and there they sometimes prolonged their stay for a few days, until the inevitable warning of the pursuivants' approach drove them once more on to the road. In recent years most of the houses had been furnished with secret cupboards where were stored the Mass vestments, altar stones, sacred vessels and books; these "priest-holes" were usually large enough to provide a hiding-place for the missionaries in case of a sudden raid; in some cases there were complete chapels with confessionals and priest's room. Many houses sheltered one of the old Marian priests who had left his cure at Elizabeth's succession, and now lived in nominal employment as secretary and butler. At this early date these seculars had no quarrel with the Fathers of the Society. The Jesuits, fresh from Rome and Continental schools, were as welcome to them as to their flocks; cut off, as they were, from episcopal control, from their reading and from intercourse with other clerics, they constantly found themselves confronted with problems to which their simple training afforded no solution; all these were brought to Campion and Persons. Their prayers were always for more Jesuits. . . .

Campion found his Catholic hosts impoverished to the verge of ruin by the recusancy fines;[8] often the household were in mourning for one or more of their number who had been removed to prison. "No other talk but of death, flight, prison, or spoil of friends," yet everywhere he was amazed at the constancy and devotion which he found. The listless, yawning days were over, the half-hour's duty perfunctorily accorded on days of obligation. Catholics no longer chose their chaplain for his speed in saying Mass, or kept Boccaccio[9] bound in the covers of their missals. Driven back to the life of the catacombs, the Church was recovering their temper. No one now complained of the length of the services, a priest reported to Father Agazzari; if a Mass did not last nearly an hour they were discontented, and if, as occasionally happened, several priests were together, the congregation would assist at five or six Masses in one morning.

Word would go round the countryside that Campion had arrived, and throughout the evening Catholics of every degree, squire and labourer and deposed cleric, would stealthily assemble. He would sit up half the night receiving each in turn, hearing their confessions and resolving their difficulties. Then before dawn a room would be prepared for Mass. Watches were set in case of alarm. The congregation knelt on the rushstrewn floor. Mass was said, communion was given. Then Campion would preach.

It needs little fancy to reconstruct the scene; the audience hushed and intent, every member of whom was risking liberty and fortune, perhaps his life, by attendance. The dusk lightened and the candles paled on the improvised altar, the tree tops outside the window took fire, as Campion spoke. The thrilling tones, the profusion of imagery, the polish and precision, the balanced, pointed argument, the whole structure

[8] RECUSANCY FINES—Those who refused to conform to the new religion and attend the Anglican Church were fined heavily. Practicing his faith in those days cost a man several thousand pounds a year.

[9] BOCCACCIO—Writer of the Italian Renaissance, famed for his *Decameron*.

and rich ornament of rhetoric which had stirred the lecture halls and collegiate chapels of Oxford and Douai, Rome, Prague, and Rheims,[10] inspired now with more than human artistry, rang through the summer dawn. And when the discourse had mounted to its peroration and the fiery voice had dropped to the quiet, traditional words of the blessing, a long silence while the priest disrobed and assumed once more his secular disguise; a hurried packing away of the altar furniture, a few words of leave taking, and then the horses' hooves clattered once more in the cobbled yard; Campion was on his way, and the Catholics dispersed to their homes.

The danger was increasingly great. *"I cannot long escape the hands of the heretics,"* said Campion, in the letter quoted above, *"The enemy have so many eyes, so many tongues, so many scouts and crafts. I am in apparel to myself very ridiculous; I often change my name also. I read letters sometimes myself that in the first front tell news that Campion is taken. . . . Threatening edicts come forth against us daily. . . . I find many neglecting their own security to have only care of my safety."*

More than once while Campion was sitting at dinner strangers would be heard at the outer doors. *"Like deer when they hear the huntsmen"* the company would leap to their feet and Campion would be rushed into hiding. Sometimes it proved to be a false alarm; sometimes the pursuivants would enter, question the inmates, and depart satis fied. The party would resume their meal and the interrupted conversation. Events of this kind were now a part of his life, but by the loyalty and discretion of his friends, and by his own resources, he escaped unmolested

[10] OXFORD, DOUAI, ROME, PRAGUE, RHEIMS—These were the various places where Campion studied, taught, and preached.

through the three-month journey, and his report ends in a triumphant mood. *"There will never want in England men that will have care of their own salvation, nor such as shall advance other men's; neither shall this Church here ever fail so long as priests and pastors shall be found for their sheep, rage man or devil never so much."*

FOR DISCUSSION

1. Discuss in detail the different reactions of the English Catholics and the Protestants to Campion's return to England. Explain the reasons for these reactions.

2. Describe the manner in which Campion traveled, as well as the countryside through which he passed.

3. Contrast the material and the spiritual condition of Campion's hosts. Discuss their attitude toward the Mass as contrasted with that of former years.

4. Explain what Waugh means, in the second paragraph, when he says that "the Society, so far, had no place in English tradition."

5. Discuss at some length the ninth paragraph and the sixth footnote.

6. Waugh's description of Campion's preaching is a splendid example of modern English prose at its best. Analyze it carefully.

7. Has Campion's thrilling prophecy of the last sentence of this selection been fulfilled? Explain.

8. Waugh has given us several quotations from Campion's own writings. Do you think that Campion was a good writer in his own right?

WORD STUDY

1. What is the relationship between the words *apathetic, pathos,* and *sympathetic?* What is the difference between *credence* and personal experience? Give several synonyms for *pottered. Livid* describes what color?

2. Discuss the rich meaning of the following expressions: *tremulous expectation; age had not yet softened the stark lines of change.*

PROJECTS

1. Trace on a map of England the journeys of Campion.

2. Could you mention some of the prominent leaders of the Counter-Reformation in England?

3. Attempt a radio or television script in which you describe the martyrdom of Campion. Base your text on the passage of Waugh's *Campion*, pp. 150-161.

RELATED READING

Richard Breen and Harry Schnibbe have written a modern drama which has as its theme the heroism of Campion. This drama can be found in *Theatre for Tomorrow.*

Many Catholic novels have been written about the persecution of Catholics during the days of Henry and Elizabeth. Among them are Monsignor Hugh Benson's *The King's Achievement, The Queen's Tragedy, Come Rack, Come Rope;* Mrs. Wilfrid Ward's *Tudor Sunset;* and *The Mass of Brother Michel* by Michael Kent.

TWENTIETH CENTURY POETRY

The first years of the twentieth century inaugurated no revolution in poetry. The big names of the late nineteenth century continued to be the big names of the early twentieth. Poets such as Thomas Hardy, A. E. Housman, Rudyard Kipling, and W. B. Yeats dominated the poetic scene.

The first two new poets arrived in 1902: Walter de la Mare, the poet of childhood and magic dreamland; and John Masefield, who poured new life into English narrative poetry with his realistic themes of the sea and the common man. W. W. Gibson discarded his earlier tendency to follow the style of Tennyson and began to write simply and realistically of miners, engineers, and shepherds.

The Catholic poets, Belloc, G. K. Chesterton, and Alfred Noyes belong to this earlier generation. Chesterton will always be remembered for his stirring narrative, *The Ballad of the White Horse,* and his *Lepanto.* Belloc rivalled Kipling in praise of his native Sussex; his sonnets and epigrams will be long remembered.

FIRST WORLD WAR YEARS

The First World War brought forth the muse of many young soldiers. Outstanding among these young poets were Wilfred Owen, Siegfried Sassoon, and Rupert Brooke. Like most of the soldiers in the First War, Sassoon entered the conflict with youthful idealism, but that idealism soon turned to horror and indignation. Both Owen and Brooke were killed in the bloody conflict. A Catholic and a true poet who survived front-line action in the war was Maurice Baring, intimate friend of Belloc and Chesterton.

The generation of post-war poets revolted against what they called the emotionalism and anti-intellectualism of Romantic and Victorian poetry. However, their revolt was more than poetic. It was a revolt against the man-centered view of life which had supplanted the God-centered view of the Middle Ages. The leaders of the revolt, following the philosophical and historical findings of Catholic and non-Catholic scholars, maintained that Western Europe had taken a wrong turn at the time of the Renaissance, which made Man, not God, the center of all things. Europe had finally and fatally gone astray at the time of the French Revolution. Under the influence of Rousseau, who denied Original Sin and wanted man to go back to the pure state of nature, the culture of Europe had broken its final link with the ancient Faith.

These young poets of revolt were not only against the spirit of Romantic poetry, but against its form and its diction. The two great exponents of the new school were T. S. Eliot and Miss Edith Sitwell. Miss Sitwell did not discard traditional meter and rhyme, but experimented in the mental effects of assonance and alliteration. Much of her early poetry was obscured imagery—but she did teach us to see things we never saw before, and she helped to freshen the diction of the English language. Her later poems have a definite Christian tone and flavor.

In 1922 T. S. Eliot's *Waste Land* was heralded as a landmark in English poetry as important as Wordsworth's *Lyrical Ballads.* Its main attraction lay in the manner in which it mirrored the disillusionment of his age and its bold innovation in versification and style. It is the voice of one crying in the wilderness of a Godless world. Eliot took the symbol of the Waste Land from the Grail legend. Despite its elaborately obscure and conventionally simple style, the lesson of the *Waste Land* is a powerful one: our culture will never bloom again until the Holy Vessel of the Grail is found. Eliot's forthcoming conversion to Anglo-Catholicism is implied in this poem. In 1928 he declared himself a classicist in literature and an Anglo-Catholic in religion. His other well known poems include: *The Love Song of J. Alfred Prufrock, Ash Wednesday, The Rock, Four Quartets,* and his dramatic poetry, *Murder in the Cathedral, The Cocktail Party,* and *The Confidential Clerk.*

SEARCH FOR THE HOLY GRAIL

The twentieth century witnessed the birth of a poetic movement in Ireland. Its major poets, W. B. Yeats, G. W. Russell (A.E.), and John M. Synge, did not go to the traditional Catholic Faith of Ireland for their themes, but to the pagan mythology of the ancient Gaels. As a result, their poetry lacks strength and virility and constitutes a sort of beautiful escapism into the twilight world of pagan legend. The Irish Catholic tradition has been kept alive in the poetry of Katherine Tynan, James Stephens, and Padraic Colum.

THE NEW GENERATION

A new generation of poets began to arrive in 1930 in the persons of W. H. Auden, Stephen Spender, and Cecil Lewis. In their earlier poetry they copied Eliot's and Gerard Manley Hopkins' techniques, but not their doctrines. All three of these poets had Leftist leanings at one time. But Auden, who became an American citizen, discarded his radicalism and began championing the cause of the Christian tradition.

Dylan Thomas, the great Welsh poet, was first caught up in the poetic imagery of the stream of consciousness and surrealistic schools. But in his later poems he became much more distinct and understandable. He gave concrete evidence in such a poem as "Vision and Prayer" of his growing interest in Christian themes.

Roy Campbell, a notable modern British Catholic poet, was a traditionalist in form and in content. The Spanish Civil War marked a crisis in his life. He fought valiantly on the side of Franco against the Loyalists when all the other young British poets were espousing the cause of the Republicans and the Communists. So convinced was Campbell that Franco and Spain had saved Europe from Communism that he became a citizen of Spain. No British poet has ever had a more thrilling and varied career. The first part of his autobiography appeared in 1953 under the title *Light on a Dark Horse.* There is sublimity and "a lyre of savage thunder" in his poetry, published under the titles *The Flaming Terrapin, The Georgiad,* and *Mithraic Emblems.*

ROY CAMPBELL'S EXCITING CAREER

To an Athlete Dying Young

A. E. HOUSMAN

A very pathetic figure is the aged and forgotten athlete as he pages through yellowed and time-worn scrapbooks which speak of his former fame. In this poem, Housman intimates that fame is less fleeting to those who die at the height of their athletic prowess.

The time you won your town the race
We chaired you through the marketplace;
Man and boy stood cheering by,
And home we brought you shoulder-high.

Today, the road all runners come,
Shoulder-high we bring you home,
And set you at your threshold down,
Townsman of a stiller town.

Smart lad, to slip betimes away
From fields where glory does not stay,
And early though the laurel grows
It withers quicker than the rose.

Eyes the shady night has shut
Cannot see the record cut,
And silence sounds no worse than cheers
After earth has stopped the ears;

Now you will not swell the rout
Of lads that wore their honors out,
Runners whom renown outran
And the name died before the man.

So set, before its echoes fade,
The fleet foot on the sill of shade,
And hold to the low lintel up
The still-defended challenge-cup.

And round that early-laureled head
Will flock to gaze the strengthless dead,
And find unwithered on its curls
The garland briefer than a girl's.

FOR APPRECIATION

1. Select the details by which the poet contrasts the victory procession with the funeral procession. Explain the meaning of: *chaired you; road all runners run; stiller town.*

2. Why is the athlete called "smart lad"? What connotation has "the laurel"? Explain the meaning of lines 19-20. Can you mention any famous athletes to whom these lines might apply? To set you thinking, we will name Jim Thorpe.

3. Can you mention some modern athletes who died young and to whom the poem as a whole can be applied? Again to set you thinking, we mention the immortal Gipp of Notre Dame.

4. Does the poem appeal to you? Why or why not?

The Lake Isle of Innisfree

WILLIAM BUTLER YEATS

Homesickness, and the sound of water, inspired this poem. Mr. Yeats has told how in his teens he formed the ambition of going to live in solitude on Innisfree, a small island in Lough Gill. Years later, ". . . when walking through Fleet Street, very homesick, I heard a little tinkle of water and saw a fountain in a shop window which balanced a little ball upon its jet, and began to remember lake water. From the sudden remembrance came my poem 'Innisfree.'"

I will arise and go now, and go to Innisfree,
And a small cabin build there, of clay and wattles made;
Nine bean rows will I have there, a hive for the honey bee,
And live alone in the bee-loud glade.

And I shall have some peace there, for peace comes dropping slow,
Dropping from the veils of the morning to where the cricket sings;
There midnight's all a-glimmer, and noon a purple glow,
And evening full of the linnet's wings.

I will arise and go now, for always night and day
I hear lake water lapping with low sounds by the shore;
While I stand on the roadway, or on the pavements gray,
I hear it in the deep heart's core.

2. WATTLES—Twigs; flexible withes.

FOR APPRECIATION

1. At the beginning of the poem, all in an instant, the vision of a secluded Robinson Crusoe life on Innisfree flashes into the speaker's mind. What details suggest the rural simplicity of the home he dreams of? What is a *glade,* and why does this word fit the atmosphere of the poem better than "woods" or "among the trees"?

2. The second stanza is more vague, giving a general impression of quiet contentment. How does it suggest that the speaker would like to spend the entire twenty-four hours of each day drinking in the beauty of the scene around him?

3. The last stanza returns to actuality—to the wistful poet instead of his dream. How can we tell that he is in the city? How can we guess that he has to stay there instead of going to Innisfree? What line do you think best expresses his longing?

4. Try to think of a childhood scene or experience that sometimes flashes vividly into your memory. What single thing—a sound or perhaps a scent—sets off the recollection? List the other details that instantly come to mind when this "flashback" occurs.

OF FORM AND STYLE

1. Thinking of the whole poem, see if you can explain how the beginning, "I will arise and go now," adds to its effectiveness even though the poet does not expect us to believe that he will actually "go."

2. What examples of *alliteration* can you find in the line about lake water in stanza 3? Notice the *a* sounds in this line, followed by *o* sounds. This repetition of vowel sounds in a sort of semi-rhyme is called *assonance.* What words in the following lines echo the same two vowels?

When You Are Old

WILLIAM BUTLER YEATS

Here is a message addressed by a young poet to the woman he loves. It is meant to be read many years later, perhaps even after the poet is dead. It will remind the woman of her former youth and loveliness, and of the man who understood and loved her best.

When you are old and gray and full of sleep,
And nodding by the fire, take down this book,
And slowly read, and dream of the soft look
Your eyes had once, and of their shadows deep;

How many loved your moments of glad grace,
And loved your beauty with love false or true,
But one man loved the pilgrim soul in you,
And loved the sorrows of your changing face;

And bending down beside the glowing bars,
Murmur, a little sadly, how Love fled
And paced upon the mountains overhead
And hid his face amid a crowd of stars.

FOR APPRECIATION

1. The poet shows that he has valued the woman's grace and beauty, just as many others have. Explain how his love was deeper and more valuable than theirs.

2. In the last stanza, what are the "glowing bars"? How does the vivid final phrase, "a crowd of stars," show us something about the sky that we might not notice for ourselves?

3. Reread the last stanza and see if you can decide what is meant by saying that love "fled." Notice particularly *where* the poet says love has gone. The stanza could mean that intense personal love has been transformed into something else, such as religious idealism, love of art, or love of humanity. In that case, what would be the reason for mentioning mountains and stars? How does this stanza suggest that the feeling of two young lovers toward each other is also a very fine and precious thing?

4. When the woman mentioned in the poem looks at "this book," she will literally receive a message written long before. All through history, men have been fascinated by the fact that something written down a long time ago is still read and understood—as if the dead author still had the power to talk to us. Give one example of a "message from the past" which has come down to us in the Bible. Then give examples of (a) a saying from Shakespeare which is often repeated; (b) an old proverbial expression; (c) a statement by some former American leader which we still use as a slogan in our national life. Members of the class who are Latin students may be able to think of an idea or phrase which was known to the ancient Romans and which we still repeat, in translation.

The Second Coming

WILLIAM BUTLER YEATS

Frankly, this is a difficult poem. But it well illustrates the second phase in the development of Yeats' poetry. In his later years, Yeats turned away from romantic and fanciful themes and the use of colorful symbols and sensuous language. Instead, he wrote in a language almost bare of ornament, used sharp and harsh words, and an almost conversational tone. He did not discard the use of symbols, but gave them a deeper intellectual significance.

The poem is written in blank verse and is divided into two sections: lines 1-8 and lines 9-22.

In the first section, we are told that the world is in disorder; it is out of joint and a change is overdue. This thought is symbolized poetically by the image of the falcon going so far away from the falconer that it has lost contact with its master. The world has lost its center of gravity, all things which should be bound together by its center have fallen apart, and anarchy is turned loose. It is plainly evident that the poet is symbolizing the rejection of God, the absolute moral order, and traditional Christianity—the rejection of which has resulted in the present world chaos. The bloody tide of war, of strife, and of disillusionment has drowned out the innocence which comes from faith. Even the best men lack conviction of the truth, and the worst are passionately intent on destroying the world.

In the second section, the poet utters the cry that surely Christ and His Revelation will be born anew. But SPIRITUS MUNDI, *the Spirit of the World, haunts the poet's sight and makes him fearful. The poet sees in the desert wasteland (the world without God) the head of a man (his rational nature) and the body of a lion (his lower nature turned ferocious) as if ready to move. Perhaps this beast who has rejected his Christian inheritance is ready for a change for the better. But desert birds or false prophets indignantly reel about him. Darkness comes again (is it the darkness of Communism?) and perhaps it is too late. But then the poet remembers. Was not mankind which was asleep to the light of Christianity for twenty centuries before the First Coming, aroused to the paradoxical nightmare of the Christian Revelation by the rocking cradle of the Infant Savior? In the last lines, the poet poses the tremendous question: Is it possible that modern mankind, laden with the Spirit of the World, is slowly creeping back to Christ?*

Turning and turning in the widening gyre
The falcon cannot hear the falconer;
Things fall apart; the centre cannot hold;
Mere anarchy is loosed upon the world,
The blood-dimmed tide is loosed, and everywhere
The ceremony of innocence is drowned;
The best lack all conviction, while the worst
Are full of passionate intensity.

Surely some revelation is at hand;
Surely the Second Coming is at hand.
The Second Coming! Hardly are those words out
When a vast image out of *Spiritus Mundi*
Troubles my sight: somewhere in sands of the desert
A shape with lion body and the head of a man,
A gaze blank and pitiless as the sun,
Is moving its slow thighs, while all about it

1. GYRE (jīr)—A circle described by a moving body.

Reel shadows of the indignant desert birds.
The darkness drops again; but now I know
That twenty centuries of stony sleep
Were vexed to nightmare by a rocking cradle,
And what rough beast, its hour come round at last,
Slouches towards Bethlehem to be born?

FOR APPRECIATION

1. Discuss in detail the economy of statement; the stark, unadorned, yet thought-packed symbols which the poet uses. Do these symbols appeal primarily to the intellect, or to the senses? Illustrate your answer by examples. Do the symbols merely suggest and imply meanings, or do they directly state the thought intended? Illustrate by examples.

2. Do you or do you not agree with the interpretation of the poem as given in the introduction? Discuss. Why could not any prose paraphrase of the poem do justice to its meaning or its striking interpretations?

3. Study carefully the meter and the rhythm of the poem. The rhythm of the iambic measure is frequently broken with a counter-rhythm. Select lines where this occurs, and give reasons for this change in movement. Study, for example, lines 6, 15, 17, and 19.

A Consecration

JOHN MASEFIELD

The poet laureate of England prefixed "A Consecration" to his collected poems. In this particular poem as well as in the majority of his other poems, he fulfills his promise of speaking for "the scorned—the rejected," "the man with too weighty a burden, too weary a load." In this respect, he has something in common with the medieval poet of the common people, William Langland.

Not of the princes and prelates with periwigged charioteers
Riding triumphantly laurelled to lap the fat of the years,—
Rather the scorned—the rejected—the men hemmed in with the spears;

The men of the tattered battalion which fights till it dies,
Dazed with the dust of the battle, the din and the cries.
The men with the broken heads and the blood running into their eyes.

Not the be-medaled Commander, beloved of the throne,
Riding cock-horse to parade when the bugles are blown,
But the lads who carried the koppie and cannot be known.

Not the ruler for me, but the ranker, the tramp of the road,
The slave with the sack on his shoulders pricked on with the goad,
The man with too weighty a burden, too weary a load.

The sailor, the stoker of steamers, the man with the clout,
The chantyman bent at the halliards putting a tune to the shout,
The drowsy man at the wheel and the tired look-out.

Others may sing of the wine and the wealth and the mirth,
The portly presence of potentates goodly in girth;—
Mine be the dirt and the dross, the dust and scum of the earth!

Theirs be the music, the colour, the glory, the gold;
Mine be a handful of ashes, a mouthful of mold.
Of the maimed, of the halt and the blind in the rain and the cold—
Of these shall my songs be fashioned, my tales be told.

9. KOPPIE—A word used in South Africa to mean kop, or small hill. The reference is to the Boer War.
13. CLOUT—Cloth or rag.
14. CHANTYMAN—The sailor who leads in the singing as the men work at the halliards (sails).

FOR APPRECIATION

1. Writers commonly speak of a "dedication" of their works to someone they wish to honor. What added meaning is there in the word "consecration" as Masefield used it in the title of his poem?

2. The poem is a series of comparisons between the powerful and the weak, the successful and the scorned, the rich and the poor. What is the comparison of the first stanza? What picture do you see? What is the meaning of the "fat of the years"?

3. In your own words, describe the picture in the second stanza; in the third stanza.

4. In the fourth stanza, how does the "ranker" offer contrast to the "ruler"? What is the meaning of "pricked on with the goad"?

5. What would Masefield think of the men mentioned in the fifth stanza? Was there anything in Masefield's own life which would lead him to sing of the toiling and suffering types of humanity? Or anything to lead him to enumerate the various seamen's jobs?

6. What is the figure of speech used in line 17? To whom does the "Theirs" of the last stanza refer? Explain the meaning of the figure of speech in line 20.

7. Which stanza presents to you the most vivid picture? Which lines best express the poet's sympathy for the workers of the world?

G. K. CHESTERTON

In Memory of G.K. Chesterton

WALTER DE LA MARE

In many ways, De la Mare is poetically akin to Chesterton, to whom he pays tribute in this thought-crammed quatrain. Like Chesterton, he revels in the innocency of childhood, in the unspeakable beauty of the world. Again, like Chesterton, there is always a serious undertone in the playfulness of his fancy, and an intense reality comes from his realization that this is "a world where sin and beauty whisper Home."

Knight of the Holy Ghost, he goes his way,
Wisdom his motley, Truth his loving jest;
The mills of Satan keep his lance in play,
Pity and innocence his heart at rest.

"In Memory of G. K. Chesterton" by Walter de la Mare, reprinted by permission of Faber and Faber, Limited, London, and the author.

FOR APPRECIATION

From your knowledge of Chesterton's life and work, explain each line of the poem. Show that it is a perfect summing up of what G. K. was. Explain "a world where sin and beauty whisper Home."

The Soldier

RUPERT BROOKE

This is one of the more famous poems inspired by World War I. Rupert Brooke, who lost his life shortly after he wrote these lines, has expressed the patriotic sentiment of millions of young Britons and Americans who fought in foreign fields.

If I should die, think only this of me;
That there's some corner of a foreign field
That is forever England. There shall be
In that rich earth a richer dust concealed;
A dust whom England bore, shaped, made aware,
Gave, once, her flowers to love, her ways to roam,
A body of England's, breathing English air,
Washed by the rivers, blest by suns of home.

And think, this heart, all evil shed away,
A pulse in the eternal mind, no less
Gives somewhere back the thoughts by England given;
Her sights and sounds; dreams happy as her day
And laughter, learnt of friends; and gentleness,
In hearts at peace, under an English heaven.

FOR APPRECIATION

1. Explain the meaning of the first three lines. What is the "richer dust" of line 4? Has the soldier returned home?

2. What meaning does Brooke give to immortality in lines 9-14? Is this Catholic or Christian? Explain.

3. What are the things about England he has appreciated most? Might one of today's servicemen think these same thoughts, substituting America and American for England and English? Discuss.

4. Is there an echo of Browning's "Home Thoughts from Abroad" in the poem? Discuss.

5. Mention some modern war poets who wrote about World War II.

Sight

W. W. GIBSON

For some years, Wilfrid Gibson lived in the East End, the slum district of London. His poems arouse sympathy for the man with the lunch pail, for the underprivileged and the unfortunate. He has been called "the twentieth-century Thomas Hood." In "Sight," he demonstrates how even a vegetable market, under the magic of a poet's inspiration, takes on a new and surprising significance. He uncovers the fires of Krakatao in a tomato and a Tyrean sunset in an orange. But there is further a stab of sympathy for the one who cannot see such beauty.

By the lamplit stall I loitered, feasting my eyes
On colors ripe and rich for the heart's desire—
Tomatoes, redder than Krakatao's fire,
Oranges like old sunsets over Tyre,
And apples golden-green as the glades of Paradise.

And as I lingered, lost in divine delight,
My heart thanked God for the goodly gift of sight
And all youth's lively senses keen and quick . . .
When suddenly, behind me in the night,
I heard the tapping of a blind man's stick.

3. KRAKATAO—Island volcano in Dutch East Indies; its eruption in 1883 has been the most tremendous in recent centuries.

4. TYRE—Famous maritime city of antiquity, in Phoenicia.

FOR APPRECIATION

1. In the first stanza, the poet uses the colors of a tomato, orange, and apple as a basis for suggesting three very dramatic and historic pictures. Explain.

2. How does the last line of the poem reinforce the effect of the whole poem? Discuss.

3. Read Gibson's sonnet "Color."

Aftermath

SIEGFRIED SASSOON

During the actual conflict of World War I and a few years after it, many a young English poet wrote idealistically of the heroic spirit of those who fought and those who fell. Among these were Rupert Brooke and Edmund Blunden. But as the vision of "a world safe for democracy" faded and the terrible disillusionment of the futility of that war was seen in its stark reality, other poets began to portray the physical horrors, the brutality, the mockery, and the black despair of world carnage. These qualities are especially dominant in the poetry of Wilfrid Owen and Siegfried Sassoon.

Have you forgotten yet?...
For the world's events have rumbled on since those gagged days,
Like traffic checked a while at the crossing of city ways:
And the haunted gap in your mind has filled with thoughts that flow
Like the clouds in the lit heavens of life; and you're a man reprieved to go,
Taking your peaceful share of Time, with joy to spare.
But the past is just the same,—and War's a bloody game....
Have you forgotten yet?...
Look down, and swear by the slain of the War that you'll never forget.

Do you remember the dark months you held the sector at Mametz—
The nights you watched and wired and dug and piled sand-bags on parapets?
Do you remember the rats; and the stench
Of corpses rotting in front of the front-line trench,—
And dawn coming, dirty-white, and chill with a hopeless rain?
Do you ever stop and ask, "Is it all going to happen again?"

10. MAMETZ—A village along the Somme River in France where a decisive battle in World War I occurred in 1916.

Do you remember that hour of din before the attack,—
And the anger, the blind compassion that seized and shook you then
As you peered at the doomed and haggard faces of your men?
Do you remember the stretcher-cases lurching back
With dying eyes and lolling heads, those ashen-gray
Masks of the lads who once were keen and gay?

Have you forgotten yet?...
Look up, and swear by the green of the Spring that you'll never forget.

FOR APPRECIATION

1. What simile does Sassoon employ to illustrate the speedy passage of events since the war days? Discuss the meaning of *game* in line 7.

2. Why would Sassoon be not likely to forget? Discuss.

3. Why does the poet fill his picture of war experiences with such sharply distressing details? What does he fear will happen? Were his fears realized? Explain. Do you think World War II was any more successful than World War I? Discuss. Is it necessary to be mindful of war in time of peace?

4. What does the word "Aftermath" mean? Explain why it is an appropriate title for the poem.

5. Explain: *haunted gap in your mind; man reprieved to go... with joy to spare.*

Dreamers

SIEGFRIED SASSOON

Sassoon bitterly protested against the false glorification of war. He was a soldier and knew the anguish and misery which are far removed from the romantic gestures of flying flags and beating drums. "Dreamers" is a vivid picture of what the soldier feels.

Soldiers are citizens of death's gray land,
Drawing no dividend from time's tomorrows.
In the great hour of destiny they stand,
Each with his feuds, and jealousies, and sorrows.
Soldiers are sworn to action; they must win
Some flaming, fatal climax with their lives.
Soldiers are dreamers; when the guns begin
They think of firelit homes, clean beds, and wives.

I see them in foul dug-outs, gnawed by rats,
And in the ruined trenches, lashed with rain,
Dreaming of things they did with balls and bats,
And mocked by hopeless longing to regain
Bank-holidays, and picture shows, and spats,
And going to the office in the train.

FOR APPRECIATION

1. What does the first line of the poem say about the lot of a soldier? In what sense is it true? What is the meaning of the second line? What is the aim or purpose of the soldier as Sassoon sees it?

2. When do soldiers become dreamers? Why? What do they dream about? Why these particular things?

3. Mention some modern movies, stories, and dramas which give a realistic picture of war.

PROJECTS

1. Write two graphic prose sketches or vignettes which you may call "A Study in Contrast." In the first, portray the dreams of home of one particular serviceman during the lull of some major military engagement. In the other, paint him in the environment of a confused world a few weeks after his return to civilian life.

2. Attempt a sonnet on the subject, "Soldier's Return." Talking to a war veteran first might help you.

The Express

STEPHEN SPENDER

The ordinary sights of our mechanized civilization seem strange and exciting to Stephen Spender. Here he tries to show us the beauty of an express train—not the kind of beauty a flower or a peaceful stream has, but a wilder, more powerful, and disturbing kind of beauty.

After the first powerful plain manifesto
The black statement of pistons, without more fuss
But gliding like a queen, she leaves the station.
Without bowing and with restrained unconcern
She passes the houses which humbly crowd outside,
The gasworks and at last the heavy page

1. MANIFESTO—Declaration; announcement.

Of death, printed by gravestones in the cemetery.
Beyond the town there lies the open country
Where, gathering speed, she acquires mystery,
The luminous self-possession of ships on ocean.
It is now she begins to sing—at first quite low
Then loud, and at last with a jazzy madness—
The song of her whistle screaming at curves,
Of deafening tunnels, brakes, innumerable bolts.
And always light, aerial, underneath
Goes the elate meter of her wheels.
Steaming through metal landscape on her lines
She plunges new eras of wild happiness
Where speed throws up strange shapes, broad curves
And parallels clean like the steel of guns.
At last, further than Edinburgh or Rome,
Beyond the crest of the world she reaches night
Where only a low streamline brightness
Of phosphorus on the tossing hills is white.
Ah, like a comet through flame she moves entranced
Wrapped in her music no bird song, no, nor bough
Breaking with honey buds, shall ever equal.

16. ELATE—Elated; joyous.

FOR APPRECIATION

1. At the beginning of the poem, the express train is slowly moving away from the depot toward the edge of town. "Powerful plain manifesto" and "black statement of pistons" suggest a vigorous outburst of some kind at the moment the train starts. What details of the train is the poet describing? Explain why a moment later the train is "gliding like a queen."

2. What realistic detail about the outskirts of a city is supplied by "the houses which *humbly* crowd outside"? Why is the cemetery mentioned *after* the gasworks?

3. What phrases suggest that the truly important characteristics of the express train begin to appear only after it has moved well into the country? What are the various sounds the poet has in mind when he says, "she begins to sing"? Why does he speak of the *meter* of the wheels?

4. What are the "parallels" in line 20? What keeps them "clean like the steel of guns"? Just as the train passes out of sight over the horizon the poet compares it to a flaming comet. The "flame" may be a figurative expression for the noise or "music" that surrounds the speeding train. What literal flame may also be seen around a steam locomotive at night?

5. What general feeling toward the environment we live in is implied in the last two lines?

6. Decide what typical spectacle of our machine age seems most impressive or thrilling to you. If you were to write a poem in praise of it, what specific details would you include?

The Unknown Citizen

W. H. AUDEN

Many modern writers have protested that in our day each human being's life is controlled by the newspapers, by advertisements, by various organizations, and by government. Swept along in the current like a soldier in an army, he can hardly make his own choices or have any individuality. Such a thought is suggested by the very title of this poem. The epitaph at the beginning suggests two things: that the man is such a nobody that he has a number rather than a name, and that he is exactly the kind of person modern society honors.

TO JS/O7/M/378
THIS MARBLE MONUMENT IS
ERECTED BY THE STATE

He was found by the Bureau of Statistics to be
One against whom there was no official complaint,
And all the reports on his conduct agree
That, in the modern sense of an old-fashioned word, he was a saint,
For in everything he did he served the Greater Community.
Except for the War till the day he retired
He worked in a factory and never got fired,
But satisfied his employers, Fudge Motors Inc.
Yet he wasn't a scab or odd in his views,
For his Union reports that he paid his dues,
(Our report on his Union shows it was sound)
And our Social Psychology workers found
That he was popular with his mates and liked a drink.
The Press are convinced that he bought a paper every day
And that his reactions to advertisements were normal in every way.
Policies taken out in his name prove that he was fully insured,
And his Health-card shows he was once in a hospital but left it cured.
Both Producers Research and High-Grade-Living declare
He was fully sensible to the advantages of the Installment Plan.
And had everything necessary to the Modern Man,

A phonograph, a radio, a car, and a frigidaire.
Our researchers into Public Opinion are content
That he held the proper opinions for the time of year;
When there was peace, he was for peace; when there was war, he went.
He was married and added five children to the population,
Which our Eugenist says was the right number for a parent of his generation,
And our teachers report that he never interfered with their education.
Was he free? Was he happy? The question is absurd:
Had anything been wrong, we should certainly have heard.

FOR APPRECIATION

1. This is a satirical poem about conformity. Notice that the citizen conformed to what his employers expected—and at the same time conformed to what his labor union expected. Point out two other statements that show him doing as he was told. What is satirical about " ... held the proper opinions for the time of year"? What is satirical about the line just following this one?

2. Why do you think the poet capitalizes so many words?

3. For fun, the poet has made the epitaph rhyme. What word rhymes with "State"? Within the poem itself, find the earlier word that rhymes with "drink."

4. Read several lines aloud, noticing how the absence of regular meter creates the effect of conversation rather than the effect we usually expect in poetry. Point out three phrases resembling prose more than traditional poetic language.

5. The poem implies that JS/07/M/378 never really thought or acted for himself, but merely followed the dictates of one group or another. What do you think about the accuracy of this idea as applied to citizens of our own country? Give an example of a person doing something just because "everybody else does." Then give an example proving that some citizens, at least, make up their minds independently of group opinion.

6. Read the concluding two lines again. What feeling do they leave in your mind about whether the citizen was or was not free and happy? Much evidence is given in the poem that he was not *free.* Explain your own opinion on whether or not such a person could be *happy.*

(FROM) *Chorus No. 1 of "The Rock"*

T. S. ELIOT

"The Rock" is a pageant on the church, men's neglect of it, and the place it has held and should hold in the life of the nation. Chorus No. 1 is a lament over the present irreligious state of mankind.

The Eagle soars in the summit of Heaven,
The Hunter with his dogs pursues his circuit.
O perpetual revolution of configured stars,
O perpetual recurrence of determined seasons,
O world of spring and autumn, birth and dying!
The endless cycle of idea and action,
Endless invention, endless experiment,
Brings knowledge of motion, but not of stillness;
Knowledge of speech, but not of silence;
Knowledge of words, and ignorance of the Word.
All our knowledge brings us nearer to our ignorance,
All our ignorance brings us nearer to death,
But nearness to death no nearer to God.
Where is the Life we have lost in living?
Where is the wisdom we have lost in knowledge?
Where is the knowledge we have lost in information?
The cycles of Heaven in twenty centuries
Bring us farther from God and nearer to the Dust.

I journeyed to London, to the timekept City,
Where the River flows, with foreign flotations.
There I was told: we have too many churches,
And too few chophouses. There I was told:
Let the vicars retire. Men do not need the Church
In the place where they work, but where they spend their Sundays.
In the City, we need no bells:
Let them waken the suburbs.
I journeyed to the suburbs, and there I was told:
We toil for six days, on the seventh we must motor
To Hindhead, or Maidenhead.
If the weather is foul we stay at home and read the papers.
In industrial districts, there I was told
Of economic laws.
In the pleasant countryside, there it seemed
That the country now is only fit for picnics.
And the Church does not seem to be wanted
In country or in suburbs; and in the town
Only for important weddings.

1-2. EAGLE . . . HUNTER WITH HIS DOGS—The constellations Aquila, Orion, and Canis Major and Canis Minor. The rotation of the earth causes these and the other stars to appear to travel a circuit around it.

29. HINDHEAD . . . MAIDENHEAD—A hill and a city, both near London.

FOR APPRECIATION

1. The beginning of the poem introduces the idea of "perpetual recurrence" of seasons and of birth and death. Then it is suggested that history, too, is only an endless cycle that is leading to no greater wisdom and no nearer to God. What does the poet mean by saying that

we have "Knowledge of words, and ignorance of the Word"? Judging from this line, what does he mean by contrasting "stillness" and "silence" in the two preceding lines?

2. What do you think is the difference between "Life" and "living" in line 14? Reread lines 15-16, and explain the difference between wisdom and knowledge; also between knowledge and information.

3. All through the second part of the poem there runs the idea that there are not very many churches in England, and also the deeper idea that there is not enough interest in religion. By its expression of both these ideas simultaneously, the poem is satirical and witty. For instance, when the city people say they have too many churches and too few chophouses, the deeper meaning is that they think prosperity—making a living—is more important than religion. Explain the deeper meaning of their belief expressed in lines 23-24.

4. What passage suggests that religion is becoming a mere social custom?

5. In every community there can be found earnestly religious people, and also those who are indifferent to religion. In your opinion, can Eliot's comments be applied to American life in general?

Journey of the Magi

T. S. ELIOT

Long after the event, one of the Magi ponders the significance of their journey to Bethlehem. The Magi went to witness a Birth, but their rebirth in Christ spelled death to their old way of life. Upon returning to their homeland, the Magi feel as aliens among a people who know not Christ, and they would gladly die.

Eliot takes his introductory lines from a sermon of Lancelot Andrewes, a seventeenth-century Anglican sermon-writer.

The description of the difficulties of the journey outwardly symbolizes the internal conflict of the Magi and suggests events to come in the life of Christ. As you read, notice the contrast between the plain, matter-of-fact account of the journey, which ends with the understatement: "it was (you may say) satisfactory"; and the spiritually transforming effect of that journey.

'A cold coming we had of it,
Just the worst time of the year
For a journey, and such a long journey:
The ways deep and the weather sharp,
The very dead of winter.'
And the camels galled, sore-footed, refractory,
Lying down in the melting snow,
There were times we regretted
The summer palaces on slopes, the terraces,
And the silken girls bringing sherbet.
Then the camel men cursing and grumbling
And running away, and wanting their liquor and women,
And the night-fires going out, and the lack of shelters,
And the cities hostile and the towns unfriendly
And the villages dirty and charging high prices:
A hard time we had of it.
At the end we preferred to travel all night,
Sleeping in snatches,
With the voices singing in our ears, saying
That this was all folly.

Then at dawn we came down to a temperate valley,
Wet, below the snow line, smelling of vegetation;
With a running stream and a water-mill beating the darkness,
And three trees on the low sky,
And an old white horse galloped away in the meadow.
Then we came to a tavern with vine-leaves over the lintel,
Six hands at an open door dicing for pieces of silver,
And feet kicking the empty wine-skins.
But there was no information, and so we continued
And arrived at evening, not a moment too soon
Finding the place; it was (you may say) satisfactory.

All this was a long time ago, I remember,
And I would do it again, but set down
This set down
This: were we led all that way for
Birth or Death? There was a Birth, certainly,
We had evidence and no doubt. I had seen birth and death,
But had thought they were different; this Birth was
Hard and bitter agony for us, like Death, our death.
We returned to our places, these Kingdoms,
But no longer at ease here, in the old dispensation,
With an alien people clutching their gods.
I should be glad of another death.

6. GALLED—Irritated.
6. REFRACTORY—Obstinate.

FOR APPRECIATION

1. Point out the contrast in mood between lines 1-8 and lines 9-10. Show how these lines suggest the sacrifice of the Magi.

2. Enumerate the particular hardships they encountered in lines 11-20. Line 21 indicates that they have traveled a long way and have at last come into a warm climate. What precise details are chosen to develop this thought?

3. Explain the prophetic symbolism of lines 24 and 27. Explain the Biblical reference in line 29.

4. In what sense was the visit of the Magi a "Birth"? In what sense was it a "Death"? Discuss the deep spiritual meaning of these lines.

To Dives

HILAIRE BELLOC

D. B. Wyndham Lewis, a modern Catholic satirist and biographer, once wrote that "if the pill is sufficiently gilded with humor and nonsense, the public will swallow anything—even the truth!" In prose and in satirical verse, such Catholic satirists as Chesterton, Belloc, J. B. Morton, Douglas Woodruff, Ronald Knox, and Anglo-Catholic C. S. Lewis have been giving the "Catholic attitude," the truth about contemporary society, and the English public have swallowed the pill with delight.

In Belloc's "To Dives" we have an example of Catholic humor with a sting, a controlled but biting contempt for the modern, self-made millionaire who has chosen Wealth as a way of life.

Dives, when you and I go down to Hell,
Where scribblers end and millionaires as well,
We shall be carrying on our separate backs
Two very large but very different packs;
And as you stagger under yours, my friend,
Down the dull shore where all our journeys end,
And go before me (as your rank demands)
Towards the infinite flat underlands,
And that dear river of forgetfulness—
Charon, a man of exquisite address
(For, as your wife's progenitors could tell,
They're very strict on etiquette in Hell),
Will, since you are a lord, observe, "My lord,
We cannot take these weighty things aboard!"
Then down they go, my wretched Dives, down—
The fifteen sorts of boots you kept for town;
The hat to meet the Devil in; the plain
But costly ties; the cases of champagne;
The solid watch, and seal, and chain, and charm;
The working model of a Burning Form
(To give the little Belials), all the three
Biscuits for Cerberus; the guarantee
From Lambeth that the Rich can never burn,

1. DIVES—Pronounced dī'vēz.

1. HELL—The hell of Greek mythology known as Hades was a dreary place where the ghosts of the dead led a vague, unsubstantial life. A few fortunate ones escaped to Elysium, while those who had offended the gods were removed to Tartarus for punishment. Hades was separated from the land of the living by the river Styx, and it was Charon's job to ferry the dead across the river. The three-headed watch-dog, Cerberus, stood guard at the entrance to Hades to prevent any of the dead from going out again. The Cocytus was another river of the infernal region.

22. GUARANTEE FROM LAMBETH—Lambeth is the official London residence of the Anglican archbishop of Canterbury. Here Belloc is satirizing the official teaching of the archbishop that, perhaps, there is no Hell and certainly it is not eternal.

And even promising a safe return;
The admirable overcoat, designed
To cross Cocytus—very warmly lined:
Sweet Dives, you will leave them all behind
And enter Hell as tattered and as bare
As was your father when he took the air
Behind a barrow-load in Leicester
Square.
Then turned to me, and noting one that
brings
With careless step a mist of shadowy
things:
Laughter and memories, and a few regrets,
Some honour, and a quantity of debts,
A doubt or two of sorts, a trust in God,
And (what will seem to you extremely odd)
His father's granfer's father's father's name,
Unspoilt, untitled, even spelt the same;
Charon, who twenty thousand times before
Has ferried Poets to the ulterior shore,
Will estimate the weight I bear, and
cry—
"Comrade" (He has himself been known to
try
His hand at Latin and Italian verse,
Much in the style of Virgil—only worse)
"We let such vain imaginaries pass!"
Then tell me, Dives, which will look the
ass—
You, or myself? Or Charon? Who can tell?
They order things so damnably in Hell.

26. COCYTUS (kô·sī´tŭs)—In Greek mythology, one of the rivers of Hades.

FOR APPRECIATION

1. Explain in detail the two different packs which the scribbler and the millionaire will carry. Which would you rather be: a millionaire or a scribbler?

2. What indications are there in the poem that Belloc is satirizing the "new rich" and the "newly titled"? Explain lines 36-38.

3. Does Belloc soften the satire in the last three lines? Discuss.

4. How does this famous line of Chesterton's express the same attitude: "I do not mind the swindle, but deprecate the swank"?

C.S. Lewis

To the Sun

ROY CAMPBELL

Since the early ages of the Church, poets have been using symbols drawn from nature to represent Christ. At various times, Our Lord has been represented as a Lamb, a Fish, a Pelican. To Joseph Mary Plunkett, the Irish poet, the whole of nature was a symbol of Our Lord. In the following poem, Roy Campbell has exquisitely drawn subtle relationships between the colors of the sun and Christ.

Oh let your shining orb grow dim,
Of Christ the mirror and the shield,
That I may gaze through you to Him,
See half the miracle revealed,
And in your seven hues behold
The Blue Man walking on the Sea,
The Green, beneath the summer tree,
Who called the children; then the Gold,
With palms; the Orange, flaring bold
With scourges: Purple in the garden
(As Greco saw): and then the Red
Torero (Him who took the toss
And rode the black horns of the cross—
But rose snow-silver from the dead!

"To the Sun" from *Collected Poems* by Roy Campbell, reprinted by permission of John Lane, The Bodley Head, Limited, London, and Henry Regnery Company.

11. GRECO—Theotocopuli, a Spanish painter of the sixteenth century. The reference is to a painting, "Christ in the Garden," done in heavy red and purple. "As Greco saw" means "as the artist conceived it."
12. TORERO—A Spanish bullfighter on foot.

FOR APPRECIATION

1. Examine carefully the implied metaphor of the white light of the sun broken into its prismatic rays. Is there any relationship between such a figure and the liturgical year which "breaks down" Christ, the Way, the Truth, and the Life, into the various mysteries of His life?

2. Is it natural to make such comparisons between those we love and external objects? Give some examples from modern song writers.

3. Compare Campbell's use of color with that of W. W. Gibson in "Sight."

4. Explain the implied figure in lines 12-14.

5. For other religiously beautiful comparisons, read the opening stanzas of Thompson's "Ode to the Setting Sun."

ESSAYS

If broadly defined as "any short piece of nonfiction," the essay is the most prominent form of modern prose writing. This is because the definition includes the articles that fill our magazines. Modern articles, of course, do not pretend to the literary merits of essays by Bacon or Addison. They differ also in subject matter, being more full of specific information. They consist of recently gathered facts about places, people, and events. A sound, well-written article can supersede all earlier articles on its topic—but may be out of date within weeks or months.

Side by side with factual articles, present day magazines continue to carry the type of essay that makes judgments, expresses personal tastes or opinions, or recollects and describes personal experiences. Editorials, book reviews, and historical and cultural studies are examples of this form. Oftentimes these articles are given permanence when their authors publish them in book form.

Virginia Woolf's *The Common Reader* contains some of the finest essays in literary criticism that appeared in the twentieth century. E. V. Lucas was a follower of Lamb's personal, whimsical style of writing. Among many other non-Catholic British writers who have produced brilliant essays are George Orwell, Rebecca West, E. M. Forster, and Dylan Thomas. On any list of Catholic twentieth-century essayists and prose writers must be included: G. K. Chesterton, Hilaire Belloc, Monsignor Ronald Knox, Arnold Lunn, Eric Gill, Caryll Houselander, Douglas Woodruff, Frank Sheed, Martin D'Arcy, S.J., and the two Dominicans, Bede Jarrett and Vincent McNabb.

A very frequent type of the modern essay is the humorous sketch. A. P. Herbert, J. B. Priestley, and Stephen Leacock are three of the best known humorous essayists. Short humorous pieces find a constant market in newspapers and in magazines like the famous English weekly, *Punch.*

Christopher Dawson is England's greatest Catholic historian of culture. Barbara Ward, in her *Faith and Freedom,* has given a penetrating analysis of the great ideas and movements which have made Western culture. Winston Churchill, who was as skillful a master of English prose as he was a statesman, has written an outstanding example of the *eye-witness* historical account in his *The Second World War.*

THE PATH TO ROME

HILAIRE BELLOC

Hilaire Belloc's literary reputation can rest secure upon his travel essays, The Cruise of the Nona, The Four Men, Hills and the Sea, *and* The Path to Rome. *In all of these, we have some of the loveliest lyrical prose in all English letters. In these works, Belloc views the universe as a thoroughly Catholic universe. He sees physical nature as something good to be reverenced, but not to be worshiped for its own sake. He loved the sea and the hills and the mountains because he saw in them the seal of God's power, and he beheld in them a great sacrament symbolizing the beauty and majesty of the Creator.*

Belloc's The Path to Rome *is the best of all travel books. It breathes the refreshing spirit of a Catholic at home in Christendom. Belloc tramps through the Alps down into the Italian plains, and his heart expands under the graciousness of Catholic skies. The book abounds in his adventure and in good humor. He exults in existence and manifests a zest for living, as he lyrically expresses his love of the mountains, good companionship, wine, and all the other great gifts of God.*

Two passages from The Path to Rome *have been selected for our study: The first is a description of the Alps as seen from the Jura mountains; the second is a description of dawn as he sees the plains of Tuscany from a mountain ridge.*

DESCRIPTION OF ALPS

The wood went up darkly and the path branched here and there so that I was soon uncertain of my way, but I followed generally what seemed to me the most southerly course, and so came at last up steeply through a dip or ravine that ended high on the crest of the ridge.

Just as I came to the end of the rise, after perhaps an hour, perhaps two, of that great curtain of forest which had held the mountain side, the trees fell away to brushwood, there was a gate, and then the path was lost upon a fine open sward which was the very top of the Jura and the coping of that multiple wall which defends the

Selections from *The Path to Rome* by Hilaire Belloc, reprinted by permission of Henry Regnery Company.

Swiss Plain. I had crossed it straight from edge to edge, never turning out of my way.

It was too marshy to lie down on it, so I stood a moment to breathe and look about me.

It was evident that nothing higher remained, for though a new line of wood —firs and beeches—stood before me, yet nothing appeared above them, and I knew that they must be the fringe of the descent. I approached this edge of wood, and saw that it had a rough fence of post and rails bounding it, and as I was looking for the entry of a path (for my original path was lost, as such tracks are, in the damp grass of the little down) there came to me one of those great revelations which betray to us suddenly the higher things and stand afterwards firm in our minds.

There, on this upper meadow, where so far I had felt nothing but the ordinary gladness of The Summit, I had a vision.

What was it I saw? If you think I saw this or that, and if you think I am inventing the words, you know nothing of men.

I saw between the branches of the trees in front of me a sight in the sky that made me stop breathing, just as great danger at sea, or great surprise in love, or a great deliverance will make a man stop breathing. I saw something I had known in the West as a boy, something I had never seen so grandly discovered as was this. In between the branches of the trees was a great promise of unexpected lights beyond.

I pushed left and right along that edge of the forest and along the fence that bound it, until I found a place where the pine-trees stopped, leaving a gap, and where on the right, beyond the gap, was a tree whose leaves had failed; there the ground broke away steeply below me, and the beeches fell, one below the other, like a vast cascade, towards the limestone cliffs that dipped down still further, beyond my sight. I looked through this framing hollow and praised God. For there below me, thousands of feet below me, was what seemed an illimitable plain; at the end of that world was an horizon, and the dim bluish sky that overhangs an horizon.

There was brume[1] in it and thickness. One saw the sky beyond the edge of the world getting purer as the vault rose. But right up—a belt in that empyrean—ran peak and field and needle of intense ice, remote, remote from the world. Sky beneath them and sky above them, a steadfast legion, they glittered as though with the armour of the immovable armies of Heaven. Two days' march, three days' march away, they stood up like the walls of Eden. I say it again, they stopped my breath. I had seen them.

So little are we, we men: so much are we immersed in our muddy and immediate interests that we think, by numbers and recitals, to comprehend distance or time, or any of our limiting infinities. Here were these magnificent creatures of God, I mean the Alps, which now for the first time I saw from the height of the Jura; and because they were fifty or sixty miles away, and because they were a mile or two high, they were become something different from us others, and could strike one motionless with the awe of supernatural things. Up there in the sky, to which only clouds belong and birds and the last trembling colours of pure light, they stood fast and hard; not moving as do the things of the sky. They were as distant as the little upper clouds of summer, as fine and tenuous; but in their reflection and in their quality as it were of weapons (like spears and

[1]BRUME—Mist or fog.

shields of an unknown array) they occupied the sky with a sublime invasion: and the things proper to the sky were forgotten by me in their presence as I gazed.

To what emotion shall I compare this astonishment? So, in first love one finds that *this* can belong to *me*.

Their sharp steadfastness and their clean uplifted lines compelled my adoration. Up there, the sky above and below them, part of the sky, but part of us, the great peaks made communion between that homing creeping part of me which loves vineyards and dances and a slow movement among pastures, and that other part which is only properly at home in Heaven. I say that this kind of description is useless, and that it is better to address prayers to such things than to attempt to interpret them for others.

These, the great Alps, seen thus, link one in some way to one's immortality. Nor is it possible to convey, or even to suggest, those few fifty miles, and those few thousand feet; there is something more. Let me put it thus: that from the height of Weissenstein[2] I saw, as it were, my religion. I mean, humility, the fear of death, the terror of height and of distance, the glory of God, the infinite potentiality of reception whence springs that divine thirst of the soul; my aspiration also towards completion, and my confidence in the dual destiny. For I know that we laughers have a gross cousinship with the most high, and it is this contrast and perpetual quarrel which feeds a spring of merriment in the soul of a sane man.

[2] WEISSENSTEIN—A ridge of the Jura mountains.

Since I could now see such a wonder and it could work such things in my mind, therefore, some day I should be part of it. That is what I felt.

DESCRIPTION OF SUNRISE

I have waited for the dawn a hundred times, attended by that mournful, colourless spirit which haunts the last hours of darkness; and influenced especially by the great timeless apathy that hangs round the first uncertain promise of increasing light. For there is an hour before daylight when men die, and when there is nothing above the soul or around it, when even the stars fail. And this long and dreadful expectation I had thought to be worst when one was alone at sea in a small boat without wind; drifting beyond one's harbour in the ebb of the outer channel tide, and sogging back at the first flow on the broad, confused movement of a sea without any waves. In such lonely mornings I have watched the Owers light turning, and I have counted up my gulf of time, and wondered that moments could be so stretched out in the clueless mind. I have prayed for the morning or for a little draught of wind, and this I have thought, I say, the extreme of absorption into emptiness and longing.

But now, on this ridge, dragging myself on to the main road, I found a deeper abyss of isolation and despairing fatigue than I had ever known, and I came near to turning eastward and imploring the hastening of light, as men pray continually without reason for things that can but come in a due order. I still went forward a little, because when I sat down my loneliness oppressed me like a misfortune; and because my feet, going painfully and slowly, yet gave a little balance and rhythm to the movement of my mind.

I heard no sound of animals or birds. I passed several fields, deserted in the half-darkness; and in some I felt the hay, but always found it wringing wet with dew, nor could I discover a good shelter from the wind that blew off the upper snow of the summits. For a little space of time there fell upon me, as I crept along the road, that shadow of sleep which numbs the mind, but it could not compel me to lie down, and I accepted it only as a partial and beneficent oblivion which covered my desolation and suffering as a thin, transparent cloud may cover an evil moon.

Then suddenly the sky grew lighter upon every side. That cheating gloom (which I think the clouds in purgatory must reflect) lifted from the valley as though to a slow order given by some calm and good influence that was marshalling in the day. Their colours came back to things; the trees recovered their shape, life, and trembling; here and there, on the face of the mountain opposite, the mists by their movement took part in the new life, and I thought I heard for the first time the tumbling water far below me in the ravine. That subtle barrier was drawn which marks to-day from yesterday; all the night and its despondency became the past and entered memory. The road before me, the pass on my left (my last ridge, and the entry into Tuscany), the mass of the great hills, had become mixed into the increasing light, that is, into the familiar and invigorating Present which I have always found capable of opening the doors of the future with a gesture of victory.

My pain either left me, or I ceased to notice it, and seeing a little way before me a bank above the road, and a fine grove of sparse and dominant chestnuts, I climbed up thither and turned, standing to the east.

There, without any warning of colours, or of the heraldry that we have in the north, the sky was a great field of pure light, and without doubt it was all woven through, as was my mind watching it, with security and gladness. Into this field, as I watched it, rose the sun.

The air became warmer almost sud denly. The splendour and health of the new day left me all in repose, and persuaded or compelled me to immediate sleep.

I found therefore in the short grass, and on the scented earth beneath one of my trees, a place for lying down; I stretched myself out upon it, and lapsed into a profound slumber, which nothing but a vague and tenuous delight separated from complete forgetfulness. If the last confusion of thought, before sleep possessed me, was a kind of prayer—and certainly I was in the mood of gratitude and of adoration—this prayer was of course to God, from whom every good proceeds, but partly (idolatrously) to the Sun, which, of all the things He has made, seems, of what we at least can discover, the most complete and glorious.

FOR APPRECIATION

DESCRIPTION OF ALPS

1. Describe in detail the *point of view* from which Belloc describes the Alps.

2. Explain in your own words Belloc's first reaction to this "vision."

3. What physical details of the Alps did Belloc select to describe the immensity and beauty of the scene? What was Belloc's emotional reaction to the scene? What was his personal religious reaction? Explain in detail.

4. Study the imagery contained in these expressions: *they occupied the sky with a sublime invasion.* Is this expression consistent with the other figures, *steadfast legion, armour of the immovable armies, spears and shields,* previously used in this description? Explain.

DESCRIPTION OF SUNRISE

1. The *mood* expressed in paragraphs 1, 2, and 3 is entirely different from that of paragraphs 4, 5, and 6. What are these predominant moods? Select those details which Belloc uses to describe these moods.

2. Would you say that Belloc gives us description through the use of many individual *concrete, physical* details of the sunrise, or does he try to convey a particular *impression* suggesting an intangible and indescribable atmosphere? Discuss.

3. Would you say that word-painting is much more difficult than painting with oils or water color? Explain. What are the tools which a literary artist must employ in word-painting? Would you say that no one who had not seen what Belloc saw could describe the scene which he paints? Explain. Does he effectively capture the fugitive effects of fleeting loveliness in the scene? Explain your answer by selecting phrases and sentences from the descriptive passages.

WORD STUDY

Explain the meaning of the expression *beneficent oblivion.* Give three synonyms for *tenuous.* Give the origin of *sward.* Discuss the connotation of *cheating gloom.*

RELATED READING

Everything that Belloc stands for is contained in his essay "A Remaining Christmas," which may be found in his *Conversation with a Cat.*

The mature student who would understand Belloc, the man and his work, should read Frederick Wilhelmsen's brief but brilliant analysis in his *Hilaire Belloc.*

REMINISCENCES OF CHILDHOOD

DYLAN THOMAS

Dylan Thomas tells us in his "Reminiscences of Childhood" that "the memories of childhood have no order and no end." As you read the essay, you will see how convincingly he has written of many things shared by all in that world of childhood where trifles are tremendous and tragedies are frequent but fleeting, where the physical confines of home and neighborhood take on, at times, the aspect of a magic world of high adventure and, at other times, become the twilight borderland between the unexplainable adult world and the world of childhood reality with its swift succession of apparently unrelated moments and events.

I like very much people telling me about their childhood, but they'll have to be quick or else I'll be telling them about mine.

I was born in a large Welsh town at the beginning of the Great War[1]—an ugly, lovely town (or so it was and is to me), crawling, sprawling by a long and splendid curving shore where truant boys and sandfield boys and old men from nowhere, beachcombed, idled and paddled, watched the dock-bound ships or the ships steaming away into wonder and India, magic and China, countries bright with oranges and loud with lions; threw stones into the sea for the barking outcast dogs; made castles and forts and harbours and race tracks in the sand; and on Saturday summer afternoons listened to the brass band, watched the Punch and Judy, or hung about on the fringes of the crowd to hear the fierce religious speakers who shouted at the sea, as though it were wicked and wrong to roll in and out like that, white-horsed and full of fishes.

One man, I remember, used to take off his hat and set fire to his hair every now and then, but I do not remember what it proved, if it proved anything at all, except that he was a very interesting man.

This sea-town was my world; outside a strange Wales, coal-pitted, mountained, river-run, full, so far as I knew, of choirs and football teams and sheep and storybook tall hats and red flannel petticoats, moved about its business which was none of mine.

Beyond that unknown Wales with its wild names like peals of bells in the darkness, and its mountain men clothed in the skins of animals perhaps and always singing, lay England which was London and the

[1]GREAT WAR—The author is here referring to World War I.

country called the Front, from which many of our neighbours never came back. It was a country to which only young men travelled.

At the beginning, the only "front" I knew was the little lobby before our front door. I could not understand how so many people never returned from there, but later I grew to know more, though still without understanding, and carried a wooden rifle in the park and shot down the invisible unknown enemy like a flock of wild birds. And the park itself was a world within the world of the sea-town. Quite near where I lived, so near that on summer evenings I could listen in my bed to the voices of older children playing ball on the sloping paper-littered bank, the park was full of terrors and treasures. Though it was only a little park, it held within its borders of old tall trees, notched with our names and shabby from our climbing, as many secret places, caverns and forests, prairies and deserts, as a country somewhere at the end of the sea.

And though we would explore it one day, armed and desperate, from end to end, from the robbers' den to the pirates' cabin, the highwayman's inn to the cattle ranch, or the hidden room in the undergrowth, where we held beetle races, and lit the wood fires and roasted potatoes and talked about Africa, and the makes of motor cars, yet still the next day, it remained as unexplored as the Poles—a country just born and always changing.

There were many secret societies but you could belong only to one; and in blood or red ink, and a rusty pocketknife, with, of course, an instrument to remove stones from horses' feet, you signed your name at the foot of a terrible document, swore death to all the other societies, crossed your heart that you would divulge no secret and that if you did, you would consent to torture by slow fire, and undertook to carry out by yourself a feat of either daring or endurance. You could take your choice: would you climb to the top of the tallest and most dangerous tree, and from there hurl stones and insults at grown-up passers-by, especially postmen, or any other men in uniform? Or would you ring every doorbell in the terrace, not forgetting the doorbell of the man with the red face who kept dogs and ran fast? Or would you swim in the reservoir, which was forbidden and had angry swans, or would you eat a whole old jam jar full of mud?

There were many more alternatives. I chose one of endurance and for half an hour, it may have been longer or shorter, held up off the ground a very heavy broken pram we had found in a bush. I thought my back would break and the half hour felt like a day, but I preferred it to braving the red face and the dogs, or to swallowing tadpoles.

We knew every inhabitant of the park, every regular visitor, every nursemaid, every gardener, every old man. We knew the hour when the alarming retired policeman came in to look at the dahlias and the hour when the old lady arrived in the Bath chair with six Pekinese, and a pale girl to read aloud to her. I think she read the newspaper, but we always said she read the *Wizard*. The face of the old man who sat summer and winter on the bench looking over the reservoir, I can see clearly now and I wrote a poem long long after I'd left the park and the sea-town called: "The Hunchback in the Park."

And that park grew up with me; that small world widened as I learned its secrets and boundaries, as I discovered new refuges and ambushes in its woods and jungles;

hidden homes and lairs for the multitudes of imagination, for cowboys and Indians, and the tall terrible half-people who rode on nightmares through my bedroom. But it was not the only world—that world of rockery, gravel path, playbank, bowling green, bandstands, reservoir, dahlia garden, where an ancient keeper, known as Smoky, was the whiskered snake in the grass one must keep off. There was another world where with my friends I used to dawdle on half holidays along the bent and Devon-facing seashore, hoping for gold watches or the skull of a sheep or a message in a bottle to be washed up with the tide; and another where we used to wander whistling through the packed streets, stale as station sandwiches, round the impressive gasworks and the slaughter house, past by the blackened monument and the museum that should have been in a museum. Or we scratched at a kind of cricket on the bald and cindery surface of the recreation ground, or we took a tram that shook like an iron jelly down to the gaunt pier, there to clamber under the pier, hanging perilously on to its skeleton legs or to run along to the end where patient men with the seaward eyes of the dockside unemployed capped and mufflered, dangling from their mouths pipes that had long gone out, angled over the edge for unpleasant tasting fish.

Never was there such a town as ours, I thought, as we fought on the sandhills with rough boys or dared each other to climb up the scaffolding of half-built houses soon to be called Laburnum Beaches. Never was there such a town, I thought, for the smell of fish and chips on Saturday evenings; for the Saturday afternoon cinema matinees where we shouted and hissed our threepences away; for the crowds in the streets with leeks in their hats on international nights; for the park, the inexhaustible and mysterious, bushy red-Indian hiding park where the hunchback sat alone and the groves were blue with sailors. The memories of childhood have no order, and so I remember that never was there such a dame school as ours, so firm and kind and smelling of galoshes, with the sweet and fumbled music of the piano lessons drifting down from up-stairs to the lonely schoolroom, where only the sometimes tearful wicked sat over undone sums, or to repeat a little crime—the pulling of a girl's hair during geography, the sly shin kick under the table during English literature. Behind the school was a narrow lane where only the oldest and boldest threw pebbles at windows, scuffled and boasted, fibbed about their relations—

"My father's got a chauffeur."

"What's he want a chauffeur for? He hasn't got a car."

"My father's the richest man in the town."

"My father's the richest man in Wales."

"My father owns the world."

And swapped gob-stoppers for slings, old knives for marbles, kite strings for foreign stamps.

The lane was always the place to tell your secrets; if you did not have any, you invented them. Occasionally now I dream that I am turning out of school into the lane of confidences when I say to the boys of my class, "At last, I have a real secret."

"What is it—what is it?"

"I can fly."

And when they do not believe me, I flap my arms and slowly leave the ground only a few inches at first, then gaining air until I fly waving my cap level with the upper windows of the school, peering in until the mistress at the piano screams and the metronome falls to the ground and stops, and there is no more time.

And I fly over the trees and chimneys of my town, over the dockyards skimming the masts and funnels, over Inkerman Street, Sebastopol Street, and the street where all the women wear men's caps, over the trees of the everlasting park, where a brass band shakes the leaves and sends them showering down on to the nurses and the children, the cripples and the idlers, and the gardeners, and the shouting boys: over the yellow seashore, and the stone-chasing dogs, and the old men, and the singing sea.

The memories of childhood have no order, and no end.

FOR DISCUSSION

1. Thomas writes that the town of his birth was "an *ugly, lovely* town." Does he stress the "ugly" or the "lovely" aspect of the town? Explain.

2. Precisely what did the outside world of Wales mean to the author? What was his childhood "front"? Enumerate the "terrors and the treasures" of the park. Describe some of the daily visitors to the park.

3. What were some of the ordeals a young boy had to undergo to be initiated into the secret societies? What particular ordeal did the author choose?

4. What particular experiences does the author describe which have something in common with the experiences of every young boy?

5. In what particular way does the author connect the events of his childhood with the dreams of manhood? Is it true that childhood memories often form the substance of later dreams? Discuss.

FOR APPRECIATION

1. Select and study those passages from the essay which effectively show that a child views the world as touched with magic.

2. Read aloud two or three paragraphs. Try to capture the rhythm and the singing quality of his prose.

3. By his use of imagery, Thomas *suggests* reality; he does not describe it *literally.* Study the following expressions for their power of suggestion and state to what particular sense they appeal: the sea is *white-horsed and full of fishes; storybook tall hats and red flannel petticoats; Wales with its wild names like peals of bells in the darkness; I think she read the newspaper, but we always said she read the* Wizard; *tall terrible half-people who rode on nightmares through my bedroom; I used to dawdle on half holidays along the bent and Devon-facing shore; tram that shook like iron jelly; gaunt pier* (with its) *skeleton legs; the groves were blue with sailors; the sweet and fumbled music of the piano lesson.*

THE ROMANCE OF ORTHODOXY

GILBERT K. CHESTERTON

Chesterton's ORTHODOXY *is a mature book, but it is also an important book. The selection given below must "be chewed and digested"; but it will well repay study, for it is one of the finest passages Chesterton has written and one of the best in modern prose. Chesterton has a way of compressing a whole movement, an entire century, in one sentence. Here we have the fine gold of Chesterton's thought and style, a brief but brilliant synthesis of the balance and romance of Orthodoxy as the sane and permanent ideal in a fickle and changing universe.*

The thesis of Chesterton's ORTHODOXY, *written ten years before his conversion to Catholicism, is that "the central Christian theology (sufficiently expressed in the Apostles' Creed) is the best root and energy of sound ethics." Christianity represents a new balance that constitutes a liberation. The idea of the pagan balance, as expressed by the best Greeks and Romans, was to enforce moderation by getting rid of extremes. Christianity combined in a perfect balance furious opposites. "The more I considered Christianity," writes G. K., "the more I felt that while it had established a law and order, the chief aim of that order was to give room for good things to run wild."*

This was the big fact about Christian ethics; the discovery of the new balance. Paganism had been like a pillar of marble, upright because proportioned with symmetry. Christianity was like a huge and ragged and romantic rock, which, though it sways on its pedestal at a touch, yet, because its exaggerated excrescences exactly balance each other, is enthroned there for a thousand years. In a Gothic cathedral the columns were all different, but they were all necessary. Every support seemed an accidental and fantastic support; every buttress was a flying buttress. So in Christendom apparent accidents balanced. Becket[1] wore a hair shirt under his gold and crimson, and there is much to be said for the combination; for Becket got the benefit of the hair shirt while the people in the street got the benefit of the crimson and gold. It is at least better than the manner of the modern millionaire, who has the black and the drab outwardly for others, and the gold next his heart. But the balance was not always in one man's body as in Becket's; the balance was often distributed over the whole body of Christendom. Because a man prayed and fasted on the Northern snows, flowers could be flung at his festival in the Southern cities; and because fanatics drank water on the sands of Syria, men could still drink cider in the orchards of England. This is what makes Christendom at once so much more perplexing and so much more interesting than the Pagan empire; just as Amiens Cathedral is not better but more interesting than the Parthenon.[2] If anyone wants a modern proof of all this, let him consider the curious fact that, under Christianity, Europe (while remaining a unity) has broken up into individual nations. Patriotism is a perfect example of this deliberate balancing of one emphasis against another emphasis. The instinct of the Pagan empire would have said, "You shall all be Roman citizens, and grow alike; let the German grow less slow and reverent; the Frenchman less experimental and swift." But the instinct of Christian Europe says, "Let the German remain slow and reverent, that the Frenchman may the more safely be swift and experimental. We will make an equipoise out of these excesses. The absurdity called Germany shall correct the insanity called France."

Last and most important, it is exactly this which explains what is so inexplicable to all the modern critics of the history of Christianity. I mean the monstrous wars about small points of theology, the earthquakes of emotion about a gesture or a word. It was only a matter of an inch; but an inch is everything when you are balancing. The Church could not afford to swerve a

[1]BECKET—St. Thomas à Becket was both the Chancellor of the realm and later archbishop of Canterbury under Henry II. He was murdered in his cathedral by four retainers of the king because he consistently opposed Henry's encroachments upon the rights of the Church. See *The Canterbury Tales* of Chaucer and T. S. Eliot's *Murder in the Cathedral.*

[2]PARTHENON—The Doric temple of Athena, perfect product of Greek architecture.

hair's breadth on some things if she was to continue her great and daring experiment of the irregular equilibrium. Once let one idea become less powerful and some other idea would become too powerful. It was no flock of sheep the Christian shepherd was leading, but a herd of bulls and tigers, of terrible ideals and devouring doctrines, each one of them strong enough to turn to a false religion and lay waste the world. Remember that the Church went in specifically for dangerous ideas; she was a lion tamer. The idea of birth through a Holy Spirit, of the death of a divine being, of the forgiveness of sins, or the fulfillment of prophecies, are ideas which, anyone can see, need but a touch to turn them into something blasphemous or ferocious. The smallest link was let drop by the artificers of the Mediterranean, and the lion of ancestral pessimism burst his chain in the forgotten forests of the north.[3] Of these theological equalisations I have to speak afterwards. Here it is enough to notice that if some small mistake were made in doctrine, huge blunders might be made in human happiness. A sentence phrased wrong about the nature of symbolism would have broken all the best statues in Europe.[4] A slip in the definitions might stop all the dances; might wither all the Christmas trees or break all the Easter eggs. Doctrines had to be defined within strict limits, even in order that man might enjoy general human liberties. The Church had to be careful, if only that the world might be careless.

This is the thrilling romance of Orthodoxy. People have fallen into a foolish habit of speaking of orthodoxy as something heavy, humdrum, and safe. There never was anything so perilous or so exciting as orthodoxy. It was sanity: and to be sane is more dramatic than to be mad. It was the equilibrium of a man behind madly rushing horses, seeming to stoop this way and to sway that, yet in every attitude having the grace of statuary and the accuracy of arithmetic. The Church in its early days went fierce and fast with any warhorse; yet it is utterly unhistoric to say that she merely went mad along one idea, like a vulgar fanaticism. She swerved to left and right, so exactly as to avoid enormous obstacles. She left on one hand the huge bulk of Arianism,[5] buttressed by all the worldly powers to make Christianity too worldly. The next instant she was swerving to avoid an orientalism,[6] which would have made it too unworldly. The orthodox Church never took the tame course or accepted the conventions; the orthodox Church was never respectable. It would have been easier to have accepted the earthly power of the Arians. It would have been easy, in the Calvinistic seventeenth century, to fall into the bottomless pit of predestination. It is easy to be a madman; it is easy to be a heretic. It is always easy to

[3]THE SMALLEST LINK ... FORGOTTEN FORESTS OF THE NORTH—Chesterton is referring here to the doctrines of Calvin and Knox. The southern peoples of Europe are by nature light-hearted; the Nordics rather somber and gloomy.

[4]BROKEN ALL THE BEST STATUES IN EUROPE—A reference to the Iconoclast heresy of the eighth and ninth centuries which rejected the use and veneration of images.

[5]ARIANISM—The first great heresy in the Church. It denied the divinity of Christ and was condemned at the Council of Nicea in 325. It had the support of most of the rulers in Christendom.

[6]ORIENTALISM—No doubt Chesterton has reference here to the Monophysite heresy which taught there was one nature in Christ, the divine nature. The Orientals, in general, tend toward the mystical, the hidden, the other-worldly, and the occult. The Western mind is more practical.

let the age have its head; the difficult thing is to keep one's own. It is always easy to be a modernist; as it is easy to be a snob. To have fallen into any of those open traps of error and exaggeration which fashion after fashion and sect after sect set along the historic path of Christendom—that would indeed have been simple. It is always simple to fall; there are an infinity of angles at which one falls; only one at which one stands. To have fallen into any one of the fads from Gnosticism to Christian Science[7] would indeed have been obvious and tame. But to have avoided them all has been one whirling adventure; and in my vision the heavenly chariot flies thundering through the ages, the dull heresies sprawling and prostrate, the wild truth reeling but erect.

[7]GNOSTICISM TO CHRISTIAN SCIENCE—The Gnostics were the first heretics to deny the divinity of Christ. St. John's Gospel was written to prove them wrong. Christian Science denies the existence of cause and effect outside the mind. Hence Christian Scientists argue that all organic sickness is imaginary.

FOR DISCUSSION

1. In his *G. K. Chesterton,* Maurice Evans analyzes Chesterton's style and discovers that he is: *(a)* a writer of brilliant epigrams; *(b)* a master of the paradox; *(c)* an artist in the use of vivid imagery and alliteration; *(d)* a writer with a deep love for solid and concrete things; *(e)* an author capable of packing into a single sentence an historical movement, a life of a man, or an entire book. Keeping the above elements in mind, choose sentences from the passage which clearly illustrate each of these qualities.

2. Chesterton has defined a paradox as "a truth standing on its head to attract attention." Discuss this definition and apply some of Chesterton's paradoxes to it.

3. G. K. gives us example after example to prove his point that Christianity is the discovery of a new balance. Enumerate some of these examples.

4. What are the differences between classical and Gothic architecture? Do you think the Gothic better expresses the Catholic ideal? Explain. What is a flying buttress?

5. Discuss these statements: *(a)* "It is at least better than the manner of the modern millionaire, who has the black and drab outwardly for others, and the gold next his heart." *(b)* "To be sane is more dramatic than to be mad."

6. Study carefully the figure which Chesterton uses to illustrate the romance of Orthodoxy. Is it vivid, striking, graphic, powerful, convincing? Why?

7. In the passage, Chesterton refers to St. Thomas à Becket. Is there any similarity between Thomas à Becket and Thomas More? Explain.

PROJECTS

1. Make an outline and write a formal essay on the topic: "To be a Christian is more thrilling than to be a pagan."

2. Read Chesterton's essays "On Lying in Bed" and "Laughter." Discuss their humor and satire.

RELATED READING

Read at least the first chapter of Chesterton's *Autobiography.* An interesting introduction to Chesterton, Belloc, and Maurice Baring is given in Calvert Alexander's *The Catholic Literary Revival.*

MODERN DRAMA

After languishing for almost a century—except for the sparkling operettas of Gilbert and Sullivan—English drama began to revive in the 1890s. The daring challenges to unjust social conditions and existing moral standards, which were presented in Ibsen's realistic dramas, served as models for the social criticisms of Galsworthy and G. B. Shaw. In his *Strife, Justice,* and *The Silver Snuff-box,* Galsworthy re-echoed some of the thinking of the Norwegian dramatist's *The Doll's House, Hedda Gabler,* and *The Idiot.* On the other hand, disapproval of the realistic themes of Ibsen were expressed in the romantic fantasies of James M. Barrie.

Ibsen introduced the intellectual discussion to the stage, and G. B. Shaw seized upon this device to preach his own social doctrines. Shaw had been a prominent leader of the Fabian Society, a group of English Socialists who advanced their own ideas on social and economic problems. But soon Shaw evolved his own theory of man and society, and with wit, satire, and prejudice pronounced judgment on all things under the sun. He satirized war in *Arms and the Man;* made fun of medical science in *The Doctor's Dilemma;* and suggested in *Pygmalion* that the "higher" classes in England were superior to the "lower" only in their pronunciation of words. One of his finest plays, *St. Joan,* has as its theme the justification of Protestant individualism.

Shaw was a brilliant technician, an egotist whose wit was sparkling and whose satire was biting, trenchant and, at times, uproariously funny. But he substituted for revealed religion the religion of the Superman,[1] with himself as its prophet and high priest. Graham Greene has written of Shaw that "he plays the fool at enormous length. ...Ideas are adopted for the sake of their own paradoxes and are discarded as soon as they cease to startle. He gives his audience a sense of intellectual activity—but they often imagine they have exercised their brains when they had really done no more than strain their eyes at the startling convolutions of a tumbler."

SIR JAMES BARRIE

In the early years of the century, Sir James Barrie was a popular fiction writer who used his native Scotland as a background for realistic stories with a tragic undertone. His *Sentimental Tommy* and his sensitive biography of his mother, *Margaret Ogilvy,* are the best of his prose works. But Barrie is known more for his dramas. He openly protested against the realism of the Ibsen imitators and was prompted to write plays with fancy and romance as their theme. Barrie will always remain immortal as the creator of *Peter Pan* with its Never-Never Land. The best of his longer dramas are *Dear Brutus* and *Quality Street.* These plays, as well as his one-act plays, have been frequently presented in the movies and on television.

[1] SUPERMAN—Shaw conceived God as a growing Life Force, an imperfect power striving to become perfect. As the instrument of the Life Force, man must help God perfect Himself. Shaw said that man should so live that when he dies God is in man's debt.

THE IRISH THEATER MOVEMENT

One of the most interesting movements in the history of twentieth-century drama has been the rise and success of the Irish National Theater. Stirred by the political nationalistic movement and by the activities of "little theater" groups throughout the world, several writers of Irish nationality undertook to preserve Irish folklore and the traditional legends through the medium of the drama. Led by William B. Yeats and Lady Gregory, they took over the Abbey Theater, from which came some of the finest plays and actors of the twentieth century.

John M. Synge, who died at the early age of thirty-eight, was the most successful in capturing the real spirit of the Irish peasant. He took realistic material and clothed it in a language which expressed verbal beauty, irony, and satire. In his best-known one-act play, *Riders to the Sea,* he wrote of the humble folk whose daily battle is with the sea. Because he lived among them, Synge caught that blending of stark realism and mysticism which belongs to those who spend their days close to the beauty and despair of the sea.

The realism of the English and continental drama influenced the Abbey Group in 1910, and the poetic and imaginative dramas of Yeats were heard less and less. Other Irish playwrights were discovered, the most conspicuous of whom was Sean O'Casey. His *Juno and the Paycock* brought him international fame, as did his *Plough and the Stars.* These tragicomedies present the seamiest side of London tenement life in alternating scenes of sparkling comedy and stark tragedy. Contrary to what one might expect, O'Casey is not a Catholic nor a Christian, but an atheist. According to his biography, published in 1954, he appeared to have deep sympathies for the Reds and a deep hatred for the traditional Faith of his homeland.

Other well-known Irish dramatists whose plays were witnessed by the Abbey Theater audience are: George Shields, Frank O'Connor, Lord Dunsany, Daniel Corkery, Paul Vincent Carroll, Lennox Robinson, and Bryan MacMahon.

THE POETS IN THE THEATER

Poetry, the traditional medium of expression in the fifteenth, sixteenth, seventeenth, and eighteenth centuries, returned to the drama in the 1930s, when the theater ceased to be the exclusive hunting ground for the realists. The poetic movement was stimulated with the publication of T. S. Eliot's *Murder in the Cathedral.* The drama is an old Greek tragedy transplanted into medieval Canterbury. Eliot wrote the play to aid restoration of Canterbury Cathedral in England, where the murder of St. Thomas à Becket actually occurred in 1170. Eliot opens the play with Thomas' return to England. The women of Canterbury, in the manner of the old Greek chorus, chant a warning of death and destruction which will follow his homecoming. Uncertain about the course he will follow, Thomas listens to four tempters who offer him in turn: easy living and good times; temporal authority, which he had once enjoyed as Chancellor before he was forced to flee from England; leadership of a titled group out to overthrow the throne; and finally, martyrdom. The climax of the play is the dramatic murder scene at the high altar. As in the Elizabethan play, the poetry builds a unique atmosphere, much more effective than lights and setting.

In 1932, the *Group Theater* was formed for the express purpose of reviving poetry in drama, especially through the expression of religious themes. Recalling the days when the Church and dramatic art were on friendly terms, English churchmen (mostly Anglican) encouraged the poet-dramatist by commissioning plays for performance under church sponsorship. It might be said that the stage followed where the church led. Christopher Fry, like Eliot, wrote his earliest plays for religious festivals, as did other poetic dramatists such as Ronald Duncan, Norman Nicholson, Anne Ridler, and James Birdie. It is important to note that such impressive religious plays as Fry's *A Sleep of Prisoners* and *The Boy with a Cart* have been frequently and successfully staged by amateur dramatic groups, and by college and high school dramatic clubs in the United States—evidence that poetic drama is appreciated by youthful actors and audiences.

Fry's *The Lady's Not for Burning* was made famous by the acting of John Gielgud, Britain's outstanding actor. In this play Fry demonstrated a talent for pouring out phrases like liquid silver. His poetic imagination, like a rocket, illuminates a galaxy of words and metaphors which recall the great Elizabethans. The play combines the piety as well as the raucous realism of the medieval morality and mystery play—but throughout it all there is the breath of spiritual sensitivity.

Two noted playwrights of more recent years are Noel Coward and a much younger author, Terence Rattigan. Perhaps Noel Coward is the best craftsman in modern drama. *Journey's End* by R. C. Sherriff is one of the most powerful plays ever written on the theme of war.

NOEL COWARD

TERRANCE RATTIGAN